WITH PEN AND SABER

Also by Robert J. Trout:

They Followed the Plume: The Story of J. E. B. Stuart and His Staff

WITH PEN AND SABER

The Letters and Diaries
of J. E. B. Stuart's Staff Officers

ROBERT J. TROUT

STACKPOLE
BOOKS

Published by
STACKPOLE BOOKS
5067 Ritter Road
Mechancisburg, PA 17055

Printed in the United States of America

10 9 8 7 6 5 4 3 2 1

First edition

Library of Congress Cataloging-in-Publication Data

With pen and saber: the letters and diaries of J. E. B. Stuart's staff officers/edited by Robert
   J. Trout.—1st ed.
        p. cm.
   Includes bibliographical references and index.
   ISBN 0-8117-1930-8
   1. Confederate States of America. Army. Cavalry—Officers—Correspondence.
2. United States—History—Civil War, 1861–1865—Cavalry operations—Sources.
3. Stuart, Jeb, 1833–1864—Correspondence. I. Trout, Robert J., 1947–
E546.5.W66 1995
973.7'82—dc20   95-1753
                                                                              CIP

*To the descendants of those
who rode with Stuart*

CONTENTS

METHODOLOGY

[ ] Brackets indicate material added by the editor.

( ) Parentheses are part of the original text.

———— [word illegible] indicates material that could not be deciphered.

Initial misspellings of words are identified with [*sic*]; misspelled place names are followed by the correct spellings in brackets. Repetitions of errors are not marked. Abbreviations are spelled out in brackets for clarity if necessary.

ACKNOWLEDGMENTS

THE COMPILATION OF MATERIAL APPEARING IN THIS WORK WOULD NOT HAVE been possible without the cooperation of many individuals and institutions. The editor's sincere gratitude is extended to Mr. Staige D. Blackford (W. W. Blackford), Mrs. Sally-Bruce McClatchey (W. W. Blackford), Mrs. Isobel Smith Stewart (W. D. Farley), Judge Peter Wilson Hairston (P. W. Hairston), Mrs. Robert E. Osth (P. H. Powers), Mr. Philip Henry Powers Jr. (P. H. Powers), and Mr. James S. Patton (F. S. Robertson), descendants of Stuart's staff officers.

The willingness of Ms. Jennifer Young, Mr. Scott C. Mauger, and my wife, Judith, to share their time, talents, and expertise is greatly appreciated.

The letters of Peter W. Hairston, part of the Peter Wilson Hairston Papers, along with the letters of Richard Channing Price and the letter of Heros von Borcke, part of the R. Channing Price Papers, and the letters of William W. Blackford, part of the Blackford Family Papers, are housed in the Southern Historical Collection, Library of the University of North Carolina at Chapel Hill, and appear with that institution's permission.

The letters of Frank Smith Robertson are a part of the Wyndham Robertson Papers and are in the Department of Special Collections, University of Chicago Library, which granted permission for their publication.

The July 15, 1862, letter from Dabney Ball to Stuart is reproduced by permission of the Huntington Library, San Marino, California.

The Philip H. Powers letters of July 4, 22, and 23, 1861, April 2, 3, and 27, 1862, May 12 and 15, 1862, December 17, 20, and 25, 1862, March 17, 1863, May 6, 1863, December 26, 1863, February 6 and 21, 1864, and May 4, 9, 11, 15, and 17, 1864, are printed with the permission of Mr. Lewis Leigh. Copies are housed in the U. S. Army Military History Institute in Carlisle, Pennsylvania. The Powers letters of April 6, 14, 17, and 21, 1862, and January 1 and 29, 1863, are printed with the permission of Mrs. Robert E. Osth. The November 11, 1861, letter from Stuart to Powers is reproduced through the courtesy of Mr. Philip H. Powers Jr.

The Chiswell Dabney letters appear with the permission of the Virginia Historical Society, Richmond, Virginia.

The William D. Farley letter appears through the courtesy of Mrs. Isobel Smith Stewart.

The diary and letter of James Hardeman Stuart are printed here with the permission of the Mississippi Department of Archives and History.

John Esten Cooke's War Diaries, 1862-1864, are from the John Esten Cooke Papers in the Special Collections Library at Duke University, Durham, North Carolina, which granted permission for their publication.

The Alexander Robinson Boteler Diary is part of the William Elizabeth Brooks Collection in the Library of Congress.

The poetry of William W. Blackford is printed with the permission of Mr. Staige D. Blackford.

INTRODUCTION

AMONG THE MOST INTERESTING BOOKS PUBLISHED ON THE CIVIL WAR period are those that present the letters or diaries of soldiers who fought in the great conflict. Unlike reminiscences and memoirs written years after the war, when memories may have become clouded, most letters and diary entries were written immediately after the writer had participated in or witnessed some event. There are some cases in which the writer even took the time to record his thoughts while the battle raged around him. Additionally, what was recorded often reflected the everyday occurrences in a soldier's life in camp and on the march, his opinions on the political and the military situation, and his concerns for his family back home. Such accounts are vital to the historian.

An individual soldier's view becomes even more valuable if he had the opportunity to observe and record the words and actions of the war's more famous personages. These behind-the-scenes glimpses of the war's great leaders often reveal the personal side of their nature rather than just their performance as military commanders.

For those who have an interest in Robert E. Lee's great cavalry commander, Maj. Gen. James Ewell Brown ("Jeb") Stuart, the letters and diaries of a number of Stuart's staff officers have long supplied material for biographies and articles on the "Beau Sabre of the Confederacy." The focus, however, has often been on those letters and diary entries that recount Stuart's battles or raids; these in reality make up only a small percentage of what is available. Most of the material has never appeared in print, even though references to Stuart abound.

Besides contributing information on Stuart, the letters and diaries also furnish insights into the lives of the men who rode closest to one of the Confederacy's great military commanders. The topics of family, home, and friends appear in almost every letter and, along with explanations of official duties, comments on personal health, news of fellow officers, and descriptions of cavalry headquarters, provide an intimate look at the life these men led during this crucial period in our country's history.

The men whose writings are included in this volume came from all walks of life. They ranged in age from seventeen to over forty-five. Some were married; others were not. Most lived to go home again, but two sacrificed all for their country. None had any idea that decades from their time others would be reading what they had written. They did not censor their words, but wrote honestly of what they felt, what they saw, and what they did. Because their letters and diaries were preserved, we have the opportunity to ride with them across the fields after the Battle of Fredericksburg, stroll among the tents of Stuart's headquarters camp, crouch low in the saddle as Yankee bullets whiz by at Brandy Station, and bemoan the lack of a good horse on which to go raiding.

Considering the importance of many of the events they wrote about, it is not surprising that sometimes the men themselves receive only a passing mention by historians, whose attention is focused on an event rather than the men who witnessed it. Some knowledge of the men whose writings follow is necessary, however, to understand and appreciate what they wrote.

Among the first to become a member of Stuart's inner circle was his brother-in-law, Peter Wilson Hairston. Born at "Oak Hill" in Pittsylvania County, Virginia, on November 25, 1819, Hairston studied law at the University of Virginia but never finished because of illness. Instead, he settled in North Carolina and spent the next several years running his plantation, "Cooleemee." He married Stuart's sister, Columbia Lafayette Stuart, on November 7, 1849, but she died on August 2, 1857, while giving birth to a daughter, who also died. Hairston married his second wife, Fanny McCoy Caldwell, "My Dear Fanny" of his letters, on June 22, 1859. Hairston's thirty-three letters from May 9 through October 11 cover the early, critical months of the Confederacy, its leaders, and the army that would one day become the Army of Northern Virginia. After the war, the economic situation forced Hairston into the mercantile business in Baltimore, Maryland, though he did manage to hold on to "Cooleemee." When his business partner died, Hairston was left to assume the responsibility of repaying the firm's debts, his partner having borrowed money from the business for personal use. Hairston repaid every cent, but the strain of the constant work and the death of his two children by Columbia took their toll. He died on February 17, 1886, and is buried at "Berry Hill," another of the family's plantations in Pittsylvania County.[1]

Another of the men who gathered around Stuart in those first days of the war was Philip Henry Powers. Much of Powers's early life after his birth on April 10, 1828, is unknown up until he was twenty, at which time he was tutoring the children of a Lorenzo Lewis at "Audley" near Berryville, Virginia. On December 28, 1852, he married Roberta Macky Smith of "Smithfield" in Clarke County, Virginia. The couple had ten children between 1854 and 1876, including twins born during the war. Powers was a member of the Clarke Cavalry before the war, and at its outbreak he enlisted with the rest of the company that became part of the 1st Virginia Cavalry. Eventually he ended up on Stuart's staff as quartermaster. Powers's declining health brought about his resignation on June 5, 1862, and he left the army for a time. When he returned, it was as a civilian aide to his brother, James. He maintained this status until April 26, 1863, when he reenlisted in the 1st Virginia and was transferred almost immediately to Stuart's head-quarters as a courier. He later served as clerk in the commissary depart-ment. By the end of the war he was a captain. Powers's letters begin in July 1861 and end in May 1864, with a number of significant gaps when he was either not with the army or at home on leave. After the war, he returned to teaching and did some farming at his home, "Auburn," in Clarke County. In 1887 he contracted typhoid fever and died on September 18. He is buried in Green Hill Cemetery, Berryville.[2]

In December 1861 the youngest man to serve on Stuart's staff, seven-teen-year-old Chiswell Dabney, arrived at cavalry headquarters for a brief visit. He became a permanent fixture in January, though he was almost im-mediately sent home with typhoid fever, which kept him from his duties through February 1862. Once he returned, Dabney participated with Stuart in all the major campaigns until November 1863, when he left the staff, having received a promotion to captain in the Adjutant General's Depart-ment. He then was appointed to the staff of Brig. Gen. James B. Gordon. Following Gordon's death he served with Brig. Gen. Rufus Barringer as inspector general. Dabney's letters cover the period from December 1861 to June 1863. After the war he was a lawyer and minister. He rests in Chatham Cemetery, Chatham, Virginia.[3]

The fourth member of the staff whose letters make a significant con-tribution to the history of Stuart and the cavalry was Richard Channing Price. Born in Richmond on February 24, 1843, Price came to Stuart with the unique ability of almost complete auditory memorization, which he had learned while working for his nearly blind father. His early war service was with the 3rd Richmond Howitzers. He joined Stuart's staff as an aide-de-camp on August 8, 1862, and rose to be a major and assistant adjutant general. His fascinating letters begin in September of that year and continue, with a few interruptions during furloughs, until April 16, 1863. His death on May 1, 1863, from a wound received in the Battle of Chancellorsville was a terrible blow to the staff and to Stuart personally. A few of Price's letters centering on Stuart's raids are among the most quoted of all of the writings of the staff officers. Price is buried in Hollywood Cemetery, Richmond, Virginia.[4]

The last officer whose letters are included in this volume served Stuart in the capacity of assistant engineer. Francis "Frank" Smith Robertson, a descendant of Pocahontas, was born in Richmond, Virginia, on January 3, 1841. He was attending the University of Virginia when the war broke out. He had earlier demonstrated his political beliefs by helping to organize the "Sons of Liberty," a military company made up of students at the university. His first attempt to join a proper military unit, the Richmond Howitzers, ended when his father made him remove his name from the rolls. Robertson was not to be deterred for long, however, and soon obtained a commission as a lieutenant in the regular army of Virginia and a two-month stint at the Virginia Military Institute, where he was educated in the duties of an officer. Fearing that the war would end, he left VMI and in June 1861 enlisted in the 48th Virginia Infantry. His service with the regiment was short. Robertson contracted "camp fever" and was out of the war until March 1863, when he joined Stuart. His nine letters from March to June 1863 cover the death of John Pelham at Kelly's Ford and the beginning of the Gettysburg Campaign at the Battle of Brandy Station. The collapse of his health following the army's return to Virginia ended his effective service with Stuart. He did recover and went on to serve on the staff of W. H. F. Lee. After the war, he farmed his beloved plantation, "The Meadows," until his death on August 10, 1926. Robertson is buried in Abingdon, Virginia.[5]

Of the four diarists, the most well known is John Esten Cooke. A famous writer even before the war, Cooke managed not only to perform his military duties, but also to continue his writing throughout the war. Cooke was born at "Ambler's Hill" in Winchester, Virginia, on November 3, 1830. His early life was much influenced by his older brother, Philip, a talented poet. John attended the University of Virginia and studied law privately. For a time he even was a member of his father's law firm, but the desire to write proved too strong. His first novel, *Avalon*, was published in 1848, and more followed. When the war began, Cooke joined the Richmond Howitzers, serving with them until January 31, 1862. By March he was a volunteer aide for Stuart, and in May he was commissioned as a lieutenant. He served as Stuart's ordnance officer and later as an assistant adjutant general. After Stuart's death, he was assigned to the staff of William N. Pendleton. Cooke's diary entries, which include the periods June-July 1862, January-May 1863, and January-April 1864, are filled with observations, opinions, battle notes, and accounts of writings-in-progress. He wrote freely and, in fact, ended one diary because he was afraid that it might be captured by the enemy and cause embarrassment for all concerned, as had a fellow officer's writings. After the war, Cooke continued to write and tried his hand at farming. He died on September 27, 1886, and is buried in Old Chapel Cemetery, Clarke County, Virginia.[6]

Like Channing Price, James Hardeman Stuart did not survive the war. A relative of the general, Stuart was born in Mississippi in either 1839 or 1841, depending on which source is consulted. He studied law at a school that eventually became the University of Mississippi, and established a practice in Jackson in 1859. At the beginning of the war he joined the Burt Rifles, which became Company K of the 18th Mississippi Infantry. Shortly after the regiment arrived in Virginia, Stuart was detached to the fledgling signal corps, where he received his training under Edward P. Alexander. On June 5, 1862, he was discharged from the 18th Mississippi, his enlistment having expired. On the eleventh he received his commission as a captain in the signal corps and an assignment to Stuart's staff. His diary begins on July 1 and gives a detailed account of events up until August 24. Hardeman Stuart was killed on the thirtieth at the Battle of Second Manassas while charging with either the 4th or 5th Texas Infantry. He is buried on the battlefield.[7]

The diary of Thomas Randolph Price Jr., the elder brother of Channing, was controversial in his day and remains so in the present. Born in Richmond on March 18, 1839, Price graduated from the University of Virginia in 1858 and entered the study of law. After a year, with his father's permission, he abandoned his law studies and journeyed to Europe to study literature and languages. Price's service in the war did not begin immediately, as he was still in Europe studying when the war broke out. He returned in December 1862, and reported to Stuart in February. His commission in the engineers was dated April 5, 1863, to rank from March 17. That he hated army life is very evident in the few diary entries that have survived. Unfortunately, he at first also wrote negatively of Stuart, a fact that came to light when his diary was "captured" and portions of it published in the *New York Times*. The incident led to his transfer from the staff to the Department of Engineers in Richmond, where he remained for the duration of the war. After the war, he taught Greek and English at various schools, including Columbia University, and was known as one of the most brilliant philologists in the United States. Price died on May 7, 1903, and is buried in Hollywood Cemetery, Richmond.[8]

The final diarist, Alexander Robinson Boteler, was born on May 16, 1815, and attended Princeton. He was a farmer and politician before the war, serving in the U.S. Congress. He resigned when the war began, and eventually served in the Confederate Congress. In February 1862 he performed a great service for President Jefferson Davis and the country by talking Stonewall Jackson out of resigning from the army over a dispute with Secretary of War Judah P. Benjamin, among others. He served as a voluntary aide-de-camp to both Jackson and Stuart, and ended his Confederate service as a presiding judge on a military court. His diary, though brief, covers the last days of Stuart and his staff in early May 1864. After the war, he again entered politics and held numerous positions. Boteler died on May 8, 1892, and is buried in Elmwood Cemetery, Shepherdstown, West Virginia.[9]

These nine, along with thirty-nine other individuals, served on the staff at various times during the three years Jeb Stuart commanded the cavalry of Jackson, Johnston, and Lee. Stuart brought them together, and when he passed from the scene the staff disbanded. What remained were memories and the words they had recorded while part of cavalry headquarters. Their memories died with them, but their words endure.

1861

—————⟶—◦—⟵—————

MAY

The war began for thousands of young men in thousands of different ways. For Capt. James Ewell Brown Stuart, it began on May 3, 1861, when he resigned his commission in the U.S. Army, stating that he did so, "From a sense of duty to my native State Virginia."[1] At the time, Stuart was in Cairo, Illinois, but events moved rapidly thereafter. By May 9 he was in Richmond, Virginia, and about to receive his commission as lieutenant colonel of infantry. In a letter written on that date to his wife, Flora, Stuart mentioned his appointment in the Provisional Army of Virginia, his assignment to Harpers Ferry, and that his cousin and brother-in-law, Peter Wilson Hairston, had agreed to serve as his volunteer aide.[2]

Though wishing to fight for the South, Hairston did not follow Stuart into the army, preferring instead to keep his civilian status, which allowed him to come and go as he wished. He had a deep concern for what was happening back in his home state, North Carolina, and feared that Federal forces might attack along the coast and march inland. Such a move would eventually threaten his wife, Fanny, their children, Betty, Sammy, and Agnes, and their home, "Cooleemee."[3] In his letters to Fanny dated May 9 and 10, Hairston gave orders to send him his horses and other items he would need for making war against North Carolina's enemies, and revealed his excitement and defiance as he prepared to join Stuart at Harpers Ferry.

Richmond Va
9 May 1861

My Dear Fanny,

I arrived here today and met with cousin James E. B. Stuart who is appointed Col. in the Army of Va and has been ordered to Harper's Ferry in the morning.[4] I have volunteered to accompany him attached to his staff for any duty that may be assigned me. The country requires every man to do his whole duty and I could not shrink from it, when I thought that by so doing I may assist in shielding North Carolina from invasion by the most merciless horde that ever plundered any country. All accounts from the North represent them there as almost frantic and appealing to the lowest and vilest ——— [word illegible] of the starving multitudes in their cities to induce them to enlist.

1

I place my entire business under your management until I return. I know that your judgment and prudence will do all that can be done under the circumstances. Your Father can aid you in North Carolina, Mr. Adams in Stokes [County, NC] and my father in Henry [County, VA]. Should my duties prevent me from returning home before the summer, you can go to Virginia and spend your time among my relatives and visit the plantation. This will be a trial to you, it is one to me but in these times our country's claims can not be denied and it is necessary to let the poorer classes know that we are willing and ready to set them the example of fighting for our country, our homes and all that man holds sacred and dear.

History never exhibited such a spectacle of demoralization as presented in the Northern mind at present. Genl. [Winfield] Scott has been the vilest of traitors to Virginia.[5] I came down in the cars today with Dr. Atkinson, who has been a long standing personal and political friend of his and no longer than the 27th of last Jan'y Genl. Scott wrote to him expressing indignation that any one should suppose that he was in favour of coercing the South, whilst he was planning the scheme for her subjugation. About the time it was reported he was to resign, it was said positively one day he was to ———— [word illegible] with Mr. McFarland in Richmond. Dr. A. [Atkinson] met with Govr. [John B.] Floyd and mentioned it to him.[6] The Govr. told him Genl. Scott would not be there that he knew personally & officially that Scott had laid before him these very plans before he left the War department.

President Davis has sent on one million of dollars to the Commissary department & orders to make provision for one hundred thousand men. Genl. [Robert E.] Lee is doing everything in his power to get things in order here but from what I hear I think he's a little uneasy. He thinks the troops are too eager for a fight and need more discipline before they are ready.

I hope it may all end well and that Virginia may escape the scourge of Maryland which is now completely overrun by Federal troops. Tennessee & Arkansas are with us and reports today from Missouri are very favourable. Kentucky is very slow.

And now my dear Fanny I wish you to send me John Goolsby and my three horses Tom, George & Sam.[7]

I wish you to get Mr. [Charles F.] Fisher to attend to it and have them sent on a freight train to this place.[8] I would thank him to employ some one if he can to come along with John and bring them to me. I want you also to send me my Sharpe's [Sharp's] rifle and old John Brown's Bowie Knife.[9] Get Mr. Plummer to make a webbing such as used for girths for saddles and place two straps of leather with buckles attached to each end so that I can throw it over my shoulder & carry it. Send the moulds & other ———— [word illegible] attached to it. They are all at Joseph's house in his care.

I send you orders enclosed on two banks for such money as may be needed for your purposes and for sending the horses to me.

Direct to the care of

Henry C. Walking

Richmond & he will aid them in forwarding them to me at Harper's Ferry— Care of Col. James E. B. Stuart. I wish some one to come on with John as I do not think he could get them through himself.

I will write to you very often and hope my dear Fanny, you will not be too uneasy about me. Direct to Harper's Ferry care of Col. James E. B. Stuart.

Yours affectionately,
Peter W. Hairston

P. S. Send Joseph with John & the horses so they can come safely to me.[10] I want my saddles also—Joseph will return after bringing it.

———— ⚔ ————

Alexandria Virginia
May 10th 1861

My Dear Fanny,

Here I am a traitorous rebel in seven miles of Lincoln['s] Head Quarters not having the fear of him before my eyes although this twenty days of grace have expired.

I expect to leave in the morning for Harper's Ferry. I do not think this place will be held much longer by the Virginia troops, as it can not be defended and the enemy, by means of their war steamers have complete possession of the river.[11]

They will not forever be allowed to advance any farther into the interior without a desperate battle. Virginia has 83,000 troops enrolled and other companies are offering themselves daily. She can get as many soldiers as she can arm and feed. Large numbers are coming in daily from the Southern States.

The ladies here make themselves very useful. They go over to Washington City, buy pistols, put them under their dresses and bring them home.

I went into a store to buy me some military articles and the young man who sold them to me said he had just seen a gentleman from Phila-

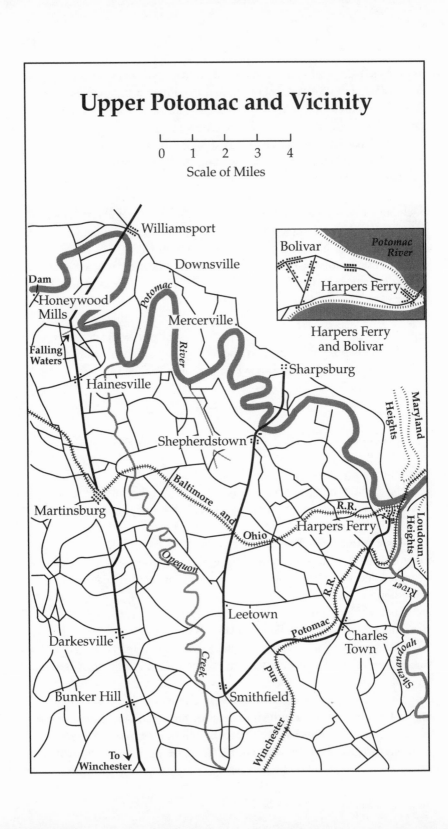

Upper Potomac and Vicinity

0   1   2   3   4
Scale of Miles

Williamsport

Downsville

Dam

Honeywood Mills

Potomac

Bolivar

Potomac River

Harpers Ferry

Harpers Ferry and Bolivar

Mercerville

River

Falling Waters

Sharpsburg

Hainesville

Maryland Heights

Shepherdstown

Baltimore and

Martinsburg

R.R.

Loudoun Heights

Ohio

Harpers Ferry

Opequon

River

Leetown

Potomac

R.R.

Charles Town

Darkesville

Creek

Shenandoah

Bunker Hill

Winchester

Smithfield

To Winchester

delphia who told him there had been a great re-action in that city in the last few days and they were now sending in to Lincoln to stop the war or they would starve to death.

They are sadly in need of vegetables in Washington City and the expenses of Lincoln's government is said to be one million per day. At this rate his government can not last long as he is getting little or no revenue from customs.

I rode out to the different camps in Richmond and saw the different companies drill. There was a company of Zouaves which reminded me of Paris.[12] The South Carolina troops were sun-burnt but very polite and well behaved.

The Louisiana Regiment is a splendid set of men I am told. I think Abraham Lincoln and his Myrmidons will have some trouble before they subjugate us; but I have no doubt they will make an attack upon Virginia before very long.[13] You need not be uneasy about me as I shall be prudent and cautious and my position will enable me to see and know every thing which is going on without being in much danger.

Give my love to Betty & Sammy and kiss the baby for me. I should like very much to see her. Tell Sammy to attend well to his drilling—it may be of great importance to him some day. And now I feel I love you truly & devotedly and I shall endeavor so to deport myself that you may not be ashamed of me and I may be worthy of you.

> Very truly &
> affectionately yours
> Peter W. Hairston

Should a letter come for me from Mr. Davis the mill-wright I wish you would have it sent to Mr. Giles so he may have the bill of timbers gotten.[14] Virginia is nothing but a camp.

On the same day that Hairston wrote to his wife, Stuart rode into Harpers Ferry and reported to Col. Thomas J. Jackson, commanding the Virginia forces there. Jackson, after soothing a ruffled Turner Ashby, who resented Stuart's superseding him in command of the cavalry, divided the mounted troops and assigned several companies to Stuart.[15] What eventually would emerge from the young lieutenant colonel's efforts to organize and train the troopers assigned to him would be the 1st Virginia Cavalry. Encamping at Bolivar, a suburb of Harpers Ferry, Stuart established a training regimen that appealed to some of the new recruits but caused others to develop a suspicious attitude toward their new commander. Nevertheless, Stuart pushed on with the drilling, knowing how important it would be in the near future.

Jackson did not retain his command at Harpers Ferry for very long. Newly appointed Brig. Gen. Joseph E. Johnston arrived on May 23 and within a short time came to appreciate Stuart's abilities. As the cavalry struggled with its training and patrol duties, constant rumors about both Federal movements and Johnston's plans circulated within the small army. Near the end of the month, almost everyone was convinced that the big battle was at hand. Included in that number was Stuart's aide, Hairston, who wrote hurriedly to his wife.

Harper's Ferry
May 31st 1861

My Dear Fanny,

We have just received marching orders in the direction of the enemy.

Should we never return, I commend my children to your charge and care and remember if I fall my last farewell was to you and my last remembrance is my affection of true and devoted love to you my darling wife, whose devotion to me has been unfaltering and in whose virtue, prudence and discretion I have unbounded confidence.

Most devotedly yours,
Peter W. Hairston

JUNE

The anticipated battle did not take place. Neither side was sure enough of itself to test the other. The early days of the month saw the routine of patrols resume. In those first few days, Stuart left Bolivar to establish a new camp at Bunker Hill between Martinsburg and Winchester. As more cavalry companies arrived, Stuart assumed a larger role in Johnston's plans. The Union forces in Maryland under Maj. Gen. Robert Patterson and those in western Virginia under Maj. Gen. George B. McClellan became the focus of Johnston's attentions, and Stuart was ordered to keep them under observation.[16] Johnston later reported, "The river was observed from the Point of Rocks to the western part of the county of Berkeley, the most distant portions by the indefatigable Stuart with his cavalry."[17]

Peter Hairston, though not obligated to follow orders because of his civilian status, participated enthusiastically in the patrols and drills with the rest of the raw recruits. Stuart used the constant patrolling to give his men the experience of facing the enemy and coming under fire. The cavalry made an advance on Martinsburg around the fifth, and while there, Hairston penned a letter to his wife giving her advice about the running of "Cooleemee," sharing his opinion of various officers, and justifying the cause for which he was fighting so far from home.

Martinsburg, VA
June 5th 1861

My Darling One,

Here we are on an expedition to this the Head Quarters of Black Republicanism in this part of the State. I will write you the particulars tomorrow after every thing is completed.

Of course if Mr. Mason does not behave himself get your father to turn him off immediately.[18] When you employ another man give him the same I am giving Mr. Giles & Mr. Orrender if you can not get him for less.[19] All wages ought to come down in these times. I am not satisfied with Joseph's conduct either from the account of John. But the peculiar circumstances of the ———— [word illegible] render me more lenient towards him. Tell my good friend the Judge that I have a deed of trust ———— [word illegible] in Davie County on the land of ———— [word illegible] & two of his Negroes should he attempt to leave the county after he is dismissed to secure my debt before he does so.

You have full powers over all my affairs while I am gone and if any of them don't do to please dismiss him at your discretion.

I wrote to your father a short time since.

I received a very kind letter from Mr. Fisher a short time since and am very much obliged to him for the interest which he took in endeavoring to get me the appointment I desired.

It makes but little difference now as the position I now occupy gives me the most pleasurable excitement, although it is a hard life as it has been raining ever since we have been in camp. But we have a tent now and are more comfortable than we were a few days ago. John is perfectly disgusted with the life.

I should have no hesitation now with Messers ———— [word illegible] & Boyden, ———— [two words illegible] what respect I might have for their ———— [word illegible] as our cause must not be endangered by any regard for persons—Inter arma leges silent.[20] The opposite party are acting upon that principle & we must do the same. We are arresting all suspicious persons here and taking their arms from them.

We are exposing our lives for what we deem the holiest cause in the world our homes and our firesides and we must tolerate no enemies in our midst, no "fire in our rear." If they are not with us, let them leave the State.

Lt. Col. Stuart is one of the bravest & noblest men I have ever seen & a fine officer. He ———— [word illegible] that eternal vigilance which is the only safety in the midst of war.

We have a host of the finest officers in the army, [Pierre Gustave

Toutant] Beauregard, [President Jefferson] Davis, [Robert E.] Lee, [Joseph E.] Johnston & others and the finest material for an army in the world.

I am struck with one thing here and that is those persons who have been accustomed to the comforts of home say less & complain less of the circumstances of the service than those who have never known any. Which shows that the mind regulates the body in a great measure & sustains us. The heart & soul of these men are entirely in the cause.

We have two very nice gentlemen from Maryland on our Staff Messers Brien & Swan.[21] They have left their property & homes to fight our cause.

If Mr. A. Boyden Jr. & wife do not trust you as they should—yield not an inch to them or any body else. ——— [Two words illegible] do they are no friends of mine neither father nor mother & thus too it is with me in the cause of the South. My love to the little ones.

Most devotedly yours

Peter W. Hairston

Between June 5 and 9, Stuart fell back to the area around Bunker Hill but maintained his pickets along the Potomac. As a result, he was quickly informed when, on the ninth, an invasion of sorts occurred at Honeywood Dam. He advanced on the enemy and shortly had them back across the river with no casualties. On that same day, Hairston found time to write to Fanny about the skirmish, among other subjects.

Camp Clover

9 June 1861

My Darling Fanny,

Yours of the 31st of May & 2nd of June came to hand today and also one from your father and one from Mr. [Col. Charles] Fisher. Tell the latter I will attend to the getting his letter across the line though it is very difficult now as our Company had an engagement last night with some more disaffected Marylanders. I was unfortunately out of it as I was left in camp to attend to the putting up of some tents. Col. Stuart had been ordered by Genl. Johnston to tear down the dam of the B. & O. Canal. While they were doing it they were fired upon & had a brisk engagement. They killed one of our horses and we wounded two or more of their men. No one was hurt on our side.

We expect every day an attack from the enemy who are now approaching & are in twelve miles of us.

I think you had better go to Pittsylvania at any time you may think proper the latter part of June or the 1st of July.

It would be safer & more satisfactory to you, for there is no telling where the destiny of this war may cast us. We are here today and there tomorrow. I know this suspense is agonizing but every man must now do his whole duty to his country. Look at Maryland look at Missouri—Their citizens not allowed the privilege of drilling or having arms. And oh! Kentucky how has she fallen from her high estate. She wavers in this conflict. I know not what fate may betide me; but this I do know far better it is to fall defending those rights so dear to us than to be the craven slave of the Northern despotism.

I have handed Mr. Fisher's letter to a very fine Maryland gentleman, who is in our corps & offers to do all he can to get it across the River.

Europe will be on our side in a short time. Austria refuses to receive Burlingame and the North is terribly afraid of England.[22] France will not be behind England in acknowledging our independence. Vallandigham of Ohio is for peace alongside of Pierce and every battle which is fought will add strength to our party.[23] We have the flower of the U. S. Army with us and every step they advance into the country after leaving Northwestern Virginia they will be harassed at every step.

I have hope and confidence in our ultimate success; although we may have to go through the fiery ordeal first.

I am glad the children are all so well. My love to them and I am most devotedly & truly yours

Peter W. Hairston

Under orders from Johnston, Stuart fell back toward Winchester on the eleventh. Patterson advanced on the sixteenth, and Johnston maneuvered to meet him. But once again the invasion was short-lived and ended with both armies retreating; the expected battle never materialized. Stuart's cavalry pickets remained alert and captured the lieutenant colonel of the 8th Pennsylvania Infantry on the nineteenth.[24] As June drew to a close, Stuart and his cavalry remained on constant watch for an invasion, which they felt could occur at any time.

Peter Hairston brought Fanny up-to-date with the unfolding events in four letters written between the fifteenth and the nineteenth. His topics ranged from giving directions for the making of two uniform jackets to his disappointment in Johnston's withdrawal to Winchester. He hinted at the frustration he felt over not having come to grips with the enemy, and shared his opinions of two Northern officers, George B. McClellan and George H. Thomas.[25] Fanny's constant anxiety over him finally bore fruit in an invitation to join him in Winchester, but only if conditions permitted.

Winchester
15 June 1861

My Dear Fanny,

Night before last we left Camp Clover by the orders of Genl. Johnston and marched all night without any supper. About day-break we stopped & had a short nap & marched on to this place without breakfast. On getting here I was so overcome with fatigue that I had one of my old headaches the first I have had since I have been in the service. I came to this hotel to rest and refresh myself and was very much gratified to meet Richard [Caldwell] who told me the baby was very sick and insisted upon my going to Richmond.[26] But I knew she was quite well as you had written to me. After remaining here about two hours the regiment received orders through a telegraphic dispatch from Genl. Johnston to march again to meet him as he is withdrawing his forces from Harper's Ferry, considering this a better strategical point and to meet McLelland's [Maj. Gen. George B. McClellan] command about 12,000 strong which is now marching down through Western Virginia. He is the finest officer in the Northern army and has always been bitterly opposed to the abolitionists and ———— [word illegible] of Philadelphia. I knew his father Dr. McLelland [Dr. George McClellan] then and always found him warm in his sympathies with the South. He built up the Jefferson Medical School then with Southern patronage. His son, however, is now led away by ambition and the love of glory to take up arms against us. His advance guard is now at Romney about forty miles from this place where they attempted to rob the bank; but all the valuables had been removed. They even robbed and insulted the ladies, deprived them of their watches and jewelry.[27] They are a parcel of robbers & thieves and the soul of no Northern man rises higher, as a gentleman well said today, than what he can make by any thing.

Troops are marching through here now on their way up to meet them and drive them back among them is the Regiment from Tennessee and Col. [Ambrose P.] Hill's from this state.[28] Our Regiment 1 Va. Cav. Vols. has gone to meet Genl. Johnston & bring up his rear. I expect to join them again this evening.

Richard tells me you are not at all uneasy about me and have only come to Richmond on a pleasure trip. Really & truly being uneasy does not do any good. I do not expect to be in Richmond until next month unless I am sent as bearer of dispatches which cousin James [Stuart] has promised to do if he meets with an opportunity.

I wish you to have me two roundabouts made of blue flannel with gilded buttons with the Va. coat of arms on them.[29] If I can not get these any metal buttons will do and if you can not get the flannel any good of a dark color which is suitable for summer. Have a band or strip of gold lace about 1/2 in. wide and 2 1/2 or 3 inches long put on each shoulder then coat buttons up straight in front. I do not need the ———— [two words illegible] but a couple of grey flannel or checked shirts would be very acceptable. Send them here to the care of Lt. Col. James E. B. Stuart 1 Regt. Va. Cav. Vols. either by express or any other ———— [word illegible] you can.

They took Richard [Caldwell] up as a spy in Harper's Ferry and he had to show his pass from President Davis before they would let him go. He therefore think[s] them all a set of boobies except a Mr. Kercheval whom he has met & who wears an old hat & slip-shod shoes & who takes good care of & waits on him.

We burnt the tressel [*sic*] work of the Baltimore & Ohio R. R. at Martinsburg as we came by. It was a magnificent sight at night & illuminated the whole town.

Richard says you had some idea of going to a private boarding house. Mr. Duval's just by the Exchange is a good one. Write me particularly where you are so I can address my letters. Should you leave Richmond it is getting so late. I think you had better take the Rail-Road to Danville & go to Pittsylvania as it will be too warm soon to be in North Carolina.

Let me know what your movements & intentions are. I will keep you well informed of what we do & expect. At present I do not know where [we] will be ordered.

My love & a thousand kisses to the dear little ones—Very truly devotedly & affectionately yours—

Peter W. Hairston

Under a large Oak
in Berkeley Co. Virginia
18 June 1861

My Darling Pet,

Here under this wide spreading oak, which has been bed-room, parlour, kitchen & dining room for the past night, I sit down to write to you. I have been unable to do so for the last two days, as we have been so on the wing.

The enemy have crossed at Williamsport and yesterday we presented the anomalous spectacle of each army withdrawing from the other.[30] They are 18,000 strong we are about 10,000. Genl. Johnston has fallen back upon a strong position near Winchester. We make a scout today in direction of the enemy. Yesterday some of our pickets run theirs into camp where they procured re-inforcements and then run ours back. We can get a chance at their cavalry we will give them an awful thrashing as they are commanded by Col. [George H.] Thomas who is a Virginia traitor & who is a fat old man who can not ride without holding on to the pommel of the saddle.

My heart sunk within me on yesterday when Genl. Johnston drew back as I was anxious to drive the invaders from our soil. They are committing devastation wherever they go. A young man, now in our camp said they stole his horse on yesterday and he went there to get him back. While he was there 10 of our men rode up in sight of them when it was reported the Virginians were advancing and produced the utmost consternation among them.

We will hover around them and watch their movements and tote them into the trap Genl. Johnston has set for them. When they waded the Potomac, they sang Dixie land.

We have slept on the ground without shelter for the two last nights—with our arms by our side.

We have amusing times around our camp fires at night talking the adventures of the day and cracking jokes. The Staff are all pleasant & genteel men, so are most of the Captains.

Tell Bettie, I want to see her very much & the little one. I was amused at John [Goolsby] yesterday. We all thought we were to have a brush with the enemy. I was sent with a message to Genl. Johnston & ordered John to keep with the baggage wagon. When I returned I found the men drawn up near Martinsburg awaiting the approach of the enemy. There was John along with them, having borrowed a double barrel gun from some one and ready to shoot if he had an opportunity.

Your devotion has but strengthened & confirmed that love which I have always borne you.

I remain most affectionately truly & devotedly yours

Peter W. Hairston

◂┄ ≡◈≡ ┄▸

Near Martinsburg
Berkeley Co. Va.
June 19th 1861

My Dear Wife,

Every thing is now perfectly quiet in camp and nothing particularly to do, the whole force having retired across the river on yesterday before we arrived.

I was disappointed as three times we have expected to have a brush with them and each time we have not met them. I wished to capture a military saddle.

We do not know the cause of their retiring. One report is that Jeff. Davis was marching on Washington City and they would be needed there. Another that they were afraid of our force. They were alarmed by the 10 of our men who run their pickets into camp & the reports of the number of Genl. Johnston['s] army.

Their whole program evidently changed.

> In haste most
> devotedly yours
> Peter W. Hairston

━━ ≋♦≋ ━━

> Camp Jeff. Davis
> 19 June 1861

My Darling Fanny,

I received your letter of the 13th today and write to you in haste to-day. I suppose Richard [Caldwell] has relieved you of your anxiety before this. If, however, you still suffer so much anxiety, if you can get safely by the Manassas Junction & have the funds you can come on to Winchester.

This country is freed of the enemy for the present. Our pickets have just brought in Lt. Col. [Samuel] Bowman of the 8th Regt. of Pennsylvania Volunteers and his Aide-de-Camp ———— [word illegible]. They say that they merely rode across the river to say they had been in Virginia, when our pickets who were ever on the alert arrested them and brought them into camp. From them we learn that Patterson's command is retreating en-route for Washington City.

We treat them very kindly & send them on to Genl. Johnston.

> Most devotedly yours
> Peter W. Hairston

JULY

The month began with the fight the Confederates had been expecting for most of May and June. It did not develop into a major battle, however. On July 2 Patterson again crossed the Potomac and pushed back Jackson, who put up some resistance at Falling Waters. Stuart and the 1st Virginia managed to get in their licks at the enemy, with Stuart virtually single-handedly capturing a total of forty-nine men.[31] Despite this success, the Confederates were forced to retreat, and the two armies again settled down to a staring match for almost two weeks.

Among the men who had become members of Stuart's headquarters entourage was Philip Henry Powers. He had joined the 1st Virginia as a member of the Clarke Cavalry, which became Company D in the regiment. He passed through the skirmish at Falling Waters and wrote his beloved wife, Roberta, on Independence Day concerning the tumultuous events he had experienced and what he anticipated would happen over the next several days.

Camp at Big Spring
July 4th

My Dear Wife,[32]

Though within 2 miles of the enemy, who are in Martinsburg and just this side, I seize the first leisure moment for two days to write you a line merely to assure you of my safety thus far. We have had a stirring and exciting time for the 2 days past. Tuesday morning [July 2] we heard that the enemy were coming at Wmport [Williamsport]—Col. Stuart instantly had us in the saddle and marched down to meet them keeping on their flank— almost before we knew it we came upon their lines. And finding one Company of about fifty men detached and resting under a tree—we charged them surrounded and captured every man of them except four who ran and were killed. One fellow was creeping away under cover of a fence when he was shot dead by the only Negro in our party.[33] However we made a most narrow escape for we had hardly started our prisoners, when a whole regiment of infantry came up to the place where the skirmish had taken place and pursued us. We were too fast for them—And got off with all the prisoners—their arms and accoutrements.

About this time Col. Jackson's command met the enemy and a skirmish ensued. We could hear the firing but could not see the engagement as we were on the flank and most of the time in the woods. Col. Jackson retired in a short time and we continued to watch the enemy until they went into Camp on the grounds we occupied the night before.

We camped first outside Martinsburg—sleeping on the ground without blankets or food. Our baggage being at Bunker's Hill. You may imagine the comfort of our position! However I managed to sleep some, though I had a terrible headache.

Yesterday morning the enemy advanced upon Martinsburg, and we retired before them keeping just without range of their guns. They are in large force, though we cannot exactly estimate their numbers. They marched upon the place in battle array. Their ———— [word illegible] gleaming in the sun as their lines hurried through the fields their main column in the road.

We retired thro' M'burg [Martinsburg]—Sadly I assure you. I could hardly refrain from shedding tears when I saw weeping women hurrying out and all in alarm. God will yet vindicate the right—And enable us to drive these invaders from our soil.

I imagine Genl Johnston wishes to draw them from the river before he gives them battle. What our movement will be today I cannot tell. We are now resting and our pickets watching the enemy.

I had expected to come home this week. Of course you will not expect or desire it now. Had I time I might write you many incidents worth mentioning that have occurred, but the man who is to take this is waiting. I only ask you not to be uneasy about me. I am well, and shall take care of myself and discharge my duty to the best of my ability. God bless you my dear—and protect you and my little children. I heard from you thro' some of [Capt. William A.] Morgan's Company.[34]

> Ever yours
> P. H. Powers

Peter Hairston continued to write to his wife, Fanny, throughout the month. His correspondence of the ninth confirms that Stuart was continuing his aggressive scouting and that, in Hairston's mind at least, the Federals were becoming disenchanted with the war, though they were not ready to permit the South to go its own way just yet. By the eleventh and twelfth he was admitting that the military situation, except for Stuart's brief forays, had stagnated on his front. The focus of his letters changes to camp events and personal opinions and observations. Hairston's letter of the fifteenth indicates that the Confederates were intensifying their preparations to defend Winchester when Patterson advanced. Reinforcements were moving up and entrenchments were being dug. All indications were that the big fight was at hand. It was, but not at Winchester. Hairston and many others in Johnston's command would soon be headed east toward Manassas Junction and Bull Run.

> Bunker Hill
> Berkeley Co. Va.
> 9 July 1861

My Darling Fanny,

Yours of the 5th came to hand today.

It is two coupons of $30 each which I wish you to send to Cousin Elizabeth Stuart.[35] The coupons Grandma sent were received by Mr. Watkins and placed in the Farmer's Bank of Va by him to be collected for me. I am very much obliged to her for them and all her other kindnesses to me and was very much gratified to hear that father thought so much of me.

My life here is certainly very stirring & eventful. All day yesterday we were scouting around the camp of the enemy to cut off some of their straggling parties. Today by a flag of truce I was in their lines to carry a letter from Lt. Col. [Samuel] Bowman [8th Pennsylvania Infantry] to his wife and so far from getting any thanks from their officers for it was cooly told the matter was not of sufficient importance to enter their lines with a flag of truce. They are very sanguine of success and think by their numbers to overwhelm us.

Genl. Johnston is fortifying himself at Winchester to meet the enemy who will probably advance in a few days to attack him. If they do there will be a hard fight. If he is victorious it will be a great blow to the enemy. If he is defeated he can fall back upon Manassas & join his forces to those of Beauregard.

I do not have the opportunity of writing to you every day as we are moving about so much. I send this to Danville as you requested in your last.

My love to all the family & a kiss for the children. I hope Sammy will be a good boy & a blessing & comfort to you.

My fondest & most devoted love is yours & I think of you day & night. Do not leave home, however, to come to me under any circumstances unless I write to you to do so for you are safer where you are than anywhere else in the United States. My great hopes are that the North may become dissatisfied with the incessant drain made upon her resources & after a while grant us peace. There seems to be no prospect of this now, however. And most of the Northern army being persons who are thrown out of employment & being in an enemy's country it is not safe for ladies to be anywhere near them. We have surgeons with every regiment who take good care of the sick and wounded.

> Most devotedly &
> truly yours
> Peter W. Hairston

━•━ ≡◆≡ ━•━

> Camp near Bunker Hill
> July 11th 1861

My Dear Fanny,

There is nothing new here. Genl. Johnston is still in Winchester with his army while the Federal forces are quiet in Martinsburg. We are halfway between the two places watching the enemy.

We have been expecting their advance for some days but they show no disposition to do so and it is now reported they will not now advance ——— [word illegible] two weeks.

Many amusing incidents happen in camp & some very tragical. On yesterday a man accidentally shot himself and is suffering very much today.

The federalists have appointed new officers in Berkeley County & have taken the whole affairs in their own hands. They pretend they are here to protect the property & yet are destroying it whenever they can. In the ——— [word illegible] where they are, they have got the people out and some of them are reported to be starving for want of food. If they over-run the South I will go to Chile for I will not live in a conquered country particularly subject to the Yankees. Before this can be done, however, we should imitate the Russians in the burning of Moscow & desolate the whole country before them to starve them.[36]

I am very well & with my love to all the family & a kiss to the children I remain

most devotedly yours
Peter W. Hairston

Bunker Hill
12 July 1861

My Dear Fanny,

The man who shot himself died last night. One of his last requests was that we should whip the Yankees out of Virginia.

Yesterday our scout brought in two Yankees whom they had captured and had a skirmish with a foraging party of the enemy in which they killed two or three of the enemy and no one hurt on our side although one man had two buckshot holes through his hat.

The enemy were in the road and took deliberate aim with their muskets, but shot over their heads and then our men charged upon them and killed them with their pistols when they fled to some woods.

Both armies are still in status quo neither moving but both receiving reinforcements.

I have heard that Genl. Johnston says he had rather die then retreat further than Winchester.

The first regiment of Cavalry is getting so popular that every one wishes to join it. Since we have done such good service, whenever we go to Head Quarters we are received with the utmost courtesy.

Most affectionately yours
Peter W. Hairston

Winchester
15 July 1861

My Darling Fanny,

I came over here day before yesterday and was surprised to meet Sam Harden.[37] His brother Watt has been very sick and is about leaving for Henry [County, Virginia].[38] On the day we expected to have the fight this side of Martinsburg he left a sick bed to join his company and this completely prostrated him.

I saw the Pittsylvania Regiment [38th Virginia Infantry] on yesterday and felt at home among so many familiar faces. Unfortunately one of their men was accidently [sic] shot. He was from Mecklenburg Virginia.

We are daily receiving reinforcements. A large Alabama regiment 1150 strong came in on yesterday & Genl. [Brig. Gen. Edmund Kirby] Smith the Adjutant Genl. told me they were expecting Mr. [Col. Charles] Fisher's Regiment [6th North Carolina Infantry] from North Carolina which he remarked was one of the finest in the State.[39]

A rumor reached here on yesterday that Col. [Brig. Gen. Robert S.] Garnett had an engagement with McClellan and was worsted but we here [sic] so many rumors that I do not know what to believe.[40] There seems no nearer prospect of a conflict here than there was the first day I came out. Each side, however, is making active preparations & the conflict when it does come will no doubt be hotly contested on both sides.

Tell Grand Ma I have just met with John Pryor of Miss[issippi] a son of Gree Pryor an old friend of hers. He gave me the sheet of paper upon which I am writing.

We have about 4,000 militia throwing up breast works. They are getting tolerably well drilled & behind those breastworks will fight well. [Robert C.] Stanard's battery has just arrived from Richmond. He has a finely drilled company.[41]

My love to the family and a kiss to the children.

I remain most devotedly & truly yours

Peter W. Hairston

On July 15 Patterson again advanced, but Stuart was not caught napping, and reported the enemy's forward movement to Johnston at Winchester. The Federal push reached Bunker Hill, nine miles from Winchester, where Patterson encamped until the seventeenth. On that date he made a move to his left toward Smithfield. Johnston did not respond, instead acting on orders he had received on July 18 directing him to move his forces to assist General Beauregard, who was facing the advance of Brig. Gen. Irvin McDowell's army toward Manassas Junction.

Stuart and the 1st Virginia were ordered to screen Johnston's movement and, if possible, rejoin the army at Manassas. The cavalry performed its duty masterfully and reached the battlefield at Bull Run in plenty of time to contribute to the Confederate victory there.

On the day after the battle, Philip H. Powers took the opportunity to write and assure his wife that he had survived the day's holocaust. He described the horror of the battlefield and talked of his wish for peace, a topic that would continue to grow in his future correspondence. The following day he wrote again recounting the aftermath of the battle and his feelings concerning what he had experienced.

Unlike Powers, William Willis Blackford did not focus on the horror of the battlefield, but instead gave a vivid description of his involvement in the war's first major engagement.[42] *Blackford was the 1st Virginia's adjutant, appointed by Stuart sometime in late June or early July, though his commission was dated July 21 when he received it. A man of innumerable talents who later became Stuart's engineer officer, Blackford reported his participation in the battle in a letter to his uncle on the twenty-seventh.*

July 22, 1861

You see to-day my beloved wife I have sent you hurried notes on my safety—and our glorious victory. Just now Richmond came up, and I will send another by him.[43] I have not time to write the particulars of the battle—Can only say it raged for hours with incarnate fury. That our Regiment at one time was in the thickest of it but our losses not very heavy. The Clarke cavalry behaved very well and were much praised by Col. Stuart.

The field of Battle after the fight presented the most awful sight you can imagine. I was sent over it with an order and at some parts found it difficult to ride among the dead without treading on them. Greatly mangled Crying Oh my God what a sight!—And what a Sin. About 4 the enemy fled in utter confusion leaving every thing behind them. Baggage of every description was strewn for miles—Muskets Cannon wagons ambulances are now on the road for ten miles from the scene of action and are being collected and brought in. Within a few hundred yards of where we are now is a church wh[ich] they took possession of for a hospital. In and around are 279 dead & wounded—many out in the drenching rain will die before morning. Around are arms and legs.[44]

But why continue the awful description. The sight of one tenth of what I have seen ought to make every one satisfied with the war and ready for peace.

Our men have provided themselves with all kinds of spoils—I have only taken Pistols and a few small articles one of which I send my little daughter Alice in this letter.

They were amply provided with every comfort in the way of clothing and little conveniences; all of wh[ich] they threw away to expedite their flight.

They had 50,000 men in the fight—we only 15,000—our main force never getting in—Gen. Johnston told Col. Stuart last night that the Va troops under Jackson won the day.[45]

Our loss is very heavy. I met with ——— [name illegible] after his Reg. had been in the fight—And with tears in his eyes he told me his men were cut to pieces & his dearest friends dead. I had no time to get names for the balls were falling thick and fast around. Today I learn that the loss of the Reg. is not as heavy as was 1st supposed. But as we are encamped some 7 miles from the Junction [Manassas] I cannot find out accurately who is killed and who is safe.

Richmond waits—Farewell. God bless you and save this poor country from another such battle.

Ever Yours
P. H. Powers

———

Camp at Fairfax
Ct House
July 23rd 1861

My Dearest Wife,

Several Clarke men, among them Kneller were in our camp for a short time this evening but I was so busy I had not time even to drop you a line and fearing less the same thing may occur again I write tonight though excessively fatigued.[46] Yesterday we had a drenching rain all day and most of last night, and being without our tents we could not escape the rain and wind. We broke our camp, however, about midnight and marched to this place accompanied by two regiments of infantry and one battery of artillery. I was glad to leave for as I wrote you we were near by a hospital of the enemy where were over 300 of their wounded, dead and dying. Many of them necessarily left out in all the inclemency of the weather to die. To pass by it was enough to soften and sicken the hardest heart. I will not dwell upon the awful scene. The Battle was nothing to this afterpiece. The excitement of the contest, the cheering of the soldiers the triumph of victory rid the battle field of many of its terrors. Nothing—Nothing could lessen the horrors of the field by moonlight. Enough—I cannot, I will not describe it—May God in His infinite mercy avert a second such calamity. Our march, after we got beyond the scenes of the fight, was rather cheering than otherwise. For twelve miles the road was literally strewn with every description of baggage, wagons, ambulances, barrels of sugar, crackers, ground coffee & thousands of axes, spades, shovels, picks, arms by the thousand—clothing of every description—cooking utensils, in fact every thing—and all left behind to expedite their flight—which was never stopped until they reached Washington.

Our troops have been busily engaged in appropriating every thing they might possibly need, from a pin cushion to the finest army tent. In this place we found collected in several houses clothing enough to fill every room in our house. Their Army was splendidly equipped, with every possible convenience and comfort. But I cannot account for their utter confusion and panic.

Their own papers give our Regiment the credit of turning the tide of victory on our side. The papers, if you can see them, will give you all particulars of the day.

Speaking just now of spoils, I only have taken what was necessary, and in some few little notions. Tell your brother I sent by Kneller a revolver, a very good one I think, but different from any I have ever seen.[47] I did not get the mould but any gun smith can make him a pair or large buck shot may answer.

I took several very fine ones.

I do not know what our next move will be, but suppose it will be upon Alexandria. All I desire is to drive them from our soil, and secure peace. I would not shed another drop.

When you can—write me & send by private convenience—There will be some one coming to the Army almost daily from Clarke—and I feel very anxious to hear from you. I have not seen Edmond and Hartwell yet, but know they were not hurt our cavalry being the only cavalry that charged the enemy. I cannot write more. Farewell! I pray that my wife and little children may be protected and comforted at all times—

Ever Yours

P. H. Powers

24th—A bright morning and a clean shirt makes a great change in a man's feeling.

I feel very well—and more cheerful.

Ever Yours

P. H. Powers

July 27, 1861
Fairfax CH
Head Q. 1st Reg.
Va, Cav.

Dear Uncle John

The great battle has been fought & won and three of us have been active participants in it. Chas. [Charles] is safe but I have not heard from Eugene.[48] I got his friend Randolph McKim to go down to look him up yesterday.[49] You can form but little idea of the ———— [two words illegible] they sustained. We have supplied the whole army with almost every thing they needed. The roads are lined with abandoned wagons filled with property of every kind. I was in the charge made by Stuart's regiment, to which we are attached. Col. Stuart has made me Adjutant of the regiment, which position is a very imposing one and the comfort of my life is much greater. I was fortunate enough to make a draw of 80 prisoners with three men. I also captured a wagon and four horses. We are now here and our Colonel is in command of this brigade consisting of two regiments of infantry and one of cavalry and a company of artillery. We lost nine men killed sixteen wounded & nineteen horses in our charge. We charged in column by fours. I was two horses length from the head when we struck the column of the enemy who were the N.Y. Fire Zouaves. We slew them at a great rate with our pistols. I doubled one fellow up by a shot in the stomach as we dashed through which was the only shot I got. I was not touched, nor my horse. I had trouble in getting back over the dead horses. Chas. [Charles] I saw after the battle and he was well. I must now close, Love to Cousin ———— [illegible] family. Your aff. [affectionate] Nephew

Wm. W. Blackford

Following the battle, the cavalry advanced to within sight of the defenses of Washington City. Stuart established picket posts at Fairfax Station, Falls Church, Munson's Hill, Upton's Hill, and Mason's Hill. Once again the two antagonists took the opportunity to regroup and prepare for what was to come. The victory at Bull Run did not give the Confederacy its independence as it had hoped. For the North, the defeat aroused a new resolve to continue the fight until it was won. July came to an end with both sides jabbing at each other's picket lines.

AUGUST

During August, Stuart continued to maintain his pickets at the key positions he had established in late July. Very little occurred other than outpost skirmishing as the postbattle lull continued. Encounters at Pohick Church on the eighteenth, at Bailey's Cross-Roads on the twenty-eighth, and at Munson's Hill on the thirty-first were typical of how Stuart and his cavalry spent the month. This type of fighting became known as petite-guerre, *the "little war," but it was just as deadly as any battle.*

Stuart was constantly on the front lines, and his staff and headquarters personnel were expected to perform accordingly. When things quieted down, training and drilling resumed, as Stuart wanted not just to maintain but to improve the efficiency of his command. In their free moments, the men took time to visit friends in other units or arrange for wives and families to visit. Stuart brought his wife, Flora, to stay at Fairfax Court House near his headquarters on the Little River Turnpike. The business of war came first, however, although compared with the din and chaos of First Manassas, August seemed like a quiet vacation.

The shock of First Manassas having somewhat subsided, Peter W. Hairston's letters of the seventeenth, eighteenth, and twenty-third reflected much of what was transpiring throughout the army as the men settled into their camps and waited for something to happen. The lack of any reference to "Cooleemee" would seem to indicate that all was well there. Each of the letters was sent from a different location, and Hairston apparently enjoyed his rounds of visitation and the new people he met. He was determined to get home for the winter months, however, and was not at all ready to make the army his permanent home.

Camp Longstreet
Fairfax County Va
17 August 1861

My Dear Fanny,

I write merely to let you know that I am well as nothing of importance has transpired since I wrote to you yesterday. I send you a letter which I received from old Genl. Stewart of Maryland for the loan of the grey.[50]

We moved camp on yesterday are now still nearer the enemy surrounded by woods.

I dined on yesterday with the members of the Washington Artillery and found them a nice set of fellows. Their Capt. [Thomas L.] Rosser I admire very much for his gallantry.[51] I expect to spend the winter at home unless North Carolina is invaded.

I rec'd a letter from your father dated the 9th. He has purchased the salt for me and directed Mr. Giles to make arrangements about the shoes.

I have received no letter from you for the last several days.

I remain most
affectionately yours
Peter W. Hairston

Vicinity of Alexandria and Washington City

0 1 2 3 4
Scale of Miles

Dranesville

Georgetown

Leesburg and Alexandria

Turnpike

Loudoun and Hampshire

Potomac River

Langley

Turnpike

Chain Bridge

Lewinsville

Georgetown

Vienna

R.R.

Ball's Cross Roads

Arlington

Mill's Cross Roads

Falls Church

Upton's Hill

Ft. Runyon

Fairfax Court House

Munson's Hill

Little River

Mason's Hill

Bailey's Cross Roads

Annadale

Turnpike

Fairfax Station

Orange

and

Alexandria R.R.

Alexandria

Pohick Creek

Accotink Creek

Telegraph Road

Pohick Church

Accotink

Potomac River

Richmond
18 August 1861

My Dear Fanny,

I have met since I have been here the Episcopal clergyman Dr. [William N.] Pendleton and the Methodist preacher Dr. [Dabney] Ball of whom you have heard me speak as being two men whom I admired.[52] The latter has given me a long account of the Regiment since I left. [Robert] Swan is very unpopular so much so that some of the Captains have refused to serve under him as Major & Stuart has applied to have him transferred to another Regiment.

I dined today with Mr. & Mrs. Ficklin. They had some very nice melons for dinner. I made your apology for not returning their visit.

Col. [Robert C.] Puryear called to see me today.[53] He said he saw the President on yesterday and had a conversation with him about another cavalry Regiment and the President told him it would be impossible to arm one. I expect to call to see him tomorrow myself.

Gov. [Thomas] Morehead is unwell.[54]

No news of any interest today—a perfect lull in the storm. We are expecting every day to hear of Lee having a fight with Rosencrantz [Brig. Gen. William S. Rosecrans].[55]

I should like so much to see the children & yourself.

Most devotedly yours
Peter W. Hairston

Mr. Harrison's
Prince William Co Va
23 August 1861

My Dear Fanny,

The morning after my arrival at the Junction [Manassas Junction], I borrowed a horse and rode over to the camp of the 11th N.C. Regiment which was several miles off to find Julius.[56] Upon arriving there I found he had been removed to the country and being upon a borrowed horse, I had to return & go to the camp of 1st Cavalry some 15 miles distant.

Yesterday I rode up here & found Julius at this place a distance of some 22 or 3 miles at a farmer's home where he is kindly cared for and is improving. His physician does not think it is typhoid fever but that it proceeds from over-exertion and some bilious symptoms. He was very much alarmed at first and very nervous which with a desponding temperament militated against a recovery. He is now hopeful and cheerful this morning—pulse good and skin pleasant with a disposition to sleep and his tongue clearing off.

I find the movements of the army completely paralyzed by sickness. Not less than ten thousand men are on the sick list. Most of them at first having the measles & then being exposed produces the typhoid symptoms. The forces here are too largely overestimated being not over 53,000 men when they are all well.

Reports of sickness in the Northern army is [sic] even worse than it is in our own. McClellan is calling for men and telling them not to wait for their clothing & provisions but to come in to Washington even before their Regiments are full merely as skeleton regiments. This demonstrates severe alarm. He too has to contend against the jealousy of [Maj. Gen. Winfield] Scott, [Brig. Gen. Irvin] McDowell & all the older Genls. whom he has superseded and it will no doubt break him down ultimately, tho he may make some bold and daring movements.[57]

They are already saying of him what has he ever accomplished in a military point of view except to overcome some 1500 men in Western Virginia with 15,000.

Prince Napoleon does [not] appear to have made a very favorable impression here. Capt. Fauntleroy told me he looked around stupidly at everything and left as soon as he could.[58]

I had a very pleasing interview on yesterday with Genl. Johnston. He treated me with ———— [word illegible] courtesy as I thought. I laughed at him about the conversation he had with the men about the onions. He told me it was true and occurred near Harper's Ferry, just about the time he left there. They were some Kentuckians in ———— [word illegible] the many small gardens which surround that place.

I felt complimented that he should concur in a remark which I made from what I had observed in my limited experience in the army. It was this that I thought the smooth bored musket with the bayonet was about as good a weapon as the soldier could have. He gave a very decided assent and said he thought the expectations from the improvements in arms and long bearing guns were entirely too great. To have about one fifth of the men armed with them to bring on the engagement and to be used at long distance in its commencement was ample.

A good many of the officers have resigned, however, he would not give them leave of absence to go home.

I met John [Goolsby] on yesterday going down to camp with my horse quite lame from the injury which he received in being put on board the cars.

The wanton destruction of property and the desolation produced in Fairfax County by the Northern troops is disturbing to behold. Many families are completely ruined and have had to take refuge elsewhere.

No wonder the vengeance of the Almighty should be aroused against a people who thus violate all other dictates of his teachings.

Several of the U. S. officers who fought against us at the battle of Manassas have resigned & come over to our side. That victory is quite a knock down argument in our favour.

Julius [Caldwell] has sent in his resignation, because he says he can not stand camp life.

There is some dissatisfaction in our Regiment owing to the appointment of Swan as Major and from other causes. The men say they & their horses are worked too hard. I found, however, on going to Mr. [Col. Charles] Fisher's Regiment [6th North Carolina] the same state of things had existed there and they had complained of him in a similar manner. Now, however, they say they know how much he did for them and can see the difference between when he was ———— [word illegible] and now. They are very anxious to find out into whose hands they will fall and say they will never get a man who will take the same care of them that he did— that he performed the office of a subordinate and attended to every thing. He would be constantly doing something. It was his nature.

We have a cool bright day after a hard rain last night.

Remind the children of me often. Kiss them for me and do not let the baby forget me.

I am uneasy about you as I have not heard from you since I left home.

> Most truly & devotedly
> yours
> Peter W. Hairston

SEPTEMBER

August turned to September with little variation in the routine that had been established shortly after the Battle of First Manassas. The troops manning the outposts of both armies traded goods, words, insults, and occasional shots as each side waited for something to happen. Stuart and the cavalry continued to be in the forefront of the army fighting off enemy incursions, making scouts and small forays, and at times escorting the commanding generals along the picket lines to observe the enemy.

From the number and frequency of Peter Hairston's letters during this month (he wrote fourteen over a twenty-seven-day period), Stuart's voluntary aide evidently had plenty of time to record his thoughts. The wide range of topics in just the first four letters would also seem to indicate that Hairston had many leisure hours to fill. Of special interest are his observations on the impact of the war on the people living between Manassas Junction and the Potomac River and his comments on Antonia Ford, reputed Confederate spy and soon to be "honorary aide-de-camp" for Stuart.[59]

Camp Bee
3 Septr. 1861

My Dear Fanny,

I merely write to say that I am well.

We moved our camp on yesterday a few miles below Fairfax Court House on the road to Falls Church.

Genl. [Pierre Gustave Toutant] Beauregard visited Munson's Hill the position we are holding. He is a small man of foreign aspect.

I have had the blues ever since I heard of the foray upon North Carolina.[60] It would have better not to have thrown up any fortifications, than such as they did make, so as not to attract their attention. I am afraid now they will treat the whole Southern coast in the same manner and subject it to their piracy.

I am very anxious to hear from the children not having heard in several days.

Most affectionately yours
Peter W. Hairston

◆━━◆≣◆◆

Fairfax Co Va
4th Septr. 1861

My Dear Fanny,

A severe headache on yesterday renders me feverish and nervous to day, so I shall remain quietly in quarters.

I heard yesterday one of the most romantic incidents of the war. Miss [Antonia] Ford of Fairfax Court House having received information thro' the Federal officers who took up quarters in her mother's house, that the enemy intended to make an attack on the 18th of July on Manassas and their plan of attack, procured permission the night before to visit her grandmother who lived six miles off. She then procured an old and rough-going horse and made her way to Manassas where she was taken prisoner by Capt. [Thomas L.] Rosser of the Washington Artillery from New Orleans. He carried her to Genl. Beauregard and she revealed to him their plan of attack which enabled him to place his men in ambush and commit such havoc on the enemy on the 18th.

On yesterday I saw a beautiful bouquet which she had sent Capt. Rosser and I would not be surprised if the matter ended by her leading him Captive. She is said to be beautiful and accomplished and I know him to be a brave and gallant man.[61]

I saw at Fairfax Co. Ho. Mrs. Thomas who is sister to Jackson who killed [Col. E. Elmer] Ellsworth in Alexandria.[62] His wife also lives there.

Many families in this country have left their homes and gone off some at the approach of our army and some at that of the enemy. It will be a howling wilderness for some time after the close of the war.

One of Genl. Beauregard's spies came into our camp last night and gave me information that the Federal government ——— [word illegible] sending reinforcements to forts Hatteras & Clark. I will telegraph the information to Govr. [Henry T.] Clark.[63]

I have not heard from you in several days and feel restless and uneasy about the children.

> Most affectionately &
> truly yours
> Peter W. Hairston

Camp Bee
5 Septr. 1861

My Dear Fanny,

Not having heard from you for several days renders me restless and uneasy.

Nothing of importance occurred in our department on yesterday except the visit of Genl. Johnston who was visiting the outposts.

I hear that Beauregard and himself intend to move their Head Quarters to Fairfax Court House some twelve miles in advance of their present position. Whether this movement indicates any change of policy is more than I can say as they keep these things very closely concealed.

There was some firing yesterday upon the enemy just above the falls of the Potomac. We run them away from their guns and out of their encampment, but being across the river and our men having no means of crossing could not get their guns.[64]

We have received two more companies of Artillery and I am told they are making some very large guns in Richmond to be placed along the Potomac to stop the navigation of that river.

John [Goolsby] found the great _General_ Stewart of Maryland on yesterday at Fairfax Court House and recaptured his horse, in very much the same condition as when he left him with the General.

The General gave him a very amusing account of his riding him over the toes of the Yankees. He said he was recaptured by our men and they treated him worse than the Yankees did before they found out who he was. All the Northern officers to whom he was conducted were his personal friends, some of whom he had frequently entertained at his home.

All letters which have my name written on the back you have to pay the postage of, at home.

The enclosed letter was written by the sister of Mr. Watkins commission merchant in Richmond.

All soldiers become more or less demoralized and trespass upon the inhabitants of the country through which they pass. Dr. [Dabney] Ball and myself were conducting a Regiment of Tennesseeans through a road in the neighborhood and very much to our chagrin and mortification they would get out into the fields and commit depredations.

Last night I was awakened by some of our soldiers cursing, having become excited over a game of cards.

This is a sorry & gloomy day in camp.

With a kiss for the children & my best love for yourself

>   I remain
>   most affectionately
>   yours
>   Peter W. Hairston

Camp Bee
Fairfax Co. Va
8 Septr. 1861

My Dear Fanny,

"I have seen th? wars," such was the language on yesterday of quite a good looking lady with two little children. She lives just upon the contested ground between the two armies. Her husband wished to join our army but she objected and retained him at home. The northern army came. He was pointed out to them as a disloyal citizen by some of the northern people settled in this county, was arrested by them, refusing to take the oath of allegiance, has been off hand confined ———— [word illegible]. She refused permission to see him or have any communication with him. Now she wishes she had permitted him to join our army. Mrs. Rockford's case, I have no doubt, will be that of many ladies before this war is ended. They will wish they had permitted their husbands to join the army. They stole from her a favorite horse, which was very gentle and which she had been accustomed to drive. Now she says she feels safe as she is surrounded by

Southern soldiers. Upon her door is written "This house belongs to a Southern man," and a guard is placed over her property to protect it from depredation. Around her were the emblems of her faith, the Rosary, the Crucifix, the picture of the Virgin Mary and one of the finest copies of the Douay version of the Bible I have ever seen. The houses all around her are deserted the inhabitants, being Northerners, having fled at the approach of our army, leaving every thing behind, which now plainly shows the marks of desolation which follow in the footsteps of an army.

We have a report in camp that Govr. [John B.] Floyd had gained another victory; with considerable loss of life on both sides and that he had driven the Northern forces nearly out of the Kanawha valley.[65]

Our pickets and those of the enemy are continually firing at each other. On yesterday we had a Tennesseean shot.

We are expecting Genls. Johnston & Beauregard to move their Head Quarters to Fairfax Co. Ho. This is an onward movement. Rumor through camp says President Davis prevented the pursuit of the enemy by our troops after the battle of Manassas.[66]

Napoleon said there was as much in following up the consequences of a victory as in gaining it.

With my love & kisses to the children I remain

most devotedly

yours

Peter W. Hairston

The period of relative calm was broken somewhat on the eleventh when Union colonel Isaac I. Stevens of the 79th New York Infantry with a mixed force of 1,800 men made a reconnaissance from Chain Bridge to Lewinsville, Virginia.[67] Stuart with less than a third of that number caught the enemy on the flank and rear near Lewinsville.[68] The Federal force retreated after suffering a few casualties. Stuart reported no loss. Hairston's letter of the thirteenth commented on this action, mentioning the "cowardly" conduct of the Union troops, his continuing concern for the defense of the Southern coastline, and the rumored difficulties the North was having getting men to join the regular army.

Camp Bee

13 Septr. 1861

My Dear Fanny,

The cowardice of the Northern troops is beyond what I could have conceived. We heard on yesterday after the fight of the day before [the skirmish at Lewinsville], their officers attempted to make a stand at a house just beyond where we saw them but the men broke and would not do so.

The second time still farther on they made the attempt with a similar result, and the infantry again broke and ran when they charged them with their own cavalry to stop them; but instead of doing so were fired upon by their own infantry and had quite [a] skirmish among themselves.[69]

From a copy of the New York Herald of the 9th which some men who have escaped from Alexandria brought in, I see that the Northern people still talk and vote blood and thunder against us and wish to drive off our army here by making their raids upon our coast. I hope, however, they will be defeated in this and in addition to our forces here each state will raise an army for coast defence [sic].

This New York Herald admits the difficulty of getting recruits in New York for the regular army. It says "the reduction of the standard from 5 ft. 4 1/2 inches to 5 ft. 3 inches has not had the effect which was expected to have, of increasing the number of recruits, although a great proportion of those enlisted would have been refused under the old regulations. Not more than ten men were booked in New York last week for general service, and the regimental officers were scarcely more successful."

Our only difficulty is getting arms. We could get as many men as we want if we could only procure a supply of the former.

These men who have escaped from Alexandria state the acts of the Officials there as very tyrannical and the military to have completely abolished the civil authorities. They say it is the first time they have felt like freemen for several weeks.

The reports from Maryland state that King Bombo was never more despotic than Lincoln and his ——— [word illegible] on them.

Most affectionately yours
Peter W. Hairston

Following the clash at Lewinsville, with the exception of the usual scouting and skirmishing, a quiet period again permitted the armies to peacefully speculate about and prepare for their opponent's next move. In his next several letters, Peter Hairston discussed some of the unique individuals he met during his rounds of the camps and shared an intimate conversation he had with Joseph E. Johnston, which amply illustrates the influential people he rubbed elbows with as a civilian volunteer. He continued to voice his views on the political and military situations as he saw them, criticizing President Davis and Robert E. Lee as well as predicting a possible assassination attempt on Lincoln. He apparently enjoyed army life and admitted as much to Fanny. At the same time, he assured her that for all his patriotic feelings he would be home for the winter.

Camp Bee
16 Septr. 1861

My Dear Fanny,

The firing of cannon which we heard on yesterday proved to be nothing but the enemy firing off their guns in and around Washington City. They were practising I suppose. Reports say their army is thoroughly demoralized and never will fight unless it is behind entrenchments. They are calling upon the militia of the states beginning with 80,000 from New York. This rabble will be a poor dependence for them.

Our pickets and those of the enemy are in a few hundred yards of each other. Sometimes you will hear a Yankee cry out "Damned rebel." The Southerner will reply "Bull Run" and sometimes they will shoot each other and occasionally take a drink together.

There is a club foot Texan an independent scouter who has killed a number.

Among the persons whom I saw at Munson's Hill on yesterday was Capt. Todd, Mrs. Lincoln's brother. He says Lincoln has not a single relation on his side. That his brother-in-law White of Ky [Kentucky] telegraphed to him, (when he issued his proclamation giving the South twenty days to return to allegiance), if he would allow him (White) 3 days of grace as he could not make up his mind in the twenty days.

I have received from your father a very unfortunate letter begging me to return home. I can not resist his importunities, but expect to return in some three or four weeks to remain until Spring, unless the invasion of North Carolina by the enemy shall call me before. I fear President Davis's great desire to settle the controversy without the effusion of blood will be wrongly construed by our enemy.

I hope you will retain Laura—with love and kisses for the children. I remain

Most affectionately
yours
Peter W. Hairston

Java coffee is hard to get

Camp Longstreet
19 Septr. 1861

My Dear Fanny,

On yesterday the Generals Johnston, Beauregard and Longstreet surveyed all the outposts of the army towards the Potomac. What is brewing I do not know; but I have an opinion founded upon conjecture of the position of the army alone, that as soon as the navigation of the Potomac is closed by our batteries now ——— [word illegible] upon its banks—we will do something. I had a conversation with Genl. Johnston.

"How do you do Col. Hairston."

"Genl—You give me a rank to which I am not entitled."

"I know very well, I tried to get it for you."

"I am very much obliged to you General for your kindness and regret that you did not succeed."

As to your suggestion about raising the company and being elected one of its field officers that would have been the proper course at first. But when I proposed doing so I was informed by Judge [Thomas] Ruffin that no more companies would be received and President Davis himself told me he could arm no more.[70]

I have written to you regularly—nearly every day and certainly every other day.

You might pay a flying visit to Cooleemee but had better not remain there until after frost.

I want warm shirts and drawers of any suitable woolen goods—and am not particular about them so they are warm & strong. I am glad that you are so anxious to be a good wife and hope you will not make any more such wishes as you did about me.

I fear from what I hear Genl. Lee has permitted Rosencrantz [Rosecrans] to attack Floyd without making a demonstration against him.[71]

I received a letter from Richard [Caldwell] on yesterday begging me to come home.

I think I had as well get rid of Moses.

With a kiss for the little ones I remain

Most affectionately
yours
Peter W. Hairston

I have drawn on the bank in Salisburg $250 for the salt & balance due Shoe. of last year—$400—

—•— ☱♦☱ —•—

Camp Longstreet
20th Septr. 1861

My Dear Fanny,

Yesterday was the most quiet day we have had in a long time. Nothing exciting or interesting having occurred.

I met Mrs. Bradley Johnson riding in an open Jersey wagon.[72] She had been down to Munson's Hill on a visit to her husband.

I send you a note which I have just received from Julius [Caldwell].

The Navigation of the Potomac is now or will be stopped in a few days, when I hope the Govt. at Washington may look out for squalls.

Last night our "fighting parson" as he is familiarly called in camp, had a prayer meeting. The Rev. Doctor [Dabney] Ball is quite a character— one of the bravest, coolest and most determined men I have known. We have an Episcopal clergyman called the "foraging parson", but have had him sent out of our jurisdiction. He belonged to the Maryland Regt.[73]

The tyranny of Lincoln is arousing up such a deep rooted animosity against him that I should not be surprised to hear that he was assassinated.

I saw an old man on yesterday upwards of 80 years of age who has been a strong Union man said yesterday, that he was willing to volunteer to overturn his government.

Remember me to the family with love and kisses to the children

I remain
Most affectionately
yours
Peter W. Hairston

—•— ☱♦☱ —•—

Camp Longstreet
Fairfax Co. Va
22 Septr. 1861

My Dear Fanny,

I received yours of the 15th enclosing Francy's on yesterday. Her letter is a remarkable production for a child of her age and a model of its kind.

Tell Sam Harden I met with Genl. Jackson on yesterday and he was enquiring very particularly after him and his battery. He wished to know if he was in the service.[74]

I do not wish this war to end until this mercenary horde which have invaded us have been driven back to their dens and learned that lesson of humiliation which we will be sure to teach them and all the Southern blood which they have shed shall be fully avenged.

It is true this military life is very attractive to me, its excitement and its dangers have a fascination about them; but I should prefer the comfort and quiet of home if I thought them consistent with honor and duty—but woe unto those Southerners who now falter in the time of their country's direst need.

Last night we had quite a storm. I hope it caught some of the cowardly wretches on the coast of North Carolina and sunk their vessels to the bottom of the sea, with all on board.

A federalist enquired of one of our men, "Where we got our arms"— "At Bull Run" was the reply.

Our "fighting parson" Dabney Ball tells an amusing anecdote of himself. He was at Cape May one summer and was invited to preach. He accepted the invitation; but on repairing to the room designated he found a gay assemblage of persons—ladies and gentlemen in ball room attire—the former with bouquets in their hands and engaged in lively conversation. He was invited up to the piano, took his seat behind it as a reading desk. Soon he had to call the congregation to order. He did not understand the matter until the next morning he saw in the newspaper, the joke of the service. Some wag had circulated the report there was to be a ball there that night. After the services were over his friends came up to him and tried to apologize but did not know how.

The [Richmond] Examiner does not publish my letters; but adopts many of them editorially, which I consider quite a compliment.

> very affectionately &
> truly yours
> Peter W. Hairston

I would like to engage Laura upon the same terms I offered before if you think they would be acceptable to her. You said nothing about what had become of her or your cousin Sam.

All is perfectly quiet in camp and on the line to day.

⊷—≖◆≖—⊶

> Fairfax Co. Va
> 24th Septr. 1861

My Dear Fanny,

It has been several days since I have received any letter from you. I was surprised day before yesterday upon seeing Sam Harden arrive in camp. He says that [James Thomas] Watt [Hairston] has returned to his company.

We rode up to day to see Robt. Wilson.[75] He says he can stand more fatigue than he could before he went home. He is looking remarkably well.

I must confess that I do not understand President Davis' Policy. I have hear[d] that before the battle of Manassas Genl. Beauregard submitted a plan of operations to him to unite his forces with those of Johnston and [Brig. Gen. Theophilus H.] Holmes and whip them at Manassas.[76] Let Genl. Johnston pursue them into Maryland and cut off [Maj. Gen. Nathaniel P.] Banks column and then send reinforcements to Lee.[77] This conception was one worthy of Napoleon and had it been executed I believe would have ended the campaign.

President Davis, however, for reasons known only to himself did not adopt the plan and here we are no nearer the end than we were at first. What he expects to gain by this inactive policy I can not conceive. Floyd's brilliant exploits in the West are all we have to redeem our cause in that direction Lee as yet having done nothing.

I would not be surprised to hear any day that we had stirring times here as Genl. Johnston has directed Col. Stuart not to consider his present picket stations as permanent; but to feel the enemy.

Some of our pickets had made an agreement with the enemy's not to fire at each other—which was violated by those of the enemy. An old Dutch Captain came over under a flag of truce to apologize for it. Stuart told him to clear out and if he ever caught him there again he would have him shot. The Dutchman said something about what McClellan had told, "I have nothing to do with McClellan, sir, but to whip him when I can catch him." At this the Dutchman left in high ———— [word illegible].

I am very anxious to hear from you. Our Cavalry is always in the advance hence it does most of the skirmishing. It is dull, however, now as we have not had one in more than a week.

Tell Sam Wilson I saw his uncle Alexander today and he was quite well.[78]

> Love & Kisses
> to the children
> Most affectionately yours
> Peter W. Hairston

Cousin Flora Stuart [Jeb's wife] called to see me while I was writing this letter—brought me some ginger cobbler she had made and sent her love to you

Stuart's actions at First Manassas and Lewinsville and his vigilance as the commander of the troops in the army's forward positions did not go unnoticed. On September 24 he was promoted to brigadier general. Almost immediately, Stuart began to look around his regimental headquarters for men he could make officers on his staff. Several who

*had joined the regiment in August and September were candidates, as were others
who had been with Stuart since the beginning.*

*One of the men to whom he offered a commission was Peter Hairston. Though
Hairston rejoiced in Stuart's promotion, he wanted no part of the captaincy offered
him. As October approached, he gave strong indications in his letters that his time
with Stuart was drawing to a close. His apprehension over conditions at home and
Fanny's distress over the possibility that he might be wounded or killed increased.
With all this on his mind, he still took the opportunity to express again his opinion
of Davis's running of the war and of Lee's defeat in West Virginia. New members
of the headquarters company also drew his attention as Redmond Burke and George
Freaner joined Stuart's circle of future staff officers.[79]*

Fairfax Co. Va
26 Septr. 1861

My Dear Fanny,

I received yours of the 21st last evening and am sorry to see you are so
nervous and low spirited. I expect to come home next month. You need
not send me those winter clothes until I come.

I want you to engage Laura to teach the children. It is time they were
going to school. I received a letter from your father a few days ago. He is
still regretting the Union, when every day but convinces me we remained
in it much longer than we ought. He had visited Cooleemee Hill and reports every thing going on well there.

I saw Sam Harden day before yesterday. I think he has no idea of joining the army or raising his company. I can get the position of aid-de-Camp
[*sic*] with the title and pay of Captain but that would bind me to the service. I therefore think my present position preferable when I can come and
go as I please.

We had another little brush with the enemy on yesterday; but owing
to the tardiness of Col. [Joseph B.] Kershaw of S. C. who led the attacking
column, we inflicted little or no loss upon the enemy, when we had a fine
opportunity of inflicting severe loss, and would have done it; if we had been
the attacking column.[80] I am of the opinion that Virginians and North
Carolinians form our best fighting material. Fred Brodnax could do his state
some service by raising a company and defending the coast from invasion.

I am very anxious to write Frances a letter but really scarcely know
how to pen one to her. Ordinary subjects would have no interest for her
and I fear to trespass upon her feelings.

I think I mentioned to you on former occasion that an Irishman and
myself brought up the rear when we were driven out of our camp near
Bunker Hill. I fear the enemy captured him on yesterday. He was sent as

a scout and the probabilities are he rode into their lines thinking they were ours. Burke was a useful man to us and I regret his capture if it is the case.

> With love & kisses to
> the children
> I remain
> most devotedly yours
> Peter W. Hairston

> Fairfax Co. Va
> 27 Septr. 1861

My Dear Fanny,

The weather is wet and blustering and last night the wind blew in gusts around our tent, our only protection from the storm. Nevertheless I slept well and soundly, although, I had just heard through a man who had escaped from Washington City that the enemy intended to fast and pray on yesterday and fight us to day. It is now, however, after dinner and still no sign of them, nor do I believe they intend to make their appearance.

Your anxiety, I know is very natural—it is true I have been exposed to dangers but have escaped entirely unhurt. I am not a reckless man—neither do I take credit to myself for being a very bold man—but I have tried to do my duty and I think a man is always safe in the line of his duty.

This absence does not ———— [word illegible] me from you or home but only intensifies my love for you and the children and I sincerely & truly wish the situation of the country was such as to permit me to return to it and remain with you.

I hope this storm may catch some of those northern marauding parties upon our coast and overwhelm them.

A Mr. Freaner a talented lawyer from Maryland has arrived in our camp having made his escape from Maryland a few days ago. He represents the system of espionage which they are under in that state as very harassing. He watched his opportunity and passed through their outposts.

A young man from Maryland has just told me that a gentleman in Baltimore has some large mirrors in his home and behind those mirrors he has places opened in his walls and filled with arms. The aperture is then ceiled [sic] up and papered over.

There is no one in the tent with me but our "fighting parson" and the storm is howling around us. His wife has been writing him letters about going into battle; but he says it is just as much his duty to fight as it is to preach and pray. A true, brave, genuine man is the Rev. Dabney Ball. We had a ride home late last night through the dark, after taking supper at his uncle's who tho' having been a strong union man is fast getting his feelings wound up in our cause not withstanding the war ———— [word illegible] so heavily upon the people of this part of the country.

> With love and kisses for
> the children I remain
> most affectionately, truly
> & devotedly yours
> Peter W. Hairston

⊷ ☒◈☒ ⊶

> Fairfax Co. Va
> 28 Septr. 1861

My Dear Fanny,

I feel lonely this cold windy day and should like to be at home. I have received no letter from you for two days and this adds to my feelings of depression.

Genl. Johnston is concentrating his forces and consequently has withdrawn some of the outposts which we held. This is to prevent the enemy from attacking those points and inflicting injury upon us which we could not prevent.

Through the Northern papers we have accounts of another brilliant victory by Mccullock [Brig. Gen. Ben McCulloch] in Missouri at Lexington.[81] They report their own loss at 300 killed 4000 taken prisoners and 6000 stand of arms. They state his loss in killed and wounded at more as they fought behind intrenchments.

Lee has done nothing in the West. If you recollect in a conversation with your cousin Sam I remarked I did not think him a man for the field although he may be a very skillful engineer. I think it is perfectly ridiculous, his having published a long account of a brilliant campaign which he intended to make if it had not failed. I think this shows vanity without greatness.[82]

We had the reporter for the Dispatch to dine with us to day. He is taking notes for his paper. I gave him a few items about the first Cavalry.

The President has conferred a Brigadier Generalship upon Stuart. He has offered me the position of his Aid-de-Camp [sic], but I think I shall decline it as it would subject me to the rules and regulations of war and I could not come home when I wished.

I regret very much that I did not raise a Regiment for myself at the commencement of the war. I know I could lead them into battle much better than many of the colonels whom I see here.

Women are remarkable creations. Our Major [Robert Swan] is a dissipated, gambling untruthful man. His wife is a sincere graceful and dignified lady. Yet she appears to be perfectly devoted to him—tho there is such a wide contrast in their characters. He is one of those fussy men who would worry my life out of me if I had to live with him.

A talented member of the Maryland Legislature Mr. Freaner has just made his escape and joined us.

With love & kisses to the children

I remain

Most affectionately yours

Peter W. Hairston

Why do you not spend some of your time with Grand Ma?

Fairfax Co. Va

29 Septr. 1861

My Dear Fanny,

I have nothing of interest to communicate. The enemy have occupied all the advance posts from which we withdrew our forces. This was a precautionary measure on our part as we wished to ——— [word illegible] them on into the country and prevent them from gaining any advantage over us by turning the flank of our forces stationed at those points. I regretted our falling back from those positions as I had assisted in taking them from the enemy, but I have such entire confidence in the sagacity of Genl. Johnston I feel that the present movement is all right.

I am coming home soon and do not expect to return to the army again unless I receive such an appointment as will comport with my dignity and standing at home as I feel confident I have the courage and capacity to command them and the inferior position which I have held here has given me no opportunity to distinguish myself as I could have done had I a command. Had I acted like Mr. [Col. Charles] Fisher I could probably have been a General by this time whereas now I will have to begin anew.

I will come into the bosum [sic] of my family where I know I am loved and appreciated.

I do not think President Davis is pushing on the war with that vigor which he might. Had he kept our army actively employed and the enemy engaged they would not have had time to make those raids upon our coast. His health, I fear, is too feeble for the labour which he has to undergo.

Cousin Flora, to whom I delivered your message, says she would gladly accept it, but likes to stay with the Genl. as long as she can.

Our Chaplain [Rev. Dabney Ball] has just delivered us a sermon on the duty of patience in our trials and disappointments. It was very appropriate to the occasion.

> With love & kisses to
> the children
> I am most devotedly
> yours
> Peter W. Hairston

OCTOBER

Gen. Joseph E. Johnston's orders in late September to pull back from the advanced positions that the army had held since shortly after First Manassas caused some discontent among those units who had manned them for so many weeks. Except for the tentative advance of the Federal forces, little occurred out of the ordinary for Stuart and the cavalry. Enemy reconnaissances to Pohick Church on the third and along the Little River Turnpike on the fifteenth were not even mentioned in any Confederate reports.

Over the same time period, changes were taking place at Stuart's headquarters in regard to organizing the new cavalry brigade, forming the general's staff, and settling into new quarters, which were soon dubbed Camp "Qui Vive."[83] Little occurred to disturb the progress of these projects. Stuart and the cavalry rejoiced in the Confederate victory at Ball's Bluff and continued with patrols, drills, and other duties. The relative quiet hid the preparations that both armies were making. For some, the war may have seemed far away; for others, it was just across the no-man's-land between the picket lines.

Over the first several days of the month, Hairston wrote five letters. They are newsy and relatively short. In only one does he mention coming home, though he was definitely working toward that end. His descriptions of the battlefield of First Manassas in his letter of the sixth painted a stark image of the horror of the war.

> Camp Beverly at
> Mrs. Chichester's
> Fairfax Co. Va
> 2nd October 1861

My Dear Fanny,

Since we have been promoted, we have actually got to living in a house. After so long living in a tent this civilized life is rather strange to us.

Mrs. Chichester is a very pious old lady, member of the Episcopal Church—she assembles her family around the breakfast table and just after they have finished their breakfast she reads a chapter from the bible [sic] and has prayers.

Yesterday was remarkably quiet, nothing going on.

We are just on the eve of a dress parade to take leave of the Regiment. It has taken place and the men gone thru cheers for the newly made general.

Capt. W. E. Jones is the new Colonel.[84]

It is raining hard.

We have good news from [Robert E.] Lee in the West at last.

Tell Sammy h[is] uncle James [Jeb Stuart] has won a reputation of which he may well be proud in after years.

Most devotedly yours
Peter W. Hairston

Camp Beverly
3 October 1861

My Dear Fanny,

We had a very quiet night. Watt Hairston has resigned his position as Captain not being able to stand the fatigue of marching. He has purchased a horse, bridle and saddle in order to get John Hairston into the cavalry. This arm of the service is now very popular since our success.

Watt tells me it will be sometime next week before the batteries at Evansport are completed—which will stop the passage up and down the Potomac. He also informed me we have five hundred boats sunk in the water at that point to be used when needed. Their batteries are now so completely masked the Federals can not see what is going on.

Genl. Stuart made his valedictory address to his regiment on yesterday which was well received,

I remain truly &
affectionately yours
Peter W. Hairston

P. S. We caught four Yankees on yesterday two infantry & two cavalry.[85]

Camp Beverly
October 4th 1861

My Dear Fanny,

The President reviewed several brigades of the army on yesterday and then left for Richmond it is stated to remain a few days and then return. For what purpose I do not know.

I saw in the New York Times of the 1st instant that the enemy had another Kilkenny affair—the day after we fell back from Fall's [Falls] Church.

They advanced in the night to take possession when by some accident or other one company mistook one of their own for our men when they fired into it and had quite a battle. About one hundred men were killed and wounded.[86]

We are having beautiful weather and ought to be marching against the enemy; but here we are still inactive--waiting for those batteries on the Potomac to be unmasked.

Our falling back from Munson's Hill and Fall's Church appears to have alarmed and puzzled the Northern Army more than any thing else. They say & say truly it was not weakness which caused us to retire and are completely at a loss to know what the strategic movement meant.

With love and kisses for the children I remain

> Most affectionately
> yours
> Peter W. Hairston

P. S. No letter from you in 3 or 4 days

> Camp Beverly
> 6 October 1861

My Dear Fanny,

Day before yesterday I rode, with Watt, to visit the battle field of Manassas and returned on yesterday.

It presents a horrid spectacle. Many of the bodies were slightly buried and the rains have washed the dirt from some buried in the gullies and from others the hogs have rooted the dirt away and thus left their bodies partially exposed with their ———— [word illegible] scattered about and exposing clothes, shoes and other things belonging to them. I could plainly distinguish the red pants of the Zouaves among many of them.

I met with Gus Henderson, (now a Lieut in a Mississippi Cavalry Co.) on the field.

I send you a piece of cedar plucked from a tree near the spot where Mr. [Col. Charles] Fisher fell. The cedar post planted there to mark the spot is fast being cut away by persons taking mementoes from the field.

President Davis has intimated his course—I am told—to be to let the enemy do all the attacking. He told the Mississippi troops, which acted as a body guard for him while here, on taking leave of them and thanking them for their attentions to him that in the hour of danger, he would be with them.

I do not like this inactive policy of his—if he were to keep them engaged here on the line—he would prevent their marauding expeditions on the coast. He said if we did not have a battle here before long, he would send a part of the forces South to protect that Section.

If the enemy are permitted to get possession of our coast the war will be a long protracted one.

I expect to go to Dumfries tomorrow to visit Evansport and the batteries along the river. They will be completed in a few days and unmasked when if we do not have a fight I shall despair of having one here soon.

I shall visit with home before long

Yours affectionately

Peter W. Hairston.

➤┄ ⊨◆⊒ ┄◄

Camp Beverly

October 7th 1861

My Dear Fanny,

Every thing is very quiet here with fine weather overhead.

I expect to meet Watt to day to visit our batteries upon the Potomac at Evansport near Dumfries. The impression is they will be unmasked to day or tomorrow, when the navigation of the Potomac will entirely cease.

It is bad to lend things. Yesterday I lent my saddle to a young Lt. under the express agreement he was to send it back to me last night and this morning I have to go after it. Had the enemy come last night I should have to ——— [word illegible] take it à la ——— [two words illegible].

Day before yesterday, we threw some shell into the enemy's camp and come very near killing a General so some of the neighbors report—as having been informed by their pickets.[87]

Ink is scarce. I am writing with a pencil taken from the Yankees.

With love & kisses for the children

I remain

most affectionately yours,

Peter W. Hairston

Aware of the imminent loss of his aide, Stuart made a final effort to retain Hairston with an appeal to his and his wife's patriotism, but to no avail. In the end Hairston received his permission to leave, and Stuart graciously gave him a strong letter of recommendation. Although the permission must have been just a formality considering Hairston's civilian status, it and Stuart's letter of recommendation show the re-

*spect both men had for each other. For whatever reasons, the two never served to-
gether again, though Hairston did return to the army, again as a civilian voluntary
aide, this time with Maj. Gen. Jubal A. Early.*[88]

I go to day to the Court House to get my permission to leave for home.
                                        Camp Beverly
                                        11 October 1861
My Dear Fanny,
    My life has been so eventful for the last few days that I have not been
able to write, but telegraphed to you on yesterday.
    I had made an arrangement to go to Evansport, to see our batteries
erected there. Watt who was to meet me failed to come, so I performed
the trip alone. A picket guard of the 6th North Carolina Regiment stopped
me and sent me into camp. I there found Col. [William D.] Pender who
has just united himself to the Episcopal Church.[89] I also met Minnie Scales
there.[90] She sent her love to you and enjoys camp life as she is living in a
tent with her husband—and says she never had such health. No sore throat
and eat [sic] what she pleases. It rained very hard the night before I was
there and the floor of the tent was wet; but she suffered no inconvenience
from it—had no cold. I spent a pleasant afternoon with the 6th.
    Col. Pender rode down to the batteries with me. We saw Genl. [Brig.
Gen. William H. C.] Whiting and his wife, who was a Miss Walker from
Wilmington.[91] She is also living in a tent, but has a plank floor and carpets.
They both knew your father and Genl. Whiting remarked that military men
were said to be very strict with their subordinates; but the Judge was stricter
with his than any military man he knew.
    We passed Dumfries an old dilapidated town which was once very
flourishing and vessels came up to it, but now there is nothing but a small
stream near—the port having been filled up by the debris and washings from
the hillsides. The batteries are at a place called Evansport about one mile—
two miles before Dumfries and so masked by pine trees the enemy has been
unable to find them out. They will command the river completely as they
are mounted with 40 pounders and the river here is 1 7/8 miles wide.
    They are now ready for unmasking and only awaiting communications
from Genl. Johnston to do so. The Genl. thinks McClellan must fight and
show their hand as the Potomac River will be closed through which the
enemy draws most of their supplies.
    At Evansport I met with Genl. [Brig. Gen. Theophilus] Holmes—
brother-in-law to Mr. Witman—who gave me a cordial invitation to visit
him. He used strong language in regard to the Hatteras affair and says he

preaches daily to the North Carolina Regiments under him that the recollection of the Hatteras affair must be wiped out whenever an opportunity offers.

A Mr. Fergusson, member of parliament, has been on a visit to Genl. Johnston. These Englishmen of standing visiting us has some meaning—I presume.

President Davis thinks the North will soon get to using the Guillotine among themselves, and from information gathered from deserters and some escaped prisoners I would not be surprised. These represent a great dissatisfaction with Lincoln and discontent in their army. Their men are saying they wish to go home as they think this war useless and unnecessary as they never can conquer us.

Genl. Stuart directs me to say to you <u>If I neglect the higher duties of the Patriot to be a daily companion to you, I would make you a husband to be ashamed of in after life.</u>

Write that, he says, on your mantle place whenever you think I ought to be with you read it.

I made a very important scout on yesterday. It was reported to Head Quarters the enemy were in strong force at Springfield Station on the Rail Road and were using the cars in bringing out more men from Alexandria. This was two miles beyond our lines. I took ten men and proceeded cautiously down there where I found there was no enemy and they never had been there; but men using the cars to a station two miles below there to bring provisions out to their troops and carry wood into Alexandria.[92]

For this I deserve some credit. Our escaped prisoner represents the enemy as having 185 regiments in their army of the Potomac and the Politicians of the North as dissatisfied with McClellan as they were with [Maj. Gen. Winfield] Scott. [Maj. Gen. John C.] Fremont is certainly to be court-martialled and this brings out the fact their 50,000 men in the West was nothing but a ——— [word illegible] of brag. He only had 8,000.[93]

> With love & kisses for
> the children
> I remain most devotedly
> yours
> Peter W. Hairston

Head. Qrs Cavalry
Brigade
Camp Beverly
Oct 12th 1861

This is to certify that Peter W. Hairston of North Carolina, has for the past five months been associated with me as volunteer aid [*sic*], during that time he has borne the hardships and privations of outdoor campaign with the most commendable zeal and cheerfulness. His duties with the 1st Cavalry have time and again brought him in the presence of the enemy, and he has never failed to show determined courage—intelligent apprehension of orders, and conspicuous daring. As an aide his services have been invaluable.

On the battlefield of Manassas, he was constantly exposed to a destructive fire, but bore himself handsomely throughout, having twice crossed the battlefield bearing dispatches from me to our Generals. In several less important engagements with the enemy both in the valley of the Shenandoah and Potomac, he has received for his gallant and efficient conduct my high commendation.

He has been long enough a close observer of cavalry drill and outpost service to make him particularly efficient in that duty, and I hope the country will continue to have his services, but in a much higher grade than that heretofore filled. Given under my hand at the Head quarters Cavalry Brigade, Army of the Potomac Confederate States of America the day and year above written.

J. E. B. Stuart
Brig. Gen'l

NOVEMBER

The final two months of 1861 continued with the advances, retreats, skirmishes, and scouts that had become the pattern of warfare between the two armies. Another Federal reconnaissance to Pohick Church on November 12 was followed by the capture of a Union foraging party by Maj. William T. Martin, commanding the Jeff Davis Legion, on the sixteenth.[94] Lt. Col. Fitz Lee and a detachment of the 1st Virginia Cavalry skirmished on the road between Falls Church and Fairfax Court House on the eighteenth, killing seven Federals and capturing ten.[95] Lee's horse was killed under him during the brief but hard-fought encounter. Much of this ground was continually and obstinately contested by both sides. On the twenty-sixth, the 1st North Carolina Cavalry, led by Col. Robert Ransom Jr., clashed with the enemy's cavalry near Vienna, killing and wounding several and capturing twenty-six.[96] More fighting occurred on the twenty-sixth and twenty-seventh near Dranesville and on the twenty-seventh near Fairfax Court House, as blue and gray cavalry and infantry wrestled for control of the "land between."[97]

Around Stuart's headquarters, the search for staff officers continued. The general was having some difficulty in filling the position of quartermaster. Stuart's first choice had been Roger W. Steger of the 1st Virginia Cavalry.[98] *Unfortunately, Steger could not fill his bond as required and was forced to resign from a position that technically he had never held.*[99] *To replace him, Stuart turned to Philip H. Powers, who had been attached to the 1st Virginia Cavalry's headquarters when Stuart was the regiment's colonel. There were delays, but Powers would not encounter the difficulties Steger had in filling his bond and eventually would assume the post. Stuart's letter to his soon-to-be quartermaster included instructions and advice, and revealed Stuart's concern for both Powers and the execution of the duties of the position.*

Hd Qrs Cavalry Brigade
Camp Qui Vive
Nov. 11, 1861

Dear Powers—

I received your letter to-night in which you tell me there will be delay about your commission, and then no doubt about your bond but not if you have your sureties ready to sign it as soon as the commission issues; but your time can be very profitably employed in learning the duties getting your blanks, and finding out at what point & in what quantities supplies needed can be obtained. Your expenses thus incurred will be legitimate items of account against Confederate States to be included in your accounts after you get commissioned. I wish your attention directed to the subject of copper bugles without keys for our cavalry two for every company we need them very much. See if you can what chance there is to get them. I hear there are factories of such things in New Orleans. Perhaps Col. [Abraham C.] Myers the acting Quartermaster Genl can inform you.[100]

As for explicit instructions I would not actually know where to begin. You are specially charged with the procurement of those supplies rather peculiar in such immense quantities to Cavalry such as forage & horse shoes & nails. 15,000 horseshoes are required to shoe the Cavalry once around. You can easily estimate from our strength the number of pounds of corn & hay we need for <u>daily</u> consumption, which you will have to furnish, when the supply is entirely exhausted, you have the whole state & C. S. at your command, and as your labor is Herculean—you must have agents of your own selection that you can rely upon, you will have too to have an eye to the Rail Road & see that they are prompt & careful, instead of slow & neglectful as I fear they too often are.

Remember there is no virtue so much in requisition for a Quartermaster as <u>Patience.</u> Indomitable energy and untiring industry without patience will wear you out. You must not attempt to do everything yourself, superintend generally, the business is too extensive for your labor to be spared for a single place. Lupton ought to be with you, he is useless here.

I have been very favorably impressed with Edmund Harrison, & hope he will get the appointment of Capt under you.[101]

Matters are as when you left. I have just returned from an expedition to the vicinity of Acotink [Accotink] Village where I hoped to bag a Regiment of Yankees but they had left long before my arrival.[102]

We brought back a pet coon.[103]

Col. [William E. "Grumble"] Jones the other day made a scout near Binn's & bagged 7 Yankees.[104] You forgot to resign your position as Sergt major—date it Novr. 1st 1861. Col. [G. W.] Custis Lee, the President's Aid [*sic*] is my most intimate friend & was my classmate at West Point.[105] I haven't seen him for a long time but I hope if you see him you will give him my regards—& tell him how proud I would be to have him inspect my outposts. Tell him to come down. Give much love to Mr. Steger. Tell Roger that while I regret deeply the circumstances which compelled him to resign, I honor the self denying impulse that prompted his course. If you see Gov. [John] Letcher tell him not to forget to have 4 12pdr Howitzers for me very soon—my artillery will be in the field soon.[106]

Don't forget the Bugles—

The staff join in regards

Yours truly
J. E. B. Stuart

DECEMBER

The coming of December brought nothing new to the struggle. On the second at Annandale, Col. Charles W. Field, with a detachment of his 6th Virginia Cavalry, made a dash at the Federal picket line that left 4 of the enemy dead and another 15 prisoners.[107] On the sixth at Gunnell's Farm near Dranesville and on the eighteenth near Pohick Church, the petite guerre continued. Stuart reported a number of these smaller actions, though for the most part he was not involved. On the twentieth, however, while in command of a foraging expedition of about 1,200 infantry and a few cavalry, he found himself confronted at Dranesville by almost 4,000 of the enemy. Outnumbered and with a wagon train to protect, Stuart managed to break free after suffering 194 casualties to the Union's 68. Stuart would have much rather ended the year with a victory, but considering the odds against him, he could be thankful that things had not gone worse.[108]

*One of the young men who fought at Dranesville was soon to become a familiar
sight around Stuart's headquarters. Chiswell Dabney, all of seventeen, had experienced his first real fight. With the exuberance of youth he wrote to his mother, who
undoubtedly did not share his enthusiasm, about his trial by fire.*

December 24th 1861

Hd. Qrs. Cav. Brig.

Dear Mother [Mrs. Elizabeth T. Dabney]

I received your very affectionate & kind letter this morning & as I have
not written to you before I set down now promptly to answer it. I wrote
to Aggie day before yesterday giving her an account of my first battle, which
they (the officers) say was more hotly contested than that of Bull Run, in
fact we fought for two hours & a half with 2000 men, an enimy [sic] of
15,000 strong, saved our wagons, & fell back, in perfect order with a loss
of only 193 killed wounded & missing. The next day we went back &
brought off all our killed & the wounded that we left the day before; which
was only about 12. The enimy lost about 250 or 300 men & stopped firing
at the same instant we did at least they fired only one gun more than we
did, & didn't pursue us at all which proved that they were as much crippled
as we were if not more.

Gen. Stuart has made out his report in which he mentions me amongst
others who were of good service to him on that day, & Gen. [Joseph E.]
Johnston also did me the honor of enquireing [sic] of Gen. Stuart who I
was & where I came from as he only knew me before as a certain Dabney.
I had to escort him home (Gen. Johnston) the other night & the old gentleman very politely asked me in his quarters but as it was quite late at night
I refused.

Gen. Stuart['s] staff consist[s] of Capt. [Luke Tiernan] Brien of Maryland a young man Wm. [William Eskridge] Towles[109] from Louisiana who
by the way is a relative of ours, he & I sleep together & mess together that
is we all mess together with the Gen. & lastly Mr. [Redmond] Burke the
great scout who was taken prisoner by the Yankees some days ago & carried to Washington but very romantically made his escape, an account of
which you will find in the Richmond Dispatch.

I wish you could possibly do it send one hand trunk to put my things
in as my valise is too small. I will have to get a uniform from somewhere
as I thing [think] this one which I have will give out shortly. You tell me
in your letter to make myself comfortable & I can assure you I am in as
good quarters as I want. I have a nice large room to sleep in & with Towles'es
[sic] bed clothes & mine combined I sleep very comfortably & after rideing
[sic] as much as I do very soundly. I haven't been out of my saddle a whole

day with the exception of one or two since I have been down here. You also seem to think that because I am young I cannot stand the hardships of military life, but with several conversations with officers that I had they all agree the young men of my age stand it better than any others in fact I could cite hundreds of instances of the kind. Give my very best love to Bettie & tell her that Gen. Stuart enquired after her the very second question he asked me was how is Cousin Bettie which I answered to the best of my knowledge. Give my love to Charley when you write to him & tell him to be sure & leave that North Western Army as soon as he possibly can, & tell him also to join Stuart if he wants to be under a brave chivalrous & energetick [sic] commander for he possesses all the qualities in the highest degree.

I went with the Gen. to Drainsville [Dranesville] to get our dead with only two regiments of infantry & a few cavalry but the Yankees had left that morning early so we took quiet possession of the field & got all our killed & wounded but while I was there in the town of Drainesville [Dranesville] the Gen. & myself rode up to where there were several very pretty young ladies & commenced talking with them they admired my horse very much & said they would like to ride uptown to their home so I jumped off & offered my horse to the best looking one & another officer lent his to another & they mounted & rode all down the lines of Infantry we walking by their sides. It was the first lady I ever saw on my horse & I think the horse become the lady & the lady became the horse so they both looked very well. You must have a very merry Xmast [Christmas] at Vaucluse.[110] I wish I could be there but that is impossible. I suppose the girls will stay in Lynchburg with Nannie during Xmast week. Give my very best to all at home & tell them that I would be very glad to see them. I am very well myself & hope you are all well too. I believe that I have told you everything I can think [of] so good buy [sic] my dear Mother. I remain as ever your most affectionate son

Chiswell Dabney

P.O. I would be very glad if you would send me a box of things for new years.

The year did not end quietly. Again on the twenty-fourth and twenty-fifth there was skirmishing near Fairfax Court House. Not even Christmas passed with "peace on earth, good will to men." [111]

The new year would be little different.

1862

JANUARY TO MARCH

The new year began quietly, with little more happening than outposts and pickets exchanging pleasantries, tobacco, coffee, and at times occasional shots if the situation warranted. The cold weather had much to do with the lack of activity on the part of both armies as January passed peacefully into February.

On February 3, however, the calm was interrupted by a Federal reconnaissance toward Occoquan Village in the midst of a snowstorm. Stuart himself was not involved in the brief skirmish that ensued on the outskirts of the village, though some of his cavalry pickets came under fire as the Federals made their way back to their own lines past Pohick Church. Quiet again reigned until the twenty-fourth, when Confederate infantry struck a Federal picket post about a mile beyond Pohick Church near Lewis' Chapel.[1] The Confederates filed no reports on either of these actions.

March opened with a skirmish on the fifth near the familiar ground around Pohick Church, though the Confederates involved were probably infantry and not Stuart's cavalry. From the seventh through the ninth, the Confederates withdrew their forces from around Evansport, Dumfries, Manassas, and Occoquan, giving up positions they had held since the summer of 1861. Stuart and the cavalry brought off their tents and equipment and by the thirteenth had established a new picket line from Warrenton down to the Brentsville Road to alert the army of the Federal advance that was sure to follow. Between the fourteenth and sixteenth, the line was probed but not penetrated by a Federal reconnaissance near Warrenton Station and along Cedar Run.[2]

This stalemate continued until near the end of the month, as Stuart maintained his cavalry pickets from the Blue Ridge to near the Potomac. On the twenty-eighth, skirmishing took place along Cedar Run. The following day a Federal force under the command of Brig. Gen. Oliver O. Howard marched toward Bealeton as Stuart withdrew over the Rappahannock River and joined forces with Maj. Gen. Richard S. Ewell's infantry division. By dawn of the thirtieth, the Federals were retreating, and Stuart hurried his troopers across the river in pursuit. The enemy finally encamped around Warrenton Junction.[3] Stuart settled down to watch them and spent the thirty-first writing his report.[4]

There are no letters or diary entries by any member of Stuart's staff from January through March. During these months the staff increased in size, and by the be-

ginning of April it consisted of Maj. Philip Henry Powers, quartermaster; Maj. Dabney Ball, commissary officer; Capt. Luke Tiernan Brien, assistant adjutant general; Lt. John Pelham, commander of the Stuart Horse Artillery; Surgeon Talcott Eliason, medical director; Lt. James Thomas Watt Hairston, acting assistant adjutant general; Lt. Chiswell Dabney, aide-de-camp; Lt. John Esten Cooke, voluntary aide; Lt. Redmond Burke, voluntary aide; and Lt. William Eskridge Towles, voluntary aide.[5]

APRIL

Through early April, Stuart continued his observation of the Federals as Gen. Joseph E. Johnston tried to determine Federal major general George B. McClellan's plan. At last Johnston decided that the main Federal thrust would come up the peninsula between the York and the James rivers. Immediately he began to prepare to move his army to the vicinity of Yorktown, where he could oppose McClellan. The Confederate cavalry had performed well under Stuart's command and would need to continue to do so if the move was to be successful. Among those who would help coordinate the move was the cavalry's new quartermaster, Maj. Philip H. Powers.

Powers had become Stuart's quartermaster on March 18. He had left the 1st Virginia Cavalry, where he had held the rank of sergeant major, to join the staff. During the last days of March and the beginning of April, he began to assume the duties of his new position. As he penned his letters to his wife, Roberta, on the second and third, he knew nothing of the hurried activity that was soon to come, and focused on how he was settling into his office and some of his activities. He also made a reference to dyspepsia, one of a series of illnesses that were to plague him continually for months.

Culpeper Ct House
April 2nd 1862

My Dearest Wife,

I was fortunate enough to reach this place without difficulty last night and to get very good lodgings—and this morning I write trusting to get my letter off by the return train. Mr. Ballard and Sis F. met Willie at Gordonsville on his way to Richmond.[6] I did not have time to see him. Mr. B. [Ballard] said he was very sick—his case aggravated by the bite of a dog on his thigh, which had enflamed. Poor fellow. I hope and trust he may recover. At Orange Court House I met with Mr. H. Willis and he came on with me to this place. We slept together by which I had a very <u>comfortable</u> bed fellow. He left Jefferson the day of Jackson's fight and passed through the lines safely—has been to Nelson County on business and is now on the return home. Of course he brings the latest news from our county. He says the enemy have committed no outrages whatever—have not interfered with

private property or citizens—have made no arrests except of persons connected with the Army. Stores have been opened at ———— [word illegible]
and Winchester from which the citizens are allowed to purchase salt gro-
ceries & etc. at reduced prices. He says a great many Negroes have run off,
but when he left not one of your Father's had left him. He knew nothing
of our children—I shall write a few lines by him to Miss Hall—or Miss
Ware—telling them of your whereabouts. If you have any intimation of
Jackson's falling back south or east of Staunton you had better go to Staunton
before he effects his movement. Write to me as soon as you get this and
direct to Culpeper Ct H. care of Gen. Stuart's Cavalry Brigade. He is at
Brandy Station five miles below this—I shall join him to day.

I have not time to write more. Give love to all. Tell Alice she must
learn to write now and write to me.[7] I sent you a pencil letter written on
the cars yesterday by Wm [William] Donaghe who intended stopping in
C'ville [Charlottesville]. In that I told you to direct to Gordonsville but the
mails are running sometimes to this place.

God bless you my dear wife and be your stay and comfort in all your
trials, ever pray,

Yours As Ever
P. H. Powers

━━ ≡◆≡ ━━

Culpeper Ct House
April 3rd 1862

My Dearest Wife,

The irregularity of the mails is such that I know not whether to write
or not, and yet I do not feel satisfied unless at least making an effort to
communicate with you. I sent you a letter yesterday by mail which I hope
you receive. After writing it I rode to Genl Stuart's Hd. Qrs. near Brandy
Station in the fine new house of James Barbour.[8] I managed to see many
of my old friends—visited the Clarke Cavalry—and found them as dirty as
any set of men I ever saw. I have not the time to mention the individual
members—nor do I suppose you care to hear. I am ordered for the present
to fix my quarters here. Major [Dabney] Ball [commissary officer] and myself
and employees have a large office and are reasonably comfortable—though
I have not been in office except at night. Today I went up to Rapidan,
some 15 miles in the cars, on business, expecting to return in the evening
train. There was no evening train, and I had to foot it—quite a walk, but
it did not tire one much. I will not tell you any thing of my business until
I find out more about it. I know I shall experience many difficulties and

trials—but I hope to endure them. I will do my best—no man can do more. The dispepsia [sic] is still troubling me—and our bread is awful. Edmund Harrison is here. I am much afraid he will not suit me. He is too careless—and too fond of ease—this is entre nous.[9] Hasty is also here tonight. He is well but dirty.

I had a telegram from Mr. Ballard to-day stating that William [Ballard] and Lelia [Powers] were better.[10] I have not as yet learned to write while so much talking is going on—so must close—Friday morning—I append a line this beautiful morning my own dear wife merely to say that I am well. I hope to hear from you by the first mail. I saw a Baltimore Sun yesterday of the 28th which contained a list of the prisoners taken in Jackson's fight—among them was Bushrod Washington and George Washington was among the names of the wounded in Winchester.[11] Several of the Bartons were named as either wounded or prisoners.

I know nothing of our movements but hardly think the enemy will advance on this line—and now my dear I must stop. I have much before me to day. If I could only think of you as being cheerful and contented, could only hear from you and our poor little ones I could bear the hardships of this war with a better spirit—could you see our soldiers however exposed more for a month to all the privations of constant bivouac and short rations my privations would seem light indeed. Give much love to all. Kiss Alice for me. And love most particularly to Aunt June—

To the care of Him, who alone can comfort you, I commit you my beloved—praying that He may lead you into perfect submission to His Will.

Ever Yours
P. H. Powers

In obedience to his order from Johnston, Stuart, who had his headquarters near Brandy Station in the home c^f James Barbour, made preparations during the second week of the month to once again screen the army's movements and then withdraw to rejoin it. By the evening of the twelfth, Stuart and his brigade were encamped seven miles outside of Richmond headed for Yorktown, where they arrived on the eighteenth. The entire operation was kept from the majority of the officers and their men until the time for its execution. Though the terrain of the Peninsula would limit the cavalry's role in the campaign, for the remainder of the month Stuart tried to prepare his troopers for what lay ahead.

That the movement and its destination were not widely known is evident from Powers's letters of the sixth and fourteenth. He had no idea what was going on behind the scenes at cavalry headquarters. He wrote his wife once from Richmond on the seventeenth and again after settling into a new camp near Yorktown. He also penned a letter to his sister. His letters of the twenty-first and twenty-seventh revealed a growing despondency over his work. *From the beginning, he had doubted as to whether he had done the right thing in leaving the 1st Virginia to accept the quartermaster position. The responsibilities soon began to weigh heavily upon him, and his health began to suffer almost immediately. The cavalry's transfer to the Peninsula with its damp climate contributed to his weakening physical condition. The letters reflected his growing depression throughout the remaining days of the month.*

Culpeper Ct House
April 6, 1862

My Dear Wife,

This beautiful Sabbath morning though very much indisposed from dispepsia [*sic*] which depresses my spirits most distressingly and totally incapacitates me for business, I must attempt a short letter to you.

I have sent you several since I left Richmond but as yet have heard not a word from you. I find our brigade in such a condition that the business of my department is worrying almost to desperation. A thousand times have I regretted ever aspiring to anything above the simple position of Sgt. Major. That carried with it no responsibility and but little work. The circumstances of our Brigade changed so since I left and affairs have been managed so badly that as yet everything seems confusion to me. With the help of God however, I will do my best to discharge faithfully the duties which have fallen upon me. But, Oh my wife, you cannot conceive of the intense longing of my heart for you, for my children and for a quiet home. Will I ever enjoy any one of these blessings again?

A discussion has sprung up in my office and I must close for the present—I ought not to write you feeling as I do today for I know how sad your own heart is and how much you need cheering words, but bear with me. When I feel strong and healthy again my buoyancy of spirits may return and then I will write differently. Now I am weaker than you—

Though feeling very unwell this morning, after being interrupted in my letter, and though I was compelled to meet Gen. Stuart at the depot, when I heard the Church Bell I could not resist going in. The Church reminded me of our old Wickliffe, and when the little Melodeon played one of our old familiar airs, I could hardly control my feelings, but feel as you have often felt like resting my head somewhere and having a good cry. But the Car whistled, and I had to leave to meet Gen. Stuart. Alas! that in this war there should be no sabbath. No day of rest. But blessed hope, "there remaineth a rest for the people of God." I will not write more now but perhaps add a line in the morning when I feel better—

Monday morning [the seventh]. I only open, my dear, to add a line. I feel much better this morning though the stomach is still at fault. I saw yesterday evening Dr. Fauntleroy and Philip Meade, just from Clarke, left White Post Friday morning. They represent but a small force of the enemy in Clarke. None South of Berryville. They could tell nothing of our particular friends but I infer nothing is very wrong with them or they would have heard. The Yankees have taken some horses, and many negroes have gone off, but beyond this they mention no particular outrages. Nat Meade was one of the committee appointed to bury the dead after Jackson's fight. The total number left on the field was 83. They confirm the reports of the immense loss of the enemy.

I have no time to write more. Give love to all. Kiss my little Alice and may God keep you in charge, my own wife, ever prays your devoted husband

P. H. Powers

◆─ ⊠◆⊠ ─◆

Richmond
April 14, 1862

My dearest Wife,

Very much to my surprise I find myself in the City again. Our Brigade encamped within 7 miles of the city Sat. night. Yesterday afternoon I was sent in, in order to be here early this morning to attend to some business and I have gotten up early enough to write you, knowing that I will have neither time nor opportunity but this. I can't say that I have experienced any pleasure in marching to Richmond. I am glad to see our friends again, but you, my beloved, are away, and the rejoicing of others at meeting with their loved ones but adds poignancy to the Constant pain I feel at being separated from you and my little ones. Still I am glad you are not here. I could see you but for a moment. The grief of another parting would have to be borne. Oh, my Wife! I cannot tell you how often, how deeply I have thought of you during our march from Culpeper here. How ardently I have wished that our route might be towards the Valley!

We took up our march on Tuesday last without an hour's preliminary notice, and with no intimation of where or how far we were to go. Thru the terrible storm of Wednesday and Wednesday night, the men were exposed to all its inclemency. We brought not a wagon, not a tent. Not even a change of clothing and ate what we could get. We marched to Rapidan the first night, Louisa Courthouse the 2nd, Trinity Church the 3rd, and here the 4th. So much for the generalities of this, to me, very unnecessary march.

As to my own individual discomfort and trouble, it was small. I rode several hours in advance for the Column every day, selecting a Camp, and getting in forage for the horses by night. Fortunately I was very successful in my arrangements and though attended with considerable labor and worry, yet my position gave me an opportunity of getting good meals on the roadside, and good quarters at night and I feel much better than before we started. Have nearly worked off the dyspepsia.

Where are we going? That is the question. We all supposed we were hurrying to the Peninsula, where the great battle of the War seems to be impending, but it is now intimated that our services are not needed there, that they have enough Cavalry, and that we will probably be sent to Suffolk or N. Carolina. These are only rumors.

I sent you a letter from Louisa Ct. House written in Culpeper and until I got here I had not heard a word from you since you left. We had no mails to Culpeper after the letter I sent you from there. I hope to get a letter from you while we are encamped near here. Saturday I gave James $100 to send you by the 1st opportunity.[12] We sent it out yesterday by Major Macgruder.

They say here that you are only waiting to hear from me to take up your line of march also towards Clarke [County]. If I thought it possible to have you where I could either hear from you regularly or see you sometimes I should ask you to go to that place, but as I feel assured that our campaign will be a very active one, that I shall be unable to see or hear from you, I am still of the opinion that you had better get to Clarke if possible. At the same time, if you prefer remaining on this side with our friends whether here or elsewhere, think you will be happier or better satisfied, I interpose no objection.

Would to God, my dear, that I could take you and my little ones and flee to some quiet corner of the earth, there to pass the remainder of my life where neither wars nor rumors of wars might be heard of. I am tired. I long for rest and for peace. I am writing from Brother William's. He is quite unwell and Lelia is still very ill and cannot last much longer. I was sorry to hear that brother James had forgotten to send my likeness to you. I have a vast amount of business to get thru with today so must close.

Give much love to all and take to yourself, my dear wife, that which is yours. My love to Alice. I will tell Jim to write to you as soon as our destination is ascertained. God help you my dear, yours

P. H. Powers

Richmond,
Tuesday morning
April 17th 1862

My Ever Dear Wife,

While waiting for the omnibus I write a line. I shall get off this morning. William Ballard is ill at Culpeper and Mr. B. [Ballard] and sister F. [Fanny] go up with me.[13] Lelia is worse, tho better this morning than yesterday. James had determined last night to resign, perhaps he will change his mind this morning. Capt. Preston told me he saw you safely arrived at Charlottesville. I do trust, my beloved, that you are comfortable and contented. I have no words to express my dear, my feeling since you left. This is the hardest blow yet. You are before me all the time and the weight, almost unbearable, presses upon me unceasingly. But God is good, to Him I can trust you, Mr. Ballard and brother William both insist that you return to Richmond if you have any difficulty in getting on. And I hope you will do so. I know they will take care of you. Do not hesitate to apply to any of my friends for assistance. They all love you as one of their own and in these times we must not be proud. Should you want money before I see you, either draw on Brother William, or borrow from Mr. Lobban.[14] I hope some change will soon take place, which will enable you to get home, for I still feel that if separated from you, which is almost certain, I would prefer your being with our dear little children. I had the likeness taken for you and left with brother James to send to you by first opportunity. If you can have a small one of yourself taken in Charlottesville do so. Some opportunity will occur of sending it.

Mrs. Stuart rec'd a telegraph from the general yesterday telling her to come to Brandy Station with her children. That does not look like an early advance of the enemy. Brandy is beyond Culpeper. He also stated that he had pursued the enemy nearly to Warrenton Junction, capturing some 40 officers and men. Gen. Joe. Johnston was in Richmond yesterday. The Bell rings. Give love to all and oh, my wife, be brave, and trust all to Him, who abates the storm to the Shorn Lamb. A trustful cheerful spirit will conduce to your health and alleviate your trials. For my sake and the sake of our little children, be courageous. The end will come after a while. Kiss my Alice. Tell her to learn fast. Write me and direct to Gordonsville, I will try and get it by someone, or if you hear of anyone going to Culpeper Courthouse.

Good bye,
Ever yours
P. H. Powers

Camp New Yorktown
April 21, 1862

My Beloved Wife,

Since leaving Richmond I have been so driven by difficulties, conse-
quent on a forced march thru poor country that I have not even attempted
to write you. I feel as if I were separated from you by an immensity of
distance. At times as if I had lost you altogether. And I can hardly bear up
against the pressure that weighs me down almost to destruction. But God
is merciful and thru Him I yet hope for a brighter day and a happy reunion
with my loved ones once more.

I wrote to you from Richmond. We stayed near there until last Wednesday then marched hurriedly down here. Arriving at our present location 6
miles from Yorktown Friday morning. What we were brought for I cannot conceive unless to gratify Genl Stuart's ambition to get in a fight. The
ground does not admit of the operations of Cavalry except to a very limited extent. The supplies are very scant and difficult to get and both men
and horses are in a fair way to starve if we are kept here long. The impression seemed to be that a great battle was to be fought here but I somewhat
doubt it. If I could only hear from you, only know where you are. It may
not be, His will be done. Pray for me my wife and pray for your self that
God in His infinite mercy may sustain us in all our trials.

With love to all
ever yours
P. H. Powers

⊷ ⫘✦⫘ ⊶

Hd. Qrs. Cavalry
Brigade
Camp Forlorn
April 27th, 1862

Dear Sister Mary,[15]

Since I have been in the service it has been my custom, rarely deviated
from, to write to Bert [Roberta, his wife] always on Sunday evening. 'Tis
useless to write to her now for from what I hear communication is most
probably broken between Richmond and Staunton and I suppose I will
hear from her and my little darlings no more until this terrible strife is ended.
As I cannot write to her I turn my pen to you knowing that you also will
be glad to hear of my condition in this the most "forlorn" of all places.
Well I am as yet neither <u>entirely</u> devoured by <u>ticks</u>, nor swamped in mire
though I have been in eminent and repeated peril from both. I had sup-

posed that Manassas excelled the world in the depth and filth of the mud. I had not then experienced the soil of Warwick County.

The weather has been despicable since our sojourn in this encampment. Cold rains nearly every day. And our men have not a tent. I have managed to make myself passably comfortable. Sleeping in a neighboring farm house when the weather was very bad, and at other times in a very comfortable tent which is only allowed to Quarter Masters and Commissaries. They ought to have some perquisites to compensate for the insessant [sic] worry incident to their duties.

I have seen your brother Col. [John E.] Johnson several times: his quarters are not more than a mile off.[16] I understood yesterday that he was not reelected; he did not expect to be as he told me a day or two ago. He had been kept too much from his Regiment. A great number of old officers are thrown out in the reorganization very much I think to the detriment of the service. But this democracy hydra-headed monster it has ruined our government, and now its baneful influence is rapidly demoralizing our Army. I sometimes almost wish for an autocrat to crush it out.

We are expecting a battle. The lines of the two armies stretching across the Peninsula, in many places not more than 500 yards apart; from which an interchange of shots is continuously going on, night and day. But still the fight does not come off. I am almost afraid this is only a feint. That a heavy force will hold us here while the advance upon Richmond will be made elsewhere. I do not like the appearance of things ——— [word illegible]. Our army and government appear to me to some extent in confusion. And nothing but hard fighting and successful fighting and that right off can extricate us.

Edmund [Harrison] mentioned in a note that my wife had been heard from, that she was in Staunton, and would get home. This is all I have heard. I hope she may reach Clarke safely. I shall be better satisfied when I know she and the children are together and at home once more. I hardly dare think of them now.

When I reflect upon what this unholy war ——— [three or more words illegible] broken up and scattered all the sources of my earthly happiness; in the bitterness of spirit I could curse those who originated it. But God is good and just. To His will we must submit—my time runs out—

Give much love to all. I hope brother William is ——— [word illegible] ere this. It would be a comfort to hear from you. And our nearest office for the present is "Grove Wharf."

Kiss the little ones

Very Affectionately
Yours
P. H. Powers

MAY

May found Stuart and the cavalry in the vicinity of Yorktown, with the Confederate forces soon to begin their withdrawal up the Peninsula toward Richmond. In his report of May 13, Stuart recorded that on the third he was entrusted with the rear guard and established his line along Skiff Creek. About noon on the fourth, the Federals began their advance up Telegraph Road, driving back the 4th Virginia Cavalry under Lt. Col. Williams C. Wickham. Stuart mounted a countermove and drove back the Union cavalry, but he was forced to retreat toward Williamsburg when Federal infantry appeared.[17] Meanwhile, Wickham and the 4th Virginia, along with the Wise Legion Cavalry and the Hampton Legion Cavalry, engaged the Federals near Fort Magruder southeast of Williamsburg. In driving them back, Wickham was severely wounded.[18]

On the fifth, the Battle of Williamsburg was fought. The Confederate rear guard of Maj. Gen. James Longstreet's infantry and Stuart's cavalry offered stubborn resistance to gain time for the rest of the army to continue its withdrawal. Stuart was stationed near Fort Magruder and had the pleasure of seeing the Stuart Horse Artillery under the "gallant Pelham" in action for the first time. After dark brought an end to the fighting, the Confederates withdrew.[19]

During the first week of the month, a dashing young South Carolinian joined Stuart. William Downs Farley was destined to become one of the most celebrated members of the staff.[20] His actions during the Battle of Williamsburg were but a few of the daring exploits he performed while riding with Stuart.

New Kent C. H.
May 9th, 1862.
5 o'clock A.M.

My dear Mother [Mrs. William R. Farley]:

Knowing how anxious you would feel about Hugh [William's brother] and me when you heard about the Battle of Williamsburg, I write this the first opportunity.[21] We are both uninjured—

Hugh's Brigade was not engaged. I made two very narrow escapes the day before the battle: lost my own horse, lay concealed in the bushes for half an hour, then joined in a fight against the enemy's Cavalry with our Cavalry; captured another horse,—splendid fellow; was again cut off by the enemy, was chased for a mile and had my horse wounded in two places; had to take to the woods for second time, on foot I worked my way by eleven or twelve o'clock at night to our friends.

Monday morning [May 5], having no horse, I told General Stuart I would go into the fight with the Infantry, capture another horse and then act as his aide again.

Went into the 19th Miss. Regt—then on picket in front of the enemy—killed four men before the battle commenced; one of them the Capt.

of the 47th N.Y.[22] Have his sword, a fine one. Soon afterwards the whole Regt. advanced, made a charge, the Col. was killed we kept advancing and falling back, fighting all the time, and steadily driving the enemy before us.[23] This part of the Battlefield is universally considered the hottest. Two of the flag bearers of the 19th Miss. were shot down in succession, I caught up the colors myself and bore them for some time, until one of the Officers of the Regt. requested me to give them to a member of the Regt. I did so, he was immediately shot down; another took it, and I <u>think</u> he was wounded.[24]

There was considerable confusion in this part of the field on account of the death and absence of Field Officers; and I actually took command of the 19th Miss., the 9th Ala., and some shattered companies from other Regts. Leaping upon the stumps and logs, I discovered that the enemy's battery was silenced by our cannon from the Forts. Shouting to the men to come on and take it, we did so.[25] Running forward some distance in front, and our own Forts not knowing (on account of the smoke) that we were friends who had taken the enemy's battery, continued firing upon us, and I was struck by a piece of our own shells in the breast, and knocked down, but not much hurt. I leaped up and caught one of the Yankee Officer's fine horses which was left with the battery, and rode full speed to our Forts and stopped them from firing upon us; then went to Gen'ls Johnston, Longstreet, and Stuart—who I found together, and communicated the first joyful intelligence that we had whipped the enemy and taken their battery.[26] The enemy afterwards received reinforcements and continued the fight until night.

It was considered necessary by our Genl's. to continue a backward movement, chiefly on account of nothing to eat for our army; so we had to leave that night, and left almost all of our wounded at Williamsburg. We sent some fifteen of our Doctors under a flag of truce to attend to them.

We had a considerable fight with the enemy (day before yesterday 7th) who had landed from their gun boats to our right and drove them back, killing and capturing some two or three hundred of them.[27]

I have written this in great haste, on my saddle. I have slept and ate little for several days, but am perfectly well and can stand anything. Hugh is looking finely.

I had, in the hottest of the fight all day, only one ball to touch even my clothing; that was done while carrying the flag; the blow from the shell hurt me a little that night but I do not feel it now.

God bless you all and keep the detestable Yankees from your home. Pray for the Success of our Confederacy.

Your Aff. Son,
W. D. Farley

Over the next several days, the cavalry and its commander received the praise of various officers as it performed its rear-guard duties. The retreat continued until the army was about twenty-five miles from Richmond. Here the Confederates awaited the slow advance of the Federals, everyone thinking another battle would soon be fought.

The conditions on the Peninsula under which the armies lived, moved, and struggled dulled the patriotic fervor of men on both sides, and many longed for peace, rest, and loved ones. Philip H. Powers was among those who had reached the end of their strength and resolve. He continued on solely from a sense of duty. But the war had taken a terrible toll on him physically, emotionally, and mentally. Farley's letter, filled with the fire of youth, stands in sharp contrast to Powers's letters dated the twelfth and fifteenth, which depicted a man depressed over the war and his seemingly endless duties as the cavalry's quartermaster.

New Kent County
May 12, 1862

My Ever Dear Wife,

I know it is extremely doubtful about your ever receiving this but my conscience reproved me for not having tried to send you letters oftimes than I have done since we have been on the Peninsula. I have written several times and have received one letter from you dated the 23rd April. Our service has been such for the last month, moving all the time in the saddle night and day and bivouacking wherever night overtook us without tents and removed from Post Offices that it seemed folly to attempt to write and to send letters to uncertain points.

Today however I saw Hite Opie and he told me of your still being in Staunton a week ago and of the communications between Richmond and Staunton still being open. I write this hoping it may reach you there. Hite informed me of your sickness. I trust by this you are well again and that Jackson's victory may so far clear the Valley of the enemy as to enable you to reach Clarke.[28] I shall be better satisfied when I know you are once more with our little ones and near our old home. But I cannot see how you are to manage it, unless the enemy leave the Valley road open. Still you are with friends. I know you will act for the best.

Of myself now I know you wish me to write. And yet I hardly dare venture. Physically I have been generally very well. My comfort as a soldier has been generally sufficiently provided for but from the constant pressure of business attended by insuperable difficulties ever present added to the awful horrors of this war presenting the sad picture of ruin and woe and death every hour and at every step my mind sometimes seems to be overwhelmed and I am almost reduced to desperation. Were it not for your beloved image my own dear wife and the vision of my poor little children

I would rush into the thickest of the fight and shut out all these horrors by death. But thanks be to our All ruling Providence these dark thoughts are generally dispelled by the hope that I shall yet fold you in my arms and live in peace with you and our children—and that hope saves me. I shall take care of myself. Preserve my life if possible and work to discharge the duty I owe my country.

You have heard the particulars of the battle of Williamsburg. I will not go over the horrors of that day—except so far as I was interested. I had been stationed in Williamsburg for several days preceding that of the battle. The day was terrible—a cold heavy rain all day. I was unwell but went on the field and remained until 1 o'clock then became so sick from wet and cold that I left and went back to my quarters and to bed. The victory was clearly ours though the ground did not admit of our profiting much by it. Our loss was very severe and all our dead, and I fear many of the wounded, left on the field. That night our army withdrew; the Cavalry leaving Williamsburg about sunrise. Our wounded were left. You have no conception of the roads. My horse several times sunk so deep in the mud that with great difficulty I could get him out. It reminded me of the Yankee retreat at Bull Run. Our soldiers having fought all day in a drenching rain were too fatigued to carry their knapsacks and blankets; they threw them away and for a mile or two the road side was strewn with baggage. Many wagons stuck in the mud and were left. Tents were standing and ever shame to whoever did it. Several fine pieces of artillery were abandoned by the road side—and so we marched—the Cavalry covering the retreat. Slowly the enemy followed us, afraid to come within striking distance. Nothing was left after the first few miles, but we were five days getting to this point— 25 miles from Richmond—and here for three days we have expected another battle but the enemy does not come. He is either afraid or not ready. The march had discouraged me more than anything during the war. I have seen our soldiers worn out—weary—almost starving. At New Kent Ct House I saw our commissary draw 20 bushels of corn to parch for his men! They had nothing else. But this was bad management. The government had provisions in abundance but they were not in reach. The retrograde movement had been retarded by the battle and the close pursuit of the enemy. But it is over. Now must come the great battle either here or nearer Richmond.

At New Kent Ct House Edmund [Harrison] joined me and brought your letter. I can hardly tell how rejoiced I was to hear from you, but it made me sad; I cried over it like a little child.

You tell me to save my pay. Have you any idea of the price of living in this barren peninsula? Bacon . 75 Butter $1 etc. An Officer must buy his rations and our commissariat is getting too poor to furnish anything but a little flour and hard biscuit, and very scant allowance of bacon. I have had to buy a horse at a high price never having found mine—though I heard of her in Culpeper. I have a beautiful mare now—bought near Yorktown and if I get safely out of the war hope to give her to you for your own riding horse. She would suit you exactly. You will have heard of Lelia's death. I have not heard from Richmond except through Edmund and I only saw him for ten minutes—had to send him back at once on business.

I must close—it is late. I write in a deserted house near the road side and by the light of a candle which cost me .25! I often think of the many letters I wrote you last spring and summer. It was a pleasure to write then. I knew you would get my letters and my spirit had not been broken by the war. Well would it have been for me if I had retained my position in the 1st Reg [1st Virginia Cavalry]. Promotion would have been certain, and I should have been spared the unceasing troubles of a Quartermaster of cavalry. But all I recon [*sic*] I hope is for the best. I must stop. Remember me to our kind friends in Staunton. Kiss my little girl—bravely war against the cares and troubles which would crush you. And look forward with the hope which alone sustains me to that day when we shall once more be united and in peace. May God bless you my own wife!

Ever yours

P. H. Powers

—•— ≡◆≡ —•—

New Kent

May 15th 1862

My Dear Wife,

I received yesterday a letter from Sis Frances enclosing one from you to her and asking me to write to you to return to R. [Richmond]. I cannot advise it. The people of R. I understand are in utter consternation at the approach of the Yankees and I believe the city will ultimately fall. Should you return there, I might perhaps catch a glimpse of you, but that would be all. And what then? In a month or less I may be 500 miles from here. No if you are comfortable remain where you are and give up all hope of seeing me during the war. My business is such that I can never expect to leave the Brigade except on business and for very short periods. I long to see you my dear, to fold you once more in my arms but confess it would be but little satisfaction to see you for a moment, and be torn away at once. My spirits are broken, the buoyancy of my disposition gone and the incessant worry of this Quartermaster's business will, I believe, drive me to desperation. To you I shall say remain in Staunton if you can and when possible join our children. Endeavor to make yourself comfortable and do not think too much of me. I am too selfish not to look out for my own comfort and safety. I detest this war. Curse its origination and will not if I can possibly help it allow it to drag me into continual misery and discomfort. Our Cavalry service has got to be odious. Continually in the rear of our army we have to subsist by plundering and stealing and many a home has been made desolate by the approach of Stuart's Cavalry. The standing order is impress everything that may fall into the enemy's hands. And thus we march with the wailing of women and children constantly ringing in our ears. Oh God! When will the end of these things be?

Last night Louisa Ann brought a letter from you dated April 26th and advertised it in the R. Post Office.[29] You should always direct your letters to the care of some one in Richmond. I am sorry I did not write oftener while near Yorktown and Louisa [Court House], but I thought the communication was interrupted and indeed had but very few opportunities of sending to Richmond and fewer opportunities of writing. If I could sit down and write you as I used to do when Sergeant Major of the 1st Regt. it would be now as then a great pleasure to write to you daily but times are changed. I am changed. I cannot write cheerfully when every thing looks so dark and hopeless.

We are still some 24 miles from Richmond daily expecting a great battle to come off. Every day pickets dash in saying the enemy is advancing. But they come not. They are either afraid or determined to worry us out by strategic movement. I wish it could be settled by one great battle. Our troops are generally in good spirits but suffering many privations and hardships—half rations and no tents. I myself as usual have an abundance. Edmund [Harrison] sent me a box from R. yesterday with eatables. My quarters are in a deserted house where I can have a fire and a bed-stead without a mattress to sleep on. My body does not suffer. I have an excellent servant to wait on me, a fine horse to ride, and am under little or no military restraints; but my mind never rests. I shall send this letter perhaps by private hands and hope you get it. I think the Valley will be cleared of the enemy before long and you will be enabled to get home. Keep your spirits up. Hope for a brighter day and do not suffer the fast of not hearing from me to weigh upon you.

I will write oftener hereafter.

Give love to all friends.

Kiss my little daughter and tell her to learn fast.

May God protect you my own precious wife!

Ever yours
P. H. Powers

Like Farley, another young officer at cavalry headquarters was not feeling the weight of the war or responsibility as was Powers. Chiswell Dabney showed no depression or anxiety, and in fact, seemed to be looking forward to the struggle that many predicted lay ahead. Dabney believed the titanic battle for Richmond was close at hand. His own recent adventures only heightened the expectancy he was feeling. He also believed that the Yanks would be beaten back and the capital saved.

Hd Qrs Cavalry Brigade
May 18th 1862

Dear Mother [Mrs. Elizabeth T. Dabney]

I received a letter from Aggie enclosed with one from you in which you desire me to reply to it immediately & as I have time now for the purpose I will commence although I cannot say that I will finish today, as I commenced yesterday to write & was interrupted by the enimy [sic] advanceing [sic] upon us. I had to get up & ride to get out of their way, went over to the 4th [Virginia Cavalry] Regt to carry an order & the Yankees get between me & the Genl [Stuart] & I had to ride about twenty miles to get back to him which I did without any adventure. They followed us to the Bottoms bridge on the Chickahominy where they stopped, we having burnt the bridge, fired upon them & they went back in a hurry dropping their caps in every direction.

I wrote you a letter after the battle of Williamsburg from New Kent Co Ho [Court House] thinking that perhaps you would like to know how I came out of it. I will here state that I am well & sound and ready to fight the Yankees before Richmond. Look out for a great battle. We are going to whip the Yankees sure. We have been having daily fights ever since we left Williamsburg and this has been the only quiet day I have had for some time. Aggie asked me to tell her about the Campaign. Tell her I havn't [sic] room or time to give her a full exposé of all I know & think but that I am pretty certain we will have a fight in a few days immediately before Richmond & whip the Yankees.

My mare is in very bad condition & I think she is in foal which will render her unfit for service but I shall let my boy take her. I hired a boy yesterday from Mr. Savage of this county (Henrico) for $12 a month.

I just write a few lines to let you know how I am here. After when I have more time & a better opportunity I will tell you everything about my Peninsular Campaign. I am writing on the bare ground so you must excuse my scribbling.

Your most
affectionate son
C Dabney

The battle many had hoped for failed to materialize. Johnston again withdrew to within a few miles of Richmond. With its church spires at their backs, the Confederates determined to stop the Federal advance and save the city. The Union army's thrust toward Richmond had stretched supply lines almost to the breaking point. Time was needed to gather strength for the final assault. Exhaustion brought a temporary halt to the fighting except for the usual minor skirmishes that had become almost routine for the cavalry. The month ended with the opening phase of the Battle of Seven Pines on the thirty-first.

JUNE

Although Stuart had no opportunity to use his cavalry during the fighting of May 31 and June 1, Major Generals James Longstreet and Gustavus W. Smith praised him for what personal assistance he did provide.[30] During the fighting on the thirty-first, the Confederate commander, Gen. Joseph E. Johnston, was severely wounded. His successor was Gen. Robert E. Lee, who immediately began to take steps to drive back the Federal army. He was soon dubbed the "King of Spades," as he set his men to digging fortifications to defend the Confederate capital. This "ground offensive" gave the impression of a static defense of Richmond to many observers. But behind closed doors, plans were being laid that would earn Lee a different reputation entirely. Those plans included Stuart and his cavalry.

Things were also happening behind the scenes at cavalry headquarters and elsewhere. Stuart was ever on the lookout for talented young men to add to his growing staff. Positions were available, but not just anyone would do. As the month of June began, James Hardeman Stuart and Frank Smith Robertson entered the ranks of prospective staff officers. Of the two, Hardeman Stuart was much closer to filling one of those positions, since General Stuart had been working through various departments in Richmond to arrange for his double third cousin to join his staff as soon as Hardeman's commission was confirmed. Hardeman's letter of the fourth showed that Stuart was successful in his lobbying.

Robertson, however, would have a longer wait, because his health had been seriously impaired during his service as a lieutenant with the 48th Virginia Infantry. Stuart had offered Robertson a position on his staff while visiting the bedridden young man at his home. Robertson's impatience at being incapacitated while the war raged on is quite evident in his letter of the seventh, as is his reluctance to accept the position Stuart had offered.

Richmond Va.
June 4th '62

Dear Aunt Ann,

I have this day received my appointment as Captain in the Signal Corps. My old chum [Capt. Robert E.] Wilbourn being equally fortunate.[31] I have been sick for some days past. I think I am improving now. Nothing new. Yankees in a few miles of Richmond but they will <u>never</u> take the city. Oscar is well.[32] Love to all at home & Rose Corrage. I am ordered to report to Genl Stuart and will be attached to his staff. I am

Affectly
Your Nephew
J. Hardeman Stuart

Capt. J. Hardeman Stuart
Signal Corps
Richmond, Va.
Care of Genl J. E. B. Stuart

◆◆◆

The Meadows
June 7th '62

Dear Pa [Wyndham Robertson],[33]

Your letter reached us yesterday & confirmed my fears of your detention. We also received three or four Richmond papers, bringing the first news from that point for several days—the wires were down & it was impossible to even hear why the train was detained. I suppose ere this you are safe in Richmond & really I begin to feel very much like being there too.

I find it impossible to become reconciled to leading this quiet, inactive life at home, even when convinced it is best.[34] I have however improved very much since my arrival here & with the exception of occasional pain in my heart & arm, feel almost as strong as ever—a week longer I hope will enable me once more to take the field—in what capacity however I find it hard to determine. Infantry is the arm of service I prefer, but without an office, not suited either to my health or inclination—Cavalry I would rather enter as a private, than any thing else, but I know no company in which I am well enough acquainted to make it agreable [sic]—while the place offered me by Gen. Stuart is one I should rather not accept, if my health admits of service elsewhere. Please find out the usual outfit of a volunteer Aid [sic] & let me know. I think it probable an aid to Gen. Stuart would require horses.

I am glad you have determined to have the young horses broken—with the assistance of Sam, I shall go to work to morrow.[35]

Your affec't Son
Frank

There actually was little opportunity for Stuart to work on assignments to his staff. Lee's plans would keep him occupied for quite some time. On the eleventh, Stuart

received orders from Lee that confirmed their discussion of the previous day. Lee wanted Stuart to conduct a reconnaissance in force of the Federal army's right flank in order to determine whether it was vulnerable to attack. With 1,200 men and two guns of the Stuart Horse Artillery under 1st Lt. James Breathed, Stuart set off on the twelfth on what became known as the Chickahominy Raid. He not only completed his mission successfully, returning on the fifteenth with the information Lee desired, but also performed the unprecedented feat of riding around the entire Federal army.[36]

Among the gallant troopers who made the famous ride was Aide-de-Camp Chiswell Dabney. After almost a week had passed he finally laid down his saber and took up his pen to write his mother about the raid. Frequently in the middle of the action, Dabney was able to recount the fall of the brave Captain William Latané, the only Confederate fatality of the expedition, and give a list of his "captures."[37] *That he thoroughly enjoyed the trip is quite evident.*

Hd Qrs Cavalry Brigade
June 18th 1862

Dear Mother [Mrs. Elizabeth T. Dabney]

I have been intending to write to you for the past three days but have been so busy that I could not find time to do so, but I shall now try to make amends by writing you a long letter.

———— [word illegible] I started with Genl' Stuart last Thursday to make a foray. I did not know where, neither did I care, marched all that day & camped that night in Hanover. Next morning we started early to try to make a visit to the rear of the grand army. We proceeded to Hanover Co. Ho. [Court House] where we came upon the enimies [sic] pickets. They very soon withdrew though loseing [sic] one man a seargeant [sic] of Cavalry. We next came upon the enimy [sic] beyond the old battle ground where the Fredericksburg army fought some time since. There both parties charged upon each other at a gallop, pistol & sabre we used very freely & here it was that the lamented Capt. Latane [sic] fell pierced with three balls. When I got to him he had just breathed his last. I found his sword bent by a blow from the enimies sabres, having been struck from his hand & sticking in the ground. I gave it to one of his men & told them to send it to his family.

From here it was an almost continual charge to the enimies encampment. They always flying before us. We burnt up their camp and a great deal of very fine clothing. I got my negroe [sic] boy a splendid suit of cavalry uniform & a pair of boots. I also procured myself a pair of very fine pants which are exactly the color of our uniform pants. This saved just twenty five dollars which I would have had to pay for a pair in Richmond. We also captured $5000 in Federal bank notes.

I am sorry to say that during this melee I lost my spur, my glove & my

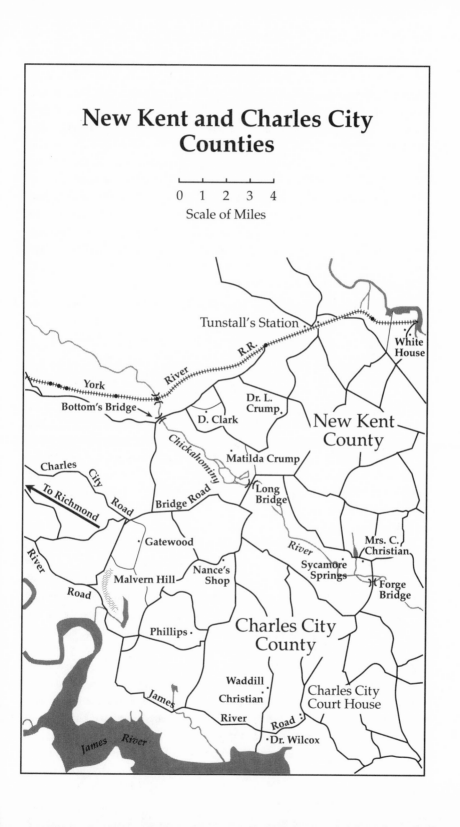

New Kent and Charles City Counties

0   1   2   3   4
Scale of Miles

Tunstall's Station

White House

York

R.R.

River

Bottom's Bridge

Dr. L. Crump

D. Clark

New Kent County

Charles

City

Chickahominy

Matilda Crump

To Richmond

Road

Bridge Road

Long Bridge

Gatewood

River

Mrs. C. Christian

River

Malvern Hill

Nance's Shop

Sycamore Springs

Forge Bridge

Road

Phillips

Charles City County

James

Waddill Christian

Charles City Court House

River

Road

James River

Dr. Wilcox

purse with $200 in it, also my commission, the latter, however, the Adjutant General told me the other [day] he would renew for me, but I must say that the pleasure of having the immediate command of a party to burn a large train of Yankee wagons was more than equivalent to my loss. I had laid up that money to buy me another horse with, but all my calculations are knocked in the head now.

I received a letter from Bettie some time since. She sayes [sic] that all are well with her. She also askes [sic] me whether I could not write to her occasionally. Tell her when you write next I will do so whenever I can. Give her my best love. Whilst we were on our expedition we traveled two days & two nights with[out] stopping to eat or sleep & I tell you I was about as tired as you ever ———— [word illegible] any individual.

Good-by. We are going to whip the Yankees like the mischief in a few days. In the mean time I remain as ever your most affectionate son

Chis Dabney

PS Give my love to all at home & tell Charley to make haste & cure his rheumaticks [sic] if he wishes to go to Washington with us.

C Dabney

The cavalry rested for a few days and then on the twenty-fourth received Lee's orders for the coming campaign. The following day, Stuart set off to rendezvous with Stonewall Jackson. The cavalry's role was to safeguard Jackson's route of march and provide him with information on the position of the Federal force in his front. In the fighting around Mechanicsville on the twenty-sixth and Gaines's Mill on the twenty-seventh, the cavalry rendered what assistance it could as the infantry of the two armies grappled with each other.

An opportunity for the cavalry to take a more active part presented itself on the twenty-eighth. Lee ordered Stuart to attack the Federal army's supply lines, which were centered on the "White House," home of Lee's son, Col. W. H. F. "Rooney" Lee, along the Pamunkey River.[38] Stuart reached the "White House" on the twenty-ninth, only to find the Federals gone, tons of supplies destroyed, and Rooney's home in ashes. The next day, he marched to Forge Bridge, where the Stuart Horse Artillery briefly clashed with Federal artillery. With darkness approaching, Stuart bivouacked for the night.[39]

Participating in this whirlwind of events was the cavalry's new ordnance officer, John Esten Cooke, another of Stuart's relatives on the staff, this time by marriage. Cooke had been a writer of romantic novels but had had little time for writing since the war had begun. On the twenty-eighth, however, he started to jot down some observations in a small notebook. In this diary, he recorded many interesting facts concerning the fighting in the latter part of June and Stuart's and Jackson's roles in it. There is little of the writer's usual romanticism in the brief, terse entries written during lulls in the battles, and they stand in sharp contrast to his other writings.

From John Esten Cooke's Journal
Memo on the Field
Cold Harbor—*June 28 Under our tree Hd. Qrs.*
Yesterday a hot fight—in it at day as far as aid [*sic*] to cavalry Genl could be.[40] The shelling hotter than I ever knew it.

At night "Stonewall" came and lay down between me & Gen. Stuart. S. "Where is your staff, Genl?"

J. "Off somewhere in comfortable quarters—I am playing orderly to-night."

Again he—Jackson—said:

"Yesterday was the <u>most terrific fire</u> of musketry I ever heard. The cannonading was much hotter than <u>I</u> liked."

Today the fight will doubtless be renewed with fury. We are whipping them. Yesterday I sat dinner in Gen. [Brig. Gen. Philip St. George] Cooke's Hd. Qrs. vacated.[41] He pitched his tent in the yard—said Mrs. Johnson near here—and came in the house but once. His horse pickets was [*sic*] excellent.—Pitiè!

June 29th—About to leave Old Cold Harbor. Here under the tree where night before last I heard S. & J. [Stuart and Jackson] discuss the situation & lay the plan now being executed to cut off McClellan's retreat to the Pamunkey or James.

Went to Richmond last evening to change horses—mine broken down. Got a fresh one & follow with the staff this morning. The enemy burning everything at "White House."

A furious battle—I saw my dear boy Nat before and after—he had a button shot off the breast of his coat. I could have kissed the dirty noble, splendid youngster![42]

Poor [Lt. D. T.] Webster killed—[Maj. Brisco G.] Baldwin looking very blue—met him near the enemy's battery.[43] [Col. James Walkinshaw] Allen too of the 2nd Va. [Infantry] with whom I shook hands in the morning "for the first and last time."[44]

En route!

Memoranda:[45]

Orapax July 7th 1862[46]

Left 1st Regt. camp where Ordnance wagons were at sunrise June 27th—on Brook road—with Dr. [Talcott] Eliason, to follow Gen. Stuart.[47] Felt the way thro' Ashland, Hanover C. H. and by [Brig. Gen. Lawrence O.] Branch's battlefield toward Mechanicsville.[48] On roadside in some old pines met with 2nd Va. [Infantry] Col. [James W.] Allen, Jackson's old brigade, and was introduced to him by Dr. Eliason. Shook hands with him "the first time and the last time"—he was killed in the afternoon. Looked for and found my dear boy Natty—dirty, gallant, smiling, my noble splendid fellow. Also Willie Randolph, Frank Whiting and the Clarke [County] boys. The drum beat and I got into the saddle. Came to old building & saw prisoners—bucktails etc. arriving.[49] Rode on and reached 1st Cavalry. Dined hastily at Mrs. Johnson's small house in field—Gen. Cooke's Hd. Qrs. His tent had been in yard—he "came in the house only once." His Cavalry Picket posts etc. excellent. He is wretched, they say, and hopes the first ball will kill him. Pushed on to small house near (perhaps) Beulah Church. Found Gen. Stuart's staff, but continued with 1st Regt., finding the Gen. This was on the road in rear of Old Cold Harbor. Cavalry drawn up in fields there. Battle commencing hotly. Volunteered to go and find out what was the state of things. Galloped over by Cold Harbor, to house used for hospital toward Cold Harbor and observed and inquired. Returned and found Gen. Jackson on a log near old tumble down log house in front nearly of Cold Harbor. Old sun-yellowed, tilt-forward cap, dingy coat.

"General, I am on Gen. Stuart's staff. He wishes to know your dispositions."

"Wait a moment"—briefly & courteously.

"Gen. Stuart is just across there—he could ride over."

"Ask him to gallop over" —in same brief cut off tones.

In the saddle, galloping back, met Stuart near the house. Heavy fire of shell, Jackson changed his position, Stuart talking with him. Then the hot battle [Battle of Gaines's Mill]. Cavalry moving and taking position. Met Alex Boteler who had lost his coat—followed Stuart here, there, everywhere. Shells very quick and hot: evidently directed at Cavalry by signal man up a tree. Sent about with orders. [Capt. John] Pelham with a gun sent forward into field to left of front of Cold Harbor. Opened hotly— batteries of enemy replied. Shelling still hotter. Sent by Stuart to order up Cobb Legion—a squadron—to support Pelham. [Col. Thomas R. R.] Cobb had changed his position, and gone into the woods to avoid the shells.[50] Could find him nowhere. Galloped back to report and saw battery rushing from field by road in front of Cold Harbor to rear. In five minutes some twenty shells burst around me—my exact range. Got out of it. Joined Stuart and Jackson near Tree Hd. Qrs. Pelham still fighting like a trump. Reported: Stuart, Jackson others & myself went forward toward Pelham—musketry terrible. Artillery duel in full roar. Shells hot and furious. Enemy's battery at last quieter. Sent to order battery to left of road to advance in echelon on hill to left of Pelham. Shell bursting among them. Capt. ———— [name illegible] "all his guns but two had burst."—"Well, bring the two—limber to the front—forward."

"Where?"

"On the hill to the left."

"That's in front of our own guns."

"Come on—limber to the front—cease firing—I'll show you the position."[51]

Galloped back. Enemy trying it last time: Firing terrible. Stuart and Jackson in thickest of it. Felt excited but no flinching and remember my prayers. "Bless and keep me and all whom I love. Preserve me O blessed Father but if it be thy will that I should fall, preserve my soul for Jesus my Redeemer's sake." Not flurried one particle—never cooler in my life. Laughing and voice steady—a sure sign with me. I never have lost selfpossession [*sic*] or resolve in any fight yet "tho' I say it."

Night coming on—separated from Stuart—could barely distinguish persons with my glasses. To Jones Christian.[52]

"Rather hot, Lieutenant."

"Yes—very."

Found Stuart's flag-bearer, and one or two escort. Stuck to me, as their Com'dg officer. Shelling awful—whiz—whis-is-is-is-is-is-bang. Whiz! bang! Whiz! bang! Whizzzz!—Whirr-rr-rr!

"Captain we had better go to the rear—hadn't we?"

"No we had better go forward. "

Went forward. Night. Our guns belching flame, and throwing shovel fulls of firey [*sic*] cinders from muzzles. Enemy's batteries silenced: found Stuart—rode forward with him and Jackson to where the enemy had fired the fence and bushes on left of road to draw our fire.

Rode back with Gen. Stuart to Cold Harbor. Ordered to take com'd and inform Cavalry of position. Man run over by wagon—well jammed. Stuart returned and we laid down under the first big tree on the right going toward Mechanicsville.

That night heavy firing again, and Jackson lying between me and Stuart consulting what road to follow and cut them off. (Forgot to say that when we were at the burning fence on side of road, D. H. Hill's men were heard cheering as they ran the enemy down the big hill where their 12 guns were—just above the abattis [*sic*] which our men charged, over a deep stream and took—then the battery.)[53]

Next morning [June 28], mounted to follow the Gen. with staff, but he ordered us to remain and galloped to Jackson. Went with Capt. Von Borcke to New Cold Harbor turned to left on Roslyn road and saw my dear boy Nat, with his coat torn in the breast by a ball which cut a brass button in two.[54] I have it. Dead Yankees as thick as leaves. Hundreds of red legged Zouaves lying on their backs—toes up. No pity for them— thinking of Nat. My boy smiling and modest. [*Margin notation*: Message from

Stuart to take charge of artillery taken from enemy—turned over to Gen. Hill.]

Forgot to say, met Jackson at New Cold Harbor who directed me to 1st Brigade. Came back, found Gen. Stuart gone, staff & A.A. Gen. [Luke Tiernan Brien] remaining under tree—horse broke down—determined to go back and get Carson's—set out about 12 or so.[55] Took Mechanicsville & Strawberry hill road—met Patterson on Brook[56]—went to Richmond—mounted sorel [sic]—saw mammy—started back—reached Tree Hd. Qrs. toward 11 P.M. (30 or more miles) Next morning [June 29] rode over battle field with Timberlake etc.[57]—saw 20 or 30 dead horses where their battery was, above the terrible ditch and abattis [sic]—found Jackson sitting on a log with Maj. [Jasper S.] Whiting[58]—Shook hands and inquired Stuart's direction—White House—followed with party—took up Yankee prisoners, ——— [word illegible] and Jimmy Riley[59] whom—— [two initials illegible]—I left at Hopkins' Mill—stopped to snack at pretty Misses Baker's house—pushed on and reached White House, finding the Gen. and—the flies.

Collected arms—eat every thing that ever was eatin [sic]—will not try to describe the wild, tragic, loathsome Chaos of Sutler's houses, tents, hospital tents, cars, stores burning and smelling an awful stench. Put my arms in a wagon with pressed team—turned it over to Lt. Waller of 9th Cavalry.[60] Started after the Gen. with [Capt. James Hardeman] Stuart and found him near Dr. Crump's with 1st Regt. Followed to Mrs. [Stanhope] Crump's with 1st Regt. then tried to go on but found my horse about to founder.[61]

The Gen. went on—I stopping to try and get a horse from Mrs. Stanhope Crump's. None. Went to Freeman Clark's on hill beyond—Extraordinary scene—Clark, son 16 year[s] old, Mrs. Clark, Miss Clark—all wringing their hands, all crying, all wailing piteously, clamorously, "Don't take our horse!—Ohhhh! Don't take our horse!" ad infinitum and ad nauseam. I told Clark he was as great a baby as his son, and finding that the words, "Madam, I don't intend to take your horse," impressed no idea on Miss Clark's mind, I turned round and went back. Mrs. Crump—Dr.— wasn't quite as gracious as when Gen. Stuart was present—lent me a horse with some difficulty—old, white, hard going—to ride to Bob's for another & I left mine, whom I could not make travel one mile an hour with the spur. He could not have walked in fact one mile more possibly. Came here—sent that old idiot Ben for Carson's horse—he stole or lost my saddle—returned last night—and here I am, in the midst of a drenching rain, about to start myself. Sent Betty who brot [sic] my horse.[62]

Was Stuart at the heavy fight last evening? I don't know. I was not. But Mon Genèrl, "thou cans't not say I did it." "'Twas the horse I mounted in an evil hour."—Dear Sal, charmed to see me and I her.[63]

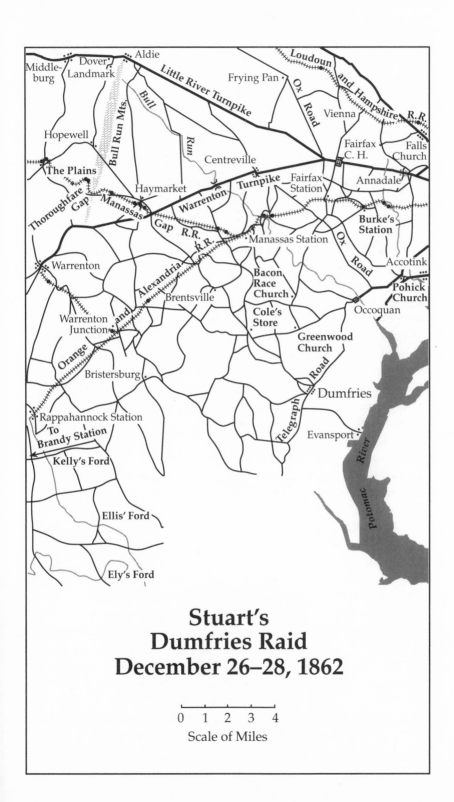

Middle-
burg
Dover
Landmark
Aldie
Little River Turnpike
Frying Pan
Loudoun
and Hampshire
R.R.
Ox Road
Vienna
Bull Run Mts.
Bull Run
Hopewell
The Plains
Centreville
Fairfax
C. H.
Falls
Church
Thoroughfare Gap
Haymarket
Manassas
Turnpike
Warrenton
Gap
R.R.
R.R.
Fairfax
Station
Annadale
Manassas Station
Burke's
Station
Ox Road
Accotink
Warrenton
Alexandria and
Brentsville
Bacon
Race
Church
Cole's
Store
Occoquan
Pohick
Church
Warrenton
Junction
Orange
Greenwood
Church
Bristersburg
Telegraph Road
Dumfries
Rappahannock Station
To
Brandy Station
Evansport
River
Kelly's Ford
Potomac
Ellis' Ford
Ely's Ford

Stuart's
Dumfries Raid
December 26–28, 1862

0 1 2 3 4
Scale of Miles

God protect my dear boy Nat whom I nearly kissed yonder.
A hot, tremendous battle was Cold Harbor. The "On to Richmond"
lags Genl McClellan!

JULY

*On July 1 Lee ordered Stuart and his cavalry across the Chickahominy to cooperate
with the Confederate forces on that side of the river. The Federals were encountered
after dark beyond Nance's Shop, scattered, and pursued toward Haxall's Landing
until a large camp was seen. After realizing that all had been done that could be
done, Stuart let his men rest. They were exhausted from a march of forty-two miles
and a brush with the enemy. Most of the next day was consumed in marching to
Haxall's and gathering up prisoners and arms. That night Pelham indicated in a
message to Stuart that Evelynton Heights, a plateau overlooking the Federals' encampment, could be occupied.*[64] *Stuart seized the opportunity and held the position
from 9 A.M. to 2 P.M. on the third, maintaining intermittent fire from one of
Pelham's guns and cavalry sharpshooters. The troops of Maj. Gen. James Longstreet,
which were to relieve the cavalry, unfortunately took the wrong road, and Stuart was
forced at last to abandon the ground, Pelham having fired his last round and the
sharpshooters their last cartridge. For the remainder of the day, the cavalry pulled
back to replenish its exhausted supplies.*[65]

*As July began, James Hardeman Stuart, who finally was established on his
cousin's staff, started keeping a diary of what transpired around him. From his entries, it is easy to see that Stuart kept his staff busy and on the move as long as there
was any chance to strike at the enemy. In the early days of the month, Hardeman
was called to do many different tasks but mainly those of courier.*

From James Hardeman Stuart's Diary

July 1 '62—Moved from the White House on the Pamunkey by way
of Talleysville to Forge bridge—here Capt. Pelham's battery "Stuart's Horse
Artillery" was in engagement with the Yankees posted on the other side;
our practice was very good. Bivouacked on the farm of Lt. Jones Christian.

July 2nd—Marched from Forge XXX Bottom's Bridge.

Jones played hard, & our ranks the day before—I found "Stonewall" a
man six feet in height, with a fine eye, quick & energetic in his speech,
goodness stamped on his countenance. On delivering my message, he said,
"Tell Gen. Stuart I am without rations myself. The trains have not come
up. Have put an officer specially to hurrying them up—when they come
I will do the best I can for him. Tell the Gen'l if he has not received contrary orders from Gen. Lee to come over with his cavalry, leaving enough
troops to picket the country toward White Oak Swamp, & pick up strag-

glers." Back I went in the driving rain to Gen'l Stuart (six miles) & reported. He sent me back with a message to Col. [Laurence S.] Baker . . . then while . . . horse ate . . . (subsequently the Gen'l halted) until he came on when I conducted him to Gen'l Jackson.[66] Shortly after meeting Gen'l Jackson, Gen. Stuart sent me back to Col. William T. Martin of Jeff Davis Legion near Rock's house, making near 24 miles I had traveled that morning. I stopped & dried my clothes. I joined Gen'l Stuart in the evening. The Yankees had abandoned their strong position on Malvern Hill & retreated down river.

July 4th—Marched toward Westover—occupied Evelington [Evelynton] Heights commanding the Yankee's camps; shelled the enemy. Count Zaluski's rocket battery brought into action for the 1st time.[67] The Count waked them up with his "infernal machine," the enemy soon commenced to reply with Parrot guns, had the infantry to advance—when we, having nothing but one howitzer in action, were compelled to retire. Gen. Longstreet's Division came (?) miles.

From July 4 through 10, scouting, skirmishing, and establishing a line of cavalry outposts kept Stuart and his troopers busy. Once the outposts were fixed, Stuart withdrew part of his command on the twelfth. He established his headquarters first near Atlee Station and then, on the twenty-first, at Hanover Court House, where rest, refitting, and reviews became the orders for the days that followed.[68]

The Federal cavalry probed Stuart's lines on the twenty-second near Verdon Station and again on the twenty-third. Stuart and 2,000 troopers responded to the latter incursion with a move toward Fredericksburg, but they returned in time for Stuart to receive notice of his promotion to major general on the twenty-fifth.[69] Several of his staff also received equally deserved promotions. The cavalry underwent a reorganization on the twenty-eighth from one brigade to two, with Wade Hampton of South Carolina and Fitzhugh Lee of Virginia receiving promotions to brigadier general. The last hot days of July were spent in the camps around Hanover Court House.[70]

On the fifteenth, Stuart received a letter of resignation from his commissary officer, Dabney Ball. The "Fighting Parson" was upset over a reprimand he had received from Stuart for not having rations available to issue to the cavalry. Stuart accepted the resignation, but the two men remained friends. Ball would return to the staff later in the war in the unofficial capacity of chaplain of the cavalry corps.

For the remainder of the month, Hardeman Stuart had to contend with trying to piece together his signal corps detachment, which was to be his main role under Stuart while still galloping here and there on various missions for the general. His diary entries showed that not all was excitement and derring-do, but sometimes just "Quiet time. Nothing stirring."

John Esten Cooke's diary for July contains entries for only four days, but it lends support to Hardeman Stuart's, as many of the same locations and individuals were mentioned. Cooke had his own duties and concerns as a member of the staff, however, not the least of which was his failure to receive one of the promotions granted to the staff. Sadly, he was to remain a captain throughout the war.

From James Hardeman Stuart's Diary

July 5th—Passed the day at Phillip's [Phillips'] farm. Nothing of importance took place. Gen. Jackson's command came up.

July 6th—Went to Mr. Christian's farm. In the evening the artillery marched to Dr. Wilcox's on the James River & shelled the transports.[71]

From John Esten Cooke's Journal

Major Phillips'—Charles City [County]

July 6, 1862—Rode all night to get here to the big fight which don't [*sic*] come off. McClellan burrowing under protection of his gun boats — —— [word illegible]!

Find my return creates a sensation. News reached Hd. Qrs. a day or so after my horse broke down at Crumps [Crump's], that Captain Cooke with another officer had picked up some Yankee stragglers in that region and proceeded toward Long Bridge where 200 of the enemy fired on the unfortunate captain killing him out & out. They then took off his boots and buried him. All belived [*sic*] it—Capt. Von Borck [Heros von Borcke] says he cried, and wanted to go after my remains—[William D.] Farley too.

Not this time mes amis! Here I am writing on the grass under the locusts the Gen. sleeping yonder.

From James Hardeman Stuart's Diary

July 7th—Headquarters at Mr. Waddel's [Waddill's], the Gen'l staying at Mr. Christian's.

July 8th—Marched back by ——— [word illegible] Shop to Gatewood, where headquarters were established. The Gen. went to Richmond—stayed that night at "Montebello."

From John Esten Cooke's Journal

Waddell's [Waddill's] Farm Hd. Qrs. July 8

Saw yesterday on picket just in front of the enemy my dear boy Natty and the Clarke boys—and my dear old Walter, with his white havelock, red face, and full uniform, sword & all, in the hot pine woods! He was greatly glad to see me & I him.

———— [name illegible] retreats with [Brig. Gen. Francis E.] Patterson to Nance's Shop—where he says he will "make a stand."[72]

Mon Capitaine Von Borcke captures a member of the 9th Cavalry![73]

Night—July 8—Phillips

Poor whippoorwill cries plaintively as I write by moonlight under my tree on the eve of leaving this fine & beautiful country of Charles City [County].

This evening left Mrs. Christian's and road [*sic*] alone with both Gen. and Stonewall to see the last brigade drawn in.

We go—'tis <u>pity</u>!

Green Meadows—July 9, 1862

Here on the way to somewhere—after a ride from Phillips [*sic*], this the "———— [word illegible] forest"—breakfast! Hairston calling "Come General!"[74]

Gatewood July 9th

10 at night.

Under my tree by the light of the full white moon I write my brief line. Yonder a soldier is singing "We are gay & happy still"—very clearly and finely. It was sung last for me at the good old Bower by my dear friend Holmes— ———— [two words illegible] merry, being gay and happy truly. He sleeps well, after the bloody field of Manassas where he fell. O how sweet and mournful it sounded—for it has ceased. He is yonder beyond the stars, in a happier world.

Richmond—July 14

Very sick from bile at Gatewood and came up with troops ———— [word illegible]. I having had two days here with my dear boy Natty— how I love him! He has just gone with Miss Lewis—and I am en route for Hd Qrs. at Atlee's Station.

———— ≡◆≡ ————

Atlee's Station
July 15, 1862

Dear General [Stuart],

I should have replied to your letter by the courier who brought it to me yesterday, but meeting him on the road as I was moving to this place, it was out of my power. I have the honour to report, in response to the inquiry it contained, that Col. [Thomas L.] Rosser's Reg't rec'd their rations yesterday, by his Commissary. Also that "arrangements" have been made to supply the three regiments east of Richmond that your orders specified, and also others who are there. I am now at this place where I expect to have supplies today for those in this vicinity.

I send herewith my resignation as commissary in the C.S. Army which you will please do me the kindness to approve and forward immediately to the government. Hoping you may speedily fill the place with someone whose manner of doing business will be less annoying to you, and who will not be so "disconcerted and diverted" from the high and responsible duty of feeding the men.

> I am with
> Great Respect—
> Your obt. svt.
> Dabney Ball
> Major & C.S.

P.S. I will continue to attend to duty for a few days as best I may, if it is your wish I should, till the government has time to act. D. B.

From James Hardeman Stuart's Diary

July 9th—All quiet. Gen'l Stuart returned in the evening. The Yankees drove in our picket at Nance's Shop.

July 10th—Marched to Richmond.

July 11th—Stayed with Capt. R. E. Wilbourn, my old classmate & friend. Met Dan P. Bestor & Edward Stuart, who had come on to join my "Signal Corps."[75]

12th—Stayed with Wilbourn. Left in evening for headquarters Atlee Station, Va. Cent. R. R. [Virginia Central Railroad].

13–14–15–16—Quiet time. Nothing stirring.

17—Brigade drill. Misses Price & Winston at HdQrs.[76]

18—Gen'l went to Richmond. Lord Seymour, the son of the Duke of Somerset, whom I first saw at Phillips, called. Was not at HdQrs. & did not make his acquaintance.

July 19–20–21—Doing nothing else but dancing attendance on the Qr. masters in Richmond, & [?] race. The Gen'l left on the 21st for Hanover C. H.

22–26—Dancing attendance on Q. Ms. & Capt. Barker trying to get my Signal Corps rigged out.[77] Left on 26th for Hanover C. H.

27—Service at HdQrs. Capt. [Norman] FitzHugh's son baptized.[78] The Gen'l acted as Godfather.

28th—Gen'l Stuart received his commission as Maj. Gen. in the P. A.

C. S. [Provisional Army of the Confederate States] Spent the evening at Dr. [Lucien B.] Price's. Made the acquaintance of two nice young ladies, his daughters. The Dr's farm caught fire while we were in the parlor & the Gen'l & staff rushed out—was the first of the staff at the barn & set the negroes to work. Dr. did not lose much.[79]

29—Brigade drill. Did not go as I wish to save my horse. The Gen'l with the rest of his staff spent the evening at Dr. Price's.

30—Nothing new.

31—Gen'l went to Richmond.

Near the end of the month, another officer, Richard Channing Price, was preparing to join Stuart's staff. In his letter of the twenty-ninth, the giant Prussian, Heros von Borcke, made a valiant attempt to explain to the newly appointed aide-de-camp just what he would require to carry out his duties. Von Borcke's difficulties with the English language were still somewhat of a handicap in his correspondence. One only can wonder if Price was able to read between the lines, and if he arrived in camp properly outfitted.

29 of July 1862

Sir

Maj. Genl J E B Stuart directs me to send you a list of what articles you will require to have as an officer in the Staff

very respectfully

Heros von Borcke

AAG.

Equipment suitable for an Officer
of Cavallerie

A good Horse wich [sic] can be bot [sic] in Richmond or among the Rgts, the cost will be 400–500 Doll

A good Jenifer saddle and bridle, wich can be bot at the ordonance [sic] store for 62 Doll.

Arms will be sabre & Pistol, wich will cost from 80 to 100 Doll.

A Uniform trimed [sic] with yellow (Cav) or buff (Staff) either coat or jacket 80 to 100 Doll.

Good Cavalry Boots with Spurs 50 Doll

Grey or Black Hat 15 Doll.

Saddle Blanket and other Blanket 20 Doll

Oilcloth Coat 25–30 Doll

Several little things not mentioned

(little Vallise [sic], Comb, brushe [sic] etc etc)

AUGUST

After a quiet beginning, August became a month of increasing activity for Stuart and the cavalry. A new adversary to the north of Richmond had attracted Robert E. Lee's attention. Maj. Gen. John Pope had been placed in charge of a large Federal force and had begun to demonstrate along the lines of the Orange & Alexandria and the Virginia Central railroads with the intent of easing the pressure on McClellan, who was still encamped on the Peninsula.[80]

Stuart felt that a response should be made to counteract Pope's raids. The abortive Verdon expedition in late July having failed to accomplish all he had desired, Stuart started on the fourth with Fitz Lee's brigade and the Stuart Horse Artillery toward Bowling Green. He hoped to get in the enemy's rear on the Telegraph Road and possibly destroy transports on the Rappahannock near Port Royal. He camped east of Bowling Green on the night of the fourth and reached Port Royal the next day. Finding no transports on the river, he turned toward Fredericksburg and camped at Grace. On the sixth, Stuart moved to Massaponax Church on the Telegraph Road and struck a Federal Infantry column, which netted him eleven wagons, about eighty-five prisoners, and some horses. Stuart then turned toward Bowling Green, where he encamped for the night, and returned to Hanover Court House the following day. His staff suffered one casualty: Redmond Burke was shot in the wrist.[81]

For Hardeman Stuart, the brief foray gave him something more to write about in his diary than "dancing attendance on the Qr. masters in Richmond." His duties early in the month still were not associated with his staff position as signal corps officer, but at least Stuart kept him busy.

From James Hardeman Stuart's Diary

Aug. 1—Gen'l sent me to Richmond as bearer of dispatches to Gen. R. E. Lee, General in Chief. The livery stable keeper charged me $5.00 for a buggy to ride two miles. Made the acquaintance of Capts. DeLisle & DeLauey, who went with me to HdQrs. They formerly belonged to St. Paul's Battalion, La.

Aug. 2nd—Drew my pay from 1st July to Aug 2, '62—$143.00 at $139.00 per month.

Aug. 3rd—Service by Parson Landstreet M. E. C. [Methodist Episcopal Church].[82]

Aug. 4—Left on a scout. Went as far as Bowling Green cty [city], seat of Caroline County & bivouacked. Took dinner that day with Mr. Digarnette Brs. of the M. C. [Methodist Church]. Had most excellent music from some young ladies. Chatted some time with them.

5th—Marched to Port Royal—the people along the road delighted to see us. We were a little too late for a party of Yankees who had been there that morning. Stopped a few minutes at Mr. Bernard's (Gaymont [Gay

Mont]), a most charming place on a hill commanding the country for many miles around.[83] It is an Eden if there is one on earth. You could see the Rappahannock winding for miles from N.E. to S.W. Beyond the highlands seemed to meet the blue heavens, while around were broad fields & high hills. What a beautiful place. Oh, if only I was the fortunate owner of such a paradise. How happy I should be with ————. Stopped at Rappahannock Academy about 2 o'clock for half an hour here. I saw eleven prisoners whom we had captured, a part of those who had been at Port Royal & at Dr. Bernard's in the morning. On the person of one of the Yankees was found a watch which he had stolen from Mr. Bernard's negro cook.[84] We slept that night at Round Oak Church my saddle for my pillow. Edward was quite tired. On the evening of this day one of the 3rd Regt. Va. Cav. was unfortunately shot by a member of the 9th. From a high eminence saw the steeples of the churches of Fredericksburg eight miles distant. Major von Borcke had an adventure with a rattlesnake. The reptile crawled over his arm while he slept. He awoke & killed him with his sabre.[85]

6th—Went to Massaponax Church seven miles from Fredericksburg. Saw wagons driven rapidly up the road toward the city. Gen'l Stuart sent a squadron in pursuit, & one or two squadrons down the road. We captured eleven wagons & eighty-five prisoners. Had two or three of our men wounded while charging the enemy. About 3 o'clock the Gen'l & staff went down the road, crossed the "Ny" creek, one of the four streams which joining form the Mattapony. They are the "Mat"—the "Ta"—the "Po"— and the "Ny." A short distance beyond the Ny we met the Blakely [Blakeley] with its elevating screw broken.[86] It had been fired at by the Yankees a number of times. The screw was broken by the heavy charges of powder. 3/4 of a mile beyond the "Ny" we saw the Yankees, & skirmishers advancing. A battery at the same time commenced to shell us. We retired, they continually advancing their battery & shelling. When we recrossed the river Gen'l Stuart sent me to Massaponax Church, 1 1/2 miles back with orders to the squadron left there, which I had hardly delivered when Major von Borcke A.A.G. galloped up & countermanded them. We started back to meet the Gen'l returning the way we came. To my surprise I found the road cleared of troops, while I had but a short time before left it crowded. I saw the rearguard 1/2 a mile in advance. I followed on rapidly. Was under the fire of a battery part of the way. The road ran along a ridge. In the plain below, I could see their skirmishers advancing, a battery training its shell on our line of march, and their horse advancing rapidly—very anxious to get near us; but they took pains to keep at a respectful distance. We accomplished our purpose, however, viz. to draw the Yankees from the Va. Cent. R. R. [Virginia Central Railroad] which they wished to destroy so as to prevent Jackson from receiving reinforcements, and then Pope falling on him at the same time. They hoped to annihilate him. The prisoners stated that [Maj. Gen. Ambrose E.] Burnside had reached Fredericksburg—in fact we captured some of his men.[87] We reached Bowling Green that night. We spent it at Dr. Roper's. Slept in his yard neath the trees. It was a beautiful night, the moon shining brightly. The dust was intolerable on that day & the day previous. My hair, eyes & beard completely filled with it. General wished to send me to Hanover C. H. with a dispatch, but not seeing me called on my cousin J. T. W. Hairston, and sent him off post haste, so that he was not with us under fire that day. All the staff were with us on this expedition except Major Norman R. FitzHugh, A.A. General—Capt. Cooke, Chief of Ordnance of the Division, and Capt. Farley, volunteer aide—and Lt. Price, three of the General's aides.

7th—Starting from Bowling Green at nine o'clock we took up the line of march for Hanover C. H. [Court House] I stopped on the way at Mr. Mason's. Heard some music by Miss Mason, a young lady of sixteen or seventeen. Had a lunch. Mounted our horses & pushed on for the C. H. A short distance past Needwood saw Edward [Stuart] on the side of the road, his horse having given out; he looking very disconsolate. I left him on his own resources, for I wished him to learn how to take care of himself, & also to teach him a lesson about his horse as I did not think he took as much care of him as I thought he should. Reached Hanover about 3. Edward came in about 5, both he & his horse looking most miserable.

8th—Was a day of rest. Did nothing but sleep.

From the eighth until the sixteenth, when Stuart, in accordance with Lee's orders, moved out to rendezvous with the army, the cavalry was granted a short respite as Pope and Jackson tangled at Cedar Mountain. Stuart did manage to become involved in the aftermath of that battle, however. On a tour of inspection, he arrived at Jackson's headquarters on the tenth. "Stonewall" put him in command of the cavalry accompanying the 2nd Corps. Stuart immediately conducted a reconnaissance that helped Jackson decide not to renew the action on the eleventh.[88]

After returning to Hanover Court House, Stuart bided his time with cavalry business until he left on the sixteenth. During this same period, Chiswell Dabney and Hardeman Stuart recovered from their exertions during the raid and recorded their thoughts. Dabney wrote to his mother, gently chastizing her for the lack of letters from home. He also included a souvenir from his recent encounter with the invader. In his diary, Hardeman Stuart contemplated mankind, bemoaned his fate at having nothing worthwhile to read, and pondered his future as a lawyer.

Hd Qrs Cavalry Division
August 13th 1862

Dear Mother [Mrs. Elizabeth T. Dabney]

I have written so often of late to you all without getting an answer that even now I write without expectation of any answer at all, but I do not ascribe it to you or any of you at home, but I do attribute it to the great irregularity in the mails. So if my letters do not reach you, do not think that I have forgotten to write to you my <u>dear Mother</u>, you all who I am so anxious to see once more at home.

Genl Stuart has just got back from Genl Jackson's. He reports a great victory for us over [Maj. Gen. John] Pope.[89] He also had conversation with several of the Yankee Generals (under a flag of truce which they came under to ask permission to bury their dead). They acknowledged themselves whiped [*sic*], but the Genl offered to bet one of their Surgeons any thing that in the next issue of the New York Herald they would claim a great victory. He would not take the bet.[90]

Three deserters from Burnside have just come in. They report him at Fredericksburg. Genl [Brig. Gen. John B.] Hood and [Maj. Gen. James] Longstreet are marching there to thrash him.[91] So you may expect ——— [word illegible] times on the Rappahannock in a very few days. I think it likely we will have to leave our pleasant camp here at Hanover Co. Ho. [Court House] tomorrow or next day. I can tell you I will hate to do it very much, for I have had an exceedingly nice time ever since I have been here, but my country first. I send enclosed three pieces of a feather which I took from a Yankee which we captured near Fredericksburg. One piece is for Aggie, one for Kitty and the other for Suanne Lemmon. Tell them I am sorry I cannot send a better souvinier [*sic*], but this is the only one which I can possibly send in a letter.

I was in a charge near Fredericksburg. We charged down the road at full speed yelling as loud as possible. The dust was so thick that I could scarsely [*sic*] see the man in front of me, but in spite of dust and minie balls we captured 70 Yankees & did not lose a man.

While Genl Stuart was with Jackson he took Genl [Brig. Gen. Beverly H.] Robertson's[92] Cavalry and got in rear of Pope's army and took prisoners in sight of his Hd. Qrs.

Good buy [*sic*] dear Mother. I will write in a day or two. In the meantime I remain your most affectionate son.

C Dabney

From James Hardeman Stuart's Diary

[August] 9th—Battle fought by Jackson, Pope & Segel [Maj. Gen. Franz Sigel] near Cedar Run, Culpeper Cty.[93] Victory perched on our banners. Gen'l Stuart sent me to Richmond with dispatches for Gen'l Lee, Gen'l [George W.] Randolph,[94] Sec. of War, & Pres't Davis. The General left for Gordonsville a short time after I did for Richmond—Major J. T. W. Hairston accompanying him.

10th—Returned from Richmond.

11th—Did nothing—*12th* Ditto.

13th—Gen'l returned this evening to HdQrs, having passed down the road to Richmond on his return from Gordonsville. On the night of the 12th Major Hairston & I received our tent ———— [word illegible] on.

14th—Did nothing. Read Wild Western stories. Joe & Sneak were quite amusing characters. Wish most heartily I had something solid to read. I could borrow I expect from Dr. Price, but he has two charming daughters, & I do not care to be at the trouble of "primping." I might get books at the country hotel over the way, but the daughter of the proprietor tells me she never read anything but <u>novels</u>, & I suppose the rest of the family have her taste. What an excellent school I am attending. I am thrown in contact with all classes of man & I shall take care to study them. "The greatest study of mankind is man." Here at my leisure I shall ———— [word illegible] my great lesson, one requiring a life long attention. I shall learn what is the motive power impelling him to action. I will read his hopes & fears. What an advantage it will be to me in life, especially if I pursue my original intention & become a lawyer. When I meet a man, to read him at a glance, to know that I am his master, for he who understands another's character by skillful management can bend him to his wishes. This dictum will hold true I am confident in the majority of cases. There are unavoidably many independent in tho·ght & action disdaining to be led, but ever aspiring to lead. Such men may be ruled by assailing them on their weak side, viz. their ambition. I did not expect to write an essay on man when I commenced to enter the events of the day, so I shall leave the subject to some philosopher. By the way, I have read "Hot Coon" by Solon Robinson. I think this book created quite a sensation at one time in Jackson [Mississippi]. It is a dirty work, which no lady should ever see. Men are so corrupt it can scarcely do them much harm. I am sorry I ever read it, for I have derived no benefit from its perusal.

15th—Nothing of interest. The 4th VA. Cav. presented Col. S. D. Lee, temporarily in command, with a fine horse.[95] Gen. Fitz Lee's Brigade (the 2nd) left this morning. The Gen'l sent [Lt. Chiswell] Dabney to Richmond on horseback. Lieut. [R. Channing] Price, the General's new aide, came today. His third visit to HdQrs. I suppose he will remain now.

When Stuart left his camp near Hanover Court House on the sixteenth, he boarded the train for Orange Court House, having ordered Fitz Lee's brigade to Raccoon Ford on the Rapidan River. At Orange he met with Robert E. Lee, and then proceeded to Verdiersville to link up with Fitz's brigade on the eighteenth before crossing the river and implementing Lee's instructions. Because orders were either unclear or misinterpreted, Fitz was late in arriving, and Stuart spent the night in Verdiersville. Early the next morning, Stuart's small party was surprised by the 1st Michigan Cavalry. All those with Stuart managed to escape. But Maj. Norman FitzHugh, who had been sent to look for Fitz Lee, had run into the Michiganders instead and was captured. Among the papers the major carried were the plans for the entrapment of Pope. Forewarned, the Federal commander temporarily withdrew beyond Lee's reach.

With Lee's plans rendered inoperative, the cavalry spent the nineteenth resting. Fitz Lee's brigade had been joined by Brig. Gen. Beverly H. Robertson's. When the cavalry moved out on the twentieth, it was Robertson who first encountered the enemy between Stevensburg and Brandy Station. The two forces clashed between Brandy Station and the river on ground that would see numerous cavalry actions over the next two years. Finally the Federal cavalry retreated across the Rappahannock to the safety of their infantry. Stuart had to be content with a handful of prisoners.[96]

A number of Stuart's staff had accompanied the general on the train as he set out on the sixteenth, but Hardeman Stuart was not among them. He left Hanover Court House on horseback in the late afternoon, and after a few stops, he caught up with Stuart on the eighteenth. Still not actually functioning as signal officer, Hardeman was assigned other duties that kept him out of the fighting as the Federals retreated, though he did witness some of the action on the twentieth.

From James Hardeman Stuart's Diary

Aug 16th—Left Hanover C. H. at 4 P.M. , & rode as far as Rev. Horace Stringfellow, passing Old Fork Church, about 120 years old. There is a place near called Helltown, noted for its rowdies. I note the place on account of its name. General left Hanover in the evening on the cars.

17—Left Mr. Stringfellow about 9 A.M. Went to Beaver Dam, from there through Col. Fontaine's to Mrs. Goodin's, where I fed my horse.[97] Passed by Gilboa Church, Dr. Phil Pendleton's, a beautiful place. After dark stopped at a house & tried to get some corn for my horse; could not get any, had to turn back & ride two miles to Dr. Perkins, where his horses were well fed, and I had a nice bed. Stringfellow Digges, of the ———— [not given] accompanying me.

18—Rose early in the morning, got breakfast, paid Dr. P $2.00, mounted & left. Passed through Louisa C. H., where Fitz Lee's Brig. was. Went by Graves' Blacksmith Shop. Went across the country to the old Lafayette Road, which commenced at Louisa C. H., crosses the Rapidan at Raccoon Ford. Went by Jackson's Shop, crossed the Plank Road for

Orange C. H. to Frederick. Went to Dr. Levorts. Found the Gen'l had passed down the Plank Road. Found him at Mrs. Crawford's, a widow lady related to a man of that name whom I left in school at Spring Ridge, Hinds Co., Miss [Mississippi]. The Gen'l had a narrow escape that morning; had to leap the fence leaving hat & haversack. Dabney followed on Dixie, leaving his pistols, leaped him with halter only. Von Borcke rushed into the road & was pursued for a hundred yards. FitzHugh was captured some miles off from that place.

19—Went from Mrs. Crawford's to Mr. Pannel's on the Rapidan.

20th—Crossed the Rapidan at Mitchell's Ford. Went to Kelly's Ford on the Rappahannock. Saw a great number of Yankees on the hill on the other side. Went to Gen. Stuart, passing through Stevensburg. Genl sent me after some mules—caught & turned them over to Col. T. [Thomas] L. Rosser of the 5th Va. Cav. HdQrs at James Barbours [near Brandy Station]. There were several brilliant cav. charges on the road from Stevensburg by Brandy Station to Cunningham's [Beverly's] Ford on the Rappahannock.

On the twenty-first, Stuart pushed across the Rappahannock and attempted to hold the crossing so that the Confederate infantry could follow. When the infantry failed to come up, the cavalry withdrew to the south side of the river and camped for the night. Following an artillery duel between the Stuart Horse Artillery and some Federal batteries at Freeman's Ford in the early hours of the twenty-second, Stuart crossed the Rappahannock over the Waterloo Bridge and moved toward Warrenton. This was the initial movement of what has become known as the Catlett's Station Raid. The object of the raid was the Federal camp at Catlett's Station, which Stuart struck later that night. He then withdrew safely to Warrenton Springs on the twenty-third, camped, and returned to Confederate lines the next day with more than 300 prisoners. John Pope's headquarters were at Catlett's Station, and he might have been captured as well had h~ been in camp. As it was, Stuart had to make do with Pope's frock coat.[98]

Hardeman Stuart finally had the opportunity to perform in the capacity of the cavalry's signal officer on the twenty-first, but the advancing Federals soon put an end to his flag waving. Thereafter he was detached from cavalry headquarters on a scout for Stuart. Gathering information as he dodged the oncoming Yankee regiments, Hardeman made his perilous assignment more bearable by visits with several loyal Confederate families who, from what he recorded in his diary, were most willing to supply his wants.

From James Hardeman Stuart's Diary

[*August*] *21st*—Went to Cunningham's [Beverly's] Ford. Had a fight of the artillery. We exploded a Yankee caisson. Used my signals for the first time. Adams was present, the rest (except Lawrence) with the wagon. Sent Lawrence to bring them up. Was out all night hunting for Gen. Jackson—found him early in the morning. Gen. [Stuart] stayed at Dr. Welford's.

22nd—Crossed at Welford's Ford over the south branch of the Rappahannock [Stuart is referring to the Hazel River]. Had an artillery duel—some of our men wounded. Went through Jeffersonton in Culpepper [Culpeper] Cty. Crossed Waterloo bridge. Part of the Cav. Div. at Hart's Mill. Gen. [Stuart] sent me to the view tree on watery mount. It rained heavily & I was completely drenched. Spent the night at Mrs. Scott's—enjoyed myself very much conversing with the young ladies, the Misses Scott.

23rd—Was scarcely out of bed in the morning when a negro ran into the room & told me the Yankees were coming. I dressed hastily & mounting my horse rode off to the top of the mountain. Sergts. [Daniel P.] Bestor & Lawrence of my Signal Corps accompanying me. I sent a servant to inform Sergt. Adams that the enemy were upon us. Went a mile into the country & sent a negro to ascertain whether any Yankees were about. He returned & reported there were none, that a party of our men had alarmed us. In the evening saw two regts of Yankee cav. come into Warrenton. I watched them until dark, when I went into the country across fields, tearing down fences & crossing bogs until I came to Mrs. Meredith's, where I stayed all night. Was most hospitably entertained.

24th—Early in the morning before I got up a courier came in with instructions for the "Signal Corps" captured from the Yankees. I could gather nothing new from them & handed them to Sergt. Adams to keep. Dressed & went out & another courier rode up to the gate inquiring for Capt. Stuart—told me that the Genl said I must return as the Yankees were advancing. I ate my breakfast & set out. When I got on the turnpike saw the Yankees a half mile off advancing. Crossed Waterloo bridge & in 3/4 of an hour the Yankees came up. Our skirmishers had a fight with them. We fired 18 rounds of shell on them, & having no more withdrew our guns. Several Regts of infantry marched down to burn the bridge.

Margin notation on final page: Learned from the country people that a Yankee force five or six thousand strong had passed down the Telegraph road. Inf. cav. & artillery—Gen. [Christopher C.] Augur's Brigade.

All day on the twenty-fifth, the 5th Virginia Cavalry under Col. Thomas L. Rosser defended the Waterloo Bridge, which Stuart had left in their care. The bridge was vitally important, being the only one still standing. That night, Stuart again met with Robert E. Lee and received orders to accompany Stonewall Jackson's movement around the right flank of Pope's army.[99]

Dutifully Stuart started with his cavalry at two o'clock the morning of the twenty-sixth to catch up with Jackson. What followed were some of the most triumphant moments in the history of the Army of Northern Virginia. Manassas Junction, stock-piled with food and supplies meant for Pope's men, fell to Jackson and the ragtag soldiers of his "foot-cavalry." Lee's great lieutenant then concealed his corps near Groveton, struck at a passing Union column to draw Pope to him, and withstood repeated Federal assaults until Lee with Longstreet's Corps arrived. Stuart and the cavalry helped screen Lee's approach and followed up after the routing Federals.[100] *He did not learn of the fate of his cousin until after the battle.*

Before Stuart had reported to Lee back on the twenty-fifth, he had sent Hardeman to capture the Federal signal station on View Tree, a small eminence near Warrenton, and establish one of his own. In this Hardeman was unsuccessful, as he was heavily outnumbered. During his scout of the Federal position, his horse was captured, and he marched on foot to rejoin the army. On the way, he fell in with either the 4th or 5th Texas Infantry. On the thirtieth, these regiments participated in the final attack against Pope's left. Hardeman Stuart was killed charging with them and was buried on the battlefield.[101]

SEPTEMBER

During the closing days of August and into early September, Stuart's cavalry enjoyed repeated successes against the Federals. A company of the 10th New York Cavalry was captured near Chantilly. In the same vicinity, Capt. Thomas Hight, Lt. Robert Clary, and their company of the 2nd U.S. Cavalry were also captured.[102]

In the action at Chantilly on September 1, the cavalry was not heavily involved, although Stuart did make an attempt to flank the enemy position by an advance on Flint Hill.[103] *Finding the enemy in possession of the hill, he withdrew. The next day, Stuart sent Hampton's Brigade and the Stuart Horse Artillery against the Federals on Flint Hill, which ·vas promptly abandoned by the retreating bluecoats. The pursuit continued until dark, when Union infantry and artillery opened fire on their pursuers from a section of woods. Stuart pulled back to Fairfax Court House and encamped for the night.*[104]

Demonstrations against the enemy toward Alexandria, Georgetown, and the Chain Bridge occupied Stuart over the next two days. On the fifth, the cavalry crossed the Potomac into Maryland at Leesburg and, keeping on the army's flank, occupied Urbana until the twelfth. While there, several advances by the enemy were met and repulsed.

Lt. R. Channing Price, aide-de-camp to Stuart, was not among the staff officers who accompanied the general into Maryland. A lame horse forced him to follow in the rear of the army, where he did not want to remain for long. When he finally rejoined Stuart, he rejoiced in the cavalry's victories and wondered about the destination of the army.

At Mr. Turleys in
Fairfax Co.
Sept 5th /62

Dear Mother [Mrs. Thomas Randolph Price Sr.][105]

I know what anxiety you must have felt on my account, but really this is the only chance I have had since leaving home of writing to you. I have passed safely through all the exposure & fighting from the Rapidan to this point, & wish that I had time to write you in detail something of the history of the last 3 weeks.

On Monday last [September 1], my horse being very lame, I left Gen. Stuart within a few miles of Fairfax C. H. just as having been joined by Jackson's Army, he was advancing towards that place. Tuesday morning I got my horse shod but found the lameness still continued: he is entirely unable to travel & I am in great trouble what to do. Gen. Stuart & the commands of Jackson & Longstreet went to Dranesville on Wednesday, & yesterday I started from the Toll-Gate where I had been staying to lead my horse on slowly to join the Army, trying to buy a horse along the road. I came into this house & staid [sic] here last night. I hear this morning that our troops started for Leesburg last night, & to-day I shall try to reach that place. I am in hopes we are on our way to Maryland. The Army of McClellan & Pope has met with the most tremendous repulse: after the retreat from the Rapidan to Manassas Junction & after our cutting their communication at Catlett's & Manassas, on Thursday, Friday & Saturday of last week, in 3 decisive fights, we drove them for miles, killing, wounding & capturing immense numbers. I don't believe there is a Yankee in Virginia, this side of Alexandria. I wish I could write more, but Mr. Turner of Goochland who takes this is about to leave. I am very well & sending love to all at home. I am your devoted son

R. Channing Price

———— ✠ ————

Head Quarters Cavalry
Division
Urbana, Frederick
County Maryland
Sept 10th 1862

Dear Mother

The Rubicon has been crossed as you will see from the heading of my letter and glad am I of it. The note I sent from Fairfax last Friday I hope you have received, as it served, though very short, to quiet your apprehensions as to me. Friday afternoon, leaving my horse with Mr. Turley, who kindly promised to care for him & keep him until such time as I can get him, I took a horse which he had picked up & offered me to ride, and started to Leesburg. I reached there about 9 o'clock & found the town blocked up with wagons & artillery moving towards the river. I went to Mr. Powell's house, but found that he & his wife had gone out on town that evening: after some trouble I got my horse in at a livery stable & taking my blanket with a South Carolina Captain I slept on the porch of a private house.

Next morning I made a start for Maryland, and reached White's Ford, where Longstreet's Corps was crossing about the middle of the day. It was a beautiful sight to see our ragged & toil-worn veterans leaving the Old Dominion which has suffered so heavily from this horrid war, and crossing to free a sister state from the Federal yoke. Getting across I heard that the Cavalry had crossed the evening before at Conrad's Ford (some distance below) & gone up to Poolsville [Poolesville]: so cutting across the country, I reached Poolsville & found that the Cavalry had camped in its vicinity the night before & gone on in the morning probably to Frederick City.

So getting on their track I rode on till after night, when reaching this place I heard that General Fitz Lee's Hd. Qrs. were here, & going to him I found to my surprise & pleasure that Gen. Stuart's were not far off. I got a nice supper at Mrs. Armstrong's, a widow of an Episcopal minister from Wheeling & who has treated me very kindly, finding out that I was a Grandson of Bishop Moore. The General has his Head Qrs. in a nice grassy yard in the village & we board at Mr. Cocka's near-by.

The people in the immediate vicinity are very Southern in feeling & recruiting is very encouraging. We are distant 7 miles from Frederick City, a place of 9 or 10,000 inhabitants, and which, Jackson having crossed before the Cavalry, entered Friday night, capturing some few sick: the Regiment of new recruits stationed there had heard of our approach & burnt about 150,000 dollar worth of Commissary stores, and then quit the place for Baltimore.

Sunday morning [September 7] the General sent me up to Frederick on some business, and I spent nearly all day there. It is quite a pretty place, but strongly tainted with Unionism. Monday I went up again with Gen. Stuart, and found every store nearly shut up. I tried in vain to get some clothes, which I need very much, as my trunk is in a wagon which was left in Leesburg. I was not with the General at the time the order was given to leave some wagons behind and consequently did not change my trunk to a wagon which was coming into Maryland. I had a chance this morning to send for it & hope I shall get it.

There is an abundance of everything in Frederick & some who went up Saturday evening got anything they wanted, boots, clothing, hats etc.

Monday & yesterday on account of difficulty about money or as some say because our Quarter Master had pressed every thing, it was difficult to find a store open. Monday evening meeting Capt. Venable in town I got permission from the General to accompany him to see the 3rd Company Howitzers, who had just gotten up & were camped about 2 miles from Frederick: leaving the General in town I rode down & found the boys all well & pleasantly camped near the banks of the Monocacy River.[106] I staid [*sic*] with them all night, & yesterday morning went to Frederick again.

Col. Bradley Johnson of the 1st Maryland Regt is recruiting for the Maryland line & I understand has gotten about 1,500 in this neighborhood: this is the most Union part of the state, & I augur very well from our success here: Col. Johnson has issued a strong Proclamation to the people of Maryland, & this morning I saw a copy of an address which Gen. Lee is about to publish for the same purpose: it is characteristic of the General, dignified, calm & calculated to set the reasons of our coming into the state in a right light before the strongest Union man in the state. The General issued a fine Order & Address to the Army while in Leesburg just before crossing, & it has had a good effect, as our troops are conducting themselves remarkably well, respecting private property, even fences. We have destroyed the elegant bridge over the Monocacy River on the Baltimore & Ohio Rail Road just at the junction of it & the road running to Frederick thus cutting off communication to Baltimore by Rail.

Our Cavalry have almost daily skirmishing with the enemy's cavalry, who have come up the Potomac River to the neighborhood of the fords at which our Army crossed. The main body of the enemy is about 10 miles from Washington at a place called Rockville, which they are fortifying rapidly. Our forces are lying quiet near the Junction resting after their great labors & preparatory to the immense work before us.

There is great curiosity to know what our destination is, but it is a profound secret. My own opinion is that after sufficient time to recruit from this part of the state, we will strike for Pennsylvania, compelling the Federal Government either to give up Washington & Baltimore to follow & arrest our career, or leave us to pursue our way unmolested through the North. Charles Minnigerode is here while I am writing having just come up with a dispatch from Brig. Gen. Lee who is commanding the cavalry some 6 or 8 miles from here in the direction of the Potomac.[107] He is very well & in case he does not write, please let his Father & Mother hear of him. Also if you see any friends of the 3rd Howitzers, tell them that they are well generally. Major Von Borcke desires to be particularly remembered to Father, Sister & yourself & says that I am too independent for him to take much care of me.

Capt [Hardeman] Stuart (our Signal Officer) having lost his horse in

98 WITH PEN AND SABER

making his escape from the Yankees near Warrenton and being unable to get one, volunteered as a private in some Mississippi Regt (his old command) on Saturday the 30th Aug't & was killed in the engagement: he was a nice fellow & his death is greatly regretted by the general & all of us.[108] I wish I could give you an account of my participation in the battles from Brandy Station to the Potomac but really I have seen so much that I could not begin to write you one. I must now close. Give my love to all at home & believe me dear Mother your devoted son

R. Channing Price

On the eleventh, the Federals began to increase the pressure against Stuart's line by backing up their cavalry with infantry. The gray cavalry drew back toward Frederick. The twelfth saw fighting along the National Road, but again Stuart's troopers held their own, taking prisoners, including Col. Augustus Moor of the 28th Ohio, and capturing a gun, although because of a lack of horses, they were unable to bring it off the field when they withdrew.[109]

Events now began to escalate rapidly. The clashes in the gaps of South Mountain, especially at Crampton's Gap on the fourteenth, involved some of Stuart's regiments and guns of the horse artillery. The Federal advance eventually proved unstoppable, and the blue columns poured through the gaps with the intention of rescuing the Union forces surrounded at Harpers Ferry. But Stonewall Jackson accepted the surrender of the garrison on the fifteenth, setting the stage for the Battle of Sharpsburg on the seventeenth.

The cavalry's role in the battle was relegated to supporting the army's flanks, with Stuart and Pelham commanding artillery in support of Jackson's Corps on the extreme left. The following day, Fitz Lee's Brigade covered the army's withdrawal across the Potomac while Stuart with Wade Hampton's Brigade created a diversion around Williamsport. On the twentieth, Stuart maintained his position on the north side of the river until dark, when he withdrew across the Potomac to the safety of Virginia.[110]

The ensuing days were relatively peaceful, and on the twenty-eighth, Stuart established his headquarters at "The Bower," home of Adam Stephen Dandridge. Here for the next several weeks, with one notable exception, the cavalry commander and his staff enjoyed a brief respite from the war. The enemy across the Potomac still had to be watched, but both armies were recuperating from their terrible encounter along Antietam Creek and remained relatively quiet.

For Channing Price, the momentous battle and the actions that followed permitted him to write only twice to his anxious family back in Richmond. His duty to his country and his general were not outweighed by that to his family, but he had been kept so busy he had not the time for correspondence. In his two letters, however, he did manage to relieve his family's fears and recount for them the doings of the army and his part in the campaign.

Near Shepherdstown Va
Sept 18th 1862

Dear Mother [Mrs. Thomas Randolph Price Sr.]

Mostly from my desire to relieve your anxiety & partly at the request of Gen. Stuart (who wishes you to let his wife hear it) I avail myself of the chance today to write you that he & I are both safe. The soil of Maryland near Sharpsburg Washington Co. has been ———— [word illegible] with the blood of thousands of our brave boys in the most terrific battle of the War on yesterday, lasting from a little after day light until darkness put an end to it.

2 days after my last letter was written from Urbana (which I hope you got) our Cavalry which for 3 or 4 days had been holding the enemy in check so as to keep possession of a high mountain in that vicinity which commands the country for miles ———— [word illegible] our forces had marched out of sight of it, began slowly to fall back. That night the 3 brigades crossed the River (Monocacy) holding the crossings, next day the General & staff spent in Frederick, and late in the evening again fell back at night. Hampton's Brigade camped near Middletown holding the gaps of the mountains nearby.

On Saturday morning we had quite a sharp fight with artillery on the mountain & the enemy advancing a very heavy force (we having nothing but cavalry & artillery) we withdrew skirmishing all the way. We now perceived that the enemy was pushing as for the purpose of relieving the garrison of Harper's Ferry, where fighting had begun today & most of Hampton's Brigade struck off towards the Ferry so as to interpose between them & General [Maj. Gen. Lafayette] McLaws who was fighting for possession of Maryland Heights.[111]

Our regiment of cavalry came on with the General to Braddock's Gap near Boonsboro, & here we were reinforced by a brigade of infantry & 6 pieces of artillery most of D. H. Hill's troops also came up during the night to hold this & adjacent gaps. We staid [*sic*] at Boonsboro all night & Sunday morning started for Crampton's Gap. Reaching it we found our cavalry holding it & soon after arriving the General sent me back to carry 2 fine maps to Gen. R. E. Lee. To my surprise I found him on the road near Boonsboro, with Longstreet's Corps coming up to the gaps.

When I got back to Crampton's Gap the enemy were in full view & the fight just commenced: hearing that the General had gone towards Maryland Heights (which had been taken by Barksdale's & Kershaw's Brigades on Saturday) I put out in that direction & going to Gen. McLaw's Hd. Qrs. found that Gen. Stuart had gone up on the Heights. I met him soon afterwards on his way back, & on reaching McLaw's Hd. Qrs., we heard that our forces had been driven from Crampton's Gap & the enemy in heavy force had crossed, thus getting between us & Gen. Longstreet at the other gap.

Gen. Stuart galloped on & a short distance from the Gap we found our troops just rallied & being reinforced. As far as I could hear one of our political Generals (Howell Cobb) was responsible for the disaster & Gen. Stuart's presence & unequalled coolness had a good effect on the men as Gen. Cobb was so violently excited as to add to the confusion prevailing. It was already dark & staying here until 10 o'clock & no fighting we came back & made Hd. Qrs. near Gen. McLaw's.[112]

Monday morning we again went out & whilst Gen. Stuart was far in front of our line of battle, examining the position of the enemy, news came by a courier of the surrender of Harper's Ferry. Such a shout as our men gave must have struck terror to the Yankees, who could hear it distinctly. The General soon started for Harper's Ferry & after staying there a short while left for Sharpsburg, leaving his Staff etc. to come in the evening.

I rode with [Lt. Chiswell] Dabney all over the place, & such a sight I never before witnessed & never expect to again. The Yankees had been drawn up on the Bolivar Heights, & their arms stacked most beautifully for upward of a mile the men were there resting in line on the slope of the hill, the artillery all parked & except for 2 regiments of our men who were guarding the ———— [word illegible] etc., not a Confederate soldier to be seen. The officers (most elegantly dressed) being allowed to retain their arms & private property were riding all over the place, presenting a singular appearance.

After staying there several hours we all took the road for Sharpsburg crossing the Potomac at a ford below Shepherdstown. Dabney & I (our horses very lame) fell behind & slept all night about 1 1/2 miles from Sharpsburg. Next day as we approached the town, a terrific cannonade commenced & after 2 hours ceased. The town was considerably damaged by shells but no one killed. Towards evening I went to the town & going to Mr. Grove's (Gen. Stuart's Hd. Qrs. the night before) got a good dinner. The General came from the field after dark having been engaged in posting batteries all day. He went back soon though to be near the front & I waited until about day with Dr. [Talcott] Eliason & the escort at Mr. Grove's. Gen. Jackson also slept on a sofa in the room with me until day. We then went out on the left wing to find the General, but so rapid & vague are his movements that we did not do [so] until late in the day: consequently I was not so much exposed as if I had been with him, but still was a good deal so. When we found him the fight on the left was over, we having dislodged the enemy & driven him some distance: on our right it was raging still. Dabney & I came back to this place last night. I to get my horse shod & he to get a fresh one.

As yet I know comparatively little of the losses, but on both sides it has been fearful. Maj. Gen. D. R. [David Rumph] Jones & Brig. Gen. [William E.] Starke were killed on our side. I hear Gen. [Lewis A.] Armistead was slightly wounded in the foot. Gen. Sam Garland was killed on Sunday at Braddock's Gap. I saw Col. W. D. Stuart in Sharpsburg Tuesday evening, he is safe but very unwell & I suppose did not go into the fight yesterday.[113] Gen. Stuart had a narrow escape on yesterday: a battery was firing at him as he was crossing a field rapidly & suddenly a regiment, which having been driven back had rallied behind a stone fence, rose & fired at him, the horse (not his own) which he was riding was struck but he escaped.

We are entirely cut off from the world; I have not seen a paper or heard any news from Richmond for more than 2 weeks. I hope that communication by Harper's Ferry & the Valley will be established. We heard yesterday that G. W. Smith & Johnston with their forces occupied Arlington Heights & if so, the blow we struck the army of McClellan yesterday may become a decided victory.

The artillery firing yesterday was the most terrific of the war, exceeding all imagination. You will hear exaggerated reports of the surrender of Harper's Ferry & I send you what I know is correct (coming from Gen. Jackson). 11,000 prisoners were taken & the negroes, camp-followers etc., swelled it to 13,000 & upwards: without seeing the position you can not understand fully the trap they were in, on one side from the Loudoun Heights, another the Maryland Heights, another from towards Martinsburg, the batteries were throwing in shell on Bolivar Heights; then A. P. Hill was marching up the ridge which terminates in Bolivar Heights, & but for the surrender, nearly every man would have been killed. Nearly the whole of the cavalry made their escape on Sunday night going by Sharpsburg & on their way capturing a portion of our wagon train near Hagerstown. We captured 73 pieces of artillery in the garrison besides stores to some little amount, the principal thing being ordnance, which we needed very much.[114]

I have not got my clothes yet, but made a ———— [word illegible] in Frederick the day we left which suits me very well. We found a large quantity of clothing intended for the Yankee Army & which we came near leaving undisturbed: I got 2 very nice linen shirts, 2 pair drawers & a quantity of good towels. There were also ———— [word illegible], socks, blankets, a few overcoats etc., but I was not so fortunate as to get any. I also got some very pretty gingham near Frederick, & if I get a chance to have it made up, can get along very well in case I do not get my trunk soon.

The commanding officer (Gen. [Col. Dixon S.] Miles) at Harper's Ferry was wounded Monday morning & died from the effects of it: we captured 3 generals I believe.[115] I wish if George Woodbridge is still in town (though I don't much expect he is) you would ask Papa to send me 50 dollars in

Confederate notes.[116] I did not have a great deal of money with me, not expecting the course of events of the last month, & not being able to draw my pay, have nearly run through what I had.

The citizens of Maryland object to ———— [two words illegible] of us but Confederate ———— [one line illegible] all of one sort, as they can not use it until the Yankees are driven out forever. Since leaving Urbana, the Union element is stronger & stronger as we approach the Pennsylvania line.

I have no time nor anything else to write & must stop. With my love to all at home & all kind friends in Richmond. I remain your ———— [word illegible] son

R. Channing Price

P. S. Some of our wagons have just come up from Winchester, and along with them Geo. Woodbridge bringing your letter. I trust that by this time you have gotten my letters from Fairfax & Urbana. At the time that Geo. Woodbridge as well as Keith Armistead left for Richmond, I was not with the Genl & so did not have a chance to write.[117] I have heard from the Battle-field to-day, but not having succeeded in getting my horse shod have not been back. Gen. Jones is not killed or hurt as I wrote you this morning. I am glad to hear that all is great to-day. I shall cross the river tomorrow I hope.

———— ≡✦≡ ————

Head. Qrs.
Cavalry Division
Hainesville, Berkeley Co.
Sept 25th 1862

Dear Sister [Ellen Price],

I am afraid that I seem to have neglected you in my letters since I left home, but really have no excuse to offer except that having had so few opportunities of writing at all, that I felt that what I was able to write, would be equally acceptable when addressed to Mama as if to yourself. I hope that Mama has received my letter from Shepherdstown & Winchester, as she no doubt would feel extremely anxious about me on hearing of the fighting on Sunday, Monday, Tuesday & Wednesday of last week.

Soon after finishing my letter at Winchester I started back towards the river & getting 5 miles from town I found our ordnance & some other wagons, as it was already night & finding Geo. Woodbridge & some other couriers who were out of horses, I spent the night with them. Sunday morning I came on & getting to Bunker Hill at dinner time went to Mr. Boyd's, where I got dinner: I also looked at a horse whilst there, as I began to see that I must have another one, even when I can get my own from Fairfax: for some time I have been riding a horse which Frank Deane picked up.[118]

After dinner I rode on 3 miles to Burkhartsville where I found Maj. [Samuel H.] Hairston's wagons: whilst there Frank Deane came from Martinsburg with orders from the General to bring the wagons there by night. Here finding I could borrow some money from Maj. Hairston QrM I determined to buy the horse from Mr. Boyd, as he seemed cheap, $125. I got a courier to go back & pay for him & bring him on next day to have him shod before coming to Martinsburg. I came on to Martinsburg and going to Dr. Summer's where the General had been, I found that he had gone to Genl Lee's, but would be probably soon back. I staid [*sic*] there a little while & found them to be very nice people & intimate friends of the Genl during his career in this country as Colonel of the 1st Va Cavalry.

A courier soon came to show Maj. Hairston the way to Head Qrs., which were about a mile from town on the Williamsport Pike. I found the staff all there, but the Genl spent the night in town. Here I heard accounts of the doings of the Genl since I left him: immediately on crossing at Shepherdstown he went to Williamsport & for 2 days Friday & Saturday with Hampton's Brigade & some artillery (amongst others, parts of both the 2nd & 3rd [Richmond] Howitzers) he kept his ground, losing not a man, & inflicting a severe loss on the enemy who attempted to overwhelm him. Saturday night he recrossed to Virginia.[119]

One of the most disastrous affairs to the Yankees that has ever occurred, was at Shepherdstown Saturday evening [the twentieth]. A very large brigade forced their way over, driving back 2 small brigades of ours stationed there; Jackson sent up A. P. Hill who attacked them furiously whilst another large brigade was coming over: Gen. Pendleton had some guns on the tremendous cliff overlooking the ford, which is a very bad & rough one. It is said to have been second only to Leesburg [Battle of Ball's Bluff] in the slaughter of the Yankees. 800 or 900 were killed, 300 prisoners & a large number wounded: our loss was very small.[120]

Genl Stuart's Hd. Qrs. are now at this place, 5 miles from Martinsburg: we came up Monday & have been here since. The cavalry are picketing at the ford & the army is resting & gathering stragglers. I started with the Genl on Tuesday to Charlestown [Charles Town], but after going a short distance, he sent me to Gen. Fitz Lee: I staid [*sic*] there all night as the Genl did not come to his quarters. Next day on coming back here I found nearly all the staff gone after the General & only [Maj. Samuel H.] Hairston, [Lt. Chiswell] Dabney, [Capt. William D.] Farley & some couriers left. The General has not yet returned.

Tell Mama that I got to my clothes the other day & they are all safe. With love to all I remain yours devotedly

R. Channing Price

OCTOBER

The quiet that had settled over the countryside at the end of September was broken on the first of the new month. Union brigadier general Alfred Pleasonton, with 700 men, crossed the Potomac at Shepherdstown with the intent of making a reconnaissance in force toward Martinsburg. He reached his goal and entered the town a little after two o'clock in the afternoon. Stuart was quick to respond and, according to von Borcke, was much disgusted that the Federals had gained possession of the town. At five o'clock, Pleasonton began his withdrawal. Stuart with Hampton and Fitz Lee's brigades, the latter under the command of Col. "Rooney" Lee, harried the blue cavalry all the way to the river but was unable to inflict any serious damage. By dark the action was over, and Stuart returned to "The Bower" at midnight.[121]

Calm again returned to Stuart's headquarters, and dances and other social events made the war seem far away. Then on the eighth, Robert E. Lee issued orders for a raid into Pennsylvania. The army's commander, Stuart, and Stonewall Jackson had been discussing such a foray for several days. Preparations were made, and with 1,800 men and four guns of the Stuart Horse Artillery under Pelham, Stuart began his expedition on the ninth. On the morning of the tenth, he crossed the Potomac heading for Chambersburg, Pennsylvania.

For Stuart's young aides-de-camp, such a raid was something to write home about, which both Channing Price and Chiswell Dabney did on the fifteenth and twenty-first, respectively. Price's role in the adventure was not a small one, as he was acting not only as aide, but also performing the duties of adjutant general. His letter shows his pride in the achievement of both the cavalry and himself. Dabney did not have all the responsibility Price bore throughout the raid, but he did contribute his share of confiscated horses and carried out all his other duties to Stuart's satisfaction.

Head Qrs.
Cavalry Division
"The Bower"
Jefferson Co.
October 15th 1862

Dear Mother [Mrs. Thomas Randolph Price Sr.],

General Stuart's long expressed desire to pay a visit to Pennsylvania & especially Chambersburg has been gratified, and safe again on old Virginia soil we find ourselves. From the beginning of last week I felt confident that some great movement was in contemplation, as Genl Stuart was sent for & had several lengthy consultations with Genls Lee & Jackson.

On Wednesday night [the eighth] I felt sure that next day would see the beginning of the movement whatever it might be, as the General directed me (at that time discharging the duties of Adjt Genl) to get all the papers requiring his attention ready for his action that night. We had a pleasant time, music & dancing, until 11 o'clock, then returned to our tents, the General finished up all his business, & about 1 o'clock, we got the music (violin banjo & bones) and gave a farewell serenade to the ladies of the "Bower."

Thursday morning [the ninth] I was at the house when the General sent for me to finish up the address to the cavalry detailed for the expedition & the orders for the government of the same.[122] I then knew exactly the object of the trip, and when soon after he started off, taking only [Lt. Chiswell] Dabney and one or two couriers, I was afraid that I would not have the pleasure of engaging in the invasion. He left orders for the rest of the staff & escort to come on with Col. [Thomas T.] Munford's command when it passed to Darksville [Darkesville], where [Brig. Gen. Fitzhugh] Lee & Munford were to rendezvous.[123]

About 2 hours afterwards we rode on & getting to Darksville, rode up towards Martinsburg with the column, but soon heard that the General was still at Darksville. [Lt. Walter Q.] Hullihen & I then turned & riding back soon met the General: he ordered us to ride on rapidly, pass the head of the column & proceed to Hedgesville, where Gen. Hampton had gone with his command from Martinsburg, see him and arrange for bivouacing [sic] Munford's & Lee's commands near the river before their arrival.[124]

Getting near the river, we had to dismount & go on foot to Gen. Hampton, whom we found on the bank of the river & every thing quiet: we then rode back & soon met Gen. Stuart & all hands soon retired to sleep, we in a strawrick: at day-break we commenced crossing, Hampton in front, Munford's command under Col. [William E. "Grumble"] Jones next, & W. H. F. Lee bringing up the rear, each having 600 cavalry, and Hampton & Lee each 2 pieces of horse artillery: at 8 o'clock we reached the Hancock & Hagerstown Turnpike, when from citizens we learned that a brigade of 5000 had just passed towards Hancock & thankful for having missed them so narrowly we pushed on by an obscure road, after capturing a signal station & some few prisoners.

About 10 o'clock we entered Pennsylvania, & the orders for the seizure of horses & public functionaries immediately went into operation: 200 out of every 600 men were detailed to visit all the houses & seize horses,

Fredericksburg
and
Hamilton's Crossing

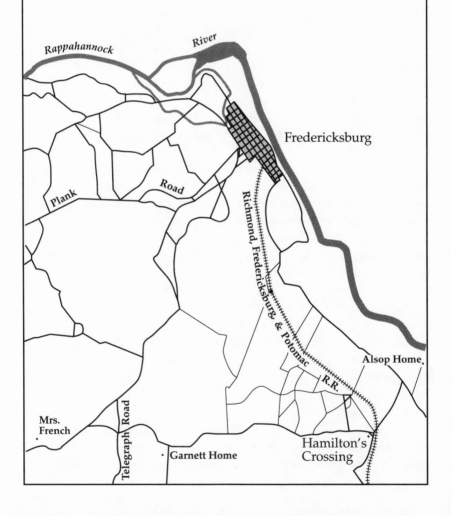

Fredericksburg

Rappahannock River

Plank Road

Richmond, Fredericksburg & Potomac R.R.

Alsop Home

Mrs. French

Telegraph Road

Garnett Home

Hamilton's Crossing

and well did they perform their duty. It was ludicrous in the extreme to see the old Dutchmen as their horses were taken in every variety of circumstances, from the stable, the threshing machine, wagons etc. I assisted in seizing a good many, giving a receipt to the effect that the horses were taken for the Army of the Confederate States, to be paid as damage by the U. S. Government: then stating their value & signing my name by command of Genl Stuart.

We soon reached Mercersburg a small town in Franklin Co. & pushed on, halting 5 or 6 miles beyond to feed: we took the corn right from the field, having no trouble about a Qr. Master buying forage. By this time the rain was falling in torrents, but we pushed on, and about 7 o'clock got to Chambersburg: it was pitchy dark & raining: we halted about 3/4 of a mile from town, put artillery in position, and Lieut. [Paul] Hamilton (Gen. Hampton's ADC) bore a flag of truce to the town.

The drums were beating calling the citizens to arms & all was in great excitement as he approached: the mayor & some other town officers met him, and after some parleying agreed to surrender unconditionally. Genl Hampton & Col. Jones then went on through the town, Gen. Lee remaining this side: Genl Stuart & staff rode in to the public square & after giving orders for the night to the Provost Guard etc., we rode back 1/2 mile to the toll house, got a cup of coffee made and then laid down on the kitchen floor to sleep, leaving our horses saddled.

I got up early, found it still raining, and went into town to get some plunder: I got to the Government Depot just as operations commenced, & supplied myself with a nice black overcoat, pair of blue pants, 1 dozen pair woolen socks, pair of boots & various other little things as much as I could carry: I rode on then to overtake the column & soon afterwards the rear guard commenced destroying all the public property left (machine shop, depot, 5 or 6000 stand of arms etc.) only clothing having been taken off: $1,000,000 it is estimated was destroyed there: we rode on passing a number of small towns, seizing horses & citizens on the way: we halted a short time to feed, and moved rapidly on: in 6 miles of Gettysburg we turned toward Emmitsburg, and at the point of turning off heard that your distinguished relative Col. [Richard H.] Rush with his regiment of lancers [6th Pennsylvania Cavalry] had just passed on to Gettysburg on the look out for us & Genl Stuart got hold of some instructions to one of his captains to keep posted of our movements: had we been a little sooner, we would have taught Col. Rush a lesson he would not have forgotten directly.

About sunset we reached Emmitsburg & such enthusiasm as we witnessed here (1/2 mile from the line of Penna) you can form no idea of; I had to mount a fresh horse here, mine being very much worn. In 22 miles

of Frederick City we were getting now where danger was to be apprehended & moved rapidly: we soon turned from the Frederick road & passed
in succession through Woodsboro, Liberty, New London, New Market &
here we crossed the B [Baltimore] & Ohio R. Road, obstructing the track
and cutting the telegraph.

We were now in 6 miles of Urbana (for some time such pleasant Hd.
Qrs. for us) & as it was getting near day-break, I hoped we were going
through it: as I had to lead my horse I rode on with the led horses, and did
not know when the Genl left the column: he took the road to Urbana with
Capt [William W.] Blackford & some others of the staff, & the column that
[road] to Hagerstown. We got here about daybreak & the General joined
us soon after: we now turned towards the [Potomac] river & at Barnesville
heard that a heavy force was awaiting us at the different fords: in about 4
miles of White's Ford (opposite Leesburg) we came in sight of a large force
drawn up to receive us, but we were between them & the ford.

Major Pelham brought up 1 piece of artillery & engaged their attention while Col. [William C.] Wickham with the column moved rapidly to
the ford: after 6 or 8 shots had been fired the General sent me rapidly to
overtake Col. Wickham & direct him to ———— [two words illegible] everything was going ———— [word illegible] at the ford which was a very
long one & much exposed both in the river & approach that a new difficulty awaited us as 500 sharpshooters were on the cliff overlooking the ford
& ready to open on us. A gun was brought up & at the first fire every
scoundrel took to his heels & the cavalry charging in as skirmishers captured a few & completely dispersed them. They also came down the tow
path endeavoring to cut us off, but one or two shots cleaned them out.[125]

Everything now being ready, the firing was kept up & the led horses,
then the cavalry & lastly the artillery moved rapidly across the river. The
Genl sent me to bring off Capt Breathed & his gun & as he was the last to
leave the enemy were closing in rapidly, no doubt thinking they had us cut
off. We all got safely across & going 3 or 4 miles halted to feed. Having
traveled all night & 2 days you may know I was tired, and after getting
something to eat laid down to sleep, but was soon roused up. we moved
on to Leesburg & the command halted & bivouaced [sic] near town. The
General & staff staid [sic] at Dr. Jackson's (in town) where we were most
hospitably entertained & I slept elegantly in a nice bed.

Monday morning [the thirteenth] I walked about a good deal, went to
see Mr. Powell's family & staid some time. About 12 o'clock we took the
road campwards & just before dark reached Snickersville at the foot of the
mountain dividing Loudoun & Jefferson Cos. Here the command halted,

Genl Stuart kept on to Genl Lee's Hd. Qrs. near Winchester, & Dabney & I came on [to] the "Bower."

About 7 miles after crossing the Shenandoah River, we stopped at Mr. Castleman's, got supper, fed our horses & slept till 12 o'clock. We then rode on 15 miles, reaching here just before day. We went directly to the house & by a serenade roused all hands. Soon after Mr. Dandridge had a cup of coffee & some bread etc. ready for us & after eating & spending a little time with the young ladies who honored us by rising early to welcome us back, Dabney & I went into one of the rooms & took a good sleep.

About the middle of the day we got up & found the General had arrived. Gen. Lee is excessively gratified at the result of the expedition & expressed warmly his thanks to the Cavalry & their gallant & noble leader.[126] Last night we had a gay time at the "Bower" after our short absence. The prisoners captured citizens & soldiers are now here at Hd. Qrs., just preparing to go to Richmond under Capt. Steven [Benjamin Stephen] White of Maryland (an attaché of the staff) who will carry this letter.[127] The results of the expedition are briefly, 1000 or 1200 horses (mostly suitable for artillery), 30 or 40 civil prisoners, about the same number of soldiers & 300 or more sick paroled in Chambersburg; the immense amount of property brought from Chambersburg in clothing etc. & 1 million dollars worth destroyed, and the moral effect which are great, teaching the Pennsylvanians something of war, & showing how J. E. B. Stuart can make McClellan's circuit at pleasure.

The whole trip was accomplished without losing a man killed or wounded & 2 or 3 prisoners. The greatest loss was Bob (the Genl's boy & 2 fine horses): he straggled behind, having been drinking & was captured I suppose.[128] I lost really all I had which was valuable as trophies, dropping my haversack & boot (both filled with little things) from my saddle during the night's march. My overcoat, pants, sabre etc. I brought safely back.

On getting here yesterday I found Major [Norman R.] Fitzhugh [FitzHugh], but I am sorry to say not my pants: he says that he directed a friend, when he left the hotel before he told you he would, to collect all the boxes sent to him & particularly mentioned a bundle from you, but he never got it: he says you may probably find them at the hotel yet, the No. of his room being 292, & if there probably in the coat room. I am sorry to lose them, as those I have though not worn out are very dirty. If you don't find them please have me another pair made & sent by Capt. White if possible; also my coat.

Everything is quiet here, the army being exactly as it was when I wrote by Lt. [Jones R.] Christian. I got your letter & Ellen's yesterday on my return & was glad to know that you had seen Christian. I delivered Ellen's message to the Genl & he requests me to say that she is still his sweet heart & sends her a leaf from the Blue Ridge as a memento of his raid into Pennsylvania. The only thing I send you is a little pocket book for stamp currency, which will do to keep for my sake until my return. Tell Eddy I had a dozen Barlow knives (one for him) which I lost.

The General orders me to tell you that I was his Chief of Staff during the expedition & discharged the duties satisfactorily. Major Von Borcke was left here much to his sorrow & [Maj. James T. W.] Hairston was Provost Marshal, so I acted adjutant. We are all delighted to get Major Fitzhugh [FitzHugh] back, as everything moves smoothly when he is about. George Woodbridge is well but did not go with us nor did Capt. [John Esten] Cooke. Frank Deane was along & is very well. Give my love to all & believe me your devoted son

R. Channing Price

In case no account of the raid is published before you get this, if you choose you can take such of my letter as will be interesting & have it published for information of all concerned. R. C. P.

—+— ≣◆≣ —+—

Hd Qrs Cavl' Division
October 21st 1862

Dear Mother [Mrs. Elizabeth T. Dabney]

As Major Hairston is about starting home, I avail myself of this opportunity of getting him to drop this letter in at Lynchburg. I wrote Aggie a letter a few days ago telling her something of our ride through Pennsylvania, but as the mails are so very uncertain I think it very doubtful whether it has ever arrived at its destination. Therefore I will give you a full account of the whole trip, knowing that it will be interesting to you.

We started from Mr. Dandriges [Adam Stephen Dandridge], our camp, on the 9th and marched towards the Potomack [sic] in a north easterly direction; after marching the whole of that day we camped about two miles from the ford that we had to cross. Next morning we started about sunrise & crossed the river with very little difficulty, there being only a very small picket which fled, leaving their horses after the first few fires. From here we mad[e] a direct line across Maryland (which if you observe on the map is very narrow) to Pennsylvania; as soon as we crossed the line, orders were issued for every available horse to be impressed into the service of the Confederate States.

Acting upon this order, being very much in want of a good horse, I sallied out together with a young English officer named Castles, to pick one fit for a Confed' to ride. After having very unceremoniously visited several jolly Dutchman's stables much to their annoyance and our pleasure, I at last found a splendid black Morgan horse. When I dismounted I call[ed] to a negroe [*sic*] to come and hold my horse but instead he commenced running away. I drew my pistol, cocked it & call[ed] to him if he moved another peg I would shoot him. This brought him to a stand still. He came up & when I informed who I was it liked to have frightened him to death. We gave him our horses to hold & went into the stable & commenced untyeing [*sic*] the horses when off started Coffee again, pursued by Castles, around the house. The race was so ridiculous that I had to sit down & laugh & Castles became more & more furious until he got his firearms out & commenced to shoot when we brought the animal to bay. By this time the man of the house came out & wanted to know who we were & what we were doing (never dreaming of rebels). I told him we were charged with the disagreeable duty of impressing all the horses of that country for the service. He commenced explaining how it was impossible for him to spare his horses & begged like a dog for half an hour. I told him this was impossible & also remarked to him that I was a very good rebel. This opened his eyes & he begged worse than ever. I said this was what we called making the <u>solid</u> <u>men</u> feel the <u>war</u>. About this time I mounted & left the gentleman to his reflections & went prancing into Mercersburg leading my old war horse Dixie who I turned over to one of the men detailed to lead horses. The poor old fellow was left during the trip & I moan his loss from the bottom of my heart.

We arrived at Chambersburg the night of the 10th, heard a great rolling of drums, thought of course there must be troops in town (at this time it was as dark as pitch & raining at that). We planted a gun in position ready to shell the place provided they did not surrender, which the[y] very soon did, unconditionally. We then marched in and took possession very quietly. By eleven o'clock Genl Stuart established Hd Qrs & down we laid on the floor, wet to the skin, to snatch a few hours of rest.

Next morning raining hard, but we were in motion early; the publick [*sic*] stores were opened & I procured myself a splendid black army overcoat, bleached castile soap, teaspoons, bridle, boots, canteens, a beautiful pocket-book, a great many U. S. postage ———— [word illegible] pocketbooks, one of which I enclosed in a letter for Aggie, doubt whether you ever got it though. The men got every thing they wanted & a great many things they did not want.

We left town about 10 o'clock after having put fire to all the railroad houses, wearehouses [sic] containing government supplies, burnt up about six thousand stand of arms. Our Caval' supplied themselves with good army pistols. We marched on through an iron region of country towards the Maryland line which we struck at a little place called Emmetesville [Emmitsburg] which by the way is as true south as Charleston, S.C. The ladies came on the street & cheered us most lustily. Some of the men were so much overjoyed that they cried & wept; this was night when we left that place, marched all night, never was so sleepy in my life. Came very near falling off my horse & breaking my neck several times.

Next morning we came upon the enimy's [sic] pickets at a little village just this side of Poolsville [Poolesville] drove them in and struck off for the Potomack where we expected to have some desperate fighting. Our position is represented on this paper. You will see that we were entirely sourrounded [sic] when we broke through the enimy except for the river side, but you see the ford was guarded by a regt of infantry. However, we shelled them away & got across without the loss of a man. I am now at the Bower, Mr. Dandriges [Dandridge] where we spend a very gay time dancing with the ladies every night. Took tea last night at the Hon. Mr. [Charles J.] Faulkner's.[129] Spent quite a nice time. Ladies very pleasant. [Remainder of letter is lost.]

Stuart had scarcely returned from his expedition when, on the sixteenth, Union brigadier general Andrew A. Humphreys, with 500 cavalry, 6,000 infantry, and six guns, crossed the Potomac at Shepherdstown on a reconnaissance in force. At the same time, Brig. Gen. Winfield S. Hancock moved toward Charles Town with another force. The enemy's advance reached Leetown and Charles Town, with Stuart's cavalry and horse artillery falling back before them. On the seventeenth, the Federals began to withdraw. Stuart followed them, exchanging skirmisher and artillery fire. Losses were light on both sides, and the Confederate cavalry resumed its former positions after the enemy had recrossed the Potomac.[130]

For the remainder of the month, brief clashes with the Federals continued as they conducted scouts to Thoroughfare Gap, Lovettsville, Manassas Junction, and Bristoe Station.[131] Cavalry headquarters remained at "The Bower" until the twenty-ninth. At that time, Robert E. Lee began to move his army across the Blue Ridge Mountains. The beautiful camp was broken up, and Stuart and his staff bade farewell to the Dandridge family and the idyllic times they had spent together over the past several weeks.

The move brought closer contact with the Federals, and sharp skirmishes erupted at Upperville on the twenty-ninth and at Snickersville, Aldie, and Mountville on the thirty-first. In all these engagements, Stuart gained the upper hand, but he was forced to fall back when a Federal force moved on his flank. The month drew to a close with the anticipation that hard fighting was ahead.[132]

Unfortunately there are no letters or diary entries from any staff member for this period. Channing Price seems to have been at headquarters part of the time but was also in Richmond until late November on furlough, cavalry business, or both.

NOVEMBER

The month of November proved to be one of the saddest for Stuart. On the third, his little daughter, Flora, died in Lynchburg.[133] The loss affected Stuart deeply but did not stop him from performing his duty. He remained with the army, feeling that he could not leave during an active campaign. Stuart also suffered the loss of another of his staff and a close personal friend when, on the twenty-fifth, Redmond Burke was ambushed and killed in Shepherdstown while on a scouting mission.

The fighting in the early days of November was incessant. From the first to the tenth, no less than twenty-seven separate skirmishes occurred.[134] Stuart was present at many of the engagements. Both the cavalry and the Stuart Horse Artillery gained his praise. There were losses: Col. William C. Wickham of the 4th Virginia Cavalry suffered a severe neck wound; Maj. William G. Delony of Cobb's Georgia Legion was wounded; and Capt. William W. Blackford, Stuart's engineer officer, suffered a leg wound.[135]

For the remainder of the month, though the number of encounters lessened somewhat, the cavalry was nevertheless kept busy repulsing enemy incursions, mounting scouts and reconnaissances, and doing picket duty. Stuart did not file a report for this time period, so details from the Confederate side are sketchy. Things did quiet enough, however, for him to invite his wife, Flora, to join him at Culpeper Court House, which she did on the tenth.

During this same period, Maj. Gen. Ambrose Burnside had replaced Maj. Gen. George B. McClellan in command of the Federal forces. The maneuvering of the armies continued until they were centered around Fredericksburg, with Lee on one side of the Rappahannock and Burnside on the other. Cavalry headquarters, dubbed Camp "No Camp," was located about five miles south of Fredericksburg on the Telegraph Road. It was to this camp that Chiswell Dabney and Channing Price returned after enjoying furloughs home. Dabney had accompanied Flora Stuart on her way to visit her husband. After performing that duty he had time for a few scouts, during which he procured some needed supplies, and on one occasion met a young lady threatened by the enemy. Price's only letter for November, while newsy, contained little mention of the fighting that occurred during the month.

Hd Qrs Cavalry Division
Camp, No Camp,
Nov' 26th 1862

Dear Mother [Mrs. Elizabeth T. Dabney]

As I am now at leisure I take advantage of it to drop you a few lines in regard to my whereabouts and what has been going on since I left Lynchburg. I arrived safely with Mrs. Stuart at Culpeper Co Ho [Court House] the same day I left you and immediately reported to Hd. Qrs. for duty. We had friquent [sic] fights with the enemy [sic] for several days, trying to find out something of the movements of the enemy. Monday we found that [Maj. Gen. Ambrose] Burnside had commenced his movement towards Fredericksburg, and Genl Stuart determined to cross the Rhock' [Rappahannock] River to ascertain exactly where his line of march was to be. We had quite a sharp fight at the crossing, but we very soon drove them away and marched on to Warrenton capturing prisoners all the way.

At Warrenton we were received with much enthusiasm by the ladies; captured here a sutlers [sic] establishment; I got segars [sic], half a dz. cans of condensed milk, fresh tomatoes, fresh cherries, gloves, boots, & handkerchiefs, in fact every thing I wanted.

We followed the enimy down the river all day, recrossed the two rivers and marched to Fredricksburg where we are now. I am now in splendid quarters, have a good tent with a stove in it & plenty to eat, in fact I have a splendid table. Then there are a country full of nice girls, many of whom I have become acquainted with. I will now tell you of quite a romantick [sic] incident that happened yesterday eavening [sic].

Major [Lewis Frank] Terrell & myself took a ride to the front—down to the Rappahannock.[136] While riding down the lines looking at the enimy we saw a lady walking on the other side. We rode down to the waters edge where it was about 200 yds wide and commenced questioning her as to the whereabouts of Burnside. She let us know every thing we wanted, in fact gave very important information. There were [sic] a whole company of Yankees on the hill so we had for the safety of the young lady to leave, but we took care to introduce ourselves. She said her name was Lucy Grey. She said the Yankees were quite civil. I am very much afraid they overheard us. If so no telling what they may do to the lady. They are capable of any thing. She promised to meet me at the same place this eavening [sic] but I expect to find the Yankees instead, but they can't get me. I [have] been here too long. The army is in fine spirits and well clothed. The men say they are going to walk right through Burnside and <u>gobble him up</u>.

Hope Pa is better. Give my love to all; & excuse this hastily written letter.

> I am your most
> affectionate son
> C. Dabney

> Hd. Qrs. Cav. Division
> Nov 30th 1862

Dear Mother [Mrs. Thomas Randolph Price Sr.],

This quiet Sunday morning I have thought it suitable for me to write to you, as I know that you (however unreasonable it may seem to me) feel always great anxiety about me. I had a stand on the platform until I reached Ashland, when I got a seat: on getting to the terminus (Hamilton's Crossing) after a little delay Maj. Ball & I found one of the men of our Qr. Master Dept. with an empty wagon & getting into it we soon arrived at the Genl's Hd. qrs. (about 4 miles) and found all well.

The General was very curious to know what had kept me so long in Richmond & was very glad to see me. I find myself perfectly afoot, as my sorrel horse is unfit to ride & do not know what I shall do for a riding animal. The horses of nearly all the staff are in a dreadful condition, and some of them who have 3 or 4 are also almost as badly off as I am. I hope to be able however to buy one in this neighborhood.

I have not been away from Hd. Qrs. since I have been up. Gen. Lee's Hd. Qrs. are not more than 1/2 a mile from us & the Corps of Gen. Longstreet is all about us. The Brigades of W. H. F. & FitzHugh [Fitzhugh] Lee are on this line, Hampton in Culpeper & Jones with Jackson.

Gen. Stuart received last night Gen. Hampton's report of a very successful little scout made by him with a small detachment of cavalry crossing the Rappahannock at ——— [word illegible] he penetrated beyond & in rear of the enemy's outposts & about daylight got in between the picket & the reserve of the squadron: after the reserve was taken, he came on up the road, capturing the picket.[137] 87 men were taken, besides 2 Captains & 3 lieuts, 100 horses & carbines, 2 flags and the best of it was that they all belonged to the 6th Regular U. S. Cavalry, (the crack Regt of their army).[138]

Gen. Stuart was off all day yesterday with Gen. R. E. Lee down the river & to-day has gone to Port Royal, expecting to be gone 2 or 3 days. There are a number of gun boats near Port Royal & I think it likely that the General will attack them to-morrow (Monday) as they are not "Iron Clads."

We have quite a nice place for Hd. Qrs. plenty of tents & are living very well. The Genl is very uneasy about little Jemmy, having heard nothing of him lately & I sent a telegraph a little while ago to Lynchburg to inquire about him.[139]

Don't forget to see about Major Von Borcke's photograph & if done get Capt. Blackford to bring it. I send a note to Taylor in relation to a pair of boots for the General, which I want you to have sent to him.

I want to go down to Fredericksburg as soon as I can to see the Yankees on the Falmouth side, as I hear you can go on the river bank & talk to them across the river.

Major Ball will carry this and I hope will go to see you, as he is a very gentlemanly person. I must now stop. Tell Ellen that the Genl was much obliged to her for her letter & candy, and says she does not know what she says when she hopes to see him soon in Richmond, as when he gets there the Yankees will not be far off. Yr. aff. son

R. Channing Price

DECEMBER

The month of "peace on earth, good will to men" opened with a continuation of the skirmishing between the armies that had marked most of November. On the second, Maj. Thomas C. Waller, with sixty troopers of the 9th Virginia Cavalry, crossed the Rappahannock near Leeds' Ferry and made a successful foray into Federal lines, coming away with a captain, a lieutenant, and forty-seven men of the 8th Pennsylvania Cavalry as prisoners.[140]

The Confederates kept busy annoying their opponents. A scout around Dumfries on the second inflicted more casualties and yielded additional prisoners. On the fourth, Pelham and two guns of the horse artillery, along with a Whitworth gun from Capt. Robert Hardaway's battery, shelled Federal gunboats on the Rappahannock near Port Royal.[141] The Federals, for their part, were not inactive, but seemed to be allowing the Confederates to have the initiative. That situation was about to change, however.

Channing Price's letters for the early days of December described the comings and goings of Stuart and the staff, as well as the activities of the cavalry. Virtually horseless, Price himself did not have much mobility and was chained to camp, where only work broke the monotony. Price bemoaned his fate but tried to maintain a positive outlook.

Hd. Qrs. Cav. Div.

Dec 1st 1862

Dear Mother,

I will add a little news this morning which may be interesting to you. soon after I finished my letter to you yesterday I heard Mr. Lawler, who had just come from Gen. Lee's Hd. Qrs. say that he had seen Gen. Jackson there & that Gens. Lee, Jackson & Longstreet had been in consultation during the morning. Last night his Corps got up & his Hd. Qrs. are about a mile from ours.[142]

The General's boy Bob has just arrived, having been with Genl Jackson for some time past. He gives a very straight and interesting account of his adventures: the horses he left at the house of a good Southern man near Hyattstown, Md. and they will be brought to Leesburg as soon as possible.

We have heard nothing from Gen. Stuart since he left us yesterday: Majors Von Borcke & Eliason are going this morning to join him & I wish I could do the same. All is quiet as yet but this will soon be broken I think, though in what way it is impossible to say. Good-bye

Yr devoted son
R. Channing Price

Hd. Qrs. Cav. Division
near Fredericksburg
Dec. 4th 1862

Dear Sister [Ellen Price],

I am afraid that Mama was more than usually anxious about me for several days after I left home last Friday as I had promised to write so quickly after my arrival: but Major Ball not going down until Tuesday accounts for her not having heard from me earlier. I hope she got my letter from him.

Capt. Blackford arrived yesterday & brought me a letter from Ma. The Negro boy I was not much surprised to hear had vamosed [*sic*] the ranche [*sic*] & am not sorry for it, as I expect he was a trifling chap.

Major Von Borcke, Dr. Eliason & Capt White started yesterday morning to join the General leaving only Major FitzHugh & myself at Hd. qrs. It was dreadfully lonesome here all day and I wished very much that I was with the General as I have found that I am always happier when with him than anywhere else in this life we are now leading: Major [L. Frank] Terrell got back late in the evening, having come up from the General in the morning to attend to some business: he told us the General would probably be back this morning, but a little while afterwards Major Von Borcke etc. arrived with him: he stopped at Gen. Lee's & soon came on to Hd. Qrs. He has been engaged for several days in flying around, reconnoitering etc. in the neighborhood of Port Royal: as yet Burnside has given no positive evidence of his intention to cross the river in our face, though several little ———— [word missing] indicate that such is his plan: one of them is this: the Genl heard they would probably throw a pontoon bridge across at a point named to him; riding along opposite to it, he discovered an Engineer Officer busily engaged in sketching on the bank of the river: the General & party drew up in line on this side & very soon the Engineer looking up, caught sight of the group watching him intently. He soon bundled up & traveled off, looking like a dog caught in the act of sheep killing.

Major Pelham, Dabney, Farley & Hullihen did not return to Hd. Qrs. with the Genl, but remained on the river some where. Gen. Jackson is at Guinney's [Guiney's] Station & his troops are in that vicinity: Gen. R. E. Lee passed our Hd. Qrs. this morning on his way to see Stonewall. Capt. Blackford went down this morning to Port Royal on some business connected with his Department.

I have not yet purchased a horse, but there are several for sale about Hd. Qrs., one of which I shall buy I think. Tell Mama, if she can, to get me a negro-boy, and if not before she can send him by Dr. Eliason who carries this letter for me, & will not be absent more than 4 or 5 days. Gen. Fitz Lee & Col. Thomas T. Munford have just left us, having been here most of the day. I have been quite busy to-day as the General, being absent for several days, necessarily found a good deal of business accumulated on his return & he, Major FitzHugh & I have been at work all day, getting it up.

You have heard I presume of the death of poor Redmond Burke by the hands of the Yankees in Shepherdstown, last Monday week. The Genl exhibits great feeling on the subject & cries almost every time allusion is made to it. He has received a letter from Mrs. Lee & one from Dr. ———— giving an account of it.[143] I this morning wrote a letter to Gen. Lee & Gov. Letcher announcing in feeling language the fact of his death & Gen. Stuart has issued a General Order to the Cavalry Division on the subject. He was a brave and true man and perfectly devoted to Gen. Stuart, and it is sad to think of his meeting his death by treachery.

Gen. Hampton & Gen. W. H. F. Lee continue to annoy the Yankees on their flanks crossing the river & capturing & killing the pickets. Col. Beale crossed the Potomac below Port Royal a few days since in boats & capturing 40 or 50 men & horses, returned in safety, swimming the horses behind the boats: Gen. Hampton on our extreme left also reports a little scout in which 3 Yankee pickets were killed & 5 (including a Lieut.) captured & brought over.[144]

Gen. Stuart sends his love to you all. Good-bye.

Your devoted brother
R. Channing Price

If Ma can send the negro before Dr. E. [Eliason] comes back & will telegraph me accordingly care Gen. Stuart, Fredericksburg, he will find a conveyance (wagon) always at Hamilton's Crossing

The Army of Northern Virginia occupied positions on the south side of the Rappahannock and waited for Burnside to make up his mind just where he wanted to cross. In the meantime, Brig. Gen. Wade Hampton continued to be a thorn in the Federal cavalry's side. On the tenth, with 520 men, he moved to strike at Dumfries in the rear of the Union army. By the morning of the thirteenth he was back, bringing with him more than fifty prisoners and seventeen sutlers' wagons.[145] The success of the raid was quickly overshadowed by the Battle of Fredericksburg, which occurred the day of his return.

The cavalry's part in the battle was minimal, but Pelham and a section of the Stuart Horse Artillery under Capt. Mathis W. Henry gained immortality by their actions in delaying the advance of an entire Federal division for two hours.[146] Pelham became, in Robert E. Lee's report, "the gallant Pelham," and Stuart and the entire staff joined in honoring the shy artillerist from Alabama.[147]

Price took time to write his mother on the seventeenth and allay her fears over his safety. In the letter, he described his actions and observations under some of the hottest firing of the day. Though his mother may have been relieved that her son was uninjured, the horror and danger that he had passed through was made crystal clear.

Elsewhere, Philip H. Powers, who had returned to the army but was not as yet a member of it, penned a brief letter to his wife. Though no longer on Stuart's staff, Powers was a frequent visitor to cavalry headquarters and would eventually return as a sergeant in the quartermaster department. He shared little detail of the battle, writing more of its aftermath. Both men were proud of their army's victory, but they also were consumed by what they had just experienced. Although Christmas was only eight days away, neither mentioned the coming holiday.

Hd. Qrs. Cavalry
Division
near Fredericksburg
Dec. 17th 1862

Dear Mother [Mrs. Thomas Randolph Price Sr.],

It has been a long time since I wrote you, but I hope that you received my telegram on Sunday morning [the fourteenth], as it would relieve you of anxiety as to my fate in the great fight of the 13th. I have heard but once from home since I left & that by Capt. Blackford: the letter which you told Dr. Eliason you had sent by mail I have never gotten, owing I suppose to the irregularity of the cars caused by the excitement of the last few days. I received the little bundle from the Doctor & was very sorry that you could not get me a servant to send by him.

I bought a horse about 10 days ago from a clerk in Major FitzHugh's office who was about to leave Hd. Qrs. for his regiment. I paid him $275 & he is a very good horse as I have proved in the past week by some of the hardest riding as I have ever had to do. My horse which I bought in the Valley is nearly well & if I had a negro to attend to them, I should be quite well fixed in that respect. Don't you think you could possibly come across one somewhere?

The accounts published in the Richmond papers of the fight are in no way reliable & though I do not flatter myself on much talent for description, still I think, that from my participation and what I have seen & heard since I can give a better idea of it than you have had. Well to begin at the beginning to make a connected story Thursday morning [the eleventh] some time before day I was aroused by the heavy cannonading in the direction of Fredericksburg, it having commenced some time before I heard it.

About sunrise we got up & as soon as we could get breakfast, started to the front, Genl Stuart having gone on a little before us to Gen. R. E. Lee's Hd. Qrs. We found Gens. Lee, Longstreet, Stuart & some others on a very commanding hill to the right of the Telegraph road this side of town, and the fog was so dense that we could only conjecture what was going on from the other side of the river. After a while the fog began to lift & just then Gen. Stuart sent me back to Hd. Qrs. to get some more couriers. On going back every thing was perfectly clear and soon afterwards commenced the grand bombardment of the town: such a cannonade I never heard before: 100 or more guns to the minute.

All the batteries were in full view & until nearly night this continued, the whole being done to drive out 1 Brigade (Barksdale's) who were keeping them [the Federal infantry] from getting across.[148] A little before sunset they succeeded in getting a number of troops across in boats, & Barksdale not being able longer to hold the bank, withdrew his men to this side of town, having inflicted a tremendous loss on the enemy & made him show his real desire to cross at Fredericksburg. They had succeeded also in getting 2 bridges over below the town & we went to Hd. Qrs. to sleep, knowing that the enemy were crossing in heavy force.

Friday morning [the twelfth] we went out again to our same position but the fog was very thick: about the middle of the day, Gen. Stuart having gone away off towards our right wing I rode along our lines in that direction to find him. After passing [Maj. Gen. George E.] Pickett's, [Maj. Gen. Lafayette] McLaws', & [Maj. Gen. John B.] Hood's Divisions, we came upon the left of Jackson's Corps (which had come up during the night) consisting of [Brig. Gen. William D.] Pender's Brigade, A. P. Hill's Division.[149] I rode to the position of the Letcher Battery where Gens. Lee & Jackson were examining the position of the enemy & the troops marching from the bridges & taking position on the left as they came up.

Gen. Lee told me that Gen. Stuart had gone out to our line of skir-

mishers to examine the enemy more closely, & pretty soon he came galloping back & joined Gen. Lee. We then rode back to Gen. Hood's position, where there was a long talk etc. and then back to our high hill. On
the way I passed thro the guns of the 1st [Richmond] Howitzer Co. , who
had just had a little artillery duel with the enemy: I saw Hugh Powell, Oby
Price and some other friends. Before returning to camp, I wrote a note to
Gen. Fitz Lee (between Spottsylvania [Spotsylvania] C. H. and Beaver Dam)
to bring the main portion of his command & unite with Gen. W. H. F.
Lee during the night on the Bowling Green & Fredericksburg road near
Hamilton's Crossing.

Next day we got up and had breakfast some time before day-light &
made our way to Hamilton's Crossing, near which we found the cavalry:
the enemy were very near the junction of the Bowling Green & Crossing
road, as we found out by riding out in the field when their sharp-shooters
opened on us. We then went on the hill to the left of the Crossing (A. P.
Hill's extreme right) & on which [Capt. William J.] Pegram's battery &
[Lt.] Jim Ellett's Section were.[150] While there the fog rose & revealed the
enemy coming up in beautiful style & forming line of battle, planting batteries etc.

I then galloped out to where Gen. Stuart was (at the junction of the 2
roads named above) & there Major Pelham had come up with 1 gun of
Henry's Horse Artillery. The enemy were in dense masses advancing straight
towards our line of battle & Pelham was exactly on their left flank with his
gun & with no support whatever: he opened on them with solid shot &
though most of them went amongst the infantry, one blew up a caisson for
the Yankees: they now opened about 15 or 20 guns on Pelham, but he
had splendid shelter for his gun & had only one man wounded I think. He
kept up his fire until he was ordered to cease so that they might come up
closer to our line: not a gun in our long line from Fredericksburg to
Hamilton's Crossing had yet fired: only Pelham with his Napoleon & soon
afterwards a Blakeley nearer the Rail Road.[151] Gen. Lee expressed his warm
admiration for Major Pelham's distinguished gallantry but said that the young
Major General (alluding to Gen. Stuart) had opened on them too soon.[152]

Everything was now quiet along our line, the rest of Jackson's Corps
(D. H. Hill's Division & [Col. J. Thompson] Brown's Artillery) had gotten
up & were in reserve, and the enemy's field batteries & his heavy guns across
the river commenced to shell in every direction to try to find our position.[153] The hill on which Pegram & Ellett were, came in for a large share
of the shelling & it was now that Jim Ellett was killed, long before they had
fired a gun. I saw his body at the Crossing soon after he was killed.

All of us except the General now got out of the way to the right of the Rail Road until the fight should commence in earnest. Gen. Stuart staid [sic] where he could see plainly when the enemy began to move & know when to begin his work, which was to bring to bear a large number of guns and break the left flank of the enemy. So soon as he began to advance, [Lt. Col. Reuben] Lindsay Walker's guns on the hill opened on their infantry & Pelham moved into the field to the right of the Rail Road with 12 or 15 rifled guns and opened an enfilading fire.[154] We now all joined the General who was near Pelham & the fight began in earnest.

Time and again we strained over the field to Gen. Jackson, Gens. W. H. F. Lee & Fitz Lee, Maj. Pelham etc. and the fight was raging now. Once when I galloped into Major Pelham's batteries to order him to advance his guns & enfilade the enemy who was now recoiling from the fierce shock of A. P. Hill's gallant men, I recognized the boys at the old gun which I have assisted so often to work: in a minute they pulled off their caps and cheered me until I left the place.

Pelham was standing between White's & Wakeham's guns & the shells were crashing in every direction. This was the last time that I saw poor Jim Utz as he was struck soon afterwards and instantly killed.[155] Pelham continued to advance his guns as the enemy retreated pouring in a terrible enfilading fire all the time: after reaching the protection of their batteries, the wretches were re-organized by the bringing up of fresh lines & again presented their front. A Parrott gun of the 2nd Howitzers & one of the Powhatan Battery now crossed the Bowling Green road & opened a very destructive fire on their flank (under the direction of Col. [Thomas L.] Rosser), Major Pelham commanding the others; I went to Genl Jackson to apprise him of this change, and returning, the neighborhood of these 2 guns was I think the hottest place from artillery fire that I have ever been in: just as I entered the field (a caisson having been blown up a few minutes before) when going up a slippery bank, a shell struck very close to my horse and rearing up he rolled over on me in the ditch.

For a moment I thought he was struck, but soon recovering himself, I found it was merely fright. Galloping to the General I found him looking on with his usual coolness: he soon started towards the Crossing & on our way met the 2 Parrotts I have mentioned above leaving the field.[156] The General was very much displeased at first, but Colonel Rosser made matters all right, by telling him that it was useless to stay there, a great many horses being killed & men wounded and ammunition nearly exhausted.

The Genl now sent me to Genl Jackson to get our ammunition replenished and not finding Gen. J. [Jackson] I was hunting about for some time before finding the ordnance train. The section of my old Company under Lieut. [2nd Lt. William P.] Payne started for the field as I passed the park of the Reserve Artillery & when I passed back I met poor Utz's section coming out: I learned for the first time their loss & taking their caisson I started back to have it filled: finding I could not do more than get the ammunition before night I sent it on and started to find the General: I did not succeed however & after dark Lieut. [Chiswell] Dabney passing we rode back to Hd. Qrs.

Sunday [the fourteenth] we were up before day & off for the field: everything was quiet & finding the 3rd [Richmond] Howitzers I staid [*sic*] some time with them. The enemy lay in full view & reach of our guns all day, but not a shot was fired from us, Gen. Lee hoping they would again make the attack.

Monday the same programme was carried out, and I spent most of the day with the boys of the Rifle section of my old Corps. Gen. Stuart was on the high hill near the R. Road all day, and I went up several times to take a look at the Yankees: their flag of truce was refused in the morning on account of informality, but in the afternoon, coming by Gen. Burnside's authority, it was granted & our men began to mingle with the Yankees on the plain. Gen. Stuart went down & a great many other officers, but I staid on the hill, looking on. A few of our dead were found, but the Yankees were thick and they were not all buried when the flag was out.

Monday night a demand for the surrender of Port Royal was made & Gen. Lee requested Gen. Stuart to start early in the morning & see what it meant. The Genl went off a little before the staff & going to Gen. Lee's, and going along slowly we met him galloping furiously from the Rail Road & learnt that the enemy had all cleared out. He sent me galloping like lightning as he expressed it to Gen. Fitz Lee to order him to throw out his sharp-shooters & pursue the enemy with his horse artillery: on getting out we found they had nearly all gone, & Gen. W. H. F. Lee marched on down to Port Royal where we soon followed: Gen. Fitz Lee moved back above town, and Pelham pushed on with the howitzers & other companies towards town. We went as far as the Barnard place (Gay Mont) 3 miles from Port Royal & found that the demand for surrender was nothing more than an attempt to divert our attention. We came on back to Hd. Qrs. that night.

I did not go on the field yesterday, as most of the staff did, but am going to-day. A large force was over all day yesterday burying the dead near town and did not succeed in completing it. I think 2500 at least were killed along their lines amongst them 2 Generals ([Brig. Gen. George D.] Bayard & [Brig. Gen. Conrad F.] Jackson).[157] Chiswell Dabney went to Lynchburg yesterday to bring Mrs. Stuart to see her brother Gen. [Brig.

Gen. John R.] Cooke who was wounded you know.[158] It is not dangerous I hope, though quite severe. Please try to get me a negro if possible. I have spun out my letter so long that I must stop. Good-bye

R. Channing Price

I forgot to tell you that the boys of the Company whom you know are all well. Alsop was not in the fight, but is well. Charley Fourquroun was & came out safe.

R. C. P.

◄─◄ ⊫◆⊨ ►─►

Camp Near
Fredericksburg
Dec. 17, 1862

My Dearest Wife [Mrs. Roberta Powers],

I wrote you very hurriedly last Saturday and sent the letter by Major Brown who was going directly to the Valley.[159] I hope you received it. At the time I wrote the battle was raging and as soon as it was finished I rode along the lines to ascertain how the day was going. The firing was incessant and grand by the time I reached our left where Jackson was engaged. The enemy were repulsed and driven with great loss into Fredericksburg and under cover of his heavy batteries on the opposite side of the river.

I spent the night with Brother James. The next day we confidently expected a <u>renewal</u> of the fight. And I again rode along our lines of battle.

The enemy were drawn up in large force and in sight; but the severe punishment he had received the day before deterred him from renewing the attack. Thus the two enemies remained all day Sunday and Monday. Monday afternoon the enemy asked permission to bury his dead, which was granted. Monday night he hurriedly and quietly withdrew the entire army across the Rappahannock leaving some 200 or 300 of his dead unburied. Yesterday morning I rode over the battlefield and counted in one place eighty-five dead bodies lying stark and cold and almost naked—a most ghastly spectacle. They had been carried to one spot for burial, but their inhuman friends had left that duty unperformed and under cover of the truce flag evacuated their position.

So ends the Battle of Fredericksburg which I suppose Burnside will claim as a great victory. Prisoners say that he ordered a renewal of the attack Sunday morning but could not get his men to come up to the scratch. His generals remonstrated with him that it was impossible to carry our position and there the On to Richmond is again stayed. Last evening Jackson's Corps moved towards Port Royal and are now between that place and Fredericksburg. What the enemy are about I have not heard—changing his base I suppose.

It is bitter cold tonight but very comfortable in our tents—a little stove keeping it warm—but not as comfortable as by your side. No other place can be. I cannot say how much I miss you. How I long to be with you again, but alas I fear we cannot be much together again until this war closes. And when will that be? God only knows—

Should you see Mrs. Hall soon, you may send word to Mr. Emitt that his brother is well. That Mr. Ratcliffe reached Camp safely. Give love to all. Kiss my little ones for me and for my sake endure the privations of your situation as cheerfully as possible. I shall take care of myself and get to you again as soon as possible.

Ever Yours
P. H. Powers

The smoke from the battle had hardly settled when Hampton was once again raiding across the Rappahannock. This time taking 465 men from various commands, he crossed the river on the seventeenth, and the following day struck at Kanky's Store and Occoquan. He came back on the nineteenth loaded with booty: 150 prisoners, twenty wagons, thirty stands of small arms, and a stand of colors. Stuart, Lee, and Secretary of War James Seddon all endorsed Hampton's modest report of the affair, Seddon marking the brigadier for further promotion.[160]

The Federal cavalry was busy too, mounting reconnaissances to Warrenton on the twenty-first and twenty-second, to Kellysville from the twenty-first to the twenty-third, and to Catlett's Station and Brentville from the twenty-first to the twenty-third. Yet with all this activity, no serious encounters between the two cavalry forces took place.[161]

Stuart got into the raiding action by striking at Dumfries and Fairfax Station. On the twenty-sixth, with 1,800 men and four guns, he crossed the Rappahannock at Kelly's Ford. After some initial bad luck, the raiders' five-day jaunt turned into a successful venture, and they returned to Culpeper Court House on the thirty-first with considerable reward for their time and energy. Military supplies as well as sutlers' treasures filled haversacks and saddlebags and hung from saddles. Wagons too accompanied the returning column, as did horses and prisoners. Stuart could be proud not only of his cavalry's accumulation of spoils, but also that he had stirred up a hornet's nest of Federal units marching and riding every which way in an attempt to cut him off. Unlike the gray cavalry, they would have little to show for their efforts.[162]

As the month and the year drew to a close, Powers and Price wrote letters that touched on the war and personal matters. Price was still in search of a servant to care for his horses, and Powers was acting as servant for his overworked brother. The recent struggle still occupied both their minds as they surveyed the ruined city of Fredericksburg and the battlefield. Christmas seemed far away. Price gave but a brief Christmas greeting at the end of his letter, and when Powers finally mentioned it, his thoughts centered on Christmases past and future more than the one that lay a few days away.

Camp Dec 20th 1862

Dear Bob[163]—

I fled from Clarke some three weeks ago on the invasion of the Yankees thinking that they intended a permanent occupancy of Winchester and our end of the Valley. I had intended leaving at any rate before Christmas and they only expedited my movements. Before reaching the Army I learned of their departure back to Harper's Ferry, but as I had parted with my family I did not care to return and undergo the pain of another leave-taking, so I came down to the Army at Fredericksburg and have been at Gen. Stuart's HdQrs. and with Brother James since. I am now with the latter giving him what assistance I can in arranging his papers the Brigade Q. M. having been absent for some time. Brother James is acting as Brigade Q. M. and consequently has much to do and much bother and trouble. I shall remain with him for the present and until something better offers. I can be of much assistance and some company and comfort to him. All of which he deserves for he has had rather a hard time since he has been in the Army.

I told Bert [Powers's wife, Roberta] when I left to send her letters to you and you would forward them to me. If any come for me enclose them to Brother James and for the present direct to Guinea's [Guiney's] Station or Depot. I feel very anxious to hear from home. When I left the Yankees were there and Bert's brother absent in Loudoun endeavoring to recover thirteen young horses which they had stolen from him a few days before. He was to have been married on the 9th Inst. [instant (this present month)] but perhaps the Yanks retained him and his horses also.

I witnessed a portion of the Battle last Saturday and as the papers have given you the details I need add nothing to their account. It was a most signal victory and the loss of the enemy immense. I rode over the right of the Battle ground on Tuesday and the dead of the enemy were there lying in heaps. I counted eighty-five in one pile unburied. We do not hear in camp where Burnside now is. There are various rumors but none reliable.

Since the battle we have moved camp and are now between F-burg and Port Royal some eight miles to the right of Guinea's Depot.

We manage to keep passably comfortable, getting an occasional mess of oysters and plenty of Ginger cakes at .50 a piece. The worst of it is Jim's servant has left and we have to do our own cooking. However I find necessity makes me a pretty good cook. I have managed to get up several very savory dinners.

If you can meet with any one coming to this brigade send us a bale of good smoking tobacco. We are entirely out. It is keeping cold but there is an abundance of wood and the troops I think are generally comfortable.

Write when you receive this and let us hear what is going on in Richmond. Jim says he has not heard from any of you since he left the Valley. With much love to Juliet and all,[164]

Yours Affly

P. H. Powers

Direct to
    Capt. J. L. Powers
        2nd Bat. Va Arty
    Fields Brigade—A. P. Hill's Division
        Guinea's Depot

⊷ ⊨✦⊨ ⊶

Hd. Qrs. Cavalry

Division

Dec. 23rd 1862

Dear Mother [Mrs. Thomas Randolph Price Sr.],

I was more than usually glad to receive your letter (dated 21st) this evening, as it has been so long since I heard anything more than a verbal message from home. Everything has been perfectly quiet with us since I wrote you last week. I rode into town the day I sent my letter with Major Von Borcke & Dr. Eliason and spent some time there, looking over our positions & other objects of interest to me, as it was the first time I had visited Fredericksburg, having neglected to do so before the fight.

Quite a large working party was over under Flag of Truce & had nearly completed the task of burying their dead. From town Dr. E. [Eliason] and I rode to the Crossing, thus passing over nearly our whole front, and I do not wonder since seeing our position from the stand-point of Burnside, that his troops and Generals rebelled at having again to "beard the lion in his den."

The town is a perfect wreck of what it was I suppose, houses burnt & battered, fences & boarding of every description torn down and laid in the streets, and on this the wretches laid the bedding stolen out of the houses and slept during their occupancy of the place. Add to all these horrors that in numbers (a hundred I suppose) of the once tastily laid off gardens and yards of Fredericksburg, the bodies of these scoundrels have been laid for their last sleep. But it is worse than useless to talk of it and as an article I glanced at in one of the Richmond papers expressed it, if we desire a bloody revenge, we have gotten it, as I do not think we have yet begun to realize the amount of damage we have inflicted on Burnside's Army.

The General has been expecting Mrs. Stuart for several days and I was much pleased to see her to-day: I went out Saturday morning to try to secure a room for her, at the General's request, in some house near Mrs. French's (where Gen. Cooke is). I succeeded in getting one at Mrs. Alsop's, a very nice place, and to-day went over with her and the General to intro-duce them, and staid [*sic*] to dinner. After dinner we went over to Mrs. French's (a very short distance) and sat some time with Gen. Cooke. He is improving very rapidly, looks pale but is sitting up in the Parlor, having only a piece of plaster on his forehead. He expects to be able to take the field in a short time. The General is up there to-night: she is only about 3/4 of a mile from Hd. Qrs.

The papers have not mentioned as they deserved the brilliant dashes which Gen. Hampton has lately been making. One which we heard of the night of the battle, resulted in 20 wagons and 50 prisoners taken at Dumfries. On the 17th in accordance with Gen. Stuart's commands he again started out, capturing a cavalry picket of 40 men, a stand of colors, 20 wagons etc. on his way, continuing his march to Occoquan, where he took 30 wagons & 100 to 150 prisoners, returning safely Saturday night I believe. Gen. Hampton was at our Hd. Qrs. yesterday and from him & his staff I got many particulars of their raids.

They got for instance 300 pair of fine boots (the General has sent Gen. Stuart one pair) boxes of champagne, claret, cheese and numerous other articles out of the sutler's wagons, which were the principal ones contain-ing anything. I carried the flag and the report of the expedition over to Gen. Lee's this morning, but did not see the General, delivering them to Gen. [Brig. Gen. Robert H.] Chilton.[165]

The pair of boots from Taylor came safely by Mrs. Stuart, and the General has disposed of them, he having gotten a very good pair from Col. [Lt. Col. James L.] Corley (captured and turned into the Qr. Mr.) and also will get those from Gen. Hampton.[166]

I hope very much you may succeed in getting me a servant but do not want you to be walking about yourself on my account, but leave it to the persons you have mentioned in your letter. I delivered Pa's messages to the General and he returns his thanks for the attention to Mrs. Towner's inter-ests and asks me to say to him that he desires him to pay for the boots at Taylor's (70 dollars) and deduct from the amount in his hands to Mrs. T's [Towner's] credit.

I have not seen anything of the [Richmond] Howitzers since the fight, but suppose they have again gone into camp near Guinea's [Guiney's] Depot as before the fight. They sustained a tremendous loss in the death of Utz: he was as gallant a fellow as ever lived and a truer friend to the Company and its interests they never had.

Mrs. Stuart said you wanted to send me a box but I am glad you did not, as she was unable to bring one for the General which she had, & is very much troubled about it. Perhaps John Esten Cooke can send it, mark it ordnance, Gen. Stuart says & it will come. I got a note from Jno. Fontaine to-day apprising me of the day fixed for his marriage & inviting me to be a groomsman: I shall try to accept, but it is hard to say positively in these times.[167] Col. W. D. Stuart was at our Hd. Qrs. a day or two ago with Gen. Hood: he looks very well: did not get into the fight nor any of Pickett's Division.

With my hearty wishes to one and all at home of a Merry Christmas & the hope that ere long I may meet you again, I remain as ever your devoted son

R. Channing Price

◆◄═◆═►◆

Camp
Near Fredericksburg
Dec. 25, 1862

My Dearest Wife [Mrs. Roberta Powers],

I hardly have the heart to wish you a Merry Christmas this beautiful Christmas morning because I well know merriment is not for you this day. But I can and do wish you a happy day and the same to our little dears who I suppose must be content with very meager gifts and very few sweet things.

I thought of them when I first awoke this morning about day and wondered what you managed to put in their stockings. Memory went back to the many happy Christmas days we have spent together with them. Alas! Will the good old times ever return again and you and I and our little ones dwell together in peace? I hope so. I believe so, but the heart sickens with the deferred hope.

As I have been Jim's chief <u>cook</u> for a week, since his servant left not much time was given me this morning for such sad reflections with the responsibility of a Christmas breakfast on my mind. So I stirred myself from a warm bed and proceeded to culinary operations. What a fall! From a Major Quartermaster to a Captain's Cook! But necessity is a hard master and you know I can do any thing I try—better cook than starve. I wish you could have been present to witness my success and partake of my viands— barbecuid [sic] rabbit, beef hash with potatoes, hot bread and coffee. If the darkies all leave us, I shall be able to render you some assistance.

We are very comfortable in camp—have good tents and wood in abundance to keep off the frost. I have been exceedingly busy for the last week assisting Jim in paying off troops. And really he needed it. He worries at every thing. Allows every trifle to ruffle his equanimity and makes himself constantly unhappy without cause. I wish from my heart he could get out of the department he is in—though I see no hope for him.

He had a letter from Robert yesterday—all well and nothing new. I have written you several times since I have been here but as yet have not heard from you. Continue to write. Some of your letters will come to hand after a while.

I wrote you some account of the great fight—but you will see from the papers how terribly whipped Burnside was, and what a commotion it has produced in Yankeedom. I think the sky brightens and our chances for peace improve. But still the war may linger on another year, or even to the end of Lincoln's term.

It is warm this morning as June and every thing bright—if I only was with you—for the day at least. I would have a happy Christmas.

We are invited to dine with Tom Ballard. And as I am interrupted I must now stop. With love to all and kisses and loving messages to my little pets.

> Very Aff'y
> Yours
> P. H. Powers

As the year drew to a close, many once familiar faces were gone. The trials and hardships of the war had brought changes to cavalry headquarters. Out of the ten men who had been on the staff at the beginning of April, five were no longer with Stuart: Philip Henry Powers, Dabney Ball, Luke Tiernan Brien, Redmond Burke, and William Eskridge Towles. Others had come and gone since April: Samuel G. Staples, James Hardeman Stuart, Jones R. Christian, and John Landstreet.[168]

To fill the gaps, Stuart, with his eye for talent, had added to the staff men he knew he could count on. As 1863 arrived, the cavalry staff consisted of Capt. W. W. Blackford, engineer officer; Capt. James L. Clark, voluntary aide; Capt. John Esten Cooke, ordnance officer; Lt. Chiswell Dabney, aide-de-camp; Surgeon Talcott Eliason, medical director; Capt. William D. Farley, voluntary aide; Maj. Norman R. FitzHugh, assistant adjutant general; Capt. Richard E. Frayser, signal officer; Lt. Henry Hagan, aide-de-camp; Maj. J. T. W. Hairston, assistant adjutant and inspector general; Maj. Samuel H. Hairston, quartermaster; Capt. J. Marshall Hanger, assistant quartermaster; Lt. Walter Q. Hullihen, aide-de-camp; Maj. William J. Johnson, commissary of subsistence; Maj. John Pelham, commander of the Stuart Horse Artillery; Lt. R. Channing Price, aide-de-camp; Maj. L. Frank Terrell, inspector; Lt. Thomas B. Turner, aide-de-camp; Maj. Heros von Borcke, inspector; and Capt. Benjamin S. White, aide-de-camp.[169]

1863

JANUARY

During the New Year holiday season until January 7, all military activity seemed suspended in and around Fredericksburg. Stuart returned from his raid to his camp near Hamilton's Crossing on January 1. His tired troopers happily sought warm campfires and cooked rations. His staff had their usual paperwork, but it did not keep them from enjoying the peace and quiet the temporary suspension of hostilities offered.

The topic around cavalry headquarters for the first week of 1863 was "the Raid." Channing Price's letter of the second provided details to his family that the newspaper-reading public was not often privileged to see. On the other hand, Philip H. Powers's letter of the first devoted not one line to the raid. Though not yet back at cavalry headquarters on a permanent basis, he was still on intimate terms with Stuart and the men of the staff, as is evidenced by the fact that Maj. Norman R. FitzHugh played postman for Powers and his wife. Personal matters, politics, and the condition of the troops occupied Powers's mind and were reflected in his letter.

Camp, Jan 1, 1863

My Dear Wife [Mrs. Roberta Powers],

Wishing you a happy New Year and many returns. I acknowledge the receipt of your letter of the 19th Oct brought up by Major FitzHugh, together with the nice collars, for which you have my thanks. You are a good wife, but rather prone at times to wish for impossibilities; to wit; that I might be quartered in Richmond during the winter. A Chateau d'Espagne. I have had the good fortune to spend one winter in Richmond with you since the war and much as I may desire to spend this one there, cannot say that such an event is at all probable. My good fortune, I hope will send me there during the winter, but my time must be spent in camp. And thankful am I, this bitter cold night that I am as comfortable here as there. Always excepting the comfort and happiness of being with my love. It has been a dreadful spell of weather and I feel for those of our soldiers who are exposed to its inclemency. Those of our troops that went to the Valley are without quarters and I suppose still marching, as I heard today that Colonel [James A.] Walker's Brigade was at Winchester.[1]

133

Doesn't your heart feel for the poor substitute men and their wives? The chivalry of the South, as Jim calls them, how will they be able to stand the hardships of Camp and the dangers of a campaign? Congress was cruel and inconsiderate with these gentlemen, and we poor devils who have volunteered to fight for them should have been allowed to die for them also. But seriously, Congress never passed an act more acceptable to the Army and one passed with more joy.[2] Perhaps it springs from a bad feeling at heart. Envy, but justice has something to do with it. Nevertheless, in regard to your letter with the question of Alice. I am perfectly willing for her to remain with Robert & Juliet during the winter, and feel very grateful to them for their kindness evinced in this and many other acts, but at present see no reason why you may not yourself pay her tuition fees.[3] I am not too proud to receive his assistance and shall doubtless avail myself of it, in many ways, if this war lasts much longer, but at present I have money enough to meet your expenses, if not too heavy, for awhile anyhow. If you think he would be hurt by a refusal, which I hardly think, you can let him have his way. It will not be much. It tends much to alleviate my anxiety and trouble in these times, to know that my brothers and sisters appreciate my difficulties and have affection enough to offer their assistance. I trust my own heart would prompt me to do even so to them, were our situations reversed.

Perhaps it may be well and proper for me to tell you at the commencement of housekeeping arrangements, exactly what means we have to depend upon. I have then in fund on notes about $7000, counting what Va. money I have as 3 for 1. My own expenses are met by my pay and allowances, and an occasional speculation on a small scale. There you have it in a nutshell. Weigh it and see what you can do with it. The above statement does not include supplies (very extensive) on hand purchased by myself or by Pink.[4] Nor your fine gold watch which you can pawn when reduced to extremities, not before. We have not much then to go upon, but with prudence it may answer for a time and with an implicit faith in the goodness of God. May we not trust Him? And if not happy, at least be thankful. My fingers are too cold to write much more. Jim spent the day with us, is rather complaining. No army news, nothing now but red orange mud. Give love to the children and all, and write me when you get to the farm and often.

May God bless you my precious wife,

Ever Yours
P. H. Powers

Hd. Qrs. Cav. Division
near Fredksburg
January 2nd 1863

Dear Sister [Ellen Price],

My not having written home during the Christmas week excited your surprise, but I hope, not your anxiety. We are all back safe from the longest, most dangerous and most brilliant expedition that the cavalry has yet given to an admiring public. I said nothing about my expecting to start Christmas day in my letter of the 23rd although I knew at that time.

Christmas Eve, large detachments from the brigades of the 2 Lees left their camps on the lower Rappahannock and marched up to the vicinity of our Hd. Qrs. so as to start Christmas day together. All being ready, the cavalry having gone on some time, about 12 o'clock Christmas day, Gen. Stuart, Dr. Eliason, Maj. Pelham, Dabney, Hullihen, Farley, Turner & myself started up the river. I stopped with the General at Mrs. French's to see Mrs. Stuart and we rode on with the escort.

After going 13 miles we crossed the Rapidan at Ely's ford & 2 or 3 miles beyond came up with Gens. Fitz & W. H. F. Lee who had halted for the night. After giving his instructions to them we jogged along to Brandy Station (about 7 miles) which we reached at 11 o'clock: here we expected to find Gen. Hampton with his detail for the scout, but he not being there, after sending him a message to report at 4 o'clock, we went to sleep on the floor of a house at the Depot: at 4 o'clock the General had us up and about day-break Col. [Matthew C.] Butler, he being in command reported to the General.[5] We got breakfast and Col. Butler taking the road to Rappahannock Station [now Remington], we went to Kelly's ford and found the Lees halted on the north bank waiting for orders. We now had 3 columns, Fitz Lee on the right, W. H. F. Lee in the centre (Gen. Stuart with him) and Butler on left. We traveled without any incident until about sunset, when the 3 columns reunited and camped near Bristowsburg [Bristersburg], Fauquier [County]. I got plenty to eat & a good sleep. Before day we resumed the march in same order for Dumfries, 20 miles distant.

When the centre got near the place, we could see wagons moving on the other side of the creek, but what force there was in the place we could not tell, it being a thickly wooded country: a gun was placed in position & the 9th Va. Cavalry pushed on down the road: they came on an infantry picket, charged it and took 9 prisoners, then pushed on towards Dumfries. The gun continued to fire and I rode with the General near the town: their infantry had formed & were pouring volley after volley into our cavalry sharp-shooters who were compelled to fall back.

We went very close to them and Minie balls whistled about us, Dr.

Eliason's horse being struck just beside me. Fitz Lee had come up the Telegraph road (capturing 9 Sutler's wagons etc.) and formed a junction with us. We got our artillery to firing & the enemy began now to show his strength, 2 guns opening on us from behind the houses of Dumfries. A large number of cavalry were dismounted and put in the woods as skirmishers: we soon found they had a considerable force, infantry & cavalry but our men held their ground. Gen. Stuart determined to charge the battery & Col Rosser swept in gallant style to our left with the 1st & 5th Va., and Col. [James W.] Watts to the right with the 2nd Va.: the force was too heavy though & no charge was made only the enemy being held in check.[6]

Finding that to take the place would require more sacrifice than it was worth, as the enemy had had 2 or 3 hours to move the stores, which we could see them doing, Gen. Stuart cut across to the Brentsville road: reaching this, Gen. W. H. F. Lee took his command to the neighborhood of Greenwood Church to camp, Gen. Hampton having come to the same vicinity from Occoquon [Occoquan] (which place he had taken with 8 or 10 wagons & some prisoners). Gen. Stuart after having seen Gen. Fitz Lee who held his own on the Brentsville road near Dumfries, waited on the road in considerable anxiety to hear of the 3rd Va. which had the wagons and prisoners in charge, and the 2nd Va., which being near town had failed to get orders to retire.

About 11 o'clock we heard that the 3rd Va. had taken a road bringing them to Coles Store and were safe: at 1 o'clock, Dabney came up having succeeded after a long ride in finding the 2nd and brought it with him. All was now safe and the results of the day were 20 wagons, 100 prisoners, about 150 horses & mules, arm etc., all of which' were started for Culpeper CH under strong guard that night. We had not a man killed, several wounded slightly and Capt. [John Washington] Bullock (5th Va.) very seriously & feared mortally: he had to be left at a house near Dumfries.[7]

Gen. Fitz Lee now moved to be near the others & we rode to Coles Store, where we expected to find Gen. Hampton, but did not. It was now 3 o'clock in the morning, we fed our horses on hay, got something to eat ourselves and then rode about 3 miles: at 4 o'clock we laid down by a big fire in the woods and slept till 6:30. At this time the General [Stuart] determined on account of the worn out condition of men and horses to return, but, on some information given by a man just from Fairfax, changed his plans.

Gen. Fitz Lee had started towards Culpeper before receiving the contrary orders and a cavalry regiment (17 Penna.) which was camped not very far from him, being reinforced by the 2nd Penna. from the other side of the Occoquon started in pursuit. Gen. [Fitz] Lee got his orders, faced about,

Gens. Hampton & W. H. F. Lee following him, and soon came on the 2 regiments, 5 to 600 men, drawn up in a field on the edge of a woods to receive him. Gen. Stuart gave the order, Col. [Maj. James H.] Drake with the 1st Va. let into them, followed by the 2nd & 3rd, and Col. Rosser with the 5th charged on their left flank.[8]

They gave one volley from their pistols, hurting not a man, and then broke: our men pursued them for 6 or 7 miles, across the Occoquon and into their camps.[9] Here Gen. Lee halted & the camp was taken possession of by our men, the tents & all of no value burn[ed] and the rest taken away. When nearly up to the Occuquon I met Gen. Stuart coming back to find out something of the firing in our rear which had been heard for some time. We soon met Gens. Hampton & Lee and ascertained that the firing came from the enemy attacking Col. Butler (2nd So. Carolina) near Bacon Race Church. A very heavy force attacked him and succeeded in cutting him off from us: a guide familiar with the country was sent him with orders how to proceed & Col. Butler knowing the roads very well got out and joined us several hours later.

The column now moved on & after crossing the Occoquon halted on the Ox Road [now Route 123] leading to Fairfax C. H. Gen. Hampton started to Occuquon with a force to capture some wagons but did not succeed in finding any. I remained at the fork of the road when the march began to deliver some orders to Gen. W. H. F. Lee and did not overtake the General until getting to Burke's Station on the O. & A. R. R. [Orange and Alexandria Railroad]. When the head of the column got here, the Genl sent 2 or 3 men ahead, who walked up into the room of the telegraph operator and with drawn pistols demanded him to surrender the office: he was dreadfully alarmed and consequently could not give a signal to Alexandria of our coming: our telegraph operator (Shepphard) then took possession of the office & for 2 or 3 hours sat there listening to the messages from [Maj. Gen. Samuel P.] Heintzelman in Alexandria to the commandant at Fairfax Station & the replies:[10] it was very ludicrous, as they were in great alarm & orders were telegraphed to destroy everything in case of our attacking them:[11] meanwhile the track was being torn up and the men helping themselves to oats & some little things found about the depot. A large number of negroes employed at the depot under guard & 20 wagons had been taken off in the evening, fearing we would attack the station.

After burning some few tents the column moved on through the woods and about 8 o'clock got into the Anandale [Annandale] Turnpike about 3 miles below Fairfax C. H. Gen. Fitz Lee took a small party and going up the railroad in 8 miles of Alexandria burnt the Accotinck [Accotink] Bridge. On the turnpike we soon encountered a small party of cavalry & our advance under Col. Rosser charged them. Lee's Brigade kept on and in about 1/2 a mile of Fairfax, a terrific volley from infantry in ambuscade was poured into the advance guard, killing 2 horses and wounding 2 men.[12]

The General was now satisfied that they had some force and were looking out for us: he started me back rapidly to meet Gen. W. H. F. Lee and turn him by a by-road towards the Falls Church road. I did so & leaving the guide with him, came back to the pike to Gen. Stuart. Hampton followed & then Fitz Lee, building immense fires before he started, which the enemy shelled vigorously for some time.

It was a beautiful night & we kept on as rapidly as possible with our artillery, wagons and 100 prisoners taken in the morning. We marched all night without anything happening of interest and at day-break passed the Frying-Pan: Gen. Stuart went in at Mrs. Ratcliffes [sic] and I kept on to Mr. Barlow's (a good Union man) where the command was to halt and feed.[13] After feeding my horse, I went into the house & got a nice breakfast with Gen. W. H. F. Lee and others. After breakfast I walked over to Mr. Turley's & spent some time with the ladies: here I heard that my horse had been sent to Loudoun for safety. About 11 o'clock we resumed our march up the Little River Turnpike & about sunset reached Dover, Loudoun Co. just after passing Aldie. Here we got plenty of forage and we got a nice supper at Col. Hamilton Rogers'. Parson Landstreet we found here.

Next morning after breakfast and attending to some business for the General, I started to look for my horse: I found a man going directly where I had been told he was & went with him: after going 3 miles, to my surprise I met Mr. Turley in the road and a gentleman with him riding my horse. Mr. Turley was in Loudoun trying to get to Fairfax to see his family and was riding down there to see our cavalry. My horse was very thin, barefooted, but had gotten over his lameness: going back a mile or so Mr. Turley had the saddle taken off, I paid Mr. Creele 10 dollars for his attention to the horse and led him to Landmark, Loudoun Co., where I had him shod. Here I heard that Gen. Stuart with the 2 Lees had gone through Middleburg to the Plains, & Hampton had taken across from Aldie to Haymarket. Saddling my little bay I rode 7 miles to the Plains, near which I found the General.

Next morning at 7 o'clock we started for Warrenton 13 miles: getting near the town we heard that the enemy were in possession & Fitz Lee with the prisoners etc. avoided it by going to the right. After a little however the Black Horse who stay in Fauquier on detached service all the time, reported that the cavalry which had marched into Warrenton in the morning, had left soon after, 2 or 3 miles out on the Warrenton Junction [now Calverton] road had drawn up in line, and finally turned & traveled back.

We now entered Warrenton, W. H. F. Lee going right through to the Waterloo road. We remained there for some time, which I spent very pleasantly with some ladies.

After getting a nice dinner, Hampton's column was reported in sight and I walked with a young lady up the street to see him pass through: he took the Springs road, General Stuart following him. Major Pelham and I staid [sic] some time at Mrs. Lucas' until the town was clear & then followed, overtaking the General at the Springs. Hampton halted a mile or so from the river, but we kept on by way of Jeffersonton, Rixeyville & our old Hd. Qrs. to Culpeper C. H. making 35 miles that day. I went with Maj. Pelham to Dr. Herndon's to see Lieut. [William M.] McGregor of the Horse Artillery who was badly wounded & left here in November.[14] We got supper & went out in the pines near the Court House where we found the General: Here reports had come that the enemy in heavy force had crossed the Rappahannock at Richards [sic] Ferry & Ellis' Ford and it was supposed were endeavoring to cut us off.

We got up before day & after arranging a long telegram to send Gen. Lee at Fredericksburg I rode into town to send it. Here however I met a courier from Col. [Laurence S.] Baker stating that the enemy had gone back the night before. This changed our plans and after getting plenty of corn to carry along & rations for the men we started for Stephensburg [Stevensburg], then on to Ely's ford, just this side of which the command halted & camped. Gen. Stuart had hurried on before we got to the head of the column & finding it impossible to overtake him, Pelham and I came on slowly getting to Hd. Qrs. about 7 o'clock last night. Here I found Mama's letter of the 25th and one from Nannie of the 26th.

The prisoners taken Sunday started from Culpeper yesterday morning, the others having gone the day before. I asked George Woodbridge who went with them to send a message to you, which I hope you got. Gen. Stuart is very much delighted with the success of the trip. Our spoils are in round numbers 250 prisoners, 250 horses, 20 wagons, 100 or so fine arms & other things too numerous to mention. We brought a fine clock & the instrument from the office at Burke's Station home: the instrument Gen. Stuart has sent to Dr. Morris in Richmond. The only thing I got was a saddle & bridle, but I recovered my horse which alone was fully worth the trip.

I forgot to mention that the little sorrel horse, that I bought in the Valley, departed this life the night before the expedition started: he died very unexpectedly to me, though I knew he was very sick: so I have only 2 horses now.

Col. Rosser went from Dover over the mountain on a visit to the

"Bower" with a picked party of 20 men. I hope he will succeed in his trip and return safely.

Tell Mama that in case she finds a boy willing to come to attend to my horses, that 15 dollars is the usual price I think. Tell Papa that his letter to Shepherdstown if sent to our Hd. Quarters will go some time or other, but there is no regularity in our communications.

Major FitzHugh went home to-day, and I am discharging his duties, and will have my hands full for some days. Major Von Borcke did not go with us, not having a horse at the time, and is very sorry about it. He desires to be remembered most kindly to you all.

Ask Mama if she sees a piece of good grey cloth soon to get me enough for a pair of pants & vest & keep it until I come down which I expect to do in about 2 weeks, if things continue quiet enough to permit it. My grey pants are completely worn out on the side where my sabre rubs & I tried to get some goods for a pair in Loudoun but failed.

I have seen the telegram of Gen. [Braxton] Bragg to-day and wait anxiously to hear further. Gen. Stuart has telegraphed Gen. [Samuel] Cooper to know what further news has been heard and I hope will get an answer this evening.[15]

The cavalry prisoners taken by us will have hard thoughts of us I reckon, as they were made to foot it all day Sunday, all night Monday, Tuesday & 35 miles Wednesday to Culpeper C. H. Gen. Stuart told them he wanted to show them what a long and hard road it was to Richmond.

Everything is quiet about here now and the enemy have had all their marching and countermarching for naught. [Maj. Gen. Daniel E.] Sickles & Ricketts moved up to Morrisville, Fauquier Co. on Wednesday [December 31].[16] A large force crossed the Rappahannock the same day & went back at night and Wednesday night after the 3rd Pennsylvania Cavalry (Sir Percy Wyndham Colonel) had skedaddled so beautifully from Warrenton, a large cavalry force entered the town to find the bird had flown.[17]

I have spun my letter out so long that I must close.

Your devoted brother

R. Channing Price
1st Lieut. & A D C

Not until the eighth did the cavalry have to stir itself to any great extent. On that date, a Federal reconnaissance to Catlett's and Rappahannock stations resulted in brief clashes near Grove Church, Elk Run, and elsewhere along the outpost line. If the purpose of the expedition was to see if Stuart was on his guard, the bluecoats found out what they wanted to know. Stuart was still vigilant and drove his curious adversaries back at all points.[18]

*After this brief interruption, which did little to upset the calm of cavalry head-
quarters, quiet again reigned. Around the campfires and in the tents of Stuart's staff,
the thoughts of the officers turned homeward. Channing Price was pleased to learn
that his brother had returned from Europe, and he was eager to see him. For W.
W. Blackford the time was one of stress and sadness as he invited his wife, Mary,
and his father-in-law to join him. He hoped the visit would help dispel the grief and
sense of loss Mary was experiencing over the death of their son.[19] He also discussed
the status of Frank Robertson, Blackford's brother-in-law. This topic was echoed in
a letter from Stuart to Robertson's father. Stuart wanted the young man on his staff,
but only under the right conditions.*

Hd. Quarters Cavalry
Division
January 6th 1863

Dear Mother [Mrs. Thomas Randolph Price Sr.],

Major Pelham is going to Richmond for a few days and I have just
tried to write a few lines to acknowledge the receipt of several letters. Your
letter of the 29th December came Sunday last from Hd. Qrs. of the Army.
The day after our return Major FitzHugh went home to spend a few days
or so. At General Stuart's request I have been discharging the duties of Adjt.
General until Major F's return on yesterday.

Saturday night I sat up very late getting through a great deal of business which had accumulated in the office during our absence & had just
retired when a courier came into my tent with a telegram; opening it I was
no less surprised than delighted by seeing the words "Thomas is here."[20] I
telegraphed you Sunday evening in relation to the servant & also put a
message to Thomas to come & see me, which I hope you got. Yesterday
I got our post man to attend to my servant & one of our ordnance wagons
going there he came up safely & ———— [two words illegible] your box &
letter. The things for Mrs. Stuart I carried to her yesterday evening & she
asked me to give you her thanks: Jemmy is better a good deal but very
fretful [remainder of letter is lost]

◄◄═╬═►►

Jan. 10th 1863
Head Qrs. Cav. Div.

Dear Sir [Wyndham Robertson],

I have written to Mary to come on and pay me a visit, hoping the
change of scene may benefit her at this time and direct her thoughts from
our poor little Landon. I wrote to ask Frank [Robertson] to accompany

her as he would find much to interest him and would I think advance his interests by so doing.

I have watched closely every opportunity to bring the mention of his joining us before the General and have had several conversations upon the subject with him. He has great reluctance to having an officer on his staff who draws no pay, and has several times asked me if you could not get Frank a commission so he would not be liable to this difficulty. I think if Frank could come on with his sister I might arrange it all—but at the same time I would not like to raise hopes in him, prematurely, for the staff is pretty full and I know that the General rejects a great many applicants constantly.

Could you not come up with Mary too? I have a very comfortable tent to myself with a good large fire place and a capital bed which you and Frank could occupy and mess with us. You need not feel the least delicacy upon this since as all the other members of the mess have had a good deal of company and I have had very little.

I wrote to Fergusen to get me a pair of large thick army blankets. Please see about them and bring or send them. Some rascal stole my best blanket the other day from under my saddle while my horse was tied in front of Gen. Lee's Head Qrs. which ——— [word illegible] me ——— [word illegible].

I hope you will be able to come as I think you would enjoy a visit to the battle field and I can make you pretty comfortable. By telegraphing to me I will meet you at Hamilton's Crossing at any time.

I wish you would enquire into the question of my promotion. Gen. Stuart has written a very strong letter of commendation and also wrote a private letter to Colonel Custis Lee upon the subject. I understand there are three majorities and one or two Lieut. Colonelcies to fill and Colonel [Jeremy F.] Gilmer the Chief Eng'r is the person to recommend.[21] I understand from [Maj. Alfred L.] Rives that my name was prominent before him.[22] If you could see him I think you might assist matters somewhat. I was favorably surprised with Colonel Gilmer and would be very glad if you could show him some attention. He seems to be a man of talent and a gentleman.

Please tell Mary to bring 1/2 doz. lbs. of candles with her.

> I remain Sir
> Yours very truly
> Wm. W. Blackford

P. S. If the enclosed letter will have time to reach Mary before she starts, according to your ——— [word illegible] from her, please forward or retain it for her.

> Wm. W. B.

Peter Wilson Hairston, volunteer aide

One of Stuart's many relatives who fought beside him during the war, Hairston could not be persuaded to accept a regular commission and a permanent position on Stuart's staff and left. He remained a civilian throughout the war but did return to the army as a volunteer aide on the staff of Jubal Early, another relative, with whom he served until the end of the war. PHOTO COURTESY OF JUDGE PETER WILSON HAIRSTON

anny McCoy Caldwell
Hairston

After marrying a man with vo children, Fanny Caldwell on found herself with a ild of her own and a antation to run as well. Like any women in the war, she ught for survival on the ome front. PHOTO COURTESY OF GE PETER WILSON HAIRSTON

Peter Wilson Hairston

Life in the postwar period was a difficult struggle for Hairston, taking him away from his beloved "Cooleemee" to Baltimore, where an unfortunate business association nearly brought financial ruin and probably was a contributing factor to his declining health. PHOTO COURTESY OF JUDGE PETER WILSON HAIRSTON

Peter Wilson Hairston's home, "Cooleemee," in North Carolina
    Unlike may plantations in the South, "Cooleemee" passed through the war unscathed. After the war, Hairston fought hard to keep it going and retain it for his descendants. Photos courtesy of Judge Peter Wilson Hairston

Philip Henry Powers and Roberta Macky Smith Powers
    After posing for their wedding portrait, Philip and Roberta settled down to rais
a family. Of their ten children, seven survived into the twentieth century, the last
living until 1971. PHOTO COURTESY OF PHILIP HENRY POWERS IV

eutenant Chiswell Dabney, aide-de-camp

The youngest member of the staff, Dabney served with Stuart until promoted d transferred to Brig. Gen. James B. Gordon's staff. He was called the "Adonis" the staff because of his handsome, youthful features. His quick mind and uberance eventually brought him promotion but took him away from the staff d the general he called "a brave, chivalrous, and energetic commander."

Philip Henry Powers as quartermaster

Though devoted to Virginia and the Confederacy, Powers viewed the war as a necessary evil to be concluded as quickly as possible. He was not a wide-eyed youth seeking glory on the battlefield, but a man separated from a family he loved. Suffering under the strain of his duties, and concerned over his family's situation, he left the army only to return and fight on to the end. PHOTO COURTESY OF PHILIP HENRY POWERS IV

Philip Henry Powers and
Roberta Macky Smith
Powers in the postwar
period
    After the war, the
Powerses returned to
Clarke County and rebuilt
their home, "Auburn,"
which had accidentally
burned during the war.
Entering the teaching
profession once again,
Philip at first taught at
Wickliffe Academy, but he
eventually established his
own school in 1868.
PHOTOS COURTESY OF PHILIP HENRY
POWERS IV

The Reverend Dabney Ball

As Stuart's quartermaster before Philip Henry Powers, Ball left Stuart's staff after receiving a rebuke from the general for not having supplies available for the cavalry at a crucial moment. Instead of parting as enemies, however, the men's friendship survived, and Ball returned to the staff late in December 1863 in the unofficial position of chaplain of the cavalry corps. PHOTO COURTESY OF NATHANIEL H. MORISON III

ɔhann August Heinrich Heros von Borcke, assistant adjutant and inspector general
    Fearsome in battle, "Von," as he was called by the general and the staff,
rovided many moments of laughter at cavalry headquarters, with his boisterous
:nse of humor and broken English. He once stated after a talk with Stonewall
ıckson, "It gives me heartburn to hear Jackson talk," when he meant to say, "It
ʿarms my heart when he talks to me." PHOTO COURTESY OF ADELE MITCHELL

Thomas Randolph Price Jr.,
assistant engineer officer
    The unfortunate publicatio[]
of portions of Price's diary le[]
to his transfer from Stuart's
staff, but not from the
friendships he had made whil[]
there. When Heros von
Borcke returned from Europe[]
to visit Virginia in 1884, Pric[]
was waiting on the dock to
greet his former comrade-in-
arms. PHOTO COURTESY OF
ADELE MITCHELL

Frank Smith Robertson,
assistant engineer officer,
shown in his captain's unifor[]
near the end of the war
    Though he remained on
the staff until Stuart's death,
Robertson's service in the
field lasted only from March
to mid-July 1863. At
Williamsport during the retre[]
from Gettysburg, he was
temporarily blinded by a fire
in a nearby warehouse and
rode off a twenty-seven-foot
bridge abutment into the
Potomac River. He spent the
night sleeping in the bottom
drawer of a bureau. PHOTO
COURTESY OF SALLY-BRUCE MCCLATCHE[]

John Esten Cooke, ordnance officer and later assistant adjutant general
   Cooke was a relative of Stuart's wife, Flora. His early relationship with his
commander became a bit stormy when he jokingly told Flora that Stuart had
shaved off his beard. From that point, however, the two did grow closer. At the
time of Stuart's death, Cooke had served him longer than had any other officer.

William Willis Blackford, engineer officer

One of Stuart's finest officers, Blackford was not just an engineer, but operated as a scout for the general on many occasions. He was reputed to have one of the best pairs of field glasses in the army. His book, *War Years with Jeb Stuart*, is a colorful and accurate account of the operations of Stuart's headquarters and the cavalry corps.

James Ewell Brown Stuart

Cavalry headquarters often rang with music and laughter, but behind the lighthearted moments were hours of hard work. Stuart demanded and received the best his staff could deliver, and those who could not meet his standards were replaced with those who could. Yet his men loved him because he asked nothing from them that he was not willing to do himself. Photo courtesy of the Valentine Museum, Richmond, Virginia

William Downs Farley, volunteer aide and scout

Farley was a daring and resourceful officer who made himself invaluable to Stuart through his behind-the-lines scouting expeditions. He accepted no pay or equipment from the Confederate army, but supplied himself entirely with what he captured from the Federals. PHOTO COURTESY OF ISOBEL E. STEWART

ichard Channing Price, aide-de-camp and later assistant adjutant general
Young, talented, and likable, Price quickly became an integral part of Stuart's
adquarters. His death at Chancellorsville might have been prevented had anyone
en equipped with a tourniquet. Following the battle, Stuart purchased tourniquets
r all his officers in the hope of preventing another such loss. PHOTO COURTESY OF THE
LENTINE MUSEUM, RICHMOND, VIRGINIA

Stuart's sister, Columbia Lafayette Stuart Hairston, first wife of Peter Wilson Hairston, and her two children, Elizabeth and Samuel. PHOTO COURTESY OF PETER W. HAIRSTON

Hd. Qrs. Cav. Div.
Jan'y 14th 1863
My much esteemed Friend [Wyndham Robertson],

I have been postponing your letter, as well as the very modest one written by your son, previously, hoping that something would turn up to enable me to accept of his services as vol. aid, but the difficulty which I have been unable to remove is the avowed determination on my part to take no vol. aids other than those who have already served with me—this avowal (entre nous)[23] was made in consequence of efforts of objectionable persons to get such positions and my being unable to get rid of their applications. This difficulty can be removed by your son's getting a commission and as officers of his experience and intelligence are needed in the Engineer & other Corps I think you ought to experience no difficulty in obtaining it and having him assigned to the Cavalry Division.

I will thus have his services without embarrassment which I very much desire. Capt. Blackford has made an elaborate sketch of the battlefield here which is to accompany Gen. Ro. E. Lee's report. It is considered excellent.

I would like very much to have a visit from you to talk over various matters of interest. Won't you come?

Believe me
sincerely your friend
J. E. B. Stuart

P. S. Please communicate this to Frank[24]

From the twentieth to the twenty-fourth, the Army of the Potomac struggled through what became known as the "Mud March." Burnside attempted to turn Lee's left flank by marching west along the Rappahannock. The weather did not cooperate. Rain came. And then more rain came. The roads turned into quagmires. Wagons sank to the axles, and it was even reported that animals sank so deep that some drowned. Others became exhausted in vain efforts to move guns and wagons. The whole exercise in futility came to an inglorious end. The army returned to its camps having accomplished nothing save provide the Confederates with an opportunity to observe how not to conduct a winter campaign.

Two days after the ill-fated "Mud March" ground to a halt, Maj. Gen. Joseph Hooker was tapped by President Lincoln to replace Burnside. Other changes rippled through the Federal army in the wake of this change in command, but for the time being, the exhausted and demoralized Union infantry was allowed to rest and regroup. For the Federal cavalry, it was scouting and patrols as usual. A brief brush with a Confederate infantry force on the twenty-sixth near Grove Church caused casualties

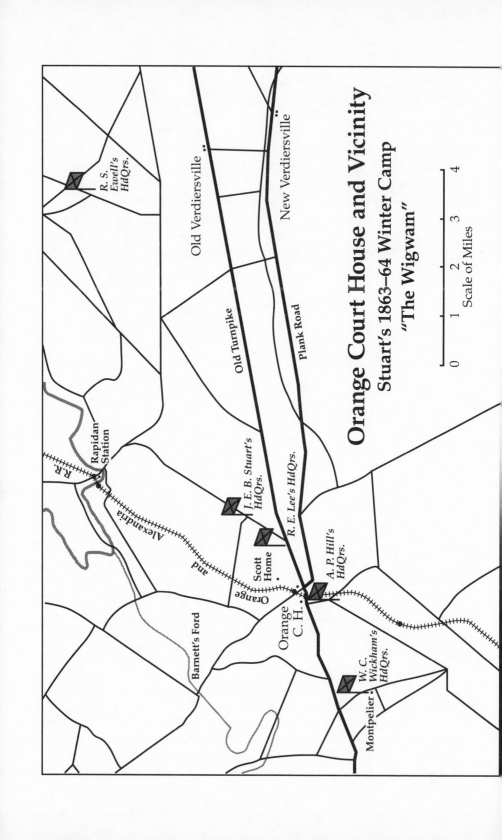

Orange Court House and Vicinity
Stuart's 1863–64 Winter Camp
"The Wigwam"

0   1   2   3   4
Scale of Miles

R. S.
Ewell's
HdQrs.

Old Verdiersville

New Verdiersville

Old Turnpike

Plank Road

R.R.

Rapidan
Station

Alexandria

J. E. B. Stuart's
HdQrs.

R. E. Lee's HdQrs.

Scott
Home

and

Orange

A. P. Hill's
HdQrs.

Orange
C. H.

Barnett's Ford

W. C.
Wickham's
HdQrs.

Montpelier

on both sides.[25] *Stuart's cavalry does not appear to have been involved in this skirmish, however. In fact, the gray troopers seemed willing to call a temporary halt to the hostilities, and eventually their blue counterparts did the same.*

On the twenty-eighth, snow came, depositing six inches on the already saturated ground. The snow changed to rain later in the day and then back to snow. Stuart's staff struggled against the cold and boredom. John Esten Cooke started up his diary again on the twenty-sixth and wrote of his activities and the goings-on in camp. He worked on his writing, visited around, and seemed to enjoy himself as much as the weather permitted. His account of a snowball fight between some of the Confederate infantry brigades gave proof of the soldier's ability to have fun even in the midst of depressing conditions.

Chiswell Dabney anticipated trouble when he returned to cavalry Headquarters. As he wrote to his mother on the twenty-eighth, he had been absent without leave for three days, having extended his furlough beyond the time granted him. On his way back he ran into John B. Fontaine's wedding party at Hanover Court House. He stayed. It would take a number of young ladies interceding on his behalf to save him. He did not mind a bit.

Channing Price returned from a visit home and wrote to his mother on the twenty-eighth to give her an account of his trip and the latest camp news. One day later, Philip H. Powers wrote his first letter to his wife in almost a month. His topics ranged from summer clothes to the fact that he had not heard from her for some time. For all three men, the war seemed to have been suspended.

From John Esten Cooke's Journal

Camp "No Camp"

Jan. 26, 1863—In forenoon, wrote 3 pp. foolscap to W̶h̶i̶g̶—army letter. Feeling dull, galloped over to Mrs. Alsop's and chatted for an hour with Miss Nannie—Back at three or four, and [Capt. William D.] Farley and [Lt. Walter Q.] Hullihen dined with Tom and myself. This evening tried an article on "Jennings Wise"—but interrupted and thrown off the track.[26]
———— [word illegible] up to the Gen'l tent several times, and chatted with him. The papers give the news of Burnside's advance. "There they are sticking in the mud now" says the Gen. "the rain of Tuesday stopped them." Our artillery is sent back, and there are no signs of a fight. What does that mean? One more fight, and I hope we will have them.

Tom is going home tomorrow, and thence to Maryland. Darkey singing "Ain't got time to tarry!" Banjo!

Camp "No Camp"

Jan. 27, '63—I have done nothing, and been nowhere today—raining incessantly. Tom has gone to mail letters at Sandy Point Maryland, and carried one from me to Mrs. ——— [name illegible], Balt. & one to Sister Willie. Reading the "Age of Chivalry" all day—interesting. This evening commenced "quiet".

Sent Miss Nannie A. [Alsop] sugar and flower [sic] to make my puddings: by ——— [name illegible] who is now spreading my bed. Banjo going as usual in the Gen.'s tent—but I believe I won't go. "Something too much of that." The Gen. has tracked me as "Tristan Joyeuse Gent." and laughs much at him.[27] Knew him by his "mighty meerschaum" [pipe] he says. I hear that the "Song of the Rebel" has taken everywhere. Bob Hunter told one thousand people he was my cousin, and [Capt. James] Dearing rode up to see the paper.[28]

Wrote 13 pp. of "Jennings Wise" last night but laid it aside. It won't do. All day now, the brigade in the pines yonder is cheering, and the band playing. [Capt. J. Marshall] Hanger came in tonight and has just gone.

The rain is pattering on my tent, and I'll stop as—No I'll add some items of recent things.

On Sunday, the 18th, I set out to visit Wattie down the river. Took the River Road, went by A. P. Hill's directed by one of his staff, and reached the Corbin House—Jackson's Head Qrs. toward dark. Chatted with Maj. [Alexander S.] Pendleton, Col. [Lt. Col. Charles J.] Faulkner, Gen. [Brig. Gen. William N.] Pendleton, and others, and found the brigade was near at hand.[29] Mistook another for it, in the woods, and left the sentinel bawling "Corporal of the guard! Post No. ———!" and pushed on—finding the Old Brigade, and Rob Randolph, Frank Whiting, Mord Lewis etc.[30] I was glad to see the old crowd about whom I had first written in the "Outlines."

Proceeded to Second Brigade and sent for Wattie who soon came. The same old coon, but bearded on the chin. He gave me an excellent supper and with some of his brother officers we talked late. He has kept a journal— ——— [word illegible] it might be called of his movements, as exact as a clock. I read that part relating to the battle of Fred'g [Fredericksburg]. I must try something of the sort. Slept together, and next morning went over to Old Brigade where I saw Willie Randolph, and Bob Hunter. Tom, who was taken prisoner in King George is in Fortress Monroe. Willie as odd and gay as ever; Bob full of fun. Liked the "Song of the Rebel," greatly. I don't.

Wattie got two days leave, and returned with me, going after dinner to see his friend "Hamilton Stone." Q. M. in [Maj. Gen. Richard H.] Anderson's Div.[31] Memo—on the way up we passed "St. Julian" where Washington chased the deer—see Judge Brooke's autobiography—and John Paul Jones often was. Must make an article of the place. Wattie returned next day after fitting himself out with McClellan saddle etc. among the couriers. Altogether a pleasant trip.

Rev. Randolph brought me letters from my darlings. Man is a character and a fairy! O! to see them once again! God grant that I may soon. We are now at the very ———— [word illegible] of the war, and if I live—but God will provide.

The "rain is on the roof"—and the banjo "tumming" as before!

Camp "No Camp"

Jan. 28, 1863—On getting up found it snowing and now the camp is one great shroud—or bridal veil as you choose. Sat in my tent all the morning, reading "Quits." First part good, didn't read second vol. as I don't care for scenes of foreign life. Snow balling in camp—with the Gen. a moment, and hailed him at dinner in Dabney's tent. Commenced article on "Band in the Pines." Stalled in the afternoon. Fitz [Maj. Norman R. FitzHugh] came in and smoked. The Gen.'s mess has split to pieces from overbulkiness. Fitz is going to mess by himself. I wouldn't mess with a dozen for pay. Commenced "Denereux." George Woodbridge and Aldrich dropping in.[32] George sat till bedtime. The papers indicate increasing disruption at the North. Heaven confuse their councils. Gen. passing on horseback going to his wife and singing "Ain't got time to tarry!" Snow still falling.

Hd Qrs Cavalry Division
January 28th 1863

Dear Mother [Mrs. Elizabeth T. Dabney]

I promised to write as soon as I arrived at Camp, but I suppose you will say from the date of my letter that I have at least made a miscalculation but listen! You remember that I intended to start the same day I left "Vaucluse" but was prevented as you have heard; the next morning I was left & consequently did not get off until Sunday eavening [*sic*]; arrived safely in Richmond, and staid [*sic*] at the "American". I there determined to carry out my original plan, of going to Fredericksburg immediately with "Felbert"[33] and my baggage; I went as far as "Guinea [Guiney's] Station" where I left my things with Major [William J.] Johnston our Divs'n Commissary requesting him to send them on by the first opportunity to Hd. Qrs., which he did. I then returned on the eavening [*sic*] train to Hanover Co. Ho. [Court House] intending to ride my horse back next morning, (I was then three day's over time) but when I got to the hotel I found John Fountaine [Fontaine] there with his wedding party, and nothing would do but for me to go, which I accordingly did; thinking like the bird that a miss was as good as a mile and nothing worse would be done for staying one more day so stay I did. When I got to Dundee who should I find there but Major

Genl J. E. B. Stuart, and before the night was over he had given me "eight days longer" to be with the bridal party, but this I must confess I owe to the young ladies who were kind enough to espouse my cause first to get pardon for the first offence and then the eight days extension. I spent one of the merryest [sic] weeks of my life here except the time we spent at Bever [Beaver] Dam where I was treated like one of the family. Hear what Cousin Molly wrote on a piece of paper & gave me when I came away;

"Dear Chiswell,

If you are ever sick or in trouble, remember Cousin Molly and Beaver Dam."

Who would not be a cousin? I intend to get wounded in the very next fight provided it don't put me altogether "hors de combat." You can't imagine what a very nice time I had there. They all enquired very affectionately after all of the family & Cousin Luisa said that she loved us all so very much. Tell Pa I staid all night with his old friend Cousin James Fountaine who was very kind to me, and enquired after all of you. Tell Annie that Felbert is very well & has been engaged cutting wood all the morning for my stove but is now in his tent & very comfortable. I think he is very much improved already & his mind is very much enlarged by what he has seen. It is snowing terribly but not very cold. I wrote to brother yesterday to try and get him to sell out the Bent Mountains to Major [Norman R.] FitzHugh, who after I had described the place to him seemed to like it very much. He will pay cash. Give my love to Betty and Edward & tell her I am going to expect her at Fredericksburg this winter. The Genl sends love to all & so do I.

Your most
affectionate Son
C. Dabney

━━◄◆►━━

Hd. Qrs.
Cavalry Division
January 28th 1863

Dear Mother [Mrs. Thomas Randolph Price Sr.],

According to promise I write at the earliest opportunity to apprise you of my safe arrival at camp. I got a seat this morning upon getting to Ashland & made the trip as comfortably as possible until reaching Hamilton's Crossing: here after wading through mud almost knee-deep, and the snow nearly blinding you, I was unable to find Ephraim, and as you may imagine was not in the best humor possible.[34] I was just coming to the conclusion that

I should have to wait with my luggage until our mail-carrier came to camp & started my horses to me, when Ephraim rode up, having started late and not arriving until 3/4 of an hour after the train. I rode to camp then & found all well & making themselves as comfortable as possible under the circumstances.

We had a merry party at dinner, considering the weather, as Chiswell and I had the General and Von Borcke with us, and the dinner consisting of cold bread, cold turkey, corn-beef, tongue, pickle, and oysters which we cooked in our tent: everything, except the oysters was brought from home by Chiswell or myself.

The General has gone quite early this evening to Mrs. Alsop's, and we are in his tent, having an uproarious time with the banjo, violin & tamborine: but in the midst of it all, I am writing this scrawl. The General is in fine spirits & looks back with great pleasure to his little frolic last week.

Everything is perfectly quiet, although there was considerable stir & movement of troops last week. We are going to have a miserable time, I fear, for the next few days, when the snow begins to melt: now it is cheerless & desolate enough, especially to those of us who have just returned from the gay scenes of last week, by getting around a comfortable fire, we try our best to forget the cold & discomfort.

I sent Mrs. Stuart's letters to her this morning by a servant: she is very well and Jemmy also, the General tells me. The General returns his hearty thanks to Eddy for his useful & pretty present. I wish you would tell Doherty or send him word to make Gen. Stuart a vest of the material he has just made for me: he can get it at the store by asking Joe, and he will make it like the blue one for the General, which suits him very well.

Do not forget about Von Borcke's photographs & mine, when Nannie [Price] comes to Richmond. My love to all & believe me as ever your devoted son

R. Channing Price

~+~ ≡♦≡ ~+~

Camp below
Fredericksburg
Jan. 29th 1863

My Dear Wife [Mrs. Roberta Powers],

If any goods can be purchased buy me some clothes for summer—flannel for shirts & drawers, socks unless I have enough.

A month, I believe has elapsed since I even attempted to send you a letter, simply because I could hear of no opportunity of sending one by private hands and it was useless to try by mail. While the enemy held Winchester. Even now I know not if this will ever reach you but I will try it. I may find someone going to the Valley. My last letter from you was dated Dec. 21. Since then I have not heard a word. I know not whether you have ever received any that I have written; though I hope you have. Such a separation would have been unendurable had I not been fully occupied night & day and thus been able to drive off thoughts of you and the children by continuous application to business.

I found Brother James' Papers in a sad state of confusion and irregularity but by laboring at them I have finally succeeded in arranging them all, and today sent them off to the Department at Richmond. This has been my occupation during this month. Comfortably fixed, after we got a servant, the time has passed not unpleasantly. I have seldom left my tent except for a daily ride of a few miles. The weather has been delightful until the last week. Now it is dreadful. All yesterday and the day before we experienced a driving snow storm, and today the snow covers everything to the depth of a foot or more. But our tent has stood the storm and kept us warm and dry [remainder of letter is lost]

From John Esten Cooke's Journal

Camp "No Camp"

Jan. 29, 1863—Snow six or eight inches deep, and the camp silent all day. The Infantry Brigades however have been snow-balling and shouting as usual—and that same old band has been playing. Scarcely out of my tent all day, and defied the weather. Remodeled "Captain Jennings Wise" and finished it. Tolerable. It makes 18 pp. Read some in "Denereux." Capt. Nelson, a nephew of Hugh N. [Maj. Hugh M. Nelson] came to pay for some cartridges, and we chatted.[35] The newspapers indicate continued changes at the North. I don't trust those cunning animals however.

Hairston (Wat) [Watt] came in and dined with me. Says he has just sold the gov't 16000 bushels of corn at $1.50. Doubts if the Gen. has anything for him to do. A better fellow than his brother [Maj. Samuel H. Hairston, Stuart's quartermaster].

Dropped in at the Gen.'s to see Cousin F. [Flora] but she had gone. Chatted, Gen. asking my opinion about Northern news. "I think," I said, "there'll be a great big thundering Spring campaign, and then it will end." Gen. replies, "If there is a Spring campaign it will last through the year, and if so, it will go on to the end of Lincoln's time." It strikes me that the high officers of the army <u>perhaps</u> are agreed among themselves to discourage <u>peace</u> reasoning—and they are right. War requires nerves always <u>strung</u>: there must be no looking forward to peace and ease: that unstrings.

We talked about Lincoln and I said he had a great deal of muscle. The Gen. agrees and says, "he has what they call iron nerve—but is not a man of ability." But this is not what I meant to set down. This was the part of the conversation which I listened to attentively.

Gen. S. "Do you know what Gen. Lee's object was at Richmond?"

I. "No."

Gen. S. "He was building the fortifications there in order to hold Richmond with a small force, and then attack McClellan's right flank. I was in favor of attacking his left flank, on the Charles City Road."

I. "From what point, General?"

Gen. S. "Well, from about White Oak Swamp."

I. "Would you have had space enough?"

Gen. S. "Yes: but the other was best. McClellan ought, when we advanced on his right flank, to have struck right for Richmond."

I. "He hadn't the nerve. Napoleon would have done it."

Gen. S. "McClellan was not the man for the occasion. His Maryland campaign was full of faults, too. He ought to have pressed on [Maj. Gen. Lafayette] McLaws after Boonsboro! That was a great oversight. If Harper's Ferry had not surrendered, we would have been in a bad way."

The Gen. had got his banjo and is going out frolicking. He's a "jolly cove!"

Camp "No Camp"

Jan. 30th '63—This morning finished the article on "Jennings Wise." It will do, and is tolerable. Took me most of the morning. Read the papers—discontent at the North increasing.

A great snowball battle among the Brigades which was worth seeing. Yesterday Hood's Texans & Georgians issued from their camp near Gen. Lee's Hdqrs. and led by Gen. [Brig. Gen. Micah] Jenkins attacked and routed [Brig. Gen. Joseph B.] Kershaw's S. Carolinians camped toward Mrs. Alsop's.[36] Inflamed with victory the Hood boys today advanced in battle array with flags flying and led by their officers against [Brig. Gen. Thomas R. R.] Cobb of [Maj. Gen. Lafayette] McLaws' Div. (as Kershaw is).[37] The camp is just back of ours in the pines. The scene was a lively and funny one. The Hoodites charged into the camp, drove out the Andersonites [Wofford] and put them to rout.[38] But they rallied got reinforcements, and drove the Hoodites from the woods, across the Telegraph road, and into the fields, with storms of balls (snow).

What was the horror of the Hoodites to see Kershaw's men, drawn up on their left flank, ready to attack. They halted and their leader rode forward and parlayed—he demanded assistance against a common foe—the

Yankee Anderson [Wofford]. A long parley, refusal at first; but compliance at last, and the combined forces attacked the enemy. Anderson was drawn up on the crest of a hill, and fought with desperation but numbers overpowered him. He fell back in confusion, his foes pursued; and burst into his camp. "Come on boys!" was the cry "here's your blankets, your cooking utensils, and everything!" Some thought they were in earnest. Then Hood as usual conquered.

The scene was a very good mimic battle. The men advanced and fell back, deployed, and charged—turned the enemy's flank, and "carried on" generally like real fighters. They had guidons for flags; and the regiments marched in very good order to the battle. There were many officers galloping about with an irresistible air of leading their men—others were shouting in furious tones to stragglers—and snow balls flew as thick as leaves in an autumn wind. I saw it from horseback, and laughed heartily. I think I will write it out for the Whig, or the News.

I write this in the afternoon. Farley and myself are going to Mrs. Alsop's about dark. I begin to feel as if I was never going to get abroad any more. At the Gen.'s tent—short chat with him—"nothing in it." I spent a pleasant evening with the Alsops. Miss Nannie had been working hard all day at my cakes and puddings, and appeared unusually amiable in my eyes. Mrs. Alsop had my bread ready and I brought it home in my overcoat pockets. Today I send after my ——— [word illegible].

Came home and smoked and chatted in Farley's tent—with Channing Price who is a good fellow. Roads horrible.

Nothing more to add, unless it be the following dialogue, viz.

Gen: displaying English Carbine "Look what my English friend brought me. That shows what they think of me in London."[39]

Moi. "What! that you are a breechloader?"

Covert smile— as of one hearing a good thing on himself. Exit Captain—to smoke as usual.

Camp "No Camp"

Jan. 31, 1863—This morning—there's tattoo! Tarra! Tarra! Tarrata! Ta Ta Ta!—rode over to Col. [Lt. Col. Briscoe G.] Baldwin's and chatted with him for half an hour.[40] Thence to Rev. Randolph's finding him out. He is ordered back to Guinea's [Guiney's Station].

Miss Nannie [Alsop] sends me cakes, pies and bread. Bless her!

Forgot my letter to the Whig, written before I rode out. It is six pages of letter paper, and describes in mock military style, the snow ball fight.

The News of this week contains my second "Outline" on Jackson. Rather inflated. This evening spent an agreeable hour or so in the Gen.'s tent with an English Captain, name not caught. He went down to Gen. Jackson's today, and was greatly pleased. He takes the staff autographs for Lady Herbert's album. Gen. S. [Stuart] again refers to Gen. Jackson's Hd. Qrs.—a room hung round with prints of racehorses, gamecocks etc. Gen. Lee says he "wishes he had a dozen Jacksons for his Lieutenants." Gen. S. again repeats that "Jackson is a man of <u>military genius</u>"—and I reply "That hits it exactly: he certainly has the knack of whipping the Yankees." I believe I am regarded as the <u>Jackson man</u> of these HdQrs.

The papers barren. They say the "radicals" are going to prosecute the war with tremendous vigor in the next 90 days. Then if they do not succeed they will "give it up."

George Woodbridge is sitting and reading near me. This has been a quiet sort of day. An excellent dinner, puddings! etc. Such are the great events of a soldier's life.

Gen. S. shouting "Good night!" Banjo lively tonight with "Jine the Cavalry" and the "Old Gray Horse" and all the repertoire! There's a violin!

FEBRUARY

Despite the rain, snow, and mud, the Federal cavalry went back to the business of war during the first week of February. A reconnaissance of the Rappahannock fords brought on a brief clash of cavalry between Kelly's Ford and Rappahannock Station on the second. For all their efforts, the blue troopers could claim only one prisoner and four horses. Between the fifth and seventh, a Union force of cavalry, infantry, and artillery advanced to burn the Rappahannock bridge near Kelly's Mills. The three regiments of cavalry and three brigades of infantry were opposed by Hampton's cavalry. Rain, hail, and snow hampered the Federals on their march to their objective, and the resulting mud made their homeward trek equally difficult. Hampton successfully defended the bridge, which was slightly damaged but refused to burn. By the seventh, everyone was back to their starting places trying to get dry.[41]

John Esten Cooke's diary entries for this time period indicated that all the goings-on along the cavalry's picket lines failed to disturb the tranquil atmosphere at Stuart's headquarters. Officers went visiting, entertained guests, and generally enjoyed the short respite the weather gave them. Cooke had an outlet in his writing and reading and took advantage of the time to pen several stories and explore some fiction. His frustration with his smoking chimney finally spilled over into action, and he fixed it with some good Virginia sod.

Chiswell Dabney's letter of the fourth confirms the relaxed atmosphere that permeated Camp "No Camp." With little to report, Dabney concentrated on his quest for butter, the snowball battles that erupted between the various infantry commands, and the ever-present mud that threatened to engulf him.

From John Esten Cooke's Journal

Camp "No Camp"

Feb. 1, 1863—Sunday, and no work, tho' I was in splendid trim for an article on "Beauregard."

In this diary I don't take the trouble to put down my official transactions. They consist of viewing and approving requisitions—corresponding with Col. Baldwin, and the Brigade Ord. officers, and supervising the ordnance rather than attending to details, which are left to my two sergeants and clerk—Aldrich, Gleason, and Booth.[42] My philosophy is to give myself as little trouble as possible. I suppose I will be rated after the war as "only an Ordnance Officer"—but I have really been aide de camp. That's not important tho'.

About 2, got tired of camp and galloped over to Mr. Garnett's to see Flora. Found them just sitting down to dinner, and dined with them. Several Fred'g [Fredericksburg] refugees, and a pleasant time. Mr. Garnett Jr. thought Gen. Stuart would find himself mistaken if he supposed the Essex girls would let him kiss them. Pink and Iday H. [Hunter] especially.[43] They never kissed people. I replied that they had honored me with that mark of affection upon sundry occasions, which rather dumbfounded him. Gen. [Brig. Gen. Robert H.] Chilton came in, and we had a chat.

Returned here and read Devereux—good but forced. In the evening Fitz [Maj. Norman R. FitzHugh] came and took tea with me, and we talked of the battle of Fred'g. Gen. Stuart came near charging the enemy's left near three o'clock. I wish he had.

Tom Turner's brother, Lt. T. [Bradshaw B. Turner] from W. H. F. Lee's [Brigade] slept with me.[44] Today when I write this, the sun is shining bright, and I am projecting a visit to "Fonthill."

Camp "No Camp"

Feb. 4, 1863—Nothing of much interest for the last three days.

Day before yesterday galloped over to Col. Baldwin's and chatted with him. Man after my own heart—likes to take long in dressing, and to do it lazily. Puts one boot half on, and then lights his pipe and studies the fire! I promised to buy Chiswell's overcoat cloth for him, and have done so—for $70. Went and came at a thundering gallop—Buck will break my neck some of these days.[45] Fitz in again chatting—I've sent to Richmond for mess things for him. Spent a smoky evening, my chimney terrible. Tried a board in front—no go. Retired—Captain [Benjamin S.] White sleeping with me. Very cold.

Yesterday commenced "A Day with Beauregard"—and wrote 19 pages.

Papers somewhat interesting. Read "Devereux." All day keeping my tent—
very cold. Gen.'s banjo going in the evening.

Today—4th—finished "Beauregard"—25 pages. Pretty good. This
makes 7 or 8 articles for the "News." Toward evening galloped over and
saw Misses French, and Miss Nannie P. [Price]. Met me most cordially.
Galloped back at sundown—and dined solus as usual. Read the "Jan'y
Messenger"—good thing of Basset French's: his letter on Jackson's summer campaign.

Spent an hour with the Gen. in his tent: recalling old battles. His re-
semblance to Longstreet is very striking: and his gayety amazing. Yesterday
Pelham brought me a letter from Pink, urging me to come down. [Francis]
Lawley's letter in the Times—backs up Pelham ———— [word illegible].[46]
Freezing cold—to bed!

━━ ⚬◆⚬ ━━

Hd Qrs Cavalry Division
February 4th 1863

Dear Mother [Mrs. Elizabeth T. Dabney]

Perhaps you will be surprised to hear from me so soon after having
received my former letter which I suppose you have already received. But
you will not be when I come to an explanation. First and foremost, while
having a conversation yesterday with the Genl and Lady [Mrs. Stuart],
amongst other things we commenced talking about the state of our different larders, and having found out by comparing notes that neither of us
had any butter, I remarked that if I could contrive any way, I was certain
that you could supply us; Mrs. Stuart said that she could arrange the matter
immediately. Thus! that as the Genl would send his servant Jacob to
Lynchburg, you could send a firkin up there and he would bring it down
to us, and that Uncle Chiswell would let you know when said servant would
arrive. Also that the Genl would take his part of the butter at the market
price. This arrangement I agreed to all except the clause about the Genl
taking his at the market price which I immediately voted down, saying that
that was impossible as neither you or I would ever agree to such an arrangement. The Genl then instructed me to say to you that he would not
offer any thing, but he certainly would not refuse such a gift if you were
pleased to send him any. So every thing being satisfactorily agreed upon, I
find myself writing this morning. Good excuse for writing is'nt [sic] it?

Tell Annie, Felbert gets along admirably and pleases me very much,
has been speculating considerably in tobacco and other things of the sort

since he has been here, made some money and thinks he will soon be a rich man, has learned quite a number of Camp songs and amuses us very much singing. He is now standing behind my chair and desires me to send his love to his mater-famillias, also to Aunt Polly—Betty &&&&&&.

The Genl sayes [sic] he is exceedingly obliged to you for the things you sent him and desires me to send his love to you all. Major [Heros] Von Borcke sayes he will take a little butter. My love to every body, the Pollys, Lucys & Bollings &&. No chance for a fight down here. Yankees stuck in the mud & can't move. Every thing is mud in these parts. We have finished my box very nearly. Von Borcke is now sitting on one corner making way with the few remaining apples and with [Lt. Richard Channing] Price to help him I think we will come to a finis today.

The army is in the best sirits [sic] I have ever seen it. We have had Brigades of Infantry out fighting each other for the last day or two, were formed in regular lines of battle with skirmishers well to the front. Went out the other day with Hood's Texas Brigade, like to have had my head knocked off, being on horse back was quite a target. We were going this way all day long, very amusing I can tell you. If the Yanks come over this river they will never get back any more. The Army of the Potomack [sic] is invincible.[47]

Good-by

Your most affectionate
son
C. Dabney

P.S.
Mud has been ancle [sic] deep in my tent for the last day or two but is improving now.

C. D.

From John Esten Cooke's Journal

Camp "No Camp"

Feb. 5, 1863—Today it snowed again and it is snowing still. Poor "Fighting Joe" [Hooker]—what can he do? Wrote out and out "The Yankee Generals," finishing it just now—25 pp. Good. The Whig contains my letter. Letters from John R. to Lil, and from Natty to Nan—God bless him! When will I see them all again? This evening Aldrich, George and Hanger sat long—time lost. White is still sleeping with me. The Gen. says there'll be a fight in a week. Maybe, but not here. Dr. Shepperson, "Bohemian" here— Gen. says he is going to move my train to Hanover and keep me here. Talk in his tent tonight about Gen. [John R.] Cooke and the John Brown times. Gen. says "——— told me Gen. Cooke was kept in complete ignorance and had <u>no choice</u>. He is unlucky." (When in ———— [word illegible])

That's true. Must close my page. Fire going out. I will write out fully his narrative about John Brown.

Camp "No Camp"

Feb. 6, 1863—Rode over and dined at Mrs. French's—pleasant time. Miss N. [Nannie Price] anxious to have ————'s address in North Carolina. Much fun with her. Camp terribly sloppy. Dr. Shepperson came in and we talked long about literature. Tom has returned and brought a boy to wait on him. I must put a back to my chimney—of sod.

Will write "The Pawnee ———— [word illegible]" and "A Glimpse of Col. Stuart" for outlines.

Today—when I write this—is splendid.

Yesterday I wrote out "Lt. Stuart and John Brown" to have by me. It is good.

Must smoke—splendid morning. I will go to Richmond I think in a few days,—and to Amelia!

Camp "No Camp"

Feb. 7, '63—Today I built a back to my chimney of sod—acts excellently, throwing the heat forward, and taking just one half the wood. The "News" ———— [word illegible] me—Stonewall is continued. About 3 I took a gallop over to Mr. Garnett's where I met Gen. Garnett and had a chat with him. A pleasant old friend. Gen. Lee wouldn't let him go to Rich'd from something Gen. Stuart had just told him. What? Flora sweet and in good spirits—talks about Gen. Cooke Jr. with cheerfulness. The Gen. came by—rode Jimmy a little—and then we returned to camp.[48] He says he is anxious to go to Europe after the war—solus: and rejoices in his stick of "Canada oak" given him by Capt. [Lewis G.] Phillips, riding with it: and tonight writing with it hooked on his left arm.[49] Says it's a great comfort to him.

Though there was skirmishing on the fringes of the armies where Confederate partisans were active and Federal expeditions to destroy or capture them were mounted, the main armies stirred little from their winter's hibernation. In Fauquier, Loudoun, Westmoreland, and Richmond counties, brief deadly encounters flared as each side attempted to establish some control over territory neither had the strength to take and hold. Some of the Confederate cavalry involved in these actions were detached from Stuart to operate in their home counties, but he did not exercise command of their independent operations once they left the army.

In mid-February, a new face was seen at cavalry headquarters. Channing Price's brother, Thomas, fresh from the salons and classrooms of Europe, joined the staff as assistant engineer officer under Blackford. Like Cooke, Tom Price too kept a diary—one that would cause problems and embarrassment for many. The dedicated philology student had yet to experience the war in any form other than what he had learned through the letters he had received from his family while in Europe and newspaper accounts. He came in the midst of a cold, damp, dismal winter with no real concept of what awaited him.

Meanwhile, needing to get away from his grim surroundings, John Esten Cooke attempted a little ruse to secure a "furlough" from Stuart. But the general was all too aware of his ordnance officer's ploy. Nevertheless, Cooke received permission to go off on an "inspection tour," during which he was royally entertained, and he returned with his spirit renewed.

From Thomas R. Price's Diary

Feb. 10, 1863—Mounted my uniform yesterday morning, buckled on my sabre and pistol, and after a farewell at home, started off on the train to begin my new life as a soldier. The day fine and mild—arrived at Hamilton Crossing, and was put down along with my baggage in a lake of mud; no conveyance at hand. Sent word by courier to ——— [word illegible], and after waiting for several hours at the Quartermaster's cabin I was sent for and carried away baggage and all. Paid my respects to Gen. J. E. B. Stuart, and was introduced ★ ★ ★ to the various members of the staff. Major FitzHugh is his adjutant; Chiswell Dabney his Aid-de-Camp [*sic*]. Gen. Stuart came to headquarters about midnight; had a great romp with his two aides, and roused up the whole camp by his singing and shouting. His conduct was held by his familiars to be the prelude to some important event; he is said to be always very gay when he is resolved upon any dashing achievement. ★ ★ ★ Mrs. Gen. Stuart ——— [word illegible] camp with her little son; she goes to R:chmond to-morrow.

Feb. 12—Nothing of importance in camp. Went to work in my new profession by tracing a map of Spotsylvania and Caroline. ★ ★ ★ Our fare is at present very bad—nothing but heavy biscuits and molasses ★ ★ ★ Oh! to be back at my favorite studies! Oh! for Berlin, or Paris, or Athens. I long so to hear again literary conversation, and have my thoughts once more directed to agreeable topics.

Feb. 13— ★ ★ ★ Dined with Gen. Stuart—his mess not much better than ours. He joked about his "stalled beef." It seems that the oxen in stall are condemned to die, and their meat finds its way to the tables even of major generals.

From John Esten Cooke's Journal

Camp "No Camp"

Feb. 14, 1863—Just returned from "Fonthill." Started down on Sunday (the 8th)—telling the Gen. I wanted to "go and inspect W. H. F. Lee's Batteries!" "Pelham has inspected them" was his cunning reply "but you can go down to Hunter's." Exactly Capt. Cooke's object.

Farley rode with me to "Hayfield"—a charming family. Old Col. Taylor, Wm. T. , Mrs. ———— [name illegible], Jim T., & Bessie and Fanny G. We struck up a relationship and had a laughing time. Next day set out alone and got to "Fonthill" about 4: galloping too much. The River road for twenty miles is spaded down for a line of defence [*sic*], and with embrasures in the bank for cannon. A notable feature of the landscape. (Negroes singing "Dixie" in a very sweet and mournful way behind my tent.) Was rec'd by all at F. [Fonthill] with the warmest affection. All there but Cousin Bob. Steve Dandridge there—a stunning youth. I staid [*sic*] there three days—smoking in ———— [two words illegible], chatting with Cousin Lettie and the girls, and enjoying myself hugely. A veritable oasis. Sadie is much grown and very gay and sweet—as is Pink. Cousin Lettie made me a sham, and I came away much urged to stay. (Darkeys changed to the "Bonnie Blue Flag!")

Started back yesterday—13th—and got to "Hayfield" at sunset—the sun crimson on the ———— [word illegible]—found that the Yankees were building a corduroy road opposite. ———— [word illegible] the setting sun shining on the Hayfield windows. Met on the road a young Mrs. Taylor I think who had been forced to "evacuate" hastily from supposed complicity in shooting Yankee pickets. Capt. (Conway) Howard & Col. [Robert M.] Mayo came at night to "Hayfield" to look after the Yankees.[50] I went down to the bank where Howard was digging rifle pickets and heard the Yankees working. Slept soundly, somewhat expecting to be waked by a cannon ball. Col. Mayo, my bed fellow aroused in the middle of the night— he commanded the reg't sent down on picket—remonstrated with him for getting up. A jolly fellow. Next morning saw Yankee Cavalry picket thro' spy glass—slapping his blue-coated arms to keep warm. Glad he was cold. Cannon sunk in the garden, and "bombproof" ———— [word illegible] behind house. Told my good friends good-bye and rode leisurely back, to find Gen. Stuart and Flora gone to Rich'd. The Gen. going up to the Valley to look after [Brig. Gen. William E.] Jones. The "News" proprietors send me funny letters about my outlines and "beg leave briefly to express their admiration of all my articles" and authorize me to draw when I choose.

Rather dull here after my good visit.

(Darkeys shifted their song to
   "Never Mind the Weather
   But get over double trouble
   I'm bound for the happy land
   Of Old John Brown!")

Fanny G. says she kissed Gen. Lee four times, and that he is the "hand-somest man in the Southern Confederacy." She said she would like to kiss Gen. Jackson, and the Gen. was told of the speech by Gen. Lee. He looked confused, laughed, and blushed! Good, noble Stonewall! <u>Memo</u>—That good story of Lt. Smith and Miss K—— C—— of their riding: she believed him—and holding him so tight that he blushed. The "Outlines From the Outpost" have got down there. Lt. Smith told Bessie that I wrote them. Has the Gen. seen them? Doubtless. Well.—I must write at once demanding copyright. They are sold too low at any rate.

The papers seem to indicate European mediation. But there will be another big fight here I suppose—before peace.

God defend the right!

As winter warmed toward spring, the war began to heat up as well. There were brief clashes at Union Mills and on the Hillsborough road four miles from Harpers Ferry on the fourteenth and a more serious affair at Hartwood Church on the twenty-fifth. The latter engagement was brought on when Brig. Gen. Fitz Lee crossed the Rappahannock at Kelly's Ford on the twenty-fourth on a reconnaissance. In all he had about 400 men from the 1st, 2nd, and 3rd Virginia Cavalry regiments. On the twenty-fifth, he drove in the enemy pickets in the vicinity of Hartwood Church, struck the reserve and main body of the enemy, and routed them to within five miles of Falmouth. Running into Federal infantry, Lee withdrew and recrossed the Rappahannock on the twenty-sixth with 150 prisoners, 5 officers, and all their horses and equipment. His own losses amounted to 14 men.[51]

The final activity for the month occurred on the twenty-seventh and twenty-eighth, when Federal colonel Percy Wyndham, with elements of the 1st New Jersey, 1st, 5th, and 6th Michigan, 18th Pennsylvania, 5th New York, and 1st Virginia (Union) Cavalry regiments, conducted a scout from Centreville to Falmouth. Seven prisoners and exhausted horses and men were all Wyndham had to show for his effort.[52]

In Stuart's camp, Tom Price began to settle somewhat into the routine of army life, though he was anything but enamored of it. He managed to obtain a furlough, which for a time gave him some relief from the camp's dreary surroundings. His entries for the middle and end of the month merely comment on what had been and was transpiring in camp and the war.

For John Esten Cooke, there was always his writing, about which he took time to record in his diary. He seemed always on the lookout for story topics, making note of them as well. Frustrated in an attempt to acquire leave, he settled for good conversation with fellow officers.

Channing Price returned from his furlough at about the same time his brother was leaving on his. Channing's account of the storm that covered the camp in a thick blanket of white provided his sister, Ellen, with some idea of what her brothers were experiencing.

In his letter of the twenty-eighth, Chiswell Dabney explained to his mother that he had overextended his furlough again and that Stuart apparently had had enough and placed him under arrest. This time there were no lovely girls to plead for him. He had to handle the problem himself. He also wrote of Stuart's visit to Richmond and the honors accorded him by the Confederate House of Delegates. Butter and horses were also topics.

Winter was not quite over. Though the pace of the war was again quickening, it had not yet dissipated the calm atmosphere that existed at cavalry headquarters. With the snow, cold and quiet reigned among the tents of Stuart's staff for at least a little while longer. Such were the "exciting" times at Camp "No Camp."

From Thomas R. Price's Diary

Feb. 17—★ ★ ★ After breakfast, Maj. Von B [Heros von Borcke], Maj. Pelham and I mounted, rode through the woods and fields across the country to strike the main road at Chancellorsville. ★ ★ ★ We crossed the Rapidan at Ely's Ford. ★ ★ ★ No food for man or horse in this barren wilderness, where the ferocity of man has conspired with an unkindly nature to render the entire country a scene of desolation. ★ ★ ★

Feb 18—Important news from headquarters. Two of the grand divisions of the Yankee army have left the Rappahannock on the 30, and are in motion. Gen. R. E. Lee says they have gone to Washington and Fortress Monroe. Our army is in consequence being dispersed. Gen. Longstreet's corps is the first to move. Gen. Pickett's division has already reached Richmond, and we passed Gen. Hood's to-day at Hanover Junction.

From John Esten Cooke's Journal

Camp "No Camp"

Feb. 18, 1863—Rain, rain! Snow, snow! Rain, rain, rain!

I have been keeping in my tent for a large part of every day—scarce going is it indeed, and writing away. Finished "My Friend Lieut. Bumpo"— and nearly an article on Miss Antonia F. [Ford] laid aside.[53] Third No. "Stonewall" better.

Last night spent the evening at Mrs. Alsop's and had a gay candy pulling. Terrel [Terrell] there—went with Farley and staid [sic] till after midnight. Miss Nannie as sweet as ever.

Hooker is gone, and ——— [word illegible] we go to establish HdQrs. between Warrenton and Aldie! ——— [word illegible]! Been reading "——— ———" [word illegible] what Capt. Bushby sent me: and am just going to write "On Picket" for Thackeray.[54]

Darkey's joking—ever.

Camp "No Camp"

Feb. 19, '63—I have finished for the "Illustrated News"—in addition to what they now have:

I. "A Day with Beauregard."	25 pp.
II. "Recollections of Jennings Wise."	23 pp.
III. "My friend Lt. Bumpo."	23 pp.
IV. "The Young Capt. of Eng. Corps."	19 pp.
V. "Some Celebrated Yankees."	<u>25 pp.</u>
	115 pp.

   and poems

I. "The Band in the Pines"

II. "Fredericksburg"

[*Margin notation*: Sent by Parson Landstreet—Feb. 21, 1863]

These are among my best pieces, and will be interesting to the citizens of the C. S. I hope.

Rumors that we will move. I must go and see Col. Baldwin.

Last night I wrote some 12 pp. of "On Picket" which I will not send to Thackeray, but make a volume of adding "Recollections of Capt. Blunderbus" as somebody else! I struck the right vein—bluff, hearty, humorous hating Yankees. Pathos can come in very well.

Camp "No Camp"

Feb. 21, 1863—Today lovely with sunshine. Yesterday the Gen. returned, and seemed glad to see us again—I was to see him. I rode over, the day before and chatted with Col. Baldwin, Maj. [Walter H.] Taylor etc.[55] The Col. said he could "biologize" any body, and turn water into whiskey. Dared him to try it. Said he could govern people's wills. I asked "Do you think you can make me do anything I don't want to—except officially?" ——— [word illegible].

Today asked the Gen. for leave to go and see Sal Duval—he "never heard it called that before" but I assured him I had no sweet heart. Said I might—but it hung fire, Taylor writing me that he "had been closeted with Gen. Lee for two hours, boring over papers"—if I'd send it in the morning he would do his best to put it thro'.—Fitz [Lee] and Col. [William C.] Wickham advise to put it in the ground if "urgent family ——— [word illegible]"—my wanting to go and see my family being urgent. Think I will. Long talk with [Sgt. William] Hoxton and Capt. Clarke [James L. Clark] a young Marylander of Pelham's staff in my tent—about Maryland especially.[56] I said it was the finest chance for conspiracy in the good old English fashion—Maryland at present ——— [two words illegible] in victory, brave, proud, restive young men in the Southern army who ought to become the emissarys [*sic*] of Jeff. Davis, and put their life on the hazard of the die to sow the seeds of armed revolt. Clarke replied that there was such a conspiracy and quoted from a letter from Mary'd [Maryland] that men were wanted "<u>Thermopylae men</u> to deluge the state in blood!"—fight her out and they were nearly ready to do so! I hope so—poor My Maryland!—it is painful: her present attitude.

Got a slip from the <u>Examiner</u> today—death of Capt. Edelin—which will give me another "Outline"—my arrest near Centreville on the way to Millers in Dec'r 1861.[57] Bringing in Bradley Johnson, and making a picture of the frightened courier etc. Humorous.

Edelin's real name was Lem. [Lemuel] Cooper & he was a lamplighter in Balt. [Baltimore]. In April 1861 when the Northern troops were passing thro' to W. [Washington] the crowd was hastily formed into companies by some ringleader who counting off 100 men said, "Who'll take command of these?" Edelin and another stepped out. The latter said, "I know how to drill them." Edelin said, "I have been thro' the Mexican War." The command was given to him, and he afterward marched his Co. out. A man of low character but brave. A great boaster. This will make an excellent article.

Long talk with Col. Wickham and Fitz [Lee] in the Gen.'s tent about the tax etc. I like Wickham—unknown I hated him. He is a cordial good fellow,—a strict soldier, and brave leader.

Wrote "On the Wing" yesterday—but will keep it.

——— ≡✦≡ ———

Hd. Qrs. Cav. Division
Near Fredericksburg
Feb. 23rd 1863

Dear Ellen [Price],

I am going to write you again to see if I cannot induce you to honor me with a letter. The General and I got safely to Hd. Qrs. on Friday last and found everything very dull and quiet.

Tell Thomas that I would have telegraphed him Friday, but the wires were down: I did telegraph him Saturday, but as I this morning got a telegram from him, suppose he did not receive it. Tell him he had best come to Fredericksburg, as on account of the severe storm of yesterday it is impossible to say when we will go to Culpeper C. H., if at all. He need not come up however I think before Wednesday by which time the snow will be somewhat melted.

We are having an awful time here as you may imagine. Chimneys & stoves smoking & snow a foot deep all outside. I was wishing all yesterday that I could be at home & did not think of having to stay in the house as I did the Sunday the General & I spent there when the rain prevented our enjoying ourselves.

Capt. Cooke is going down to-day & I have not much time: so you must take the will for the deed. Give my love to all at home & tell Nannie I expect to hear from her soon, as I believe she is in my debt. Tell Thomas that I wore his cap by mistake Friday and he can get it when he comes up. Chiswell Dabney has not come back yet, but I expect him somewhat to-day. Ask Mama please to hurry up Doherty with my jacket & send it either by Capt. Cooke or Capt. Blackford. Good-bye.

Your devoted brother

R. Channing Price

From Thomas R. Price's Diary

Feb. 27— ★ ★ ★ ★ Toward evening Gen. Stuart came into ———— [name not given] tent, and we passed a tolerably pleasant evening. The General tickled his staff and threw them down in the mud. Then we had hard-boiled eggs and stories about his different raids. He said ———— [two words illegible] that the Chickahominy raid was the most perilous and the most successful of all; that if, in his Pennsylvania raid, the enemy or the depth of water had prevented his recrossing of the Potomac, it was his intention to have boldly penetrated into the interior of Pennsylvania—to have wandered about through the country, and finally, if compelled, to have returned to Northwest Virginia. The scheme he said he had reported to Gen. Lee and the Secretary of War and if they would give him 10,000 men, he desired nothing better than to execute it in the coming spring. During my absence Gen. Fitz Hugh [Fitzhugh] Lee has executed a brilliant attack upon the Yankee cavalry. He crossed the north fork of the Rappahannock high up, at Kelly's Ford, attacked the cavalry picket at United States Ford in the rear and captured them all—fourteen killed, wounded and taken on our side. About ———— [number illegible] prisoners and a large number of horses taken.

Hd Qrs Cavl' Division
February 28th 1863

Dear Mother [Mrs. Elizabeth T. Dabney]

Betty's letter came to hand a short time ago, and for fear that she has left Vaucluse I address this to you, but if she is still there, tell her to consider this as an answer to the one she wrote.

I was very sorry to hear that she was unable to pay a visit to Fredericksburg or eaven [*sic*] to Richmond, for the Genl was very desirous of meeting her again, and seemed quite disappointed when I told him that circumstances were such as to render a visit impossible.

When the Genl was in Richmond last he was presented to the Senate and house [*sic*] of Delegates and offered a seat in the latter body. After he had spoken his thanks the members came up to be introduced, among them brother Peter. He remarked that he (brother Peter) ought to know the Genl; in reply the Genl answered, "I suppose I should as you married my old sweet-heart." Brother Peter blushed up to the eyes and for a moment was the perfect picture of confusion, but soon got over that and walked out with the Genl.

I have something to tell you which will perhaps be a surprise. The other day I was put under arrest to be closely confined eight days for being absent without leave, but talked the Genl out of it entirely, being only kept under half a day. All came from my stopping on my way from Richmond the last time to see the girls. I'll tell you more about it some other time.

If you get the butter spoken of in your last letter I'll telegraph to Uncle Chiswell to let you know when to send it to Lynchburg.

I had an old case of mine decided yesterday, which involved me to the amount of $315, but the decision was, that the amount was due by the government instead of me.

I don't know how I am to get through the spring campaign, my horses, one of them utterly useless and the other in very bad order. This service is certainly playing destruction with the equine breed.

I think I have sold brother's place on the Bent for him. I found Major [Norman R.] FitzHugh wished to buy a place, and recommended brother's. He took the matter in consideration and I wrote to brother advising him to sell, which he wrote me expecting he would do provided he can get $10,000 cash for it. The Major can pay this down I know & left this morning to go up there to look at it. I really hope that brother will leave there for the sake of his family.

Tell Annie, Felbert is gradually becoming a soldier, and I think by a little more of my training he will be first rate. He is perfectly well & sayes [*sic*] he is very well satisfied.

No fight with the Yankees for at least a month. We are all in ———— [two words illegible].

Received a letter from Aggie yesterday and answered it today; she was very well.

> Your devoted son
> C. Dabney

I am detailed on a court of inquiry and am ordered to proceed with it at once or I would make my letter longer.

MARCH

As February had closed so March opened. Skirmishing on the second at Aldie and at Independence Hill in Prince William County on the fourth heralded the coming campaign season. But it was the exploit of John S. Mosby on the ninth that fired everyone's imagination and admiration.[58] Entering Fairfax Court House in the early hours of the morning, he rode off with Federal brigadier general Edwin H. Stoughton and others as prisoners. It was but the first of many of the "Gray Ghost's" daring deeds that made him famous in the South and infamous in the North.[59] Stuart was elated with Mosby's achievement.

Though in these first few days of March the war was still on the periphery of the army, the officers of Stuart's staff knew the busy season approached. "Old Man Winter" was fading but was not going quietly. Washed-out bridges and the ever-present Virginia mud were topics that found their way into the staff officers' diary entries and letters home. All knew the peacefulness that the final days of winter had brought could not last much longer and, recognizing what lay ahead, preparations were made.

There was a new arrival at cavalry headquarters during the first week of the new month. Frank Robertson finally was fit enough to report for duty. He immediately became conscious of his need of horses, a topic that occupied much space in his first two letters home. His brother-in-law, Capt. William W. Blackford, shared his tent with the new assistant engineer officer and put him to work on a map of Fredericksburg. Robertson changed the battle's course by locating some of Robert E. Lee's troops in the wrong place via an inkblot, but he soon corrected the error.

The two Price brothers, Tom and Channing, seemed worlds apart. With the resignation of Maj. J. T. W. Hairston, Channing found himself in the adjutant general's department. His work load was increased when the general's other adjutant, Maj. Norman R. FitzHugh, took a furlough. Only a lieutenant and aide-de-camp, Channing wondered about his prospects of assuming Hairston's rank and position while at the same time envying his elder brother's luck in obtaining yet another leave. For Tom, the war continued to be an immense inconvenience. Channing recognized that his brother was bored and lacked enough work to keep him busy. But

Tom was also beginning to add entries into his diary that went beyond the frustration of being bored. He was becoming critical of his commanding officer—a situation that was soon to cause him embarrassment and regret.

John Esten Cooke managed at last to get the furlough he wanted and returned to headquarters refreshed and a little richer. His writing was selling, and he was enjoying himself. His comments on his fellow officers revealed the closeness that Stuart wanted to see among his staff. Cooke's and von Borcke's reconciliation seemed to please the young ordnance officer greatly.

From Thomas R. Price's Diary

March 1— ★ ★ ★ News received to-day that the railroad bridge over the North Anna has been washed away. All communication with Richmond has been thus cut off.

March 2—Rode in afternoon with——— [name not given] to Gen. R. E. Lee's headquarters. His quarters not more comfortable than our own— he's on the main road near the Telegraph Road—pitched in a little grove of pine saplings and half buried in the mud. A host of negro servants in his camp, washing, cooking, tending the horses, etc.

March 4—Gen. Stuart called me into his tent this evening and asked me if I had nothing better than the <u>Fairy Queen</u> to pass my evenings— offered me thereupon the use of Jomini's <u>Practice of War</u>, and a translation of an article on last Summer's campaign by the Prince de Joinville. The latter I had previously read whilst in London. ★ ★ ★ His style is clear and graphic, but his opinions are hopelessly biased and incorrect. ★ ★ ★ Gen. Stuart was with us and prattled on all the evening in his garrulous way— described how he commenced the war by capturing 50 of Patterson's advance guard on the day preceding Bull Run.

Hd. Qrs. Cav. Division
Mar. 2nd 1863

Dear Mother [Mrs. Thomas Randolph Price Sr.],

I have been rather neglectful of you I fear since I last left home. I intended to write by Maj. Hairston, but as Thomas was to come up the day the Major left I waited until he arrived: yesterday the train did not come up, a bridge having washed away, and I waited until to-day, when things are working straight again.

We have been having awful weather lately, but to-day is beautiful & bright enough to reconcile us to a good deal of bad weather.

Thomas got up in good time Friday as I had a horse to meet him & a boy to take charge of his baggage in a wagon. I have not seen a great deal of him, but I believe he is getting on as well as might be expected: the life must be a great bore to him, as besides the change from his former habits & pursuits, he has not enough work to amuse him.

I am at last regularly installed in the Adjt. Genl's office, Major FitzHugh having obtained a leave of absence for 30 days: he has not yet started, but since Friday I have been duly in charge of the office, the Major having been on a trip up the river to properly post a regiment which has just relieved Col. Wickham from picket duty above Fredericksburg. I am getting used to the harness, as I have had some experience in it before. One of the A. A. Generals on the staff tendered his resignation yesterday (Major J. T. W. Hairston) on account of ill health he states: it was approved by Gen. Stuart & I suppose will be accepted.[60] The General was talking on in a loose way yesterday to me when I went in to his tent on some business connected with the office, & asked me whom he should put in Hairston's place: this is a habit he has & generally I make no answer or some commonplace one, as I think he does not expect one, but gives utterance to his thoughts.

Now without having hinted anything to me on the subject, I merely ask you the question, how would you like to see me with a star of the A. G. Dept. on my coat? Would you rather have me as I am—1st Lieut. & Aide-de-Camp? This is all by way of digression however & must go no further than yourself.

The General was away a good part of last week at the United States Ford & staying at Maj. FitzHugh's at night:[61] he came from Gen. Lee's one afternoon in a great bustle, having just heard that the Yankee pickets at the fords above Fredericksburg had been entirely withdrawn: he started Major FitzHugh directly to United States Ford to send the squadron on picket there over the river to reconnoiter & I wrote a telegram & started a courier with a letter to Gen. Fitz Lee at Culpeper C. H. to start the next morning with his available force & cross the River, come down and see what had become of the Yankees: Gen. Stuart went off early next morning with part of his staff, leaving me in charge of Hd. Qrs. He remained up at Maj. FitzHugh's until after Gen. Lee's brilliant dash into the Yankee Cavalry: he wished to go over & meet Gen. Lee, but being uncertain as to when he would come, and remembering Vidiersville [Verdiersville] last summer, prudently remained on this side.

Gen. Lee's report states that he had only 400 men & with this force he attacked a cavalry force double or treble his own, and drove them back to their infantry line within 5 miles of Falmouth, killing & wounding a large number and taking 150 prisoners, with their horses & outfit complete. His loss was 14 killed, wounded & missing, the surgeon (Dr. Davis) of Col.

Munford's Regt. & a Lieut. in the same being the only 2 killed or mortally wounded rather & left in enemy's hands.[62]

John Fontaine is back with the brigade I notice by his name signed to some papers coming to this office; where is Lizzie now?[63] Majors Von Borcke & Pelham have been expected back for some days past with their attendants & horses, as I wrote a note to Major Von B. last week directing him to return. The river being too high to ford must be the reason I expect.

Gen. Stuart is hard at work upon his reports, being now I believe only as far as Manassas 1862. You can imagine what a labor it is this length of time to do justice to the subject.

I got a letter a few nights since from Capt. [Benjamin S.] White written at Culpeper C. H. just before he left for Loudoun, which made the mouths of our mess water and I expect would do the same in Richmond: it was to the effect that he had there (Culpeper) for us awaiting some safe chance to send, 50 lbs. butter, 80 lbs. bacon hams & 47 doz. eggs. Just to think of all this being there for us & we living on beef & bread for want of transportation for them. I hope in a day or so to make arrangements to get them.

Isn't my jacket ready? I am wearing my overcoat for the want of a jacket, as I am writing nearly all day & the light cuffs of my dress coat do not suit that very well. My old jacket is rolled up in my blanket on my saddle, as I neglected to take it out when I went from Culpeper to Richmond.

Is Nannie [Price] still with you? Tell Nannie that the General has heard of her & says that will not do. Ask her not to forget that she is in my debt for one letter, and I will try at least to answer her letters & those from home, though I have not a great deal of time to correspond.

If you have a chance, please send me some stamps, as they are hard to get up here. Thomas & the General send love. It is just before dark & I can hardly see to write. so good-bye.

From your devoted son

Channing

━•━≍◆≍━•━

Head Qr's. Cavalry
Division
March 3rd '63

Dear Pa [Wyndham Robertson],

I am once more safely ensconced in a tent as a member of the Army, and the consciousness of being once more on duty in the field brings with it a pleasure even greater than I had anticipated and for the first time in 16 months I feel comparatively happy. The position I have is not such as I should choose or prefer, but I can already see and understand its duties sufficiently to consider myself competent with steady application and practice, to fulfill them. My only fear is that my health will give way, though I shall spare no precautions to prevent it.

I find Mr. B. [Blackford] much more comfortably fixed than I had supposed and our bed is equal to any hair mattress. I superintended the making of it immediately on my arrival, and think it worth describing. We have first a long pen made airtight with mud and just wide enough for two,—in the pen we placed a layer of thick pine logs—then a layer of pine bushes—next one of straw and finally our beds and blankets.

Gen. Stuart received me very cordially and remarked how glad he was at last to have me on his staff. I thought from what he said, that he got me the position more as a means of getting me on his staff than for any assistance I might give the Engineer Corps.

Tom Price is here in the same department as myself, though ranking as a first lieutenant. He seems to know very little more about it than myself.

Mr. B. & myself rode over yesterday to see Cousin Mary Guest, who lives only about four miles from here. We found Cousin Helen & Cousin Eliza Semmes both there tho' the latter was to leave for Richmond to day. Cousin Mary was very well, but terribly distressed.

I think you had better send at once for my horses as the Spring Campaign will soon commence and I could not then do without them. Mr. Blackford is, I am sure, perfectly willing to let me use one of his as long as he can possibly get along without, but Comet is still suffering terribly with his wound and almost useless, and both the others are too miserably poor to stand hard riding without relief. I find nearly all the staff officers have two horses and they say it is impossible to accompany the Gen. on his expeditions without them. Sam will perhaps be best suited to bring them and I want Miranda and either Brenda, Bostona or Kate's mare as you choose.[64] Bostona would probably be best spared, as the other two are ladies horses and pretty good matches besides.

If you cannot get transportation in the cars I think Davidson had best try and get a pack saddle from the Quartermaster in Abingdon, or have one made and send about two hundred pounds of corn along with them. He will find it impossible to get corn along the latter part of his journey. Mr. B. thinks he had better start with only enough to do him to Lynchburg and then buy sufficient to bring him here. He says he will write to his Father, so that if Sam finds any difficulty in getting it [in Lynchburg], he can apply to him—he also thinks he had better rest there a day or two. He need bring only one halter and one old bridle and saddle for himself.

Mr. B. is very anxious to buy ——— [name of horse illegible], & desired me to ask that he may have the refusal of her, in case you think of selling—he also wishes to buy a good work horse for his wagon if you can spare one. Mr. B. has been suffering considerably with a bad cold: but is better. He sends his love to all. Give my love to all & believe me

Your affec. son, Frank

Tell Kate to write.

Please send at once for the horses, or let me know what other plan would suit better.

━━ ✠ ━━

HeadQuarters
Cavalry Division
March 7th 1863

Dear Pa [Wyndham Robertson],

I wrote to you last Tuesday asking you to send at once for my horses, but having heard nothing from you since, I fear my letter miscarried. I did not wait as long as you suggested because I found Mr. Blackford's horses in such a condition as to render it almost impossible for him to spare me the use of one. Comet is almost worthless from his wound and the other two are mere skin and bones and would require constant relief in a march. I will therefore need my horses as soon as they can be brought down [from Abingdon]. It is thought here the Gen. will soon be on the move and if he does before I get my horses, I don't know how I shall manage.

I want Miranda and any other you may deem suitable—perhaps Kate's mare or one of the Sorrels. Sam or Ben either would suit me & it would be better to bring corn along with them as I hear it is impossible to get it along the road—a bag might also be shipped to Lynchburg for the latter part of the journey.

I wrote Davidson several days since instructing him what to do in case you sent for the horses.

So far I have been perfectly well and if we remain in our present camp a few weeks longer, have little doubt of remaining so. I spend the nights as warm and comfortably as if at home and as long as that continues, have little fear of being knocked up again.

Mr. B. [Blackford] has had me busy on a map of the Battle of Fredericksburg for the last few days and I succeed much better than I anticipated. I however wound up with a huge red blot to day while designating the position of troops, making it appear as if Gen. Lee had massed about half his army in a very safe out-of-the-way place.

Mr Blackford & myself rode over to tea at Mr. Guest's yesterday evening. Cousin Helen had left for Gay Mont the day before, but a Mrs. White was staying with Cousin Mary.

Give my love to Kate and tell her she might have written—ask her to get me three or four large silk handkerchiefs if she can find them, & have them by the time I come down. Please write and let me know if you have sent for the horses & believe me

> Your affec. son
> Frank

Mr. Blackford sends his love to Sister & says he will write to morrow.

From John Esten Cooke's Journal

> Camp "No Camp"

March 8, 1863—Just returned from Richmond. I went on Tuesday the 23rd Feb.

Spent nearly two days with Sal, and about the same in Amelia. Made arrangement with Ayers for 10 ——— [word illegible] and sold " ———" [name illegible].

Went to see Gen. R. [George W. Randolph] He says, "The ——— is an arbitrary man: not a usurper but a tyrant; ruling despotically, that is, in his limits. Loving the consciousness of power—not ostentation. Irresolute, impractical, unable to see that some decision is better than none; of large views, but not magnanimous. Devout from his afflictions. Bitter in prejudices, unforgiving in temper. Lamenting yet that he was not appointed commander in chief—would have proved an immense failure. Faithful to his friends, and faithful to his enemies."

It is true of him.

Came back, and have been a little blue. The Gen. [Stuart] came and chatted with me. He is charming when he throws off business. He says of little Flora's death, "I shall never get over it. It is irreparable." Never spoke of it before but once, to me.

Staff gay and good fellows. I believe I have some. Von's away. Maj. V. B. [von Borcke] came and proposed to "make up"—I told him, willingly and shook hands.

I found a warm welcome in Amelia, and everywhere. My friends are kind indeed—but [Brig. Gen. Robert H.] Milroy![65] Oh! to go after that thief and assassin! But we will soon.

The war grows in bitterness and looms larger and darker. So be it. I for one intend to die fighting them, if necessary. It is better than having my neck under a blackguard's heel.

Camp "No Camp" still exists. When will we move.

"Tarra—tarra—tatata! There is tattoo.

━━━ ☷✦☷ ━━━

Hd. Qrs.
Cavalry Division
Army of Nor Va
Mar. 9, 1863

Dear Mother [Mrs. Thomas Randolph Price Sr.],

Alas for having made myself somewhat useful to the General! But for it I might perhaps steal a short visit to you to-day, as the General goes through Richmond on his way to Culpeper C. H. as a witness in the case of Lt. Col. [Henry C.] Pate before the court martial there.[66] However it is no use talking as I am hard at it in the department which is to be my sphere of operations until the war closes, I suppose.

The General asked me if you knew anything of an expected change in my position and rank, and I told him what you wrote me about Mrs. Stuart's letter: however agreeable it might be to surprise you, yet as Thomas goes down to-morrow, you will hear it & I might as well tell you myself: on the 4th March late in the evening, just before I closed business for the day, Genl Stuart came to my door & sent in by my orderly a paper which to my great surprise was an application for my appointment as Major in the Adjutant Genl's Dept., vice Major [J. T. W.] Hairston's resigned, to take rank from Mar. 1st. In some respects I would have preferred his waiting some time (2 or 3 weeks) to give me a fair trial in my new duties, so that hereafter in case of my not suiting him, he might not say that he took me without a trial.

However I hope as you do that I may be guided aright. The duties are somewhat confining, but in this respect there will not be much change, as without some demand for my services I very rarely quit camp for exercise merely (as Thomas does) and now having something to do to keep me here, I will never leave Hd. Qrs. How I will like the position when the campaign opens and I have at night to swing my desk out of the wagon & sitting it in the woods go to writing, remains to be seen. However enough of this, as maybe my commission will not be granted and I will let you know if it is.

Thomas is a lucky fellow, having obtained another furlough for 8 days or at least Gen. Stuart approved it just now, which is equivalent to his getting it: I reckon he thinks it a hard state of society to have to ask any one for permission to go to a wedding, but what would he have done, had he gone into the ranks as he spoke of doing and had to apply again and again for the slightest favor, as I have done, without success: again I can tell him he is a lucky fellow, only having one man to please, (and that one Genl Stuart) and getting 2 or 3 furloughs in a month. What would I have not given for the privilege of only having to ask Gen. Stuart for a leave of absence during the long period on the Peninsula, when in vain I tried to get permission to visit home. Thomas goes down to-morrow.

The presents you sent by Major Von Borcke were very acceptable. I am afraid that our supply of hams, butter & eggs has been lost: Lieut. Hullihen who took them in charge from Culpeper C. H., by some inexcusable & unheard of neglect, did not even leave his seat to see them put on the cars, and of course they did not come. I telegraphed immediately to Mr. Ballard, thinking that if the boxes went back to the hotel, he would, on seeing my name to the telegram & being told that the boxes were valuable, take some measures to find out about them: I have heard nothing from him and as I asked him to send them, if found, to the store. I want you to have some inquiries made for us. The contents are valuable, both intrinsically and for the scarcity of such things in this country: they cost about 175 dollars in Culpeper & this loss of 50 dollars apiece to the mess is a bad business in addition to the vexation of losing them. If they are found please let me know as soon as possible.

The jacket you sent me suits me very well & I was glad to get it: our horses came back the day before & I got my old one.

This morning in accordance with orders of the General, all the wagons not necessary at Hd. Qrs. & all the poor horses that could be spared were started to camp in Albermarle to recruit. I sent my little bay horse & got a very reliable & obliging boy (one of our couriers) to take care of him for me. I hope thus to have a good horse when the campaign opens, and the horses left here will fare better, getting just as much hay as the whole establishment did.

The General just called me to get my horse ready to accompany him as far as Gen. Lee's to receive what instructions may be needed to enable me to discharge business in his absence & I must close.

With my best love to all I remain your devoted son

R. Channing Price

From John Esten Cooke's Journal

Camp "No Camp"

March 10, 1863—Yesterday wrote out and out "How I was arrested"— 25 pages. It is good enough. Steve Dandridge came and dined with me— and friends dropped in. The Gen. went to Culpepper [Culpeper] via Richmond. Talked a good deal with him, and he read me a letter to Paul Hayne in answer to Paul's rending "Stuart" in which he nudged Paul about not being a soldier.[67] "That's Stuart's way." He said Genl. [Philip St. George] Cooke did try to catch him on the Chickahominy—I don't believe it. Burnet

near Cold Harbor told somebody who told Cousin Betty that when the
order to pursue Stuart reached him his hand trembled so he could not read
it—had to hand it to an aid; then that he got his men in the saddle slowly,
and next sat his dinner leisurely. I am <u>sure</u> he knew who the forager was,
and didn't <u>want</u> to find him. I told the Gen. so, but he disagreed. "Gen.
Cooke was a man who would do his duty up to the handle!" Granted but
he was a poor cavalry officer if he couldn't find the backs of 1500 cavalry
in a big road, and catch them ten miles off in 12 hours!

The Gen. says he was devoted to Gen. C. [Cooke] and he to him
"before the war." Seems to think less bitterly of him.

Likes my poem—has heard it praised, for its accuracy—"the honest face
of Hood!" Thanks Mon Generàl! He has made Fitz [Maj. Norman R.
FitzHugh] Q. M. I told him it was a cruel joke and he a rough joker.

I am about to start some thing else. Letter yesterday from Natty. Curses
on that thief and assassin Milroy: I think of the Valley constantly. God guard
them!

Last night to see the Alsops, but the ladies away. Farley and myself went
over, and returned early. Snow and rain today. When will the enemy advance. Let them try it here and they will have a good time of it.

*The war erupted in full fury on the seventeenth. Early in the morning, Brig. Gen.
William W. Averell led 2,100 Federal cavalry troops across the Rappahannock at
Kelly's Ford looking for a fight.*[68] *He found one. Met by Fitz Lee's brigade of 800
men about half a mile from the ford, the Federals at first forced back the gray cavalry.
But Lee managed to halt Averell's advance by charging the Federal line with all of
his available men. The gamble paid off; when Lee's regiments were repulsed, Averell
did not counterattack but assumed a defensive posture. Then at 5:30 P.M., Averell
withdrew. Despite his superiority in numbers, he had gone barely two miles from the
ford. Though the Federal cavalrymen had fought as hard as their Confederate counterparts, their leadership was inferior. The Confederate victory was purchased at a
high price, however. Averell counted his killed, wounded, and missing at 78; Lee
reported 133 casualties. Among them were Maj. John W. Puller of the 5th Virginia, who was killed, and Col. Thomas L. Rosser of the same regiment, who was
wounded.*[69]

*Stuart, who had been in Culpeper when the fighting began, hurried to the scene.
He did not supersede Lee in command, but instead lent his support where needed.
Only a few of his staff were with him. Majors Lewis F. Terrell and John Pelham,
along with volunteer aide Capt. Harry Gilmor, made their way toward the battle-
field, Pelham and Gilmor accompanying Stuart. Terrell fought with the guns of Capt.
James Breathed's horse artillery battery, and for a time Pelham was there too. Then
Pelham left the battery to cheer on a charging regiment and disappeared into the smoke*

and confusion of the fight. Suddenly Pelham was down on the ground. A shell had exploded above him, and a piece of it had struck him in the back of the head. Thought to be dead, Pelham was thrown over the back of a horse and walked slowly back toward Culpeper. Along the way it was discovered that he was still alive. The gallant artilleryman was taken to the home of Judge Henry Shackelford, where he died a little after midnight on the eighteenth.[70]

The days leading up to the clash at Kelly's Ford saw little going on at Camp "No Camp." In a letter to his sister, Kate, Frank Robertson again pleaded for his horses, though the lack of them did not keep him from visiting Fredericksburg to see the effects of the battle. Having finished his map, he had some time on his hands to see the sights around cavalry headquarters. Cooke, the ordnance officer, lounged around camp smoking and writing as the spirit moved him. Stuart was gone from camp, and with him had gone much of its atmosphere.

On the day of the battle, Philip H. Powers penned a letter to his wife expressing concern for her safety and regret that he had not brought her with him. He was still with his brother, James, and worried lest the conscript officers scoop him up. He intended to return to Stuart as soon as James was better.

Away on furlough, Tom Price knew nothing of the fight, though he saw the turmoil caused by the rumors of a Federal raid while he waited to catch a train back to cavalry headquarters. Amid the confusion at the station, he caught a glimpse of Robert E. Lee trying to calm the crowd.

In the wake of Kelly's Ford, Channing Price wrote to his mother, telling her all he knew of Pelham's death. He expressed, as did Cooke in his diary, his sense of loss at the passing of a gallant and accomplished officer and a close and beloved friend. Sadly he placed his name at the bottom of Stuart's General Orders No. 9.

HeadQuarters
Cavalry Division
Friday March 13th 1863

Dear Kate [Robertson],

Your long expected letter reached me today. I really began to be seriously alarmed lest your obdurate and most susceptible heart had at last succumbed to Loves keen shaft. I could not imagine what else but a severe case of smite could so long withhold your scribbling propensities, and to be candid, I still believe that something of that sort has happened. Who can it be? I am sure you will tell me, for unless it is our big cousin, I am at a loss to guess and he is or was engaged a few months ago however.

I have been hard at work (that is, in comparison with the other members of the staff) for the past week on a Map of the Battle of Fredericksburg and much to my delight, put on the finishing touches this evening. I consider it quite a masterpiece and am quite anxious to have a display of it. I am thinking seriously of riding over to Gen. Lee's HeadQuarters in the morning and showing it to him. I am confident that if he is a man of taste as reported, he would make me a Col. of Engrs. without delay. I promised to send Lou Johnston my first attempt at a map, but unfortunately I succeeded so well that Mr. Blackford refused to part with it.

Were the Mr. & Miss Dooley's the same we saw at ———— [name illegible]—if so, I sympathize most heartily with their companions. I suppose Dooley the younger contemplates creating a sensation as he carries his toothbrush.

Mr. Blackford and myself rode down to Fredericksburg yesterday it was my first visit there and I find the town even more shattered than I had anticipated. Some of the houses were mere wrecks and I suppose there were fifty that would average 50 cannon shots apiece. We rode along the bank of the river for about half a mile and had a fine view of the Yankee sentinels on the other side about 100 yards off. One of them called and asked Mr. B. if he had paid for that coat (his Yankee overcoat). Mr. B. told him, Yes, he had bought it with a bullet. Talking has been prohibited, but is still carried on to some extent. From Lee's Hill we had a magnificent view of the whole Yankee camp—with Mr. B.'s field glass, we could see accurately everything that was going on—in one place we saw an eight horse battery drilling and in another several squadrons of cavalry, and so distinctly as to distinguish the colors of the horses and the white spots about them. With the naked eye they appeared to be dark masses moving about, with no distinguishable features to denote their nature. On our way back we called to see Cousin Mary Guest.

Pa, and not Kate, to what point he obtained transportation for my horses or when they are likely to arrive—please find out & let me know at once. If they are to come to Richmond I may come down & send up what I require ———— [word illegible] by them. Also let me know when the Miss Prestons are to stay with you. Enclosed I send a ———— [word illegible] for you to fit a watch key to, I broke mine a day or two after getting here.

My love to Ma and tell her I should like to have some dried fruit if she can have some sent from home. We have nothing in the world but beef and flour for rations and something in the way of vegetables would be very acceptable. Did you get the handkerchiefs for me? Ask Cousin William if he saved some cloth. Send your letters by hand whenever possible as there is great uncertainty in the mail. Give my love to all & tell Ma I will answer her long letter soon

Your affec. brother
F. S. Robertson

P. S. The rheumatism seems to have taken quite an aversion to camp life & much to my surprise as well as delight seems to have permanently deserted me—as I have not felt his presence for a week.

From John Esten Cooke's Journal

Camp "No Camp"

March 15, 1863—This afternoon went to the funeral of poor old Mrs. French. She was a most exemplary Christian and is a Saint in heaven. They buried her near the house—to be removed here after—and we all walked to the grave. She was kind to me when I was sick. God rest her!

On the 11th wrote "Three Bands of my acquaintance." On 13th "A Walk through the Broom" for News. Tomorrow I will write "Hang him on that tree."

Memo. Howard says of Jennings Wise "His was the strongest, the most direct, the most brilliant and lucid talk, I ever heard in a young man."

Nothing doing much. The first thunder and hail storm of the season is now raging around my tent. Day follows day here, without much difference. This is my routine.

Wake about 8—find my fire burning and boots, cleaned with real Day & Martin, setting by it. Dress leisurely, gazing into the fire with one boot on or cravat in hand—an old weakness, this. Finish, and reading my bible [*sic*]. Then say my prayers. Then if breakfast isn't ready, read a novel or paper or anything.

'Lige then rushes in violently with a coffee pot—breakfast follows—of steak and biscuits nearly invariably: a strong cup of coffee—no molasses now—and I commence the real business of the day, and charm of life, smoking and reading something.

This over I go to writing and write away till three of four—or I don't write. I ride out, to Col. Baldwin's, or elsewhere, and come back, and smoke and lounge in the tents till toward dark when dinner is ready—pretty much the same—a little stewed fruit being the sole addition.

After dinner, smoke, smoke—chat chat—or read read! voila ma vie!— The storm rages and I must smoke!

━━ ▆◆▆ ━━

Camp near
Fredericksburg
March 17th 1863

My Dearest Wife [Mrs. Roberta Powers]—

Nearly a month has elapsed since I last wrote and every day since I have hoped to get some tidings of you. But alas not a word, not a line can I receive until the heart has indeed become sick with a long deferred hope. I should feel this more sensibly, but that every one I have seen in the army from Clarke [County] or Jefferson [County] tell me, they hear from home from time to time. And as no bad tidings of you come through this source, I argue that you are at least as well off as your neighbors. Still, it is a source of unnecessary anxiety and uneasiness that I cannot hear from you personally. I know my love it is no fault of yours and fully appreciate your dependence upon those who either cannot or do not know what it is to be separated for months from wife and children and confined to the monotony of a camp in winter quarters. If you would put your letters in the hands of those having friends in the Clarke Cavalry, they could be sent out and thus mailed to Richmond. Harry Bird told me he heard from his family repeatedly in that way. And Mr. Nunn tells me he frequently gets letters out. One of the Randolphs went home a few weeks ago. Staid [*sic*] two days but he could tell me nothing from our end of the county. I would attempt to run in myself, but Milroy is represented as being such a tyrant that I should fear the consequences of falling into his hands just at this time.

I must wait and bear. Sometimes I regret not having brought you away with me. Though how you could have subsisted at the present prices of everything God only knows. A major's pay would not pay your board. Flour sells in R. [Richmond] for $35 per Bll [barrel]. Bacon $1.25. Beef $1—& everything in like proportions.

I sincerely trust you are not molested by the Yankees, and are enabled to provide yourself with such comforts as you need. If there are any goods in the County do not fail to lay in a supply for me. Such as flannel, cloth for pants & coat—Hat—etc. And get Sinclair or Kable to make me a good pair of boots. Store them away—events will very probably enable me to get home before many months. They say we must have a fight here in a few weeks, and then perhaps we may clear the Valley once more. It is evident that the war will rage this Spring with greater fury than ever. May God enable our Armies to successfully resist the hordes of Vandals now being thrown against us! If we can only hold out the Campaign—all will be well.

Brother James returned from Lexington a few days ago. Whither he had gone to take Ellie—they having been in Richmond several weeks.[71] I regret to have to tell you that her health has failed to such an extent that reason has been dethroned—And she is perhaps by this time at the Asylum, under Dr. Stribling's treatment. Poor Jim! he returned perfectly miserable. He never apprehended such a sad result from her continued bad health. And was of course shocked beyond degree at her mental aberration—Doubtless her case has been aggravated by long and continued separation from him. Let us pray and trust that she may be splendidly restored.

I had intended leaving here as soon as he returned and joining the Cavalry, but I could not leave him under such a trial and consented to remain during this month—provided the Conscript Officers permitted me as I am not regularly enrolled and they have been taking up all resigned Officers of late. And enrolling them in the ranks. When I do leave here, I shall attach my self to Genl. Stuart again, and serve in the Q. M. department in some capacity. I can't stand the ranks—And besides, from much experience can render better service in some Staff Office.

All were well in Richmond when last heard from. Mildred has another son.[72]

With much love to all and many caresses for my little children whom I am longing to have in my arms more—I am, My own beloved wife

As ever
Yours
P. H. P.

❖

Hd, Qrs. Cavalry
Division
18 March 1863

Dear Mother [Mrs. Thomas Randolph Price Sr.],

I have just time to write a few lines to give you some sad news: heavy firing was heard all day yesterday up the river & as we had heard that the Yankee cavalry in large force had gone up the river, we supposed that they had attempted a crossing & had been met by Fitz Lee.

About 4 o'clock this morning Gen. Chilton sent me a letter for Gen. W. H. F. Lee which I forwarded in haste: soon after day I rode over to Gen. Lee's Hd. Qrs. & saw all the telegrams received during the night from Gen. Stuart: the Yankees crossed at Kelly's ford and were met by Gens. Stuart & Fitz Lee with part of the latter's brigade: they were repulsed with heavy loss at dark, but poor Pelham was killed.

Most of the staff have just started to the General, but I shall wait for further news. Don't be alarmed though, I think it is all over now for the present. I have no more time. I am sending a horse for Thomas.

Good-bye. Your devoted son

Channing

From Thomas R. Price's Diary

March 18—(In Richmond.) Arose before day and hurried up to the station—found there a great crowd and intense excitement. The trains had been seized by military authority, and I despaired at first of finding means of going. Gen. R. E. Lee was there in person directing the movements of troops. I heard a thousand rumors of a Yankee raid to Gordonsville and of an impending fight near Fredericksburg. ★ ★

━•━ ☰✦☷ ━•━

Headquarters
Cavalry Division,
Army Northern Va.,
March 20, 1863.

General Orders
No. 9

The Major General Commanding approaches with reluctance the painful duty of announcing to the Division its irreparable loss in the death of Major John Pelham, commanding the Horse Artillery.

He fell mortally wounded in the battle of Kellysville, (March 17th,) with the battle cry on his lips, and the light of victory beaming from his eye.

To you, his comrades, it is needless to dwell upon what you have so often witnessed—his prowess in action—already proverbial. You well know how, though young in years—a mere stripling in appearance—remarkable for his genuine modesty of deportment—he yet disclosed on the battlefield the conduct of a veteran, and displayed, in his handsome person, the most imperturbable coolness in danger.

His eye had glanced over every battle-field of this army, from the first Manassas to the moment of his death, and he was, with a single exception, a brilliant actor in all.

The memory of 'THE GALLANT PELHAM,' his many manly virtues, his noble nature and purity of character, is enshrined as a sacred legacy in the hearts of all who knew him.

His record has been bright and spotless; his career brilliant and successful.

He fell—the noblest of sacrifices—on the altar of his country, to whose glorious service he had dedicated his life from the beginning of the war.

In token of respect for his cherished memory, the Horse Artillery and Division Staff will wear the military badge of mourning for thirty days—and the senior officer of Staff, Major Von Borcke, will place his remains in the possession of his bereaved family—to whom is tendered in behalf of the Division the assurance of heartfelt sympathy in this deep tribulation.

In mourning his departure from his accustomed post of honor on the field, let us strive to imitate his virtues, and trust that what is loss to us, may be more than gain to him.

By command of Major General J. E. B. Stuart,

R. Channing Price,

Major and A.A.G.[73]

From John Esten Cooke's Journal

Camp "No Camp"

March 20, 1863—I have not had the heart to continue this journal from day to day. Poor Pelham is dead—killed in that terrific fight in Culpepper [Culpeper]. It cast a shadow over me which I could not dispel, and is a mournful thought still. He was a brave noble fellow, and I had learned to love him. So we pass.

The Gen. has not returned, and I have been working hard to add to the "Outlines," staying all day in my tent. Poor old Mrs. French died some days since. I went to her funeral; and that with a visit to Col. Baldwin, and an evening spent at Mrs. Alsop's is about the extent of my stirring out. I have been hurrying up my sketches as I soon expect to be in the saddle again. God only knows whether I shall survive, also, for the war grows desperate—and I might as well write out these things. But this is blue talk— and I'll stop it. Still Esperance!

◦—◦ ☰◊☰ ◦—◦

Hd. Qrs. Cav. Division

21 March 1863

Dear Mother [Mrs. Thomas Randolph Price Sr.],

Less than the usual interval has elapsed since my last letter & in that time Thomas has written home, but this evening, as I have nothing to do & feel like writing, I will scratch off a few lines to you.

I wrote a short note on Wednesday morning, which I suppose you received. I am still very anxious to hear our list of casualties, fearing that a good many friends in the brigade have fallen: I have received several communications from Genl Stuart & Genl Fitz Lee since the fight, but not a word as to the loss etc. on our side. Col. [Thomas L.] Rosser, I was sorry to see this morning through John Fontaine's application for a 60 days leave for him, is very badly & painfully wounded in the foot, the ball having lodged among the small bones etc. and has not been extracted. Peter Fontaine too (Adjt. of the 4th) is severely wounded in the neck by a rifle shot & 40 days is asked for him.[74] I hope sincerely that they may be spared, as both are good soldiers & officers & Col. Rosser's loss would be felt as much as any man's I know of in the Division.

I hoped the General would have come to-day, as a telegram reached here last night from Culpeper C. H. to him, which would seem to imply that he had left that place: as yet though he has not arrived, and we have not had any mail to-day, as the train if it came at all, was late: we only got yesterday's mail & papers to-day.

It is very dull & quiet at Hd. Qrs., only Capt. White, Chiswell, Thomas, Capt. Cooke, Frank Robertson & myself being here, and over us all, in spite of the hard-heartedness which war produces, a feeling of gloom is hanging, caused by the loss of one to whom all were so much attached. One of Genl Stuart's couriers who was with him during the fight, got back yesterday & from him I have all that I know of poor Pelham's death.

[Joseph L.] Minghini, soon after the fight commenced, went back to Culpeper for the General & on rejoining him on the field was told that Major Pelham had been killed or wounded, & directed by the General to hunt him up & care for him: he does not know where or how he was wounded, but after some time found him, with some surgeons attending him: he was struck on the top of the head with a piece of shell, which went out about 2 inches from where it entered, crushing the skull. Minghini got an ambulance & took him to Mrs. [Henry] Shackelford's at Culpeper C. H. where he lived perfectly unconscious & kindly watched by the ladies (friends of the Major's) until 1 o'clock in the night, when he passed off quietly & without any suffering: Genl Stuart came into town about 2 o'clock, expecting somewhat that he was still alive & was dreadfully shocked to see his dead body.[75]

Thus has passed away a man, who with faults certainly, was one of the noblest specimens I ever had the pleasure of meeting with. How his place can be supplied is hard to say but I hope the General will be able to get some one worthy to succeed him.

I have not heard a word about my promotion but suppose, from what Thomas tells me, it is sure but slow. I am afraid I shall not be able to come down to see you shortly, as furloughs have been stopped & though I might get one possibly, yet I fear Genl Stuart would not spare me now.

Capt. White got back from Loudoun a few days since bringing a good deal of coffee, so that for a little while at least we shall live very well. I haven't got my tent yet & am occupying, with Thomas, Maj. FitzHugh's. Mine got lost or mislaid at the depot, but I hope to get it soon.

With my love to all & hoping soon to hear from some of you I remain yours devotedly

Channing

Stuart and the staff felt the loss of Pelham deeply, but the war did not allow them much time to grieve. A skirmish occurred at Selecman's Ford on the twenty-second and another near Dumfries on the twenty-ninth.[76] *Though not severe, the brief clashes indicated that both armies were awakening from their long winter's sleep. During this period, Stuart's staff continued mourning for Pelham while at the same time making preparations for the campaign season. Black armbands would soon cover part of the golden sleeve braid that adorned their uniforms.*

Tom Price had returned to camp but spent little time working and more time visiting with friends and Stuart. Brother Channing worried about his increasing work load, his need for an additional horse, his uniform being retailored to fit his new rank, who Pelham's successor might be, and the new aide-de-camp who would replace him. Unlike his brother, he seemed busy enough for three men.

Cooke used his abundant free time to produce several new pieces. The scouting adventures of his friend and fellow staff officer Capt. William D. Farley found their way into several of his short stories, though Farley was given the fictitious name of Darrell. He also wrote of Pelham, who would be sadly missed.

Frank Robertson considered an offer to return to his old infantry regiment as adjutant. He was still having difficulty in obtaining a good horse, and he considered buying Pelham's if it came up for sale. The spring thaw also brought him problems; his quarters were flooded even as he wrote to his father. That the army would soon be on the move was very evident to Robertson and the rest of the staff. Now if he and Channing could only get horses, they might be able to move with it.

From Thomas R. Price's Diary

March 22— ★ ★ ★ Rode to pay a visit to Oby Price. He is a private in the First howitzers, and his camp is not far from us in the pines back of the field where Gen. Stuart held his review of Fitzhugh Lee's brigade. Found him well, and surprisingly happy and content. I have not seen him since the day I sailed from New York for Europe. He was then a neat, dapper little gentleman, with a decided penchant for the dressing and comfortable living. Now, what a change—a broad-shouldered, black-bearded, coarsely-dressed man, used to hard living and privation. His transformation is almost as singular as my own. Both show strikingly the power of circumstances and foreign influences in molding the character and pursuits of men—he the neat, precise New York merchant, converted into the artilleryman. I the retired, bookish student of philology, into a cavalry officer.

March 25—Breakfasted by invitation with Gen. Stuart. We were alone, and he was especially kind and talkative. He recounted with glee a scene which passed with Mr. [James A.] Seddon on the General's recent visit to Richmond.[77] He had requested an audience with the Secretary and the usher announced him simply as Gen. Stuart, without initials. Mr. Seddon was seated at his desk and did not rise nor look up as the General entered the room. At last the General advanced and spoke. At the sound of his voice up bounced the Secretary, all confused, and stammered out that he had taken him to be the other Gen. Steuart [Brig. Gen. George H. Steuart], of Maryland.[78]

March 25— ⋆ ⋆ About dinner-time Stonewall Jackson came over to make a visit to the General. I went out to ride and met him going away in the road between headquarters and Mr. Garnett's. He was sweeping along at an easy gallop on a large handsome bay. Passed so quickly that I had not time to distinguish his features; nothing in him to recall the caricatures which popular veneration has delighted to make of the popular hero; handsomely dressed in ———— [word illegible] General's uniform—a jaunty cap, a full black beard and a fine horse; altogether a rather dazzling vision for one used to our slovenly headquarters.

March 28— ⋆ ⋆ ⋆ The talk increased of a speedy raid to Loudoun.

------ ≖⧫≖ ------

Hd. Qrs.
Cavalry Division
25 March 1863

Dear Mother [Mrs. Thomas Randolph Price Sr.],

I intended to have written to you on yesterday, but really had such a quantity of work (correspondence etc.) incident to the return of Genl Stuart, that I could not find the time. To-day too I have been very busy, but having nearly gotten matters to rights, will have less to do hereafter.

The General got back yesterday morning much to my joy, for it has been terribly dull in his absence. I got your letter & Eddy's & one for Thomas, besides the beautiful stars sent me by the General [Stuart]: these I want to have put on my new jacket which I have scarcely ever worn, but really don't know a lady in this neighborhood whom I could ask to fix it, and as I can't expect to go to Richmond soon, I shall have to get some bungling hand to do it for me.

I really don't feel nearly as much elated by my promotion as I expected, nothing like as much as when I was taken from the ranks & made A. D. C. [aide-de-camp], but it sounded rather strange to be greeted this morning in the office by my clerks etc. in rather a low voice (not being used to it) as Major: I think it has become known to the most of the Hd. Qrs. by the General calling in a loud voice several times to-day, when something required my attention, for Major Price: it was rather unexpected to most of the staff I think, as I had not mentioned my recommendation for promotion.

The General tells me that Papa says I must go up more, as there has been a major in the family before: tell him I have gone as high as I expect or care for, as there is scarcely a chance for more promotion on the staff & I am not fitted for and would not like a position in the Line: as I am well pleased & don't think that a position on Genl Lee's staff (certainly nothing else) would tempt me to exchange. I am fond of the General, have gotten used to him & understand his character pretty well & I think he likes me & values my services.

The General desires me to inform you, in order to your relief, that the big carpet bag got up safely with its contents. He spent a delightful day at Dundee he says, no one there but the family & then rode up on the engine (to the junction) called J. E. B. Stuart.

We are living quite well now, thanks to you & Capt. White: the latter brought us 12 lbs. of fine coffee from his last trip to Loudoun & we have the finest coffee I almost ever tasted. He brought a very valuable bundle to Mrs. Stuart, bought for her in Baltimore by a friend of the Genl's: among the articles are a splendid mourning dress (Reps silk) 3 or 4 pair of elegant gaiters & a great many little & useful things. The General got a beautiful present in the shape of an elegant gold pen with "To my knight" inscribed thereon: he has also lately received from Maryland a splendid cavalry sash.

General Jackson rode up a short while before I commenced writing & got up to the General's tent before meeting any one: there he met me & I had to look some time before I could find Gen'l Stuart & when I did t'was in Capt. White's tent & told him that Stonewall had surprised him once: he dined with the General & has just left: his Hd. Qrs. are only about 2 miles from us now, having been moved last week.

Your advice about Miss May & Gen. Lee's, in general, were received & I don't think you need have any apprehension for me on that score while the war lasts.

The cape you had made for me is beautiful & I am very much pleased with it. I expect, in fact know, that our transportation will be greatly reduced this spring, and should like to send some baggage home if possible before we move: my dress coat will have to be cleaned & altered on the collar & cuffs before I again wear it, and if possible I shall send it down & get you to have new buff put on & the stars & braids arranged. I should like of all things to pay a short visit home now, but there is no one here to take my place: the General told me yesterday in speaking of his difficulty in selecting an aide-de-camp, that he did not intend keeping me in the office, but to discharge pretty much my old duties was to be my work: he will appoint another Major & A. A. G. who will take charge of the office & be Chief of Staff & this he is troubled about also. Major FitzHugh is to be Qr.

Master & the new appointed takes his place (whoever he may be): Major [Robert F.] Beckham from Warrenton & of the old Army succeeds Pelham as Chief of Artillery: he is a fine young man & I am glad we shall have him here: he was a devoted friend of poor Pelham & has been heretofore on Genl G. W. Smith's staff.[79]

Tell Eddy that I appreciate most highly his pleasant letter & shall answer it: I want him to write again: tell him to try to write well, as it has been of great service to me thus far in life. Ask Ellen if she has forgotten her promise or whether Miss Nettie keeps her too busy about her books to let her have time to write to me. Thomas is out riding my sorrel & would send much love if he knew I was writing. The Genl sends love to all.

> Your devoted son
> R. Channing Price

From John Esten Cooke's Journal

> Camp "No Camp"

March 26, 1863—The Gen. came back yesterday and had a talk with him today—he wanted to show me his general order upon poor Pelham's death. It is very excellent: terse and eloquent: in a style which the Gen. is the best hand at, of any one I ever knew. His face flushed as he read it— poor Pelham!

Staid [sic] to dinner, and Gen. Jackson came in. He is now there, chatting. What a curious eye he has—as brilliant as a diamond! He is a hero.

Gen. S. [Stuart] says he has "three times gone to Culpepper [Culpeper] with his satchel and spy glass," expecting the enemy over. They will come soon.

Today writing the "Adventures of Capt. Darrell." Wrote nearly three of them. Letters from Sal and Maria Steger. 'Old Jack' said as I went out, "Is that the author?"

> Camp "No Camp"

March 29, '63—Dined with the Gen. Chat about many things—read me his verse on "Dundee," and yesterday on poor Pelham. He gave me my poor friend's saddle. Yesterday I wrote an obituary, which with the Gen.'s verses, and general order will appear in the "Sentinel." He sent it. I wrote an outline about P. [Pelham] for the News, but threw it out, to rewrite. Fitz [Maj. Norman R. FitzHugh] returned a day or two since well and merry—the best of fellows. Channing is Adt. [adjutant]—an excellent appointment. Another letter from Saidie Hunter and one from darling Nan, just like the rascal. Cursed Milroy! O to be after him. Today (Sunday) after reading my bible [sic]—old testament—came to the resolution to kill one

Yankee at least with my own hand if possible, before I am killed or the war over. I was thinking of —————— [word illegible]; and intend to do it. God forgive me if the resolution is wrong—they have "drawn a bead" on me, often; and I may on them.

I am writing away as though in the "little room festooned with roses!" Just read "Pelham"—good. But will soon be in the saddle I think: and then— Hey for the Valley!

God guide and bless and burden us. Still, Esperance!

[*Margin notation:* On the 27th Tom [Turner] left us to go and try his luck with Mosby. Good luck to him!]

——— ≕✦≕ ———

Hd. Qrs.
Cavalry Division
Army of Nor. Va.
30th March 1863

Dear Mother [Mrs. Thomas Randolph Price Sr.],

I was so hurried yesterday that I had no time to write as I intended: I hope you received my jacket & stars, as they tell me at Hd. Qrs. they can't recognize my new rank until I mount the stars. I have begun to think that I never will receive a letter from home, as day after day passes & none comes, but hope to hear to-day by Von Borcke.

Major FitzHugh is going down to-day to complete his preparations for his new post & also to move his family to Albemarle in a few days. I hope you will see something of Lieut. [William] Hoxton, who is one of the finest young men I know: he is from Alexandria, was in Williamsburg at College when the war began: his sister is the wife of Mr. Randolph, formerly minister in Fredericksburg & he himself is a devoted admirer I believe of Sallie Munford.

I paid a very pleasant visit with Thomas yesterday evening to Hugh Powell & Oby Price: they are quite comfortable & really as I recalled, while sitting with them, the many days spent by me in the same way, I thought I could go back to the ranks of such a company with great deal better spirits than I sometimes think I could: the great objection for me, after serving as staff officer, would be the almost utter ignorance of what is passing around them, whilst I in the duties of the staff, am into, if not the secrets, at least the general plans of battles etc.

The day set apart for fasting & prayer was generally observed in the army. Thomas I suppose gave you an account of how we spent it.

Major FitzHugh will see to getting crape for the members of the division staff, which in accordance with our own wishes & Genl Orders announcing the death, we are to wear for 30 days in memory of the noble Chief of Artillery. I declare, nothing has happened in the progress of the war which I have felt more keenly than his death: although, like myself, not very demonstrative, he was sincerely attached to me I think, & I loved him almost like a brother. His was a noble character: such generosity & unselfishness I never saw in any man before & his dauntless personal courage is proverbial through our young Confederacy. Had he been spared, another great battle would have made him a General I think. But it was otherwise ordained & we must bow humbly & submissively to the decree which robs us of a cherished & loved companion & the service of one of its bravest & most devoted defenders. His successor is a very fine young man & capable officer.

I got a letter from Alsop the other day in answer to one I wrote him, enclosing one from his brother in the 9th Cavalry: he seems to be very anxious about his family, which he hears is suffering for common necessaries of life & must continue to do so, should the Yankees occupy the country any length of time.

I am looking out for a fine horse, as my new rank occasions greater expenses, with an increase of pay of 27 dollars per month: my pay is now $162 per month commencing March 1st & I have to keep 3 horses. My Robertson horse will be in fine condition I hope by the spring campaign, as I hear the horses at Camp Cripple are doing very well: if I can get a good horse soon, my sorrel will do for Ephraim to ride, & I shall then have 2 fine horses to do staff duty with: I think too I shall manage better this summer than last & will take advantage of my opportunities by capturing a horse, which will enable me to keep one horse always in reserve.

The General has not yet selected his office Adjt. Gen'l & I am still at it, and the work has been pretty heavy recently. He has offered the position of Aide-de-Camp to a young man named [Robert H.] Goldsborough from Maryland, a private in a cavalry company serving as Gen. [Jubal A.] Early's escort: he has not heard from him, as the company has gone back into the interior to recruit the horses.[80] Goldsborough is the son of a great friend of the General's in Maryland & is I think a fine young man, from what I have seen of him. He will no doubt accept the offer, as it is a place not to be scorned,—A. D. C. to the Chief of Cavalry—

The General said he would like to have Thomas as his aid [*sic*] but for having me on his personal staff & besides he thought that the Engineer Dept. was the one for Thomas to rise in, with which I agreed. The General is a singular man & I don't think Thomas would fancy the position of aid long, having to place himself so completely at the beck & call of any one, as I did when I held the position.

Give my love to all & repeat my message to Ellen.

Your devoted son

R. Channing Price

◂━ ≍◆≍ ━▸

HdQuarters Cavalry Div.

March 31st 1863

Dear Pa [Wyndham Robertson],

From all I can learn in regard to the sale of Pelham's mare, I find it will be impossible to get her in less time than two weeks if at all, & it is even doubtful if she will be sold then. I think therefore & so does Mr. Blackford that you had better buy the sorrel we were looking at & send her up by Gilbert—by railroad if transportation can be had during his short stay—if not by land. If the mare is sold before this reaches you & none others are offered more suitable than those we were looking at, I would still prefer waiting a while & stand the chances of Buying one here.

Col. [Thomas S.] Garnett came up on the train with me & informed me that Gen. [John R.] Jones, who commands his brigade, had never had his commission confirmed & was at present under arrest on charges of cowardice etc. & would probably be cashiered, & he, as senior colonel of the brigade would stand a fair chance of succeeding to the command.[81] He desired me to decide as soon as practicable, as John M. Preston was very anxious to assume the command of his company & was only acting as adjutant until the vacancy could be filled.[82] The regiment goes on picket to day & remains three days, so I shall not go down until Thursday or Friday.

We are having a dreadful day of it & one side of our tent is completely flooded. Do as you think best about the horse & write me soon. My love to all & believe me

Your affectionate son,

Frank

APRIL

Except for John Mosby, who continued to give the Federals all they could handle in the no-man's-land between the two armies, things were quiet in early April. Part of the reason was that winter weather returned with a vengeance on the fourth and blanketed the landscape with snow. Nature once again brought the struggle to a halt even before it had really started. Except for Kelly's Ford, little had happened in the way of active campaigning. And the snow meant that for a time, at least, nothing would.

John Esten Cooke found it difficult to escape the memory of John Pelham's death. A visit to relatives triggered his recollection of his friend when they shared a story concerning Pelham, and his scripting of Pelham's biography kept the "Boy Major" fresh in his mind. The black armband he wore was an ever-present reminder. Pelham was gone yet seemed everywhere.

The Price brothers tented together but otherwise led different lives at Camp "No Camp." Thomas had few duties, but Channing felt inundated by more than the snow. His letter of the fifth did mention that his brother was to be employed at last, along with Frank Robertson, on a bridge-building expedition. Channing informed his mother of Thomas's mission with just a hint of gloating satisfaction. The younger brother had no pity for his older sibling. The mountains of work and his lack of hope over acquiring a furlough pushed Channing to the point where he even accused some of his fellow officers of being mere ornaments. In truth, comparing the young adjutant's work load to that of the rest of the staff, no other officer could challenge his claim to being the workhorse of cavalry headquarters.

From John Esten Cooke's Journal

Camp "No Camp"

Ap. 3, '63—Day before yesterday, rode down in the afternoon to "Hayfield" arriving as the sun was greeting, a ball of fire behind the woods. Had a pleasant evening with my little cousins, and they told me of poor Pelham's visit there with Gen. Lee. He got by the window leaning his head upon his hand, modestly, and when Gen. Lee alluded to him, blushed. Gen. Lee said,

"I have brought these great generals here for you to look at (Jackson and Stuart) but Maj. Pelham to look at you. He is ashamed tho' because he has on a borrowed overcoat."—Poor boy!—rather <u>hero</u>! The Gen. [Stuart] has given me his saddle and I shall cling to it.

Returned yesterday, and went to Mrs. Alsop's where she had the French rolls ready. A pleasant greeting—Miss Nannie prettier than I ever saw her, in her black dress, and white handkerchief around her throat <u>ala grandma</u>. Take care Joyeuse, my boy!

Today finished "Some Pipes I have Known"—18 pp. Pretty good. The Gen. down in Hanover. Wrote "The Ballad of Sir James" March 31st!

There is cannon down the river. What?

[*Margin notation*: Wrote today "The Gallant Pelham" 24 pp.]

Hd. Qrs. Cav. Division
Army of Nor. Va.
5 April 1863

Dear Mother [Mrs. Thomas Randolph Price Sr.],

This morning I was much pleased to see the General back & got from him your note & Ellen's candy. We have been having very disagreeable times for several days, cold & windy so that you couldn't keep fires on account of the smoke, and last night when it settled down into a regular snow-storm I almost despaired of seeing spring come. Major FitzHugh's tent in which Thomas & I are staying rocked & swayed a great deal & I should not have been surprised had it come down on us in the night.

Thomas & Frank Robertson were to have started this morning for Germanna Ford, and I was a good deal amused at Thomas this morning when he got up & saw what a quantity of snow had fallen: he thought I suppose that he had to go, & the prospect was by no means encouraging I confess. Capt. Blackford has been taken quite sick, & Capt. [Charles R.] Collins is to have charge of the work I believe.[83] I suppose Thomas will go to-morrow & we will be separated for 10 days or more.

I am very anxious to run down for a few days to see you, but don't see how I am to do it: there is not a soul here who has the slightest turn for this work & I don't know how the General could supply my place in my absence. Von Borcke & [Chiswell] Dabney do very well as ornamental members of the staff, but when it comes to working & assisting the General in the many ways necessary about Hd. Qrs., they are as useless as can be imagined: as a consequence, I have to do every thing & as John Fontaine expressed it the other day, I will have a hard time to do what FitzHugh & I together used to be kept busy at.

According to the Staff Bill now before Congress, the General will not be allowed another Major & A.A.G. [assistant adjutant general], but instead of it, another A.D.C. [aide-de-camp]. I am very willing if he wishes it to be his office man, but think it would be better for him & certainly for me, to keep me in my former work, at which I had become proficient & accustomed to his wishes, and to get some one else who could suit him as well as I do in the business department.

[Chiswell] Dabney started last Monday to pay a visit to Beaver Dam, being ordered by the General to make an inspection of the 10th Va, Cavalry (between here & Beaver Dam) & also to examine the condition of the roads.[84] He had not been gone long when John Fontaine arrived, from whom I learned that none of the family were at home & I could imagine Dabney's feelings when he got there. We had a great laugh over it on his return Wednesday night: after inspecting the regiment & spending one night at Mr. Waller's, he got to Col. Fontaine's Tuesday evening & found no one there: he says he was mad enough to have killed some body, but luckily did not. The Colonel got back the next morning, but Chiswell did not stay long with him, and starting home, got here that night.

The General showed me Ellen's picture to-day & he seems to think he is well fortified with her in one pocket & Nannie [Price] in the other.

I have not bought a horse yet, but am thinking of getting Major Pelham's little mare, whom I rode the other evening & was much pleased with.

Return my sincere thanks to Ellen for the candy & tell her not to forget about the letters.

General Stuart invited us all into his tent this evening to take cake & pies of which he brought a supply from Dundee: he also brought a fine cake to Thomas.

It is getting dark & I must stop. My jacket is very beautiful & suits me very well. Give my love to all & believe me yours devotedly

R. Channing Price

From Thomas R. Price's Diary

April 5— ★ ★ Capt. ——— [name not given] came over in the evening—was present at an interesting conversation between him and Gen. Stuart. Both agreed that the next attempt of the enemy to cross would be opposite the mouth of Mine River [U.S. Ford]. The General predicted that the next battle would be fought near Chancellorsville.

The thaw in both the weather and the war came quickly. On the fourteenth and fifteenth, the Federal cavalry made thrusts at Rappahannock Bridge and Kelly's, Welford's, and Beverly Fords. Maj. Gen. George Stoneman was under orders to make a raid in the rear of Robert E. Lee's army preparatory to the Federal army's crossing of the river.[85] *Brig. Gen. W. H. F. "Rooney" Lee's brigade, along with elements from Moorman's Battery of the horse artillery, opposed the crossings. Though the Confederate defense was spirited, it would not have been able to stop Stoneman's command of more than 10,000 men. But on the evening of the fourteenth, nature intervened to frustrate the Federal offensive in the form of heavy rain and an accompanying snow thaw, which caused the Rappahannock River to rise seven feet in just a few hours. The one Federal brigade that had managed to cross the river had to be withdrawn. Lee reported his casualties as five killed and three wounded. He succeeded in capturing one officer and twenty-four privates from those Union units that had crossed the river. Other Federal casualties were unrecorded.*[86]

Following these two days of hectic activity, Stuart settled down to watch the enemy across the river. He was aware of the presence of Federal infantry, but as it remained inactive, "there was nothing inconsistent with the supposition that their appearance was a feint."[87] Everything changed on the twenty-eighth, however, when the Federals crossed in force at Kelly's Ford. This, the first movement of what would eventually result in the Battle of Chancellorsville, was undertaken by Stoneman, who was again attempting to launch a raid into the Army of Northern Virginia's rear. The situation developed through the twenty-ninth and thirtieth, as Stoneman pushed south to the Rapidan. Fighting erupted at Germanna Ford on the Rapidan, where Maj. Charles Collins, Tom Price, and Frank Robertson had been stationed on their bridge-building mission. Stuart and his cavalry responded to both the Federal cavalry's raid and Robert E. Lee's need to know the whereabouts of the main body of Federal major general "Fighting Joe" Hooker's infantry. April drew to a close with many questions unanswered on both sides. The only thing everyone was sure of was that a major battle was imminent.

Camp "No Camp" had been dismantled on the ninth and headquarters reestablished at Culpeper Court House. The move was welcomed by some and regretted by others of the staff. Leaving the old camp with its easy access to hospitable neighbors was difficult for all. On the sixteenth, Channing Price wrote what was to be his last letter. He had managed to secure a short furlough home, and his return surprised brother Tom, who had not been aware of his absence. Channing recorded the events of the fifteenth and sixteenth as he viewed them. The narrow escape he and the rest of the staff had was a topic of not only his letter but also both Tom Price's and John Esten Cooke's diary entries. Cooke's thoughts still lingered on the loss of Pelham. His depression was somewhat lifted by the headquarters move, which brought him closer to some of his other relatives. In all three of the men's writings, there was an aura of expectation. Campaigning had begun; a battle was soon to be joined.

> Hd. Qrs.
> Cavalry Division
> near Culpeper C. H.
> April 16th 1863

Dear Mother [Mrs. Thomas Randolph Price Sr.],

I expect you have been very anxious about me and [I] really feel ashamed of myself for not having written to you since leaving home, but will try to make amends now.

The General, [Maj. Robert F.] Beckham & Von Borcke got on [the train] at Hanover C. H. and we had an uninteresting quiet trip to Gordonsville; from there to Orange C. H. I passed the time more pleasantly with Miss Pearce & Miss Lee, just from the Green Springs & going to Col. Willis' at Orange C. H. We got to Culpeper late in the afternoon and here separated, Von Borcke and I going to the Virginia House, the Genl & Beckham to friends in the town. My horse arrived that evening.

Next morning Fitz Lee's Brigade marched, following the 4th Va. which had gone the day before & in the afternoon W. H. F. Lee's Brigade arrived from Orange C. H. & camped near Culpeper. A little after eight Thomas arrived at the hotel & was much surprised to hear that I had been home since I last saw him.

Sunday I heard Mr. Cole preach to a very good congregation in the Episcopal Church. Genl Fitz Lee, John Fontaine etc. were in town Sunday & the [Lt. Col. Henry C.] Pate Ct. Martial has a special meeting Sunday night to examine Gen. [Fitz] Lee. Monday morning he left to join his brigade.

Our baggage having arrived by rail Sunday evening, we proceeded Monday morning to pitch our camp etc. in a very pretty location chosen by Major Von Borcke about 1/2 a mile south of Culpeper C. H. By night we had gotten quite well fixed & about 12 o'clock I was roused by a sentinel with the information that Gen. Stuart wished me in his tent. Rising hastily I found that news had just come from our pickets on this side & scouts on the other side of the Rappahannock that a large force of Yankee Cavalry were moving up: after writing to put Gens. Fitz & W. H. F. Lee on the alert & letting Genl R. E. Lee know it, I retired with directions to rise early & put Hd. Qrs. in motion cooking etc. for the days work before us.

It was a beautiful day & the General & staff rode on slowly to the vicinity of Brandy Station, where we found the command of Gen. [W. H. F.] Lee drawn up waiting to hear positively where it was needed most: Gen. Lee had gone with the 13th Va. to Kelly's ford, and the enemy was several times handsomely repulsed there by our sharpshooters & their masses across the river driven off in confusion by one of Major Beckham's guns. They did not succeed in crossing there at all.

About 11 o'clock news came that our men at the R. R. [railroad] bridge had given way most shamefully & about a regiment & a half had crossed over. Gen. Stuart immediately put the 9th Va. & some of our artillery in motion, determined as he said to jam them right into the river: going along at a quick trot we soon came in sight of the bridge, when not altogether to our surprise we found that the scoundrels had cleared out, except a few on foot on this side: these a few shell dispersed & Capt. [William T.] Robins (Gen. Lee's Adjt.) took a party up & reoccupied the bridge at this end: in doing so he had his horse's leg broken by a carbine shot so that he had to kill him.[88]

Gen. Lee soon returned & reported all well at Kelly's & we were all lying in an open field with our horses grazing near by, looking on at an artillery duel which had been going on some time to our right & left and wondering why they did not fire at us as we were 40 or 50 & much lower & easier to hit than the batteries firing at them. Suddenly I as well as others noticed that there was a stir at the Yankee guns & several exclaimed that they are going to give us a shot. I was half reclining on the grass with Capt. [James L.] Clark's head resting on Capt. [Benjamin S.] White's gloves lying on my knee. I got up and walked into the woods to untie my horse who had gotten himself twisted in the bushes: hearing a shot I looked & a shell lit exactly where I had been lying & right into the centre of the group, throwing dirt over a good many, but not exploding and consequently not touching a man or horse. Capt. White had just picked up his gloves & assures me that it hit just where they laid: altogether it was the most wonderful escape I ever knew.

We soon mounted and scattered in the woods, the enemy firing at a limber chest coming up the road to supply our battery with ammunition. Nothing else of interest occurred that day & late in the evening we returned to camp, where we found everything gone our baggage as well as the Brigade's having been put in the cars ready to move in case we were driven back. After waiting a long time the wagon returned from the car (having upset on the way) & bringing only the General's baggage: so we all pitched in supperless to the Genl's tent & had hardly laid down when it commenced raining & continued hard all night.

Yesterday morning the staff scattered to get breakfast & I after getting some with the General started to the front. In town I met Rev. Mr. [Dabney] Ball, who kindly loaned me a splendid oil coat: getting to Brandy Station we halted & whilst there news came from Genl Lee that the enemy had forced a crossing at Beverly's ford & orders to Col. [John R.] Chambliss to push on with the cavalry to his support.[89]

It was pouring in torrents, but ahead we hurried: just as we got in sight of the ford emerging from the woods, Col. Chambliss & Gen. Lee halted the leading squadron & they with several others rode ahead to find out whether 8 or 10 men standing on the road about 50 steps from us were friends or foes: they were unable to determine & Gen. Stuart followed by us, dashed ahead of the column, took a look & gave the command "Charge": this settled the matter, the Yankees wheeled & fled down the hill, closely followed by. Col. Chambliss & his squadron: just at the foot of the hill is a mill-race which was terribly swollen: in going through this 4 or 5 Yankees fell & were drowned. There was a little delay & confusion here, it being so deep that our men could scarcely get through, several horses floundering in the water & the Yankee squadron drew up in line on the other side & fired their pistols as our men crossed single file: ahead they dashed however, the Yankees broke & Col. Chambliss pursued them to the riverbank capturing 20 & wounding 5 or 6: he then drew back his men, our sharpshooters took position & Beckham soon hurried their cavalry out of sight on the other side of the river: in this gallant little affair we had one man wounded, since dead. After waiting an hour or more, we drew back our force, except a picket, to Brandy Station, and the command went into camp at their old place last night. We had supper when we got back & after drying pretty well, except my feet slept very comfortably: it was altogether the worst days campaigning I have ever had.

Today all is quiet & I can't make out exactly what the Yankees are driving at. We have gotten fixed again to-day & I hope will continue so until the campaign really opens & we get accustomed to having no regular camp. I am getting anxious to know what has become of Ephraim: do you know anything of him? My horses are suffering for want of somebody to properly attend to them & if he does not come back soon, want another boy.

[Chiswell] Dabney started this morning to Nelson Co. to inspect Hampton's Brigade. I heard yesterday from Capt. Collins in charge where Thomas now is but have heard nothing from him since Monday. I got sister's letter to Thomas & myself while he was here & have heard nothing from home since. Major FitzHugh will go down tomorrow (probably to Richmond) on his way to Fredericksburg & I will get him to take this. The Genl sends love. Give my love to all.

> Your devoted son
> Channing

From Thomas R. Price's Diary

April 19—I think the staff made the narrowest escape Tuesday I ever saw. A shell, fired from the hills across from Rappahannock Knob, struck exactly in the midst of us, (some standing and others reclining on the ground,) but fortunately did not explode, though throwing dirt over five or six men and horses. Gens. Stuart and W. H. F. Lee were in the group, and had it exploded, one or both of them would have gone under.

From John Esten Cooke's Journal

> "Camp Pelham"
> near Culpepper
> [Culpeper]

Ap. 22, 1863—Poor, poor Pelham!

We broke up the HeadQrs. at Camp No Camp on Ap. 9: the Gen. and most of the staff going by R. R. leaving Chiswell, me etc. to come across. I spent the evenings of the 8th and 9th at Mrs. Alsop's, and was truly sorry to leave those kind friends all. Hope to see them again some of these days. On the 10th set out with 'Lige, stopped to say good-bye at the Miss French and pushed on to Capt. Beale's where I ——— [word illegible] with Miss Alice and spent the night, getting forage from [Lt. William "Henry"] Hagan's wagon. The country is bleak, bare, and was worn all through, especially there in the "Wilderness."

Next morning rode on to Germanna with Capt. Beale and saw the bridge builders. Went on—Chiswell had gone with the couriers by Ely's [Ford]—and passed Stephensburg [Stevensburg], arriving at Culpepper [Culpeper] about 2 P. M. Reported to the Gen. at Miss Shackleford's, and made the acquaintance of that gay young lady Miss Bessie. Staff all over the lavish porch opposite where we staid [sic], until Hdqrs. were established here. Went to Church next day—communed, as did the Gen. and others—God sanctify my heart. [Notation indicating date: 12th]

[Margin notation indicating date: 13th] On Monday came out here—but several, I among them—slept at the Virginia House, that night. [Margin notation indicating date: 14th] Waked in the morning by Hagan with the news that the enemy were advancing, and we set out toward Kelly's to meet him. Stopped beyond Brandy and news coming that a reg't and a half were over at Rap'k [Rappahannock] bridge. The Gen. took Col. [Richard L. T.] Beales' reg't and went after them.[90] Sent me to the Col. just as we came to the edge of the woods to tell him to "lick into 'em, and jam 'em right over the river" That they did not ——— [two words illegible] back, hurried by our Artillery. We had one man killed, and Robbin's [Capt. William T. Robins] horse was shot. Sent back; after all was quiet for am'n [ammunition] for next day—and soon after I left, the enemy brought up a gun, and threw a shot right into the crowd "the most demoralized crowd I ever did see" says Von Borcke. Next day Gen. directed me to stay in town, and personally supervise supplying of am'n. They had a small charge at Beverley's [Beverly] Ford, the enemy not standing, and caught some 30—our loss three or four wounded. I think the Kellysville fight has got them under ——— [word illegible]. I said the other day, "Hooker is falling back, looking out for May, and these alarms are only feints all along from U. S. ford up, to keep us off his rear." "I reckon that is it." ——— [word illegible] Everything is tolerably quiet but we may be in it again at any moment. I have full supplies of am'n at the Court House.

We are agreeably fixed here—Cousin Jack's within a mile or so. Took the Gen. and Von Borcke there the other evening, and slept there the night before last. Little Cooke Green has made me her victim. They are all exceedingly aff't [affectionate]. Dined yesterday at the Shacklefords'. Gay young dames.

——— [paragraph illegible].

Letter from the Valley—Oh to be there! No literature at all as yet at this camp. But I might and will write.

I believe I will go in town.

No! I'll smoke.

Esperance!
(Song I heard my African, 'Lige, singing last night—
"Jeff Davis, he got pretty young wife—
Ole Abram he got none!"
Anecdotiana.
Old Perry, Gen. Lee's body servant boy.
"Mas. Robert, why don't you have braid and wreaths on your coat,
and all like the other big officers?"
Com-in-chief with gravity
"Pshaw Perry, you don't want me to fix myself up in that way, do
you? The real generals don't have such things on their coats!"

MAY

*The Battle of Chancellorsville raged for the first four days of the month, and though
Hooker finally withdrew across the Rappahannock on the sixth, Robert E. Lee's
victory was won at a heavy cost. Stonewall Jackson fell, wounded by his own men.
He would "pass over the river and rest under the shade of the trees" on the tenth.
When A. P. Hill was also wounded, Stuart had to take command of the 2nd Corps.
He led it until the close of the campaign. The days immediately following the battle
were anticlimactic. Both armies needed time to rest and recuperate.*

*The staff did not escape the battle unscathed. On the first, while riding with
Jackson and Stuart, Channing Price was struck in the leg by a piece of shell. No
surgeon was at hand to recognize the seriousness of the wound, nor did any of the officers
have a tourniquet. The young adjutant died from loss of blood around midnight, with
his brother Tom and others present. His unique talents and engaging personality had
endeared him to many. Stuart would miss him as both an officer and a friend.*

*Others had fallen. Lt. Walter Hullihen, an aide-de-camp, had been struck in
the right shoulder. The wound incapacitated him for some time. Frank Robertson
had been "winded" by a cannonball and was fortunate that he was only temporarily
disoriented from a circumstance that had killed soldiers at other times.[91] Maj. William J. Johnson, chief of subsistence, was the only staff officer captured. He had been
stationed miles to the rear at Shannon's Crossroads, where he was performing the
duties of his office when Stoneman's raiders came to call. His time in Old Capitol
Prison was short, however, and he rejoined the staff about a month later. Shortly
after the battle, the staff learned that Tom Turner, a former aide-de-camp of Stuart's,
had been killed fighting with Mosby's command. Though his death was not directly
linked to the battle and had no effect on the staff physically, his loss was felt in spirit,
as he had been well liked.*

The final staff casualty resulting from the campaign came after the guns had fallen silent. On the twenty-second, the New York Times *published portions of Tom Price's diary, which had been "taken prisoner" when the Federals had captured the bridge-building crew with whom Price had been working. The entries printed brought embarrassment to Price, his family, and Stuart. Price left the staff to take a position in Richmond.*

Philip H. Powers finally rejoined the army and, as he had anticipated, was immediately attached to Stuart's headquarters. His letter of the sixth explained what had happened to him during the battle. The isolated position in which he had found himself at the opening of the campaign had kept him out of immediate danger. Once again he was more concerned about his family than himself.

Capt. John Esten Cooke, the ordnance officer, had been sent to Richmond to deliver a prisoner and did not return in time for the battle. It was not entirely his fault what with Stoneman's cavalry about, his lack of a horse, and rail transportation interrupted. Aide-de-camp Goldsborough was with him. Upon their return, Stuart was much amused at their "adventure." Cooke took it as such and thought to make it another of his short stories on the war. His other writing he brought to a close. Not wanting a repetition of the Tom Price incident, he ended his almost daily diary entries with a final "Esperance!"

Gordonsville
May 6th 1863

My Dearest Wife [Roberta Powers],

I think it exceedingly doubtful of this ever reaching you, but I must write a line to let you know where and how I am. Shortly after receiving your letter of the 24th March I joined the 1st Reg. Cavalry and was detailed at once at Genl. Stuart's Hd. Qrs. in the Quartermaster Department of which Major FitzHugh former Adjutant Genl. of Genl Stuart is now chief.[92] And since have been actively engaged in purchasing horses etc. I was just contemplating a trip to Warren with a view of getting to Clarke when the enemy crossed the Rappahannock and drove us from Culpeper. I need not give you any detail of the late military operation further than to say that the Enemy's cavalry have gotten between this point and Richmond cut the R. [Rail] Road at Louisa CtH. and other points below, penetrated to the James River and are running wild over that country plundering and robbing. Unfortunately we have but one Brigade of Cavalry a few infantry and two Batteries here; Genl. Stuart being somewhere below towards Fredericksburg And this force is by no means sufficient to oppose the enemy, as they have some 14000 Cavalry. However Genl. Lee has gained a glorious victory at Fredericksburg [Chancellorsville], driven the enemy across the Rappahannock and the Cavalry must leave at once if they can.

I am waiting here until the way is open. I have not heard from Jim since I left him some two weeks ago. Nor have I heard from Richmond.

I am hoping my dear wife from day to day that the tide of war may bring me nearer to you and enable me to see you once more, but now that I am regularly enlisted in the Army again I have no freedom of action, and must bear and endure with what patience and fortitude I can command, And have to beg of you, my love, to comfort me by exhibiting also that degree of Christian resignation which I know will be vouchsafed to you.

I have no time to write more at present. All is commotion here.

With love to all and more than all for your own dear self—believe me

As Ever
Yours
P. H. P.

Charlottesville May 8th 1863

I came up here yesterday on business—found all well and very glad to see me once more. Aunt Kitty [Lobban] is the same old thing as good and kind as ever. And perfectly willing to kill me with eating—She sends love and hugs. She is not so much afraid of Yanks now—Aunt Fanny lives with her now. She is very infirm and dreadfully fretful—I return to Gordonsville this morning

Yours in Haste
P. H. P.

From John Esten Cooke's Journal

Camp Orange C. H.

May 12, 1863—Hooker whipped out.

On the night of April 27th Gen. S. [Stuart] said "Cooke do you want to go to Richmond?" Reply, "Yes Sir." "Well go down and take that prisoner to Gen. [Brig. Gen. John H.] Winder."[93] "All right Sir." And poor Channing wrote me one of his last orders. I set out next morning, 28th, with the prisoner Rector—a sort of Nighthawk of the border, Mrs. Stuart & Goldsborough. At Hanover C. H. Goldsborough left us to go to Dr. Price's, and Cousin J. myself and Rector proceeded to Richmond where I turned over my lumber to Gen. W. [Winder] and by the Gen.'s permission staid [*sic*] a day to see to my uniform, Pelham's picture, a Napoleon gun etc. On 29th rumor that they were fighting at Fredericksburg—went that night to Dick Meade's cautioning servant to wake me at 6 A.M. for morning train. She failed and I was left. Ordered a new uniform in Rich'd [Richmond]—will cost 70 to make. Saw all my friends & had a pleasant time. Slept with Howard last night—paid servant from ——— [name illegible] to wake me at 5. Got off, and found Goldsborough on train. Arrived at Gordonsville expecting Gen. S. [Stuart] to fall back toward that place; enemy having crossed higher up. Found he was in parts unknown, but supposed near Vidiersville [Verdiersville]—and wagons would probably come to Orange C. H. for forage. Telegraphed Maj. Fitzhugh [FitzHugh] who had military command of trains.

"Will a forage train go up today? Lt. Goldsboro' and myself are here, and exceedingly anxious to report to the General. Please order a train if possible."

News soon came that Gen. S. [Stuart] had joined Gen. [Robert E.] Lee, and that 14,000 Yankee Cav. had cut off Gen. W. H. F. ["Rooney"] Lee and consequently G. [Goldsborough] and myself, at Gordonsville. Tried our best to get horses—begged—couldn't—loafed, feeling intense anxiety. Reported for duty on staff of Gen. Rooney [W. H. F. Lee] if he would only get me a horse. Delighted to have me, but horses difficult. John Lee applied to Maj. [Charles] Waite for me—none.[94] Willie Hoxton finally lent me a little scrub just in time to be of no use—Gen. Rooney having fallen back with his command "couldn't do anything with such a force"—enemy's. He had small regiments against full brigades. Finally rushed on by train to Gen. S. [Stuart] here, who met us, and laughed at our mishaps "he understood it all": and here is our camp, above Mrs. Thompson's; I am under my fly writing.

That was a most singular week at Gordonsville: and I think I'll write "Left behind or the Dismounted Cavaliers"—our horses having gone on toward Ginneys' [Guiney's Station] with the Hdqrs. wagons. We made the acquaintance however of the Orange refugees Mrs. Newton, Miss Robinson & others in the ———— [word illegible] near the lake, sang "Lorena," and wiled [sic] away the time.

We will go to the Valley I trust soon, and I shall see my darlings again. Natty has 14 days furlough and is going up.

Historical

Gen. S. [Stuart] says

Rosser told him last night that Jackson on his death bed had expressed a desire that he, Stuart, should succeed him in the command of his Corps.

Gen. S. [Stuart] said

"I would rather know that Jackson said that, than have the appointment."

Gen. Jackson died at Ginney's at fifteen minutes past three P. M. on the 10th May. He has gone to rejoin Him in whom he trusted. We are the unfortunates not this immortal being.

Camp Orange C. H.

May 12, '63—Poor, poor Tom [Turner]!

He was killed the other day near Warrenton. I saw this evening a letter from Mrs. [Edward Carter] Turner to Lt. G. [Goldsborough] which tells all. He was in a house, when the Yankees surprised him. He ran to his horse, but while mounting was shot in the back and through the lungs. He was taken into the house and subsequently home where he died in four days, Mrs. T. [Turner] writes "he was very calm and the most patient person I ever saw." He received the announcement of his dying condition with entire calmness and said "God have mercy on me." While he was thus sinking quietly, the house was surrounded by a party of Yankees who pushed on to his chamber, strode about the room, and felt his wounds to see if he "could be moved." This made him terribly "restless" and he never again became calm, expiring the same evening.[95]

Poor poor Tom!

God deal with them and reward them according to their works!

Camp Price, near
Culpepper [Culpeper]
C. H.

[*no date*]—I have been incessantly engaged on the "Life of Stonewall Jackson," having in about a week or ten days, got him through the Battle of Cedar Run [Cedar Mountain, August 9, 1862].

Rarely have I worked so hard—and it has been done in the midst of a thousand distractions: the care of equipping thoroughly the whole division on me: incessant calls: a very bad cold: and the wind fluttering my thin blue paper violently as I wrote. That wind is rolling through the trees now, and talking to me of other and more peaceful days. But "God's in Heaven"—and all is well.

Culpepper [Culpeper] is a pleasant little place, and Miss Nettie [Antonia] Ford is here: pretty as ever, and as sweet, though thin from the effect of her imprisonment by those outer barbarians and cowards in their bastille at Washington. She and myself are as good friends as ever. A pleasant evening at Miss Bessie Shackleford's; and at Cousin Jack's—with Cooke Green crying violently for her departing lover,

I think—but a staff officer don't [*sic*] think: has no opinions.

The wind is blowing so, I can hardly write: but I intend to seal up this journal, and send it back to Richmond for fear the Yankees will get it, and print it as they have done Tom Price's. So I write a parting page.

I am tired of the war, and want to go to the Vineyard.[96] The sight of the blue mountains yonder, makes me homesick: and I long to flee like a bird to those mountains. When shall I? I saw my dear Natty in Richmond, at Mrs. Duval's, where were the Misses Semmes, daughters of the Captain of the "Alabama": and Miss Ellen Caldwell and Bunton, whom I saw much of and went with to Gen. Winder. Natty is handsome, and an elegant boy. May God spare him in this atrocious war, and permit him to return to his mother whose heart yearns for him.

O for the mountains! When shall I be there?

Roll on, mountain wind! and bring me some far whispered words from the dear old Vineyard. Bring me a loving word from Sister, a jest from Nan, a kiss from Lettie, and a caress from Lil. Alas! it is only the fingers of the wind which play in my hair, among which are I think some gray threads.

Sentimental:—yonder is the dazzling battle flag like a big "Giant of Battle" rose; flaming in the wind beneath the tall tree. Chiswell is kicking his heels together, and making his spurs rattle, on the red blanket of our bed. Old and Young "Brown" sleeping together at present.

Perhaps—who knows?—a bugle may soon sound: and then "On to the mountains!" and—quien sabe?

Esperance! Esperance!

The remaining days of the month were given over to refitting, rest, and preparation for the summer campaign. Only light skirmishing, most of it involving Mosby and his partisans, broke the informal truce. Stuart reorganized his horse artillery and saw his cavalry command increase in strength as men returned from leaves or horse furloughs. On the twenty-second, Stuart held a grand review of his entire division. Shortly thereafter, two more brigades were placed under Stuart's command when Robert E. Lee ordered Brigadier Generals William E. Jones and Beverly H. Robertson to join Stuart. By the end of the month, there were nearly 10,000 cavalry troops encamped in and around Culpeper. Something big was in the offing.

The staff slowly regrouped after the losses of Chancellorsville and its aftermath. Tom Price was still at headquarters as late as the thirtieth but would soon be gone. Channing Price was dead, and Cooke had sent his diary to Richmond for safekeeping. The only staff officer to record any of the events as May drew to a close was Frank Robertson, Stuart's young assistant engineer. His letters of the twenty-second, twenty-fourth, and thirtieth recounted the review of the twenty-second and expressed his everyday concerns over obtaining fishing tackle and seeing that his new jacket had the proper braiding. He even wrote of returning to Germanna Ford to view where he and Tom Price had narrowly escaped capture. His last recorded thought was not of the war, but of his pay, which he asked to have sent as soon as possible. Even lowly lieutenants in the engineer corps had expenses.

HeadQuarters
Cavalry Division
Culpeper C. H.
May 22nd

Dear Pa [Wyndham Robertson],

I only have time before dark to drop you a hasty note. I reached here safely Wednesday evening being ignorant of our change of HdQuarters until I got to Orange C. H. We are now camped about half mile from the town, on a high, shady hill with a good spring & excellent pasturage near at hand & in every respect much better by the change. My horses I found much improved by their weeks [*sic*] rest, but still quite thin & sadly in need of Sam's attention.

The grand Cavalry Review took place this morning & was one of the most imposing scenes I ever witnessed. First & at the head of the collumn [*sic*] came the artillery, twelve guns strong & immediately behind, the cavalry in collumn of squadrons—Gen. Hampton's Brigade in advance—Gen. Wm. H. [F.] Lee's next & Gen. Fitz Lee's bringing up the rear—about five thousand men in all & generally well mounted.

After passing thus before the Gen. [Stuart] & staff at a slow gait, the artillery drew up in line of battle on an opposite hill where they remained until the head of the collumn again approached our position, when they unlimbered & commenced a heavy cannonade. The Cavalry Division at the same time moving up at a brisk trot & each squadron as it reached a certain point, charging with a yell that almost drowned the roar of the opposite batteries. The rush of such large bodies of men amid the booming of cannon & clashing of sabres produced a very pleasant excitement & somehow inspired me with a confidence in our cause & an assurance of eventual success, difficult to account for, now it is all over.

Gen. [George W.] Randolph & Maj. Peyton came up from Richmond to witness it, & I am very sorry I did not know certainly where it was to take place until too late to let you know in time to get here.

If Sam is only slightly indisposed, I think it probable he would recruit here as soon as in Richmond & if we made an advance movement before he was well, he might remain with the wagons, but do as you think best about him. If he comes, don't forget to send my jacket & pants by him or by any other opportunity you may have, also my hat. It is so dark I can't see to write more & we have no candles. I have gotten almost well again, but suffer a good deal with headaches. Give my love to all & write soon to

Your affec. Son
F. S. Robertson

Send me a spoon if there is a common one to be had.

HeadQuarters
Cavalry Div.
Culpeper C. H.
May 24th

Dear Kate [Robertson],

As we may be here for several weeks yet & I hear the fishing is very good in the vicinity, I write to ask you to get me some fishing tackle & send it either by Sam or in a letter. I want two lines without corks & about twelve or fifteen hooks of different sizes, not much smaller than this [drawing of small fishhook] or larger than this [drawing of larger fishhook]. I write for so many because several of the staff have requested me to get enough for them also. Wyndham will get them for you.

If my jacket is still unfinished I should like the arms to be trimed [*sic*] with buff & gold lace.[97] I directed otherwise, but the staff have all fixed up to such an alarming extent that I shall have to follow suit, or be taken for a courier. Cousin William will have it done if you will get Wyndham to tell him. I want a cord of buff [drawing of jacket sleeve appears here] run around the sleeve marking the edge of the cuffs if there were any.

Please get me a piece of sponge. I was about to say as large as your hand, but considering it a matter of serious doubt whether a common hat could contain both that & my head, a piece half the size will do.

I am going down to Germana [Germanna] to day to get my clothes & also for another purpose which I will tell you of, one of these days perhaps.

I am almost well again, but still in a bad humor—about what I can't imagine. I will write a larger letter when I return. My love to all & believe me

Your affec. brother
Frank

HeadQuarters
Cavalry Division
Culpeper C. H.
May 30th

Dear Pa [Wyndham Robertson],

Neither Mr. Blackford or myself are sure the enclosed form is filled out correctly, but I suppose with his signature there will be no difficulty in drawing pay on it. Please ask Maj. [Alfred L.] Rives to give you a blank filled out as it should be, and send it to me.

Mr. B. [Blackford], Tom Price & myself received orders to day to make a topographical survey of the North bank of the Rappahannock, extending from the Rail Road to the mouth of the Rapidan—as it is fifteen or twenty miles between, we will probably be absent several days.

I see by to day's papers that you were elected by a large majority & am glad & sorry at the same time. I should have disliked very much for you to have been defeated, but could you possibly have escaped otherwise & been allowed the quiet of private life, for a while, at any rate. I should have been much better satisfied.

I rode down down to Germana [Germanna] a few days since & inspected the battle ground. I learned from a man who lives on this side [of] the river and whose house was occupied by Yankee General [Brig. Gen. Alpheus S.] Williams, that they had five thousand men engaged, before we evacuated and that their loss was five killed and ten wounded.[98] We lost one killed and I saw the poor fellows grave as I passed by nearly in the exact spot where I dropped my sabre.

I have not heard a word from Sam since I left. Tell Kate I think she might have written. Love to all & believe me in haste

Your affec. Son

Frank

Send my pay as soon as possible

JUNE

During the first few days of the month, Stuart's cavalry continued to rest and refit. On the fifth, with all of his brigades now present, Stuart ordered another review. Robert E. Lee was to be the guest of honor, but he was unable to attend. The review went on as scheduled. Lee did want to see his cavalry, however, so on the eighth another review was held at Lee's orders. There was the usual griping and complaining among the men, but for "Marse Robert" they formed ranks and paraded one more time. On the following day, Stuart had orders to begin maneuvering north to cover the infantry's movement. Lee's army was about to take the initiative from the Federals and strike northward. But things did not go as planned.

Early on the ninth, the Federal cavalry struck across the Rappahannock with the goal of destroying Stuart's cavalry. Their commander, Brig. Gen. Alfred Pleasonton, believed that Stuart was encamped around Culpeper, when in actuality he was camped around Brandy Station.[99] Sharp fighting erupted almost immediately. The Confederates were surprised at the strength and tenacity of the Federal forces; their Union counterparts were shocked to find the Confederates so close to the river. The Battle of Brandy Station lasted the entire day, with charge answering charge until the Federals at last withdrew. Stuart was not destroyed as Pleasonton had hoped, but the blue cavalry had come of age. They had matched their longtime superiors

*blade for blade and shot for shot. The days of the Confederate cavalry's easy victories
were over.*

*Stuart's staff performed exceptionally well during the battle but again suffered
casualties. Capt. William D. Farley was mortally wounded by a cannon shot that
tore off his leg just below the knee. He died in just a few hours. Capt. Benjamin S.
White was wounded in the neck, and though he remained on duty throughout the
Gettysburg Campaign, he would eventually need months to recover completely. Lt.
Robert H. Goldsborough's inexperience resulted in his capture when he rode into a
Federal column that he mistook for Confederate. Others of the staff were in and out
of the thickest fighting of the day but fortunately emerged unhurt.*

*In a letter to his sister, Frank Robertson recounted his adventures of June 9. He
had had several close calls and was extremely disgusted with his horse, which had
almost cost him his life. He managed to ride all over the battlefield either carrying
messages for Stuart or escaping from the enemy and so had much to tell. He was
pleased with the souvenirs he had collected but saddened by the loss of friends and
fellow officers.*

*One other staff officer recorded the day's events. On the fourteenth Chiswell
Dabney penned a letter to his father, hoping to clear up some of the misinformation
that had appeared in the newspapers. Like Robertson he had some narrow escapes
and was witness to the gallantry of both sides. In the end, however, all that mattered
was that Stuart held the field. To Dabney that meant victory.*

Camp Fairleigh [Farley]
near Cul. C. H.
June 12th 1863

My Dear Kate [Robertson],

It gives me pleasure to write you that once more I have passed thro'
the thickest of the fight unscathed. We were waked on the morning of the
9th by the rattling fire of our pickets as they slowly fell back before the
heavy masses of Cavalry which the enemy were throwing across the river
at Beverly's [Beverly] Ford. Of course everything and everybody were
immediately on the stir. The wagon trains were in motion first and went
thundering to the rear mid clouds of dust—then came the cavalry regiments
at a trot with here and there a battery of artillery,—all hurrying to the front
with the greatest possible speed.

As it was some time before the Gen. Commanding changed his base,
I had ample opportunity to witness all the preparatory arrangements, both
offensive and defensive, for the coming fight. With the aid of Mr. Blackford's
glass, I saw distinctly the advance of the Yankee skirmishers and the heavy
line of battle following closely in their rear—they advanced cautiously but
boldly until within range of our batteries and the advanced skirmishers of

the supporting Regiments and squadron after squadron dashed to the front until it began to sound a little like Chancellorsville.

About this time Gen. Stuart ordered me to Brandy Station to take charge of the dismounted men of Hampton's Brigade and post them on the road leading from that point to Kelly's Ford, as he anticipated what afterwards took place, that the enemy would cross at that ford and endeavor to get in our rear. On getting to Brandy, I found Capt. [Theodore Gaillard] Barker (Hampton's Adjutant Gen.) who informed me that there were no dismounted men belonging to Hampton's Brigade on the field and I at once galloped back and reported to Gen. Stuart, who I found far to the front, immediately in rear of the skirmishers. As he seems to consider me particularly suitable to manage foot soldiers, and left me to form them in line and advance through the woods until the enemy was found, which after much difficulty I succeeded in doing.

When I next found the General he was near the old brick church [St. James Church] in the woods. He was behind one of our batteries which was playing on a column of Yankee Infantry advancing from the river to support their skirmishers who were falling back before Gen. [W. H. F.] Rooney Lee's brigade at our extreme left. We had been there I suppose 15 or 20 minutes when a courier dashed up and reported the enemy at Brandy Station, immediately in our rear and advancing rapidly upon the hill where we had been camped and which commanded the surrounding country for miles.

For the first time the Gen. looked excited and ordered me to go to Gen. Hampton as fast as a horse could go and tell him to send back to this hill a regiment at a gallop. Away I went over ditches, fences, mire and everything else at a breakneck speed for about a mile, delivered my orders, started the Regiment and returned nearly as fast with a message from General Hampton, but on reaching the place where I had left the General he was gone as also most of the cannon—the latter I could see dashing across the field at a gallop to get possession of the hill before the Yankees. From where I was I could see the most exciting scene I ever witnessed—on one side of the high hill were dense columns of Yankee Cavalry galloping up in beautiful order and on the other side our ragged troopers, one or two regiments in good order, but the rest one confused mass of flying horsemen and both sides straining every nerve and muscle to reach the hill first. The enemy however had the advantage and while one of their batteries made for the hill, another unlimbered on a slight elevation opposite and opened fire on a few of our men who had been on the hill all the while with our adjutant General (Maj. McClelland [McClellan]).[100]

I was considerably puzzled to know where to go or what to do, but concluded the General must be making for the hill with the rest, I galloped on, but on getting nearly to the top met a large body of Yankees who were sweeping everything before them. [Chiswell] Dabney (who was with me), as soon as we had recovered from our precipitate retreat, told me that the General was on the right and we rode in that direction and reached the top of the hill several hundred yards further on. When we reached the top we saw a regiment or two of our men, who had charged around the left of the hill, pursuing a large body of Yankees who were flying towards Brandy Station. I supposed at once that the hill was in our possession, on seeing our men were on the opposite side and put up my pistol and rode very composedly right into the head of the eighth Illinois who came charging and yelling around a skirt of trees, right on the heels of the twelfth Virginia Cavalry, who had taken to the most inglorious flight.

With my usual good luck I was obliged to run once more for my life, with a Yankee orderly Sergeant right at my heels popping away at my back every jump of his horse—how he happened to miss me I can't imagine, for a fairer mark or a more helpless one was never presented. I was riding Bostona and do what I could, I could neither turn her to the right or left—nor could I draw my pistol, every time I attempted to unbutton the pistol holster, she commenced blundering, absolutely it seemed on purpose, and I was forced to withdraw my hand to grasp the rein and hold her up—for at least two hundred yards this race kept up and I could see the fellow raise his pistol between his horse's ears and take deliberate aim, but fortunately I was not even grazed, though one of the balls cut a slight furrow in Bostona's leg.

Von Borcke and Dabney were both in the route [sic], but some distance ahead of me. Bostona is so awkward and difficult to turn, that when the General gives me an order to the rear and I endeavor to turn she generally manages to sweep the road clear of both staff and couriers and always produces a laugh—if I want to turn to the left, I grasp the left rein firmly and pull her head in that direction at the same time extending my left foot as far to the rear as possible and spurring most furiously—I find that the only way of accomplishing the left about wheel.

When I again joined the General the hill had been cleared of the Yankees and we had captured the battery which they had endeavored to place on top of it.[101] The fight was still raging on the left and Gen. [W. H. F.] Lee had been forced to fall back. I was again in the thickest of the fight and had nearly got to Gen. Lee with orders when he was wounded. At another time a percussion shell struck the ground about ten yards beyond a group of us who were lying in the shade of a cherry tree, and bounded right into the midst of us, stopping within a yard and a half of my head, but fortunately not exploding. I could write a great deal more about the fight but am quite tired and sleepy and you must wait till another time. Mr. Blackford was sent down to Gen. R. E. Lee at Culpeper and I did not see much of him during the fight, though he saw the most glorious thing of the day, the retaking of the hill by Col. [P. M. B.] Young of Cobb's Legion while I was skedaddling with the routed twelfth.[102]

The fight lasted from sunrise to sunset and is by far the greatest Cavalry fight of the War. Our loss was about 400, killed, wounded and missing. The Yankees about 700 and three pieces of artillery.[103] Capt. Fairleigh [Farley] (Vol. Aide) was killed, Capt. White also one of the General staff was shot through the ear and neck and Lieut. Goldsborough (regular Aide) is missing, supposed to be a prisoner, who with Pelham, Hullion [Hullihen], and [Channing] Price make a very heavy loss of a General in three months.

I think we will probably move in a day or two, I don't know certainly, but it is generally believed, across the Rappahannock. I suppose ere this you are all at the Meadows—how I would like to pay you a short visit up there, but unless I am wounded, I suppose there is little chance this summer. Write me what you are all doing & who is with you & the news up there generally. Tell Cousin Lou to take good care of small Tom. I am sure he will soon be ——— [word illegible] & she can't imagine what I have heard. My best love to all & believe me

Your affec. brother
Frank

Enclosed I send you a piece of silk from one of the Yankee flags we captured. I have also the brass spear head of a flag staff but it is too heavy to enclose. Tell Aunt Charlotte Gilbert [her grandson] is well and he and Sam are both riged [*sic*] out in Yankee clothes.

◆━◆ ≅◆≊ ◆━◆

Camp Farley
June 14th 1863

Dear Father [Rev. John B. Dabney]

Doubtless you have heard before this of the great cavalry fight at Brandy Station; and as all the accounts I have seen in the papers are erroneous I have determined to write you a short account of the facts of the case. On the morning of the 9th inst' while in camp beyond Brandy about a mile, we were suddenly waked up by firing in the direction of Beverly's ford: a courier from the picket at that place came up and reported the enimy [*sic*] crossing in heavy force and our picket being driven in rapidly.

Genl Stuart ordered me to saddle up and ride immediately to the front and ascertain the condition of affairs. When I arrived in the vicinity of the enimy I found our small party being driven back by an enormous column of the Yankees. So rapidly were we driven in that our artil' [artillery] had just time to limber up and get out of the way. This, however, they did successfully and in a few moments, (under the excellent leadership of Major [Robert F.] Beckham) got in battery and opened a terrific fire upon the enimy.

By this time Genl [William E. "Grumble"] Jones had all his command in hand and rapidly advanced and charged the Yankees driving them to the cover of the woods where they took shelter bihind [sic] their line of Infantry skirmishers. We were then in our turn compelled to retire which we no sooner commenced to do when out came the Yankees charging in fine style. This time we were driven, but reformed around our artillery, which poured such a hot fire into the enimy that they retired pell mell back into the woods.

During this time Genl Stuart had sent two regiments of Cav'l [Cavalry], the 2nd S.C. [South Carolina] and the 4th Va. [Virginia] to Stevensburg to guard the road towards Kelleys [Kelly's], but the enimy coming up from that direction in overwhelming numbers, eluded our men by keeping them engaged in front and pushed on towards Brandy. This Genl Stuart found out almost as soon as it was done, and took the proper steps to guard against an attack in that direction. All our baggage and every thing else had been moved at least an hour before this; hence the misstatement in all the papers, Viz., that Genl Stuart was surprised in his quarters by the enimy shelling him out, and the capture of valuable papers showing the exact plans of the campaign, all of which is absolutely false, and the tale of some straggler which our periodicals seem to believe rather than the authority's.

Our force was then concentrated in the direction of Brandy to meet this advance. Genl Jones took the lead, the 12th Va. and [Lt. Col. Elijah V.] White's[104] Battalion charging simulyaneously [sic] drove the enimy past their artillery and captured it, but were so much scattered by the charge and the tremendous fire of grape, shell, and canister to which they had been subjected, that when the enimies [sic] reserves charged they were driven back in utter confusion. I was with White's Battalion, and I never yet had to get out of the way so fast since I have been in the service. The feeling was awful for I dreaded being shot in the back for the enimy were only about ten steps behind me a portion of the time. One ball came between my ear and hat, but a "miss" is as good as a "mile".

By this time the men had rallyed [sic] and we returned towards the enimy, but before we got back Col. [Lunsford L.] Lomax[105] of the 11th Va. with [Brig. Gen. Wade] Hampton's Brigade on his left had charged the enemy driving them in utter confusion out from Brandy Station, the 11th Va. recapturing the artillery which we had taken. Genl W. H. F. Lee later in the day made a magnificent charge with his Brigade. He was wounded but not seriously. He charged Buford's regulars and the fight was for a time desperate but he succeeded in driving them back and taking possession of the field.

This country is open for miles—almost level without fences or ditches and the finest country for cavalry fighting I ever saw. We charged in line of battle and sabres were crossed very often. Comeing [*sic*] to the cold steel something which the infantry with all their vaunted superiority have never done yet. Of this latter arm we had none engaged at all. From all that we can learn there was upward of nine regiments of infantry and between twenty-five and thirty regiments of Cavl' making an aggregate force of about twenty thousand men. This we fought all day with one Division of Cavl' and two brigades of it not engaged scarcely at all, and succeeded in driving them before us at every point and taking undisputed possession of the field.

The enimy lost about six or seven hundred in killed, wounded and prisoners; we lost about four hundred.

Capt. Wm. [William D.] Farley of Genl Stuart's staff (one of my particular friends) killed. You see we have named our camp after him. Capt. [Benjamin S.] White, one of my mess, wounded through the neck. Lieut. [Robert H.] Goldsborough A. D. C. taken prisoner. This is our loss in the staff. Every fight seems to take one of us off. Capt. Farley had his leg completely shot off by a shell, passing through his horse and shattering Col. [Matthew C.] Butler by whose side he was riding. When he was picked up he said with a laugh, "Bring along my leg too. I wish to have that along any how."

I was so unfortunate as to lose one of my horses when the Yankees charged into Brandy. He was captured by them, my boy Felbert just having time to make his escape on the one he was riding. I think, however, I can get paid for him, but I am afraid it will be a long time. Felbert hurt himself pretty severely several days ago by being thrown from a horse which he had tried to ride without my knowledge. He is now, however, nearly well having only got a sprain, fully equiped [*sic*] himself from the last field and is wearing a jacket of a Yankee man who was killed on the ground where our Hd Qrs were in the morning. ———— [name illegible] was shot through the back. I will write whenever I have an opportunity.

> Your devoted son
> Chiswell Dabney

From Brandy Station, Stuart's cavalry moved north to screen the movement of Robert E. Lee's infantry. The cavalry actions at Aldie on the seventeenth, Middleburg on the seventeenth and nineteenth, and Upperville on the twenty-first followed. They were contested as hard as Brandy Station had been. The Federal cavalry was determined to break through Stuart's screen and find out what Lee was up to, while Stuart was equally determined that they would not.

In the fighting around Middleburg on the nineteenth, Heros von Borcke was shot in the throat while riding at Stuart's side. The wound was thought to be mortal, but the giant Prussian, with his iron constitution, survived, though his military service for the Confederacy and Stuart was over. The rest of the staff passed through the three battles unharmed.

On the twenty-fifth, Stuart set out on his third ride around a Federal army. He would cross the Potomac at Rowser's Ford, capture a 125-wagon supply train near Rockville, have a brief skirmish with Federal cavalry at Westminister, encounter Judson Kilpatrick's cavalry brigade at Hanover, and shell Carlisle before rejoining Lee at Gettysburg on July 2. June had been a very busy month for Stuart, his staff, and the cavalry.

Frank Robertson took a brief moment on the eighteenth to pen a letter to his father about Stuart's clash with the 1st Rhode Island Cavalry in Middleburg the previous day. As he explained it, his role seemed more that of an aide or courier than an engineer. Still, Robertson did as his general commanded and found himself cut off and unable to return until late at night, a circumstance he did not particularly relish.

For Chiswell Dabney the fighting had brought danger and excitement. On the twentieth he wrote to his father of the destruction of the Rhode Islanders, the wounding of Maj. Heros von Borcke, and of his near capture. He both expected the enemy any minute and at the same time did not think there would be much fighting. His uncertainty reflected the feelings of many of the gray troopers. Everyone was on edge. The waiting and watching were the hardest parts of the fighting.

> Hd. Qrs. Cav. Div.
> Rectors three miles from
> Middleburg
> June 18th '63

Dear Pa [Wyndham Robertson],

Thinking you are all anxious to hear ——— [word illegible] on our grand advance I have borrowed a sheet of paper with some difficulty & will ——— [word illegible] a few hasty lines.

On Tuesday [June 15] the bugle sounded to horse at 8 1/2 AM and we left our Hd. Qrs, near Culpeper, crossed the Rappahannock and halted at Rectortown on the Manassas Gap R. R. after a ride of 35 or 40 miles. The next day we started at daybreak & reached Middleburg about twelve o'clock where we unsaddled I presume with the intention of remaining but an hour or so after we had gotten there, two couriers dashed in & reported a heavy column of the enemy on a road to the south of town a mile off & advancing rapidly. I think it was an unexpected movement, for Fitz Lee's Brigade under command of Col. [Thomas T.] Munford had passed thro' town some time before & were fighting the Yankees about five miles beyond [at Aldie] & the approaching column was therefore coming immediately in its rear cutting Munford off from the rest of the division which had not yet gotten within several miles of the town.

The Gen. & staff mounted & dashed out of town towards our approaching reinforcements leaving only a few scattered videts [*sic*] on the road on which the Yankees were approaching to watch their movements. After riding a little upwards of half mile he [Stuart] called me & told me to go to Col. Munford with orders for him to fall back. I thought it probable I would more probably reach Washington than Col. Munford but there was no alternative & away I dashed.

On reaching town not a solitary trooper was to be seen but the women & children were scattered along the sidewalks—it was strange to see the faces which were all joy & happiness when we first went in now changed to terror & despair. I reached Col. Munford, who I found heavily engaged on his left, but steadily driving the enemy before him. On delivering my message he commenced falling back. The enemy slowly following—he sent me to report the fact to Gen. Stuart, but as I expected after proceeding a mile or so back I learned from couriers coming in that the enemy had full possession of Middleburg & were advancing down the pike to take us in the rear.

Of course the hope of getting to the Gen. was over & I returned to join Col. Munford. I found the whole brigade in motion towards Snicker's Gap & after making a detour of some 12 or 15 miles we form a junction with Gen. Stuart on the main pike about midnight. We then learned that Gen. [Beverly H.] Robertson had driven the enemy out of town [Middleburg] about an hour after they took possession. Yesterday's fight was the heaviest cavalry engagement of the war—the contending parties were constantly engaged in hand to hand combat. Our loss was however & far as can be determined remarkably small while the Yankees [*sic*] was tremendous.[106] [Remainder of letter is lost.]

Hd Qrs Cavl Divn
June 20th 1863

Dear Father [Rev. John B. Dabney]

As a courier is about starting to Culpeper I take advantage of the opportunity to drop you a few lines to let you know my whereabout and how I am. I am now at Rector's X roads Loudoun County or near Upperville Ashby's Gap. I am in fine health and spirits as we all are on account of our forward move.

Commenced skirmishing with the enimy [sic] day before yesterday and been fighting ever since. On the 18th we captured nearly all a Rode [Rhode] Island regiment, their colors, standards, and a large portion of their officers. On the same day Mosby captured a Major A. D. C. to Genl [Maj. Gen. Joseph] Hooker with very important dispatches, also a signal officer.[107] Genl Stuart sent the dispatches to Genl Lee by me, and I nearly killed my horse going, as my orders were to take them regardless of horse flesh.

We have taken up to this time about 500 of the enimy's [sic] Cavl' [Cavalry] prisoners, wounded about four hundred and killed about a hundred making their loss about a thousand. I am sorry to say that Major [Heros] von Borcke was severely wounded yesterday by a ball from a carbine. I hope not mortally. The wound is in his neck. Yesterday Major Jellet and myself while trying to communicate with Col. [Thomas L.] Rosser near the Pot House [Leithtown] ran into a Yankee detachment of ten or twenty men and came very near being captured. They gave us a volley from their carbines and sent bullets whistling by our heads. We gracefully fell back out of the way and went to Union to get a regiment to clear the way, which was very soon done.

We are expecting the enimy every minute; all our horses are saddled; but there will only be very slight skirmishing today I think. Can't tell you where to write to me as I am moving every day. Better send your letters to Richmond. Yours &c

C Dabney

JULY TO DECEMBER

Regrettably, no letters or diaries of any of Stuart's staff officers are known to exist for the time between July and late December. This period contains the Gettysburg and Mine Run campaigns and the Buckland Races, which makes the absence of records from the staff's point of view a great disappointment. There are reasons for this lack, some of which have already been mentioned.

Philip H. Powers was with Stuart's headquarters during this time, but there is only indirect evidence that he accompanied Stuart during the Gettysburg Campaign.

He was absent for various reasons for extended periods of time thereafter. He did not write frequently during this time period because he wasn't sure his letters would get through to his wife near Berryville, Virginia, and any letters he may have written may not have survived.

Frank Robertson, who rode with Stuart throughout the entire campaign, probably did not have the time to write. Once the Confederates were safe on Virginia soil after the withdrawal from Gettysburg, Robertson was sent home, having completely collapsed from a combination of exhaustion and trauma from a fall off a bridge abutment at Williamsport. Thus he never wrote his family about what he experienced, because he had the opportunity to tell them personally. So severe was Robertson's condition that he did not return to the staff for the remainder of the year. Stuart's letter of September 21 to Robertson testifies to his concern for his assistant engineer and verifies the extended time that he needed to recover.

Hd. Qrs. Cavalry Corps
Sept. 21st, 1863.

Dear Lieutenant:

I deeply regret the continuance of your illness, for I had hoped by this time you would be able to join us. I know very well that you could not be kept from your post except by inexorable necessity. It needed no surgeon's certificate to satisfy me of it.

I am glad of the present opportunity of expressing to you my sense of the usefulness, the bravery, the devotion to duty and daring for which you were distinguished during your stay with me. I sent you through fiery ordeals at Chancellorsville and elsewhere from which I scarcely hoped to see you return, but rejoiced to see you escape. You will never forget those trials and I hope the kind Providence which so signally favored you will soon see you restored to the field and to your much attached comrades.

Present my kindest regards to your father's family and believe me

Your sincere friend,
J. E. B. Stuart
Major General.

DECEMBER

By mid-December, Stuart and his staff were comfortably settled in their winter camp near Orange Court House. Much of the cavalry had been dispersed and sent home to recruit both men and horses. Those who remained took turns standing in the cold, miserable weather to watch the enemy. It was going to be a long, hard winter, and even the prospect of the coming Christmas season did little to warm the men and horses on picket duty as they tried to keep from freezing to death.

The day after Christmas, Philip H. Powers, now back at cavalry headquarters, wrote his wife. He shared with her his thoughts on the season and his depression over not being able to be with her and their children. Rumor had the enemy about to advance, but he seemed to put little stock in it. There was no mention of the new year and what it might bring. Powers and his wife already knew—the war would continue.

Camp Dec. 26th 1863

[To Mrs. Roberta Powers]

As the Christmas will be pretty well over before you receive this, I need hardly wish you a <u>merry</u> holiday. There is no holiday you will say for a poor woman with four children, a body full of ailments and pains, and a husband in the rebel army. Tis true—I have not in fact wished you much merriment, but as I have had none of the social enjoyment and pleasures usual at this season, and my mind has been much with you, I have indeed wished and prayed that you might be comfortable and happy with our Richmond friends during the season, and have longed incessantly to be with you.

Thursday, Jim & I spent a very pleasant day with our relative Ferdinand Jones—and were treated most affectionately by the ladies—his wife and daughter. He being absent. Yesterday Christmas day I had promised myself or rather my friends a bowl of Egg Nogg—but the <u>spirits</u> did not arrive— And consequently I passed a quiet and a <u>sober</u> day in my tent reading the "Woman in White"—which I finished. Jim came in last night and staid [*sic*] all night. And this morning I made the Egg Nogg—but have not been very well, and did not enjoy it—And today I have hardly left my tent.

I do not care to celebrate Christmas until I can do so with my children and my wife. When will that holiday come?

I sent you a letter by Mrs. Ballard and thought I should have had one from you tonight. And sent Jack over to H'Qrs after night to get it, but I was disappointed. I am sorry, for I am rather "out of sorts" and a letter from you would have helped me.

There is no news. I did hear of some movement going on by the enemy as if they might advance again—but have heard no details. Also heard this morning that our troops in the Valley were moving towards Winchester— but they are too few to accomplish anything in that direction. Have not heard from Clarke [County].

Major FitzHugh is still absent. Give love to all. And write me when you can. I hope the children enjoyed themselves yesterday. I thought of their stockings. Fortunate for them they were in Richmond were [*sic*] something could be had from Santa Claus. Much love for them. Excuse my poor letter my love for I am not in tune for writing tonight. And still would send you a greeting—God bless you my Dear,

Ever Yours

P. H. Powers

Stuart's staff had undergone many changes during 1863. Gone were most of the men who had been on the staff at the beginning of the year, and some had come and gone within the year: Capt. James L. Clark, aide-de-camp, had been transferred; Lt. Chiswell Dabney, aide-de-camp, had been promoted and transferred; Surgeon Talcott Eliason, medical director, had resigned because of ill health; Lt. Henry S. Farley, aide-de-camp, had been transferred; Capt. William D. Farley, voluntary aide, had been killed; Capt. Harry Gilmor, voluntary aide, had been transferred; Lt. Robert H. Goldsborough, aide-de-camp, had been captured; Lt. Col. George St. Leger Grenfell, inspector, had been transferred; Maj. J. T. W. Hairston, assistant adjutant general, and his brother, Maj. Samuel H. Hairston, quartermaster, had resigned; Lt. Walter Q. Hullihen, aide-de-camp, had been promoted and transferred; Lt. Richard B. Kennon, assistant adjutant general, had been transferred; Maj. John Pelham, commander of the Stuart Horse Artillery, and Lt. R. Channing Price, aide-de-camp and assistant adjutant general, had been killed; Lt. Thomas R. Price Jr., assistant engineer, had been transferred; Lt. Frank S. Robertson, assistant engineer, was on extended furlough; Maj. L. Frank Terrell, inspector, had resigned; Lt. Thomas B. Turner, aide-de-camp, had been transferred to Mosby's command and killed; Maj. Heros von Borcke, inspector, and Capt. Benjamin S. White, aide-de-camp, had been wounded and disabled for service.[108] *Twenty men who had been with the staff in 1863 would not begin 1864 with Stuart.*

Both old and new faces greeted the coming year as part of Stuart's staff: Rev. Dabney Ball, chaplain of the cavalry corps; Maj. Robert F. Beckham, commander of the Stuart Horse Artillery; Capt. W. W. Blackford, engineer officer; Col. Alexander R. Boteler, voluntary aide; Capt. John Esten Cooke, assistant adjutant general; Maj. Norman R. FitzHugh, assistant adjutant general; Maj. John B. Fontaine, medical director; Capt. Richard E. Frayser, signal officer; Maj. George Freaner, assistant adjutant and inspector general; Capt. Charles Grattan, ordnance officer; Lt. Henry Hagan, aide-de-camp; Capt. J. Marshall Hanger, assistant quartermaster; Maj. William J. Johnson, commissary of subsistence; Maj. Henry B. McClellan, assistant adjutant general; Capt. Garland M. Ryals, provost marshal; and Maj. Andrew R. Venable, assistant adjutant and inspector general.[109] *Before the campaign season opened in May, several of these men would also be gone.*

1864

JANUARY

Once again winter engulfed the armies. Stuart's headquarters near Orange Court House was not a big sprawling encampment, but the general's tent, dubbed the "Wigwam," was a comfortable, roomy place for the staff members to gather on cold nights and raise their voices in laughter and song. Although the social atmosphere of Orange Court House could not compare with that of Richmond, the men managed to enjoy themselves as they visited old friends and made new ones. The cold weather did not seem to depress their spirits.

Much of the cavalry had been sent home on furlough to recruit and obtain horses. Such mass leaves also served the purpose of lessening the burden on the Confederate commissary and quartermaster departments, which were constantly struggling to cope with shortages of almost everything and a scarcity of transport. Those troopers remaining with their regiments were called upon to man the picket lines and be ever ready to repulse any Federal incursions.

The cold and dreary weather seemed to bring out the best in John Singleton Mosby. With the regular cavalry hampered by thinned ranks and a lack of horses, Mosby and his partisans kept thousands of Federal infantry and cavalry occupied and constantly on the alert. Actions throughout the month in what had become known as "Mosby's Confederacy" warmed the hearts of Stuart and his staff as they read Mosby's reports or heard them directly from the "Gray Ghost" himself on his infrequent visits to Stuart's camp.

Except for the capturing of a few Federal pickets in an ambush here and there, or losing a few as occurred on the twenty-ninth, Stuart's cavalry spent a quiet month until the thirtieth, when the Federals mounted a scout from Culpeper Court House to Madison Court House. Again on the thirty-first, the area around Madison Court House was the scene of a Federal scouting expedition. The Confederate cavalry under Brig. Gen. Lunsford L. Lomax met the intruders as best they could but suffered a loss of two killed and thirty-four captured.[1] The men of Fitz Lee's and Tom Rosser's skeletal commands saw some action in the Valley.

John Esten Cooke had begun his "Life of Jackson" and was occupied with it and his usual visitations in and around the nearby communities. He evidently had given up the thought that his diary might be captured as Tom Price's had been and was back recording his thoughts and activities with his usual flair. He wrote of his

221

ongoing writing projects, the current social news, and his latest attempt to gain a promotion, which he felt he deserved.

For William W. Blackford, the month brought both good news and bad. Unlike Cooke, he would be receiving a promotion, but it would take him away from Stuart and the cavalry.[2] *In a letter to his father he expressed his feelings about leaving. He would be missed by Stuart and the staff.*

From John Esten Cooke's Journal

The Wigwam

Jan. 18, 1864—I have just returned from a ride to Orange with the Genl. and Mac [Maj. Henry B. McClellan] to see Mrs. Grinnan who goes tomorrow. Charming person. Write today the last of the chapter "Manassas" in Life of Jackson.

Letter from <u>Magnolia</u> offering me 8 columns weekly. Think of writing out my recollections of the war. Believe I will:—in natural humorous tone—no affectations of "humorous sadness."

Genl. back and great laughter. Camp gay: friends to dinner. Old Flop here—Bessie of "Hayfield" going to be married. Ca ira! And me? Esperance!

⋅—⋅ ⋙⬧⬦⬧⬪ —⋅

Jan. 23rd 1864
Head Qrs. Cav. Corps
Near Orange CH.

Dear Father [William M. Blackford],

I have been hoping for several days to be able to write you that I had received my promotion. I left Richmond yesterday and the appointment was to go into the Senate today. Mr. [Wyndham] Robertson said he would use his influence to get it through ahead of other business, so I hope it will come in a short time. I have received orders to report to the Regiment, so my commission with the Staff of General Stuart is at an end. It is with great regret that I leave him. I have been with him now for almost three years, and our relations have been most friendly, without a single exception. We have been together in almost every engagement fought by the Army of Northern Va, besides his numerous cavalry engagements and raids. I leave only two of the old staff behind me.[3] Since the second battle of Manassas five have been killed, three wounded, and two taken prisoner. One of those wounded will probably never be fit for service again and one is now in the enemy's hands. I have been ordered to Lynchburg on recruiting service and came by here to take leave and arrange about a place to leave my horses. I will probably start to Ly. [Lynchburg] on next Monday. Please let it be known that I want recruits but do not advertise yet. I do not wish to advertise until I can do so as Major. Mary will remain in Richmond for the present. Tell Eugene that I met Gen. & Mrs. [Robert E.] Rodes riding out this evening & the General inquired after him very particularly and sent his regards.[4] Give my love to Mother, Mary & Eugene.

Your aff. Son
Wm. W. Blackford

From John Esten Cooke's Journal

Wigwam near
Orange

Jan. 28. '64—Have been working enormously hard at the Jackson—and have got to Cross Keys—through the chapter headed "Ashby."[5] Some of the writing is good.

The Gen. & several staff have been up to Charlottesville, where they "inspected" and frolicked, at balls etc. An old lady, the Gen. says cautioned her daughters, young unsophisticated things, when they went to the ball "not to dance round dances or let Gen. Stuart kiss them." I wish I had gone.

Mac [Henry B. McClellan] & myself "ran the machine" here, Berkeley being Chief Engineer. Mac went over on a flag of truce to Locust Dale, and his brother Capt. McClellan on [Maj. Gen. George G.] Meade's staff hearing of his coming came to meet him, and they sat up and talked all night about things in general.[6] His brother told him he didn't blame him for taking the side where his convictions led him—but that the war would "end next summer"—meaning doubtless by our subjugation. It will take longer to do that.[7]

Letter from Kate Dan. [Dandridge], and Pennie: my Jackson a "precious gift" to Kate—Andrew dodging the enrolling officers of the Pierpont dynasty.[8] Truly the way of the stay-at-home is hard.

Poor Sweeny [Pvt. Sampson D. Sweeney] is dead—a great loss! What shall we do without him? He was a gentleman in character and manners—knew his place everywhere—had the savoir faire which makes a man graceful in the hut or the palace and was ever modest, obliging, respectful; poor fellow, he died of smallpox. Heaven rest him![9]

I think I will keep up this little diary regularly, only notes. Esperance!

Wigwam

Jan. 30, '64—My papers "complaining" etc. have come back, my private note to Gen. [G. W.] Custis [Lee] and all—with "a long string of whys and wherefores" as he says—explaining everything but their refusal to promote me.

So let it be. Two things said—and I have "no further remarks to make!"

1st Thing. I do not, on my honor, grudge the appointments of [Maj. George] Freaner, [Maj. Benjamin S.] White and [Maj. Garland M.] Ryals. They are brave soldiers, "bully boys, lads of mettle," and deserve every bit of their success. They are my warm personal friends—and good luck to 'em!

2nd Thing. I went to call on the President on New Year's day—but on my sacred word of honor as a gentleman, I then had no idea of making any application for a reconsideration of the action of the war office. The General likes me as well as if I was a ——— [word illegible], I think, and I like him as well as if he was Captain-General which he ought to be! "Good luck to him!"

Finished today Part II of the "Life of Jackson"—to the end of the Valley Campaign—563 pages. I have worked exceedingly hard on the revision so far—dovetailing the letters of papers into the reports, and making pictures as far as I could. Outstanding. The Gen. says "we must get to work"— which means his work. I will wait for McClellan's ——— [word illegible].

In doing this writing I have gone to work soon after breakfast—worked till dinner—then an hour's intermission—and then worked on till after midnight. Mind not ——— [word illegible], but my body often. Some of this my best writing. It is incomparably better than the first Ed. [edition].

Nothing stirring along the lines. We are making sawdust walks to all the tents. The Gen.'s tent excellently neat and warm. Times gay, jolly, ——— [word illegible]. In the spring we will have a lively campaign I suppose.

Weather for some days mild. delightful, May like—not cold like that at Verdiersville. Gen. Lee looking at us there in our bivouac under the pines, by the big log fire without wagons or anything—thought every brigadier and Colonel of Infantry has his wagons up—said of Gen. S. [Stuart], "What a hardy soldier!" I prefer living "under the greenwood tree" myself, when in active service. In winter quarters I like to be comfortable—in a field to be in "light marching order."

Hired 'Lige for another year at $240: a good boy. Mess bill for December $91. Charlie Lownes [Lowndes], a fine young fellow, highly recommended by Jack Wms. [Williams] has been sleeping in my tent.[10]

Wrote to Sister, Kate Dan. [Dandridge], Nan, and Pennie by Hagan who is gone to the Valley.

Ned Dan. [Dandridge] staid [sic] with me two nights lately. A fine fellow.

It is now raining. Snow soon, I reckon—and about the 10th Feb. I hope to get off and go to Fonthill.

Patter! patter!—on my tent.

Ca ira!

FEBRUARY

The bustle of activity that had marked the end of January continued into February, as the Federals probed for weaknesses along the Confederate front south of the Rapidan River. The sixth and seventh saw one such thrust escalate into a brief engagement at Morton's Ford, while skirmishing occurred at Barnett's and Culpeper fords. South of the Robertson River, the Federal cavalry ran into Lomax's weak brigade of three regiments, which they pushed back with some resistance toward the Rapidan.[11] Wade Hampton's troopers occupied the old winter encampment at Hamilton's Crossing and guarded the Rappahannock crossings from Germanna Ford to U.S. Ford. Brig. Gen. Judson Kilpatrick of the Union cavalry reported that he found Hampton's command hampered by a serious lack of horses and stated that few of the Confederate cavalry doing picket duty at the fords had horses.[12] Losses were light on both sides, and by the eighth all had returned to their winter camps.

Not a single one of the encounters at the end of January or the beginning of February disturbed either John Esten Cooke or Philip H. Powers enough to be included in their writings for the month. Cooke concerned himself with finishing Stuart's Sharpsburg and Dumfries reports, commenting on his current writing projects, reminiscing of happier times, contemplating his future, and pondering the identity of the writer of a note from "Oglethorpe Georgia." The fighting along the lines does not seem to have interrupted his daily routine.

For Powers the war existed only in the fact that it separated him from his beloved wife and family. His two letters focused on his wife's poor health, which he attributed to her mental state and the corresponding proximity of the Federals. He longed to be with her to encourage and help her and hoped for a chance to visit Richmond and see his family.

From John Esten Cooke's Journal

Wigwam

Feb. 5, 1864—On 3rd Gen. [Robert H.] Chilton and Majors Venable, Hill and Fields dined with us. ———— [word illegible] that wicked anecdote of an old fellow's asking a Va. lady who had been to the ———— [word illegible] "Whether she had been away from Virginia long enough to lose her <u>virginity!</u>"

On 4th yesterday Gen. S. [Stuart] and myself fought our way thro' Sharpsburg, he dictating uninterruptedly after the Crampton Gap fight, and some before. Report finished.

Today have commenced and nearly finished the Dumfries expedition.

Weather rainy. Singular dream last night— ———— [word illegible] up with "consuelo" and other things: in some "far land." Curious as I had forgotten that book.

Have written lately "In the Valley now!" and "The Crown" verses—
and "Thackeray" for the Portfolio papers. Both, good. Hope to go Fonthill
this month.

[Partial entry: no date, but written between fifth and twelfth.]

. . . receive and forward dispatches to Gen. [Robert E.] Lee or Gen. Stuart
and at one time thought I might have to move camp. Rather a bore to
stay behind—and the Gen. asked me if I had "felt lonely." Reply "rather."
They all came home, gay and hungry and ——— [word illegible] and Ned
Dan. [Dandridge], who had come in with young Lt. Hatcher said "I wonder what I would think if my Old Brig. did that way!" But it was the jovial
——— [word illegible]" [Surgeon John B.] Fontaine.
    [Pvt. Benjamin F.] Stringfellow is writing out his adventures, seated on
my bed.[13] He is going down this evening to see his mother in Culpeper;
having "a little raft" to get over [the Rapidan River] on. His life is a strange
one: death can't make him "back."
    Ned staid [*sic*] all night with young Hatcher. Today brilliant and beau-
tiful—too lazy to work. Gen. in high spirits and singing in his tent. Wind
blowing—sun shining. Ca Ira!

———————

Camp Sunday Night
February 6, 1864

My Dear Wife [Mrs. Roberta Powers],

    I hope to see you before this reaches you, but in case anything happens
to disappoint me, and a sad disappointment it will be, you will get my letter,
which though it may not answer for myself will yet tell you how ardently
I desire to be with you, and how earnestly I am endeavoring to get off. General Stuart returned from Hanover Junction this afternoon, and I went over
immediately to see him. He promises me an order for Richmond tomorrow—which if approved by Genl [Robert E.] Lee, will enable me to leave
on Tuesday. I hope nothing may occur to prevent; for I am unusually
anxious. I received your letter of last Sunday today. Also one from Mrs.
Ware. She had received your letter. All were well. Colonel Ware in Baltimore, but still not allowed to return home. I felt unwell this morning and
did not go to Church, but to my surprise Jim came down, his Brigade having
returned to Orange, and spent the day with me. He is very well. I was right
glad to see him. I get so tired living with people who I know care nothing

for me, that it is a real pleasure to meet with one of my own family. I have not heard from you since Bob's telegram, but hope the Yankees did not frighten you into being sick. I infer they must have either visited Marshfield or been very close to it, but as you have seen the wretches before, I judge you would not be as scared as some others would be at the sight of them.[14]

Hoping to see you before this reaches you, and praying for your safety. With love to the children and all—

Very Truly
Yours
P. H. P.

From John Esten Cooke's Journal

Wigwam, near
Orange

Feb. 12, '64—Last night we went over and spent a pleasant evening at Mrs. Scott's with Mrs. McClellan, Mrs. Berkeley, and Mrs. Taylor—pretty wife of Major Taylor.

Fun: [Pvt. William M.] Pegram and Mac playing and singing—"Bingo" "Jine the Cavalry," and all.[15] Ice cream and custard for supper!

Walked—back late.

Dr. Caney here: making us all laugh with his "Flea Story," and his account of the "Veteran Homeguard" whom he saw the other day when the alarm was given in Richmond at daylight—a big fat fellow with equipments on and musket in hand blubbering at the door, as he bade his wife farewell. Poor home guard! How they are laughed at!

Gen. [Brig. Gen. James B.] Gordon here today—a charming man.[16] My heart warms to this jovial, gallant soldier. He says he likes "Young Brown" exceedingly. Glad of it. I always knew there was more in Chiswell [Dabney] than had come out.[17]

The weather today, beautiful, brilliant, breathing balmy spring. I have just finished the falling back from the Blue Ridge in Nov. 1862, and for the moment am idle.

In a few days I hope to go to Fonthill via Fredericksburg. I dream, how I dream!—of many scenes and faces. Camp is so different from old times and persons—here it is joke or nothing: sentiment is ——— [word illegible] sentimentality. I show none but it is in my heart as before. Which light is it that shines on the windows of Hayfield in the sunset—on the porch of the Bower—on the lawn at the Vineyard: at Kennons, Glenmore, ——— [word illegible]?[18] Surely not this common place sunlight I see to-day, here in the plain bare camp!

What will be my fate after the war—if I live? Will I marry? Who can tell? I mean there is an element of uncertainty in all human things!

Things look better at the North: Through this campaign the result will begin to appear: but shall I live to see it?

I know not, and leave all issues in the hands of my Creator and re-deemer—praying that they will make me pure, and keep me unspotted from the world—and if I fall, reserve me unto heaven.

Esperance!

Wigwam near
Orange

Feb. 21, '64—Have nearly finished abstracting my ordnance accounts for three quarters. A terrific job: but now I think I have learned it—an invaluable lesson.

The Gen. for five days in Richmond. Mrs. McClellan, Berkeley and Taylor to dine with us the other day, and we had a jolly time. They are charming. This evening I went over there—Mrs. G. [Grinnan] goes tomorrow. Major T. [Taylor] a fine fellow. Suffering much with an inflamed ear.

"Jackson" has been shipped for the abstracts; for ——— [word illegible] return.

We are having a pleasant time here, good fare, and not much to do, though I am never idle. Dr. Caney has been here—a fine old boy: says I am "a devilish good fellow"—everything being with him either "devilish good" or "d——d bad."

This evening I received from "Oglethorpe Georgia" (post mark outside) the following in a beautiful feminine, rather foreign-looking hand, with a bunch of pressed flowers enclosed:

"For the sake of one who fell at 'Kellys [*sic*] Ford, March 17th '63, an unknown Georgian sends you a simple cluster of young spring flowers. You loved the 'Gallant Pelham' and your words of love and sympathy are 'immortelles' in the hearts that loved him. 'Tristan Joyeuse,' God bless you. I may never meet you, but you have a true friend in me. I know that a sad heart mourns her beloved in Virginia: I know a darkened home in Alabama tells the sorrow there: my friendship for him was pure as a sister's love, or a spirit's?—I had never heard his voice.

Your name is ever in my prayers! God bless you

'N'Importé[19]

St. Valentines Day, Georgia 1864"

Who can this be from? Curious. It is a woman—with French traces about the hand—she knows of S. D.'s [Sally Dandridge] engagement[20]—

and has never heard Pelham's voice, but prays for me, because I wrote the sketch of him in the "News!" Singular! It is impossible that the thing is a quiz. The subject is too grave, and it certainly is from Oglethorpe, Georgia—and is addressed simply "John Esten Cooke, care of Gen. J. E. B. Stuart, Army of Virginia."

Whoever you may be, O fair and kind correspondent! Thanks for your sweet words and flowers, making your letter redolent with the odours of the South! Someday we may meet. Who knows? More singular things have happened. I may meet this writer, and the owner of the ——— [three words illegible]!

━•━ ⚎◆⚎ •━━

Head Quarters
Cavalry Corps
Army of Northern
Virginia,
21st February 1864

My Dear Wife [Mrs. Roberta Powers],

I am not yet in writing trim, have had neuralgia in my head all the week and it makes me feel very uncomfortable, but I cannot allow the day to pass without sending you a line. I feel so concerned about your sickness that you are rarely now out of mind. The last of my thoughts at night and the first in the morning, longing to pierce through the space that separates us, and see you with my own eyes; hoping too each hour that it may be one of comfort to my wife. How weak we are! How incapable of helping each other in time of necessity! Each day teaches me the lesson more impressively that all our help must come from God; and I pray preserve you to me—Not that I deserve any thing at His hands, but wrath and indignation for the multitude of my continued transgressions, but for His mercy's sake, trusting in the infinity of His love and the extent of His forbearance.

I heard Mr. Davis today in an excellent sermon in little sins. It reminded me of one I heard from Dudley Tyng on the text "despise not the day of little things"—Both sermons taught how prone we are to open our heart and our conscience to small offenses until by degrees the heart becomes hard and the conscience stifled, and in rush the greater offenses by which we are lost.

Old Neill Barnett was in my tent yesterday. Came out on Monday last. Said the Yankees had certainly left Charlestown [Charles Town] but were still at Harper's Ferry. Now would be a good time to get your things out if your brother would take advantage of it, but I recon [*sic*] he will wait until later.

I am sorry you cannot get any good bread. Can't you exchange with the Bakers flour for bread? Or I think you might buy enough for yourself. I will try to get you some lard from the country. I can't send you any from our supply—not that I had rather you should have it all than myself, but it would not be right. I will write a little note to Alice. I was quite surprised, and much gratified, that she should be able to write even such a note as was hers. Encourage her to write to me. Nothing will improve her writing more. I am glad for your sake that the weather has turned warm again. I don't know how you got along Wednesday or Thursday. Major [Norman R.] FitzHugh is still absent. I may say again that I hope to come down in March. But do not expect me too certainly or too early in the month. The 1st of the month is a busy time for us. And I have much to do in the next ten days—

With much love to Mack and Jack & Billy. And more than all for your dear self.

Yours

P. H. P.

On the twenty-eighth, the Federals launched the famous Kilpatrick-Dahlgren Raid on Richmond.[21] The raid began with a skirmish at Ely's Ford on the twenty-eighth, followed by small clashes at Beaver Dam Station and Taylorsville on the twenty-ninth. Wade Hampton's Division, mostly Brig. Gen. P. M. B. Young's Brigade, offered resistance along the Federals' route of march. As February waned, the Confederates scrambled to defend their capital.[22]

In conjunction with the raid, Brig. Gen. George A. Custer carried out a diversionary attack toward Charlottesville.[23] His troopers skirmished with Confederates at Stanardsville on the twenty-ninth and later the same day ran into the Stuart Horse Artillery's winter camp at Rio Hill near Charlottesville. Without cavalry support, the meager force of artillerymen appeared doomed. But some accurate artillery fire, a little bluff, and a well-timed "cavalry" charge by the ill-armed cannoneers and drivers forced Custer back the way he had come. Stuart made an attempt to cut off the retreating Federals, but bad weather and the poor condition of the gray cavalry's horses combined to slow his pursuit.[24]

MARCH

From the first to the fourth, the Confederates fought the Union raiders at Ashland, on the Brooke Turnpike near Richmond, near Atlee's, Old Church, and Walkerton. Union commanders Col. Ulrich Dahlgren and Brig. Gen. Judson Kilpatrick had split their forces; the former was killed, but the latter made his escape. Custer brushed aside opposition at Stanardsville and Burton's Ford to return to his lines, and the whole affair was over by the fourth, though the controversy that erupted over papers found on Dahlgren still smolders.[25]

The remainder of the month was quiet except for Kilpatrick's brief foray into King and Queen County from the ninth through the twelfth. Stuart left to see what he could do to catch the raiders, but by the time he arrived, all was over and Kilpatrick was gone.[26] Stuart and his staff were honored with an invitation to a grand tournament and ball given by the officers of A. P. Hill's Corps. Stuart could not attend, but he sent members of his staff in his place.[27]

John Esten Cooke had little to write about during the month. His brief entries touched upon the Kilpatrick-Dahlgren Raid, a Federal rumor that Gen. John B. Hood would replace Stuart as cavalry commander, visitors to the camp, his near completion of "Jackson," and his awed reaction to Victor Hugo's *Les Misérables.*

From John Esten Cooke's Journal

The Wigwam near
Orange

March 7, 1864—The grand Yankee fandango is over at last. Dalgreen [Dahlgren] is shot as highwaymen deserve, and the "Dalgreen Papers" are printed.

This raid will be historic. Dalgreen sought immortality and has found it.

I was left here on Feb. 29th by the Gen. and kept forwarding and duplicating dispatches to him and Gen. Lee all night.

On March 2, he came and went to Chancellorsville—thence after the Yankees below.

I have had a jolly old time, running couriers, receiving and transmitting reports and orders day and night. I think everything is straight as a shingle. Just from Gen. Lee's Hdqrs. 10 P. M.

Gen. S. [Stuart] back.

Wigwam

March 8, 1864—Old Gen. [Maj. Gen. John] Sedgwick on hearing the report that Hood would supersede Stuart exclaimed!"[28]

"I'm glad of it! Stuart is the best cavalry officer ever foaled in North America!"

The general conviction of these Hdqrs. is that we are going to catch Kilpatrick yet. The report came last night that he was advancing from Glos'ter [Gloucester Court House] toward the Rap'k [Rappahannock]—but it turned out to be all fudge.

Wigwam

March 9, '64—Today I finished the battles around Richmond in Jackson: and when Gen. [Brig. Gen. William N.] Pendleton's notes come will finish up Manassas. The book is thus virtually done up to Maryland in Sept. 1862.

Today Gen. [Brig. Gen. Williams C.] Wickham spent several hours with us and Mrs. Stuart, Mrs. Berkeley, he, Capt. Garnett etc. dined. Gen. R. E. Lee was here before dinner in his old blue cape, and Mrs. Stuart told him laughingly how I had "dodged a little too far" (off my horse) "at Cold Harbor." "Don't tell Gen. Lee that" ——— [word illegible] cum risu:[29] but he said, "That's right—you dodge as many as you can, Captain." He's a fine old gentleman.

Tonight I went to see the Misses Bull—Miss Mary pretty, coquettish, ——— [word illegible]. Just back—banjo and ——— [word illegible] going.

Wigwam

March 13th '64—Left here again to run the ranch—Buck not being well of his ailment viz. scratches.[30]

The Gen. gone to look after Kilpatrick who advanced from F. [Fort] Monroe thro' Glos'ter [Gloucester Court House] with 6 negro regiments and his cavalry, and when Hampton telegraphed last just building a bridge over Dragon Swamp, and aiming to reach Urbana [Urbanna]. Last news is, he's gone back, burning King & Queen C. H. [Court House] on the way.

Today nine Yankees and some Confed. prisoners came from Mosby. Turned over as usual to Maj. [David B.] Bridgford.[31] Wrote to the Vineyard by the Sergeant in ch. [charge] to be forwarded by Mosby.

I am going to Fonthill probably, next week. Gen. says I can. I must start at once, as things are hurrying up.

Jackson is done (all except 1st Manassas which awaits Gen. Pendleton's notes) up to Oct. 1862—through Sharpsburg. It is much better.

Today brilliant, Maylike, the wind roaring thro' in the trees. A grand sound and stirs my blood!

The Valley! The Valley! When shall I see my own land again!

Wigwam

Night of March 13th '64—I have just finished "Jean Valjean" the last of the wretched. Infinitely mournful book!—with a pathos in three last pages too deep for tears. What a genius! Nothing in any literature is greater than some of these pictures.

A book grand, sad and unlike any other. With much that is tedious and more that is repulsive and shocking—but easily the first in pathos of modern French literature.

The effect left on the mind is intended to be, and is, salutary:—but like the death of Col. Newcome, that of Jean Valjean is infinitely sad, and leaves the heart ———— [word illegible]. What a genius! and what am I to write?

The strange thing is that Hugo with white hairs can draw that enchanting picture of love. The grandeur of Jean Valjean and the innocence of Corette are the charm of the drama. His love for her is inexpressibly charming.

Why should I try to write in the lifetime of my masters? I sit in my tent by the dying fire, and consider myself nobody.

Three last pages of the book are one long sob. Why should the Jean Valjean be trodded down by the brutal hatred of society? What a protest in favour of the "Wretched"—and sermon on repentance and the cleaning from all sin!

But God is over all.

APRIL

The calm that had marked the last two weeks of March carried over into April. There were no major engagements or even skirmishes of any importance between the contending cavalry forces, other than the usual guerrilla and scout activities, until the twenty-eighth, when the Federals mounted another brigade scouting expedition in the vicinity of Madison Court House. Information concerning Stuart's forces in the area was gathered, along with a few prisoners, before the blue column returned to its camp.[32] Though little appeared to be happening at the front, much was taking place in the rear that would make early May quite hectic.

At Stuart's headquarters, John Esten Cooke returned from a most enjoyable time among his friends. He was greeted almost immediately with the news that he was the new horse artillery inspector, an assignment he did not particularly relish but one he accepted as his duty. The batteries had to be in fighting trim for the coming campaign season, and Cooke would see to it that they were. He also celebrated the completion of "Jackson." He was pleased with the result and expected to make a few dollars on its sale.

Frank Robertson had been laid up since the Gettysburg Campaign. His health did not allow his return to cavalry headquarters, but he could still contribute. Stuart sent him some work, and Robertson's good friend Lt. Theodore S. Garnett, Stuart's new aide-de-camp, wrote to him on the thirtieth about the status of the promotion Robertson was hoping to receive.[33] Garnett also mentioned how quiet things were. The quiet would last just four more days.

From John Esten Cooke's Journal

Wigwam

Apr. 1, 1864—On March 15, in obedience to telegram from Gen. to "come down to Fred'g [Fredericksburg] on horseback as soon as Maj. [George] Freaner arrived"—set out, rode the 38 or 40 miles by sunset, and danced nearly all night, afterwards, at Miss Nelly Kelly's.

We were entertained at Mr. Slaughter's most hospitably—and after parties there, at Mr. Hart's etc. the Gen. & rest returned leaving me to go down to Essex. Went to stay a night at Mrs. Alsop's who was most kind, and staid [*sic*] three or four days—entertainments every night: charades etc. Girls of Fred. [Fredericksburg] charming—especially the Alsops who are the nicest going. But they were old friends. [Norman R.] FitzHugh of <u>Cherry Stone</u> there with me.

Went to Essex on Tuesday and was stopped at Frayser's by the snow. Arrived next day, and was warmly welcomed. Four or five charming days with the girls. That place is surely a "home of ancient peace" and warm hearts.

Pulled up stakes however on the 28th and came thro' to Orange here in two days—more than 80 miles: stopping for the night at Mrs. Alsop's: and riding the 2nd day thro' a tremendous rain.

Find Gen. W. H. F. Lee here and am charmed to see him. The Lee family are delightful people to me—personally. I take to them as to kin.

All quiet along the Rapidan. Gen. [Brig. Gen. Williams C.] Wickham dined with us yesterday.

Wigwam

Apr. 1, 1864 9 P. M.—A gay day. W. H. F. Lee here—he is a charming person: grave but cheerful, and fond of a joke. This morning being "All Fool's Day" Johnnie Fontaine poked in his head and told me that Gen. W. H. F. wanted a pair of drawers: he had none. Reply, "Gen. Lee can't wear my drawers—they are too small for me: but he can try." April Fool! Old Judge Freaner sent him handkerchiefs etc. We sent McC [Maj. Henry B. McClellan] a telegram saying that his wife had a bad sick headache and couldn't come. Rec'd [Received] at dinner table: read it: looked grave and muttered, "I don't like this!" Suddenly woke to the trick. The Gen. intended to prepare one announcing the birth of a son in the Fontaine family; and told me the plan "gleefully;" but a letter came and spoiled all.

Von Borcke came up today—a fine old boy: and all delighted to see him. He is very thin and coughs painfully. He has my deep sympathy.

Rich takes one off on "Here's your little ————" [word illegible] for the bit! Next time I'm left in charge I'll make him walk the circle.

Gen. W. H. F. goes tomorrow—says he has enjoyed his visit greatly. We have—I at least: and all. There is something charming about the Lees to me: they are highbred. I sympathize deeply with Gen. Rooney for his wife's sake, whom I always liked much. Poor fellow, he bears his loss manfully.[34]

Raining—went to see Flora today, and had a good chat. Must "to bed."

Wigwam

Ap. 10, 1864—"Jackson" is finished—all but last chapter, the ——— [word illegible], which I hope to finish on Monday.

The account of "Chancellorsville" and his wound is good I think—it is full.

The work has taken me a good while, having been commenced in November—the latter part—and occasionally <u>driven</u> ahead. It is incomparably better than the first edition and will give me some reputation I think. The bulk of the MS. is in Overton's hands at Richmond.

This is Sunday, and I am just going to church. We have had a gay time in camp—but the enemy will soon be mobilized and the campaign open. May God protect my dear ones and me.

Esperance!

Wigwam

Ap. 12, 1864— ——— [word illegible] Triomphe!!!

This very moment at about 9 P. M. on the 11th of April in the year 1864 (date to be handed down to the remotest posterity) I have finished "Jackson!!!" It makes some 1182 pp. but as the old text—also marked, or paged—is scattered through it, it will make nearer 13, or 1400 pages of my MS.—say 700 pages of letter paper size. Now that will make nearly as many printed pages 800 and such will be the size of the work if Providence permits it to be printed.

It is a good book I think, and will add to my reputation.

No news. I expect to go down tomorrow to Milford to inspect [Capt. James F.] Hart's battery: and perhaps to spend a night with Nat.[35]

My Fred'g [Fredericksburg] friends are in Richmond. Funny conversation with Flora about them, and the repetition of what friends in Richmond said ——— [word illegible].

Wrote to Nat and Sister Willie.[36]

Am tired in my back and fingers. Jackson has worked me very hard, but now the subject is off my mind.

[Surgeon John B.] Fontaine and others gone to a ball somewhere, Old

Judge Freaner just left and is coming back to chat. God bless all my dear ones.

Esperance!

Wigwam

Ap. 13, '64—See 5 pages back, a note under date of April 12 ——— in the wrong place by mistake.

Last night, just as I was finishing Jackson the Genl. sent up, and when I went down sprung the "Inspector of Horse Art." upon me.

Well—so be it. It is rather a hard thing to break the thousand ties for two years growing: but n'importe!

I hope to go to Richmond in two days—but don't know. A friend of mine is there, about whom I'm rather "imbecile."

All is in the hands of God who doeth all things well. The rest is not important.

Still Esperance!

—⬩ ▰◆▰ ⬩—

Hd. Qrs. Cav. Corps A.
N. Va.
April 18th 1864

Dear Frank [Robertson],

I send you a map of the battle of Chancellorsville, which I wish you to reduce to letter size, 2 copies. I am anxious to have it as soon as possible. Preserve the map as it is particularly valuable. Give my sincere regards to your father's family, & my condolence to [Maj. William W.] Blackford for the bereavement he has suffered.[37]

Very truly
yours,
J. E. B. Stuart

From John Esten Cooke's Journal

Camp Horse Art.
near Gordonsville

Ap. 29, 1864—On the morning of April 14, I started to inspect Hart's Battery near Milford: missed the Fred'g [Fredericksburg] train at the Junction, and went down to Taylorsville where I staid [*sic*] all night with my dear Nat. They were camped in good houses near ——— [name illegible] whose family had been very kind to Nat this winter. Long chats about getting married etc. He is a gallant boy—Cooper a good fellow.

Next morning [April 15] took the train at Taylorsville: went to Chesterfield Depot: mounted [Capt. William L.] Church's horse: and rode with [Maj. Henry S.] Farley, 5 miles, and inspected Hart.[38] Returned without loss of time to Chesterfield—[Brig. Gen. Pierce M. B.] Young's Hdqrs.— wrote my report—and just as I finished, the down train signaled, and Church told me he would endorse and forward my report. As good a fellow as ever was—Farley a good friend of mine. Memo. General "spoke highly of" my report say [Maj. Andrew R.] Venable and Freanor [Maj. George Freaner]. Gen. endorsed, "A very satisfactory report."

Went to Richmond under orders to see after packsaddles. Met old Thad. Fitzhugh at Ashland, and took a letter from him to Miss Lizzie. Expecting not to see her that night, gave it to Capt. Jones (rival) who delivered it that night in my presence.

Went first on my arrival and saw dear Mammy. She is blind in one eye, but otherwise well and gay and delighted to see me! That night went to Major French's, and saw my Fred'g [Fredericksburg] friends—saw them repeatedly thereafter! Had a good time generally: went down with them, Mrs. Gregory: Miss Net Powell, Miss Emma Dabney: and Captains Lewis, Burwell and Drs. Gregory and Temple, to Dury's [Drewry's] Bluff. A powerful position—glad I saw it. Guns splendid. Can't be taken except by flanking. A nice day. Came back and eat [sic] some cake at ——— [name illegible]. Thereafter many "pleasant walks and talks" which made it uncommonly hard to leave! Left however—having got 3 days extension from Col. Withers—on the 23rd.

Made arrangements to have "Jackson" copied by Nannie Steger, and Mr. Benjamin very politely promised to forward the MS. to London. I am having maps made, and it will bring me, I hope, at least £500 which is $50,000 or $10,000 worth of land.

Reached Corps Hdqrs. on Sunday afternoon, and on Monday fixed up and came here. Gen. and staff expressed many regrets at parting with me. Gen. said he was going to "send for me once a week." On Tuesday morning, sent Lige with the horses by the road: came down on the cars with baggage which I sent out in Capt. Oden's wagon: dined with Maj. Richards: came out: and am fixed comfortably here in a fly with the back cedared up: my desk "in position": bed all right: and with a fine set of fellows, many from Jefferson. My duties will be pleasant, I think, and once in the field, I shall have to do much riding—Hart among others, will have to be inspected—near Fred'g [Fredericksburg]! Quien sabe?[39]

Yesterday—the 28th—rode over to [Lt. Col. Carter M.] Braxton's Batt'n [Battalion] near Barboursville, to see Nat: met him on the road: turned him back: and spent a delightful day with him.[40] Afterwards rode with him on the Liberty Mills road to Gen. [Brig. Gen. Armistead L.] Long's Hdqrs. and he cut on up with me to the B. [Brock] road, and we separated.[41] My affection for Nat is greater than that which I have for any other male human being. He is taking the place of my dear Sainty—may God protect him, and enable us all to meet again at the good old Vineyard.[42]

In His hands are the issues of life and death. May He protect my dear ones and me, and bring us safely home to heaven.

Esperance!

━━ ⚔ ━━

> Head Quarters
> Cavalry Corps,
> Army of Northern
> Virginia,
> April 30th 1864

Dear Frank [Robertson],

Genl. Stuart has just now requested me to inform you that he has received a communication from Col. [Alfred L.] Rives stating that your application will be presented to Genl. [Jeremy F.] Gilmer as soon as possible for his favorable consideration.

I received your note sent by [Pvt. George] Woodbridge, & have sent one of those maps to Genl. [James B.] Gordon. You must excuse me for not informing you of this before. I trust that your promotion may be soon made now, and that you will be able to join us in the coming campaign.

There is no news of any kind up here; we are all even more quiet than we were two weeks ago.

Remember me kindly to your family and believe me,

> Your sincere friend,
> Theodore S. Garnett, Jr.

MAY

As May began, Garnett's statement about "quiet" still held true, though there were expectations that things would liven up shortly. Nothing stirred along the Rapidan or the Rappahannock, but everywhere behind the lines there was activity. Amid the comings and goings a new staff officer made his way to Stuart's camp near Orange Court House. Alexander R. Boteler, former aide to Stonewall Jackson, had consented to be a voluntary aide for Stuart. On the second, he began to record his thoughts in a diary. He was pleased to be among the men of the staff, many of whom he knew well. By the time he wrote on the third, he was making preparations for what everyone knew lay ahead.

From *Alexander Robinson Boteler's Diary*

Monday, May 2, 1864.—I left Richmond this morning by the Central Railroad for Orange Court House to resume the position of volunteer aide on the Staff of Maj. Gen. J. E. B. Stuart; likewise to report for duty as Special Commissioner to the Army of Northern Virginia under instruction from the Secretary of War in accordance with a provision of the act suspending the writ of habeas corpus.

Reached Headquarters in good time as my genial friend, the General, was at dinner with his staff in front of his tent.

Am pleased to find the greater part of his former staff still with him: Maj. [Henry B.] McClellan, Adjt. [Adjutant] and Chief of Staff; Maj. [Andrew R.] Venable, inspector; Maj. [Charles] Grattan, Ordnance Officer, with Capt. John Esten Cooke as his assistant; Maj. Fitzhugh [Norman R. FitzHugh], Corps, Dabney Ball, Chaplain, Lieuts. [Chiswell] Dabney and Hullihen (Walter Q.) whom Stuart calls "Hunny Bunny", aides, etc.⁴³ I miss that eccentric Englishman and skilled soldier of fortune, Col. [George] St. Leger Greenfel [Grenfell] who has seen so much service in all the four quarters of the globe and whose pet bulldog "the pup" was such an intolerable nuisance to everybody in camp but himself; and I am sorry not to see among the couriers, the fun-provoking face of [Pvt. Sampson D.] Sweeney, the banjo player, who contributed so much to our amusement during the last campaign, poor fellow. Since then he has died of small pox.

The camp here is the same selected last fall when we fell back from Brandy Station, but I have no idea that we will be allowed to occupy it longer than this week as we are daily in expectation of a movement by the enemy.

At a late hour retired to my former quarters in the General's tent.

Tuesday, May 3.—Spent the day in camp arranging for contingencies. Provided myself with a horse, reduced my luggage, cleaned my pistols and wrote a letter to my wife.

Sent a lot of captured Yankee newspapers to Judge [John] Perkins, M.C. from Louisiana and to other friends in Richmond.⁴⁴

Stuart gave me a characteristic autographed note of General Lee's, which illustrates a charming feature in his character—the playfulness of his disposition in social life.

At night the scouts (amongst them my remarkable young friend [Benjamin F.] Stringfellow), came in and reported that Grant's vast army is preparing to advance, that it numbers about one hundred and twenty thousand and is magnificently equipped. So the ball is about to begin. We'll have stirring times here before the week is over with more than double our effective force to contend with.

On the evening of the third, Stuart issued marching orders to his staff, and "Camp Wigwam" was broken up. Scouts had brought the news that the Federal army was crossing the rivers in force. Boteler wrote of his and Stuart's activities on the fourth as the Confederates moved to meet the Army of the Potomac in the tangle known as the Wilderness.

From Alexander Robinson Boteler's Diary

Wednesday, May 4—The news by our Scouts last night is fully confirmed this morning. The entire Yankee Army is in motion, crossing at Ely's and Germanna Fords, and by this time probably they all are over the rivers: Grant, Burnside, Meade, Warren, Hancock, and Sedgwick.[45]

Our tents were struck, wagons loaded and long before noon everything was in its proper place and everybody about the camp ready for active operations. Our mid-day meal was a merry one for all seemed glad to be relieved from the monotony of camp life in Winter Quarters.

Accompanied Gen. Stuart to Army Headquarters, taking a short cut across country which gave us several opportunities to test the jumping qualities of our horses.

Reported myself to Col. Walter Taylor and had a very kind and cordial greeting from Gen. Lee who invited us to dine with him, but as we had had our mid-day meal we declined.

Everything betokened an immediate movement at Headquarters. Noticed the General's iron gray horse "Traveller" was ready for him to mount and that he himself is looking remarkably well and as calm, as courteous and as considerate today as on the most ordinary occasions. No one would suppose from his demeanor that great events are in the gale of vast responsibilities weighing on his mind. Truly he is a grand specimen of a Christian hero—as good as he is great.

The staff of couriers having joined us, we took our leave of the Commander-in-Chief and started for the front down the Fredericksburg plank road into what is called "The Wilderness", a name that fitly applies to the locality it designates for a gloomier, wilder and more forbidding region can hardly be found this side of the Alleghenies.

For miles along the road the forests are unbroken by a single clearing and the traveller may journey on for hours without seeing a sign of human habitations. Not only do over-arching trees on either hand hem in the road and hide the sky, making it at high noon there seem more like twilight gray, but there is also on both sides a tangled mass of undergrowth apparently interminable and so densely intricate that it would be difficult for a dog to get through it. We scouted down the plank road for some miles before we were halted and then it was with unceremonious suddenness.

For while moving cautiously along, vainly trying to see beyond the thicket, our advance was suddenly fired into from the side of the road and presently under cover of another volley, which did no execution, there was an attempt to charge which, however, was promptly checked by a fire from some of our own men, and was not followed up by any further demonstration.

Having thus discovered the enemy, we slowly returned the way we had gone. By this time it was becoming quite dark and we met a courier who had been sent from camp that morning to Orange Court House, for our mail. Among the letters he brought were several for me, one of which was from Captain Tait of England enclosing a note he had brought through the lines for me from my darling daughter, J—— and which I managed to read as we rode along by the light of lucifer matches and the glow of my pipe. It was a strange place to receive news from loved ones at home, but it was all the more welcomed and lifted my heart out of the gloom of the wilderness. When we reached our lines which had taken position for the night near Mine Run at right angles with the plank road and on both sides of it we met a heavy column of our cavalry coming up to cover the right flank of the Army and as we stopped in the middle of the road, Stuart was recognized by his men who greeted him with enthusiastic shouts as regiment after regiment, following each other, filed off before him along the rear of the infantry. It was an impromptu ovation to the Chief of the Cavalry Corps and the incident, interesting in itself, was made much more so by the scenic effects of the surroundings. In fact, an artist could hardly find a finer subject for his pencil, though a picture of it, however perfect in its handling and details, would necessarily fall far short of reality in representing a scene so full of animation and excitement. Stuart himself a little in advance of us with his plumed hat in his hand, looked like an equestrian statue—both man and horse being as motionless as marble—his fine soldierly figure fully revealed in the light of the camp fires that were blazing brightly on both sides of the road as far as the eye could reach and lighting up the foreground splendidly.

The cavalry came up in columns of fours at full trot, saluting the General with a shout as they wheeled off at a gallop, toward their designated positions while the infantry, catching inspiration from their cheers, mingled their loud hurrahs with theirs in one grand chorus of twice ten thousand voices. It was really a grand spectacle to see these gallant horsemen coming toward us out of the gloom of night into the glare of the fires, making the welkin ring with their wild war cries and the earth to tremble beneath their horses [*sic*] hoofs.

Bivouacked at Verdiersville which consists, so far as we could see, of a dilapidated store house and deserted dwelling, both too dirty for human occupation so we spread our blankets under the shelter of the trees, where we slept as soundly as if on eiderdown.

The Battle of the Wilderness began on May 5, when Gen. Tom Rosser encountered Federal cavalry on the Catharpin Road. At first the blue cavalry surged ahead, but soon the Confederates drove them back to the vicinity of Todd's Tavern, where the tide turned as the Federals received reinforcements. Stuart witnessed Rosser's success but returned to the Plank Road before the Federals counterattacked. Back on the Plank Road, he helped rally retreating Confederate infantry until dark ended the fighting.[46] *Little change occurred overnight. Shortly after dawn on the sixth, the two armies began tearing at each other again. Stuart and the cavalry were heavily engaged with the Federal cavalry in much the same area as the previous day.*

In addition to Boteler, another member of Stuart's headquarters was recording his thoughts and actions during this hectic time. Philip H. Powers was now back at cavalry headquarters, but on the fourth he was laid up in his tent with neuralgia. Though weak in body, he remained strong in spirit, and he rose from his sickbed to do his duty. His long letter covering the fourth, fifth, and sixth recounted some of what he experienced during the opening phase of the Battle of the Wilderness.

Boteler too wrote of the fighting on the fifth and sixth. His descriptions are more vivid and detailed than Powers's: Lee almost captured or worse; Stuart roused from his night's rest by a false alarm; Longstreet falling at the hands of his own men. Boteler was reminded of another who had fallen among the same dense thickets a year earlier.

Wednesday—May 4

[To Mrs. Roberta Powers]

My letter had hardly reached the office and I am lying down suffering with neuralgia when I heard the Genl's clear voice say "<u>pack up</u>." I knew what was coming and sick as I was got up and went to work. We moved this afternoon some five miles towards Fredericksburg. And are in camp by the road side. I am hardly able to march, but I hate to be absent at such a time and do not wish to go to the hospital, so will struggle on—hoping the neuralgia will leave me tomorrow. I will sleep in a house tonight. The whole Army is in motion and the great battle will soon begin. These are wayside notes which I will jot down as I can and send you for a letter. Good night—

Thursday [May 5]—I have had a bad day, My love. Such a terrible pain in my eye. We moved about fifteen miles lower down the road, and by noon the battle had commenced on our left with [Lieut. Gen. Richard S.] Ewell's Corps—the firing was terrific but Genl Stuart told me a while ago that the old wooden leg soldier with his veterans whipped their 5th Yankee Corps badly—capturing 2000 prisoners and 4 guns—our loss heavy. Genl [Brig. Gen. John M.] Jones (from Charlottesville) and Genl [Brig. Gen. Leroy A.] Stafford killed.[47] Also poor William Randolph in command of the 2nd Va— that Regt is fated to lose its commanding officers—Randolph was just promoted last week.[48] I saw him & his wife at Tom Ballards. They were in fine spirits. He remarked that he thought bad luck had run with the regt long enough—he thought it would change and he escape [*sic*]. God, not luck, disposes of our lives. And he also poor fellow has fallen another martyr to Southern liberty. And his young wife so bright and happy a few days ago is today a widow and her unborn babe fatherless. Oh the dreary broken hearts that this day has made, and the blacker day that dawns tomorrow. I feel sad and Wretched over it all. My head has gotten easy but my heart grows sick when I think of the awful scenes around me. Gen. Lee & Gen. Stuart are in fine spirits. May God give us a victory and end this cruel war! This is a dreary dismal country most fitly called the Wilderness—for many miles not a house and not an open field. Nothing but a wilderness of trees and under brush and marsh—and perfectly flat. We are in a small field by the road side about 2 miles from the line of Battle. And here are Genl Lee's and Genl Stuart's HdQrs—and an <u>infinity</u> of wagons and artillery. But I must try to get a place to sleep. I am taking quinine hoping to drive off the neuralgia tomorrow. Have seen Jim today. Adieu—

Friday morning [May 6]—What a din, what an uproar!—the very heavens seem filled with sound. And in the midst of it all I sit by the road side and write to you my dear thanking God that you do not hear what I hear, nor see what I see this awful day. The battle recommenced about sun-rise and as I write seems to be raging with intense fury. Oh how my heart sickens as I listen and think of the untold misery arising from this bloody day! Have you ever imagined a battle field and its vicinity—the throng of men hurrying to & fro—the trains of wagons and artillery passing and repassing. Apparently an inextricable confusion. All is bewildering to the spectator. And yet how strange that one man's mind should control all, and bring desired results from this chaos of war. At intervals there is a perfect calm, and you might imagine all over, when suddenly the whole heavens reverberate with the clamor of the contending hosts—

Gen' Stuart has gone off in fine spirits to lead his cavalry—May God protect him this day is my earnest prayer!

It is now 8 o'clock and the last report from Genl Lee was that he was driving the enemy back handsomely. This seems evident from the sound— the firing having ceased in the center—but [Lt. Gen. Richard S.] Ewell is still keeping it up on the left. [Lt. Gen. James] Longstreet came up this morning. I think we will whip them and will be able to tell you tonight. My head is much easier today, but I feel weak. Jim took breakfast with us. We managed to have something cooked even on the verge of the battle field. 5 o'clock—so far as heard from we have been successful in the day's fight and the Yankees are falling back. The fighting has not been as continuous as I expected this morning. No artillery hardly can be used—But my impression is that the fight will be renewed tomorrow—in fact is not over for today—firing is still going on.

I am sorry to tell you Genl Longstreet was wounded in the shoulder today—they say by our own men. His wound is not considered dangerous. Genl [Brig. Gen. Micah] Jenkins was killed today and Col. J. Thompson Brown—A courier is just going off and I send this. The field of battle is between Chancellorsville and Verdiersville in the Wilderness—I will write again tomorrow—

Ever Yours
P. H. Powers

Excuse my paper

From Alexander Robinson Boteler's Diary

Thursday, May 5th—Up betimes. A tin cup of Confederate coffee and a handful of Federal "Hard Tack" broke our fast and by daylight we were in the saddle.

Skirmishing began early on our left, that wing of our Army being under command of [Lt. Gen. Richard S.] Ewell and advancing by the Orange turnpike which is nearly three miles north of the Fredericksburg plank road and running in nearly the same direction until both meet some two miles or more west of Chancellorsville, the interval between the two roads being like the rest of "The Wilderness", almost impenetrable.

The skirmishing in that direction soon resolved itself into continuous firing with occasionally a succession of volleys heavier than the rest, indicating that the forces there were fully engaged, as indeed they were to our temporary discomfiture. For in the Yankee onset [Brig. Gen. John M.] Jones Brigade was forced back and its Commander killed.

[Brig. Gen. George H.] Steuart of Maryland made a dashing charge followed up by [Brig. Gen. Junius] Daniels and [Brig. Gen. John B.] Gordon of [Maj. Gen. Robert E.] Rodes Division, which put the Yankees to flight.[49] I am very thankful that we have won the day and that I am not yet numbered with the dead. Had some interesting adventures during this eventful day. There has been great slaughter of the enemy, the ground over which we have passed being covered with their dead and wounded as well as with innumerable guns, blankets, knapsacks, overcoats, etc. which they abandoned in their retreat.

Stuart took us to the left of our line by Locust Grove where a portion of his cavalry under Rosser was on the alert and skirmishing with the advance of Burnside. After a while we returned to the plank road and in the course of the morning had an adventure which might have been of most disastrous consequences to the Confederate cause.

A little to the left of the plank road but completely hidden from it by the intervening shrubbery is an old field, scantily covered with sedge grass and a scattered growth of stunted pines. On entering it with Stuart, I noticed a group of Generals and Officers in consultation under the only large tree in the field—Generals Lee, [William N.] Pendleton, A. P. Hill, and others composing the group. As Stuart rode forward to join them, I reined up, and dismounting to rest myself in the shade of a pine bush, fell fast asleep, for I was not only fatigued, but somewhat overcome also by the heat. How long I had been napping I know not, perhaps not more than ten minutes, when I was startled by the sound of horses galloping past me, and on rising, I saw all the Generals in full flight from the field followed by their respective staffs and couriers. General Lee was galloping toward the wood on my right, and A. P. Hill on foot, was running in the same direction. I was not long in discovering the cause of the hegira, for in looking behind me toward the left, I saw a party of the enemy in the edge of the woods whose bayonets gleaming in the sunlight were decidedly too close to be comfortably contemplated; and to make matters worse my horse, having disengaged his bridle from the bush to which I had carelessly hitched it, had strayed some little distance from me and in the direction of the intrusive Yankees where he was standing ready to dash off after the rest of the party and leave me in the lurch. So cautiously keeping my horse between myself and the enemy and speaking to him gently as I approached, he allowed me to take hold of the dangling rein, and to leap into the saddle. As I galloped off, I expected every moment of course to hear a crashing volley ripping up things around me, but strange to say, not a shot was fired at any of us.

The explanation of this sudden appearance of Federal soldiers at a point where they were so utterly unlooked for, is that they were skirmishers who had advanced far beyond their own line and through a gap in ours which was soon closed up after the above-mentioned incident had revealed its existence. The little party of lost skirmishers were doubtless as much surprised as we in finding themselves in such close proximity to their enemies and consequently disappeared as quietly as they came. If they had known that General Lee and several of his Chief Commanders were within two hundred yards of them and utterly unprotected, they could with one volley have done irreparable injury to the Confederacy. But thanks to their ignorance and surprise, they did not avail themselves of the opportunity they had to destroy the head of the Army and to break its heart which they could easily have done without discovery by a single shot at point blank range.

Meanwhile there was more or less skirmishing along the entire line of battle which extended for six miles. Early in the afternoon Stuart placed us behind a line of A. P. Hill's skirmishers to advance them through the thickets where it was as much as we ourselves could do with the help of our horses to force a passage. When we came out of it, our faces were bleeding with scratches from the bushes and our clothes badly torn. Fortunately none of the staff received any injury from the concealed skirmish line of the enemy who kept up a continual fire. Between three and four o'clock, the battle began in earnest and was continued with stubborn pertinacity by both sides until nearly night—neither gaining a victory, though we steadily advanced our ground. After an eventful day, full of exciting incidents and sickening scenes of slaughter, we rode back to Parker's store. As we reached the little five acre field surrounded on all sides by the dense forest, we threw ourselves from our horses upon the ground in a state of complete exhaustion. But we were not allowed to rest long for in a few minutes after arrival, one of the couriers who had gone into the woods to hunt for a spring, came rushing toward us with the startling report that the woods were full of Yankees who would be upon us before we could get on our horses.

"You don't tell me so," exclaimed Stuart, in a tone of inimitable drollery, springing to his feet, as we all did also, seizing our arms.

"Yes, sir, I saw 'em," continued the courier, "two of 'em right down there sir." Though the report evidently taxed the General's credulity, he made his disposition of the available force at hand which all told amounted to less than thirty men, a rather disproportionate array to receive a woods full of Yankees.

But we had the benefit of a piece of artillery which happened to be passing just as the alarm was given, and which Stuart pressing into service, soon had unlimbered, loaded and placed in position, the couriers to support it with their carbines and the staff with their side arms. After a few moments of patient expectation and no Yankees showing themselves, we mounted and advanced into the woods, to learn the cause of the courier's alarm. Presently one of the men who had pushed his way through the bushes to the right of us was heard to "halt" someone. There was a sudden shout, and a rush followed by a single shot, and there came crashing through the undergrowth toward us a huge German, one of the Yankee infantrymen who seemed to be frantic from fear. After searching the woods for some time and finding no one else, we returned to our bivouac. The prisoner, crouching by the camp fire, presented a most ludicrous appearance rolling his great google eyes from one to the other as in his efforts to make himself understood, he sputtered German at us with unintelligible volubility parenthetically exclaiming, "Ach, Mein Gott, Mein Gott."

It appears, as we learned through one of the men who understood a little of his lingo, that he and a small party of his comrades had become lost in the confusion that followed [Maj. Gen. Gouverneur K.] Warren's charge on [Brig. Gen. John M.] Jones' Brigade, and had been hiding all day in the woods hoping to get back to his friends at night fall. The laughable issue of this episode gave additional zest to our frugal supper and after a soothing smoke, we were soon asleep.

Friday, May 6th.—Up and off with Stuart a little after daylight. Hard fighting from five o'clock in the morning until night with but few interruptions during the day. Neither side victorious.

When we attacked this morning the resistance was so stubborn that two of our divisions, [Maj. Gen. Henry] Heth's and [Maj. Gen. Cadmus M.] Wilcox's, had to give way, but the opportune arrival of [Maj. Gen. Lafayette] McLaws' division of Longstreet's corps followed by that of [Maj. Gen. Richard H.] Anderson and likewise of Longstreet himself, turned the tide of the battle in our favor, while at the same time it seemed to cause it to rage more fiercely than ever along the entire front.[50]

Just as Longstreet went into action he was desperately wounded and Gen. [Brig. Gen. Micah] Jenkins killed by some of our own men who mistook them for Yankees, making the same miserable blunder that caused the death of Stonewall Jackson last year in another part of this same Wilderness.

But it seems almost impossible to prevent blunders of this kind during the excitement and confusion of a battle in such a place where for more than half the time the contending forces are fighting unseen foes even when firing at short range and almost face to face.

Then too our General officers expose themselves too reckless, sometimes going as I have seen Jackson do more than once in advance of the line of skirmishers.

And General Lee today at a critical moment, wanted to lead a charge of Texans in person and would have done so if the men had let him. But they protested and seized the bridle of his horse to prevent it, shouting, "Lee to the rear. Lee to the rear." "Men," he said in reply, "This is my country as well as yours."

Just at nightfall on the plank road, a portion of our line was forced back by a furious charge and some of the men began to retreat, but General Stuart made the members of his staff, General Peyton and other officers who happened to be at hand, form a line in close order across the road, and we thus stopped what at one time began to look like a stampede.[51]

Again on the seventh, Federal and Confederate cavalry struggled along the Catharpin Road and around Todd's Tavern. Rosser's, Fitz Lee's, and James B. Gordon's Brigades were heavily engaged. Early on the eighth, after spending the night at Shady Grove Church, Stuart began moving toward Spotsylvania Court House, where Fitz Lee was fighting desperately to hold back the Federal infantry until Confederate infantry arrived. He was successful, and by five o'clock the gray line was stabilized. Stuart and his staff rode to the Old Block House to camp for the night.

The ninth brought a renewal of the infantry fighting. In the morning, Stuart was informed that the Federal cavalry was sweeping around the Confederate right flank and moving down the Telegraph Road. Fitz Lee was dispatched in pursuit, and Stuart himself followed around three o'clock in the afternoon. He rode south toward Richmond. Toward Yellow Tavern.

Neither Boteler nor Powers accompanied Stuart on his last campaign. The diary entries and letters of the two men over the next several days were at first filled with the hope that their commander would once again emerge victorious. Before long, however, shock and grief replaced that hope. Both men wrote of the disaster Stuart's death was to the country. Both wrote that they had lost more than a commander—they had lost a friend.

From Alexander Robinson Boteler's Diary

Saturday, May 7th.—This day spent like the last marching and fighting. What a curse war is. The dreadful sights I have seen this week in this Wilderness will never be banished from my memory. The woods are on fire in various places and horrible to think of hundreds of wounded men are in danger of being roasted alive. I am more than ever convinced that those who were instrumental in bringing the curse of this cruel war upon the country have committed an unpardonable crime against humanity which deserves not only the maledictions of mankind, but likewise the anathemas of an offended God.

Sunday, May 8th.—But no day of rest. Both armies pushing for Spotsylvania Court House which Fitz Lee after a gallant struggle took possession of and held until our infantry got to relieve him.

Monday, May 9th.—Up at four o'clock and after a hasty breakfast in the saddle accompanied Gen. Stuart to Spotsylvania Court House, but without any material results. Prisoners report that the Federal General [John] Sedgwick was killed today, and Stuart in expressing his sorrow told me that if he could only have been taken instead of being killed, he would most gladly have shared his blanket and last crust with him, as he was one of the best friends he had in the old army; and that when he parted from him at the beginning of the war to come to Virginia, Sedgwick shed tears and said, "Stuart, you are wrong in the step you are taking, but I cannot blame you for going to the defense of your native state. I am a Northern man and will be true to my own section."

——— ✠ ———

Spottsylvania
[Spotsylvania] CH
Monday Morning
[May 9, 1864]

My Dear Wife [Mrs. Roberta Powers],

Shortly after closing my note of yesterday we moved our train. The enemy having tried in vain to break our lines by fighting, drew off his troops Saturday night towards Fredericksburg and Spottsylvania CH necessitating a move on our side. And our Army during yesterday marched over here. A fight ensued during the day near here between Longstreet's Corps and a Corps of the enemy in which the enemy were repulsed with terrible slaughter.

The march yesterday was awful. The heat and dust were more oppressive than I ever felt before and our poor men suffered terribly—in hundreds of cases they were compelled to throw aside their blankets and clothing and numbers dropped by the wayside exhausted, but they are coming up this morning apparently eager for the fight. This war is a strange thing.

Our lines of battle this morning, from what I can judge run in a direction somewhat parallel to the Plank road and at right angle to the line we have been holding—And near Spottsylvania CH—

I believe a battle is expected, but I do not understand the position of affairs. Our Generals seem in fine spirits and the men also—While eating breakfast this morning Gen. Robert Lee rode by our fire—"Good morning gentlemen," said he. "I am glad to see you faring so well on ham, eggs and coffee." As I write they are skirmishing about one mile from where I am sitting.

I saw the old Stonewall Brigade yesterday. The Clarke and Jefferson companies lost only a few men wounded. Sam Moore was wounded in the leg and not killed as at first reported. Our loss generally has been remarkably light—while that of the enemy has been immense—they say 25000 men. Yesterday many of the prisoners taken were drunk, their army is doubtless much demoralized but Grant is obstinate and his reputation is at stake. He will fight as long as he can make his men stand to it, but God I trust will give us the final victory.

I have not succeeded in driving off the neuralgia. Suffered all day yesterday—and feel the pain coming on now. I will add to this before I send it—

Tuesday morning [May 10]—Nothing but maneuvering and skirmishing ensued yesterday. I remained quiet and felt much better than usual. Received your note enclosing that of Mrs. H. and also the bundle of <u>drawers</u>. ———— [two words illegible] are very acceptable as I have nearly suffocated with heat of late—Am glad to hear you and the babes are more comfortable than when I was with you.

We expect a battle today, but the enemy may have moved again last night. I wish it were all over. I am sick and tired and the poor wounded how they suffer. I think my head was <u>helped</u> yesterday by seeing a poor fellow with the top of his head shot off. What is my little ailing to suffering like his?

Love to all

Yours P. H. Powers

 •••• ⚔️ ••••

Wednesday
11th May 1864
Near Spottsylvania
[Spotsylvania] CH

My Dear Wife [Mrs. Roberta Powers],

I resume my notes this morning wondering if any I send in these troublous times will reach you. Yesterday we had another terrible conflict with the enemy. He assaulting our lines for eight hours in vain, being repulsed with heavy loss in every attack. About sunset he massed his troops and made a most furious assault upon our centre, succeeding in driving our men from these works, and capturing 4 pieces of artillery, but it was only a temporary success. [Maj. Gen. Jubal A.] Early's Division attacked them and drove them back with heavy strength, expediting our position and recapturing the guns.

Mr. Grant fights with determined obstinacy, but so far with no success. He cannot fight much longer unless reinforced. Every expedient is adopted to make his men fight. Yesterday before commencing the fight he issued an order to his troops which I have seen informing them that Butler had defeated the Confederates near Petersburg and [Maj. Gen. William T.] Sherman had whipped Johnston at Dalton—but he cannot persuade them that he has whipped Genl Lee and that is the main point.[52] I do not know the extent of our loss. Yesterday Genl [Brig. Gen. Henry H.] Walker (Heth's Div) and Genl [Brig. Gen. Harry T.] Hays were wounded, the former losing his foot.[53] The enemy detached his cavalry on Monday and started on a raid towards the Central RR. Gen. Stuart pursuing them. We hear that they attacked Beaver Dam destroying some stores and releasing some 380 prisoners. Gen Stuart is right up to them—but how far he will be able to damage them I cannot say. Everyone seems in good spirits. And confident of final success. I wish it were over. This is the 7th day of the fighting— I saw Jim yesterday—very despondent as usual. I suffered dreadfully with neuralgia yesterday but feel much better today. Have no pain up to this hour. Every thing is perfectly quiet this morning. Not a gun has been fired. How long the calm will last I know not.

I will add to this unless a courier leaves this morning. PHP

May 12th—Another bloody day is about closing and still this incarnate strife goes on. We were awakened this morning by the most furious firing I ever heard. The enemy taking advantage of the fog charged our left centre and ran over our works capturing some prisoners and 18 pieces of artillery, but our gallant boys reformed and recovered everything except the prisoners. I don't know how many of them. Among them however was Genl [Maj. Gen.] Ed. Johnson and Genl George Stuart [Steuart]—for eight hours the fight raged with a firing I have never heard surpassed.[54] The enemy attacking our lines again and again, but thanks to the God of battles, every time repulsed with heavy loss. A heavy rain fell during the morning and the roar of thunder and the roar of the artillery and musketry intermingled made an uproar of elements hardly conceivable. I never had such awful feelings in my life. Could only pray silently for deliverance. As the sun came out about noon and good news came in, I felt better. Tonight without knowing the extent of our loss—which however is said to be very light, as our men fought behind breast works, I feel more hopeful—and thankful at least that so far we hold our own—

Jack came in this morning brought no letters save a note from ——— [name illegible]—left all well. The Yankees were in Winchester—he said your brother still spoke of sending your things

I must close—

Ever yours
P. H. P.

Genl Stuart is still absent after the Raiders—

From Alexander Robinson Boteler's Diary

Tuesday, May 10th.[55]—In the saddle by five o'clock and all the morning with Stuart at Spotsylvania Court House, where we had a severe cavalry fight on the right in which we were successful. Several times in the course of the day, I heard Stuart say, "Where in the world is Fitz Lee? What can have become of him?"

Being uncertain as to whether those with whom we were fighting were infantry or dismounted cavalry, Stuart was unwilling to send to Gen. Lee for the aid of infantry until he had ascertained the character of the foe in front. So he turned to Channing Smith and Stringfellow, his two most valuable scouts, whose adventures would make a book more wonderful than the wildest stories of oriental fiction and said, "Go down there to the enemies [sic] lines and kill or catch one of those fellows so that I may know positively who and what they are."[56]

Before noon the Scouts came back bringing the accoutrements of a cavalryman and reported that those in our immediate front were dismounted cavalry supported by a heavy line of infantry, whereupon Stuart hesitated no longer in sending for the aid of infantry which enabled him to end the fight successfully.

When the battle was over he told us to go back to our bivouac of the night before saying that he would ride down the road to find out what had become of Fitz Lee and would probably join us before we had finished dinner.

As he was leaving he turned to me with a laugh saying, "Don't let any of those fellows get my share of the coffee, Colonel," referring to a trick that he himself had played on one of the members of his staff, and then he gaily galloped off singing, "Take your time Miss Lucy and pour your coffee out."

We returned to camp and waited some time for him to come back, but later received word of a raid of [Maj. Gen. Philip H.] Sheridan's cavalry toward Richmond, and that Fitz Lee and [James B.] Gordon of N.C. were in pursuit, and that Stuart accompanied by [Maj. Andrew R.] Venable and [Maj. Henry B.] McClellan had gone down the Telegraph Road hot foot to overtake them.[57] It was night when we got this information, but Dr. [John B.] Fontaine determined to take the chance of catching up with Stuart the next day by riding all night and so he left us.

Wednesday, May 11th.—Up early and out on the lines. Both armies in position and another fight imminent.

More or less skirmishing on both flanks all day by the cavalry under W. H. F. Lee and Rosser. In moving about from point to point, I met many of our General Officers with whom I had brief conversations, General Lee, Ewell, Early, A. P. Hill (who is not well), Pendleton, Geo. Steuart, and Johnson, N.C. Also met Mr. Huston, the special correspondent of the London Herald, with whom I had an interesting talk as we took a social smoke together. This had been an off day with me. After supper smoked a pipe and as Old Pepys says, "So to Bed," if a couple of blankets and a gum cloth spread under a tree with one's saddle for a pillow can be called a bed.

Thursday, May 12th.—Awakened at half past four o'clock by a sudden assault on a salient of earth works near our left center not far from our bivouac.

Maj. Gen. Johnston [Edward Johnson], Brig. Gen. Geo. Steuart, seventeen hundred men and eighteen guns captured. This brought on the general engagement we have been expecting which has been terrible in its duration and in the destruction of life. The battle lasted from daylight until ten o'clock at night. Our loss in officers has been heavy, but that of the rank and file comparatively light as the men were, on portions of our line, partially protected. The loss of the enemy must be enormous judging from the number of dead bodies in front of our position and in some places lying literally in heaps. It was a wild day's work. The artillery itself seemed to become tired, for I noticed that in the morning the reports of the guns were sharp, quick and vicious and that toward evening they roared more sullenly and though as loud were lazier in their utterances. This was doubtless due to the state of the atmosphere as there was rain at intervals throughout the day and at one time, when the battle was at its height, the thunder added its peals to the dreadful uproar that raged around us.

Got back to our bivouac long after dark, but had hardly lain down to rest under the shelter of a fly before we were shelled out of our uncomfortable quarters and forced to find another lodging place on the damp ground further to the rear.

There are unpleasant rumors in reference to General Stuart, it being reported that he has been mortally wounded near Richmond.

Friday, May 13th.—My worst fears are realized for he is dead. This is a terrible blow to us all. The South has lost one of its best defenders. The loss to General Lee will be irreparable for Stuart kept him constantly and correctly advised of all the enemy's movements. He was emphatically "the eyes of the Army."

This is the third friend I have lost in battle who was a master spirit in this war, and with whom I was on terms of confidential intimacy. [Brig. Gen. Turner] Ashby, Jackson, and Stuart—a glorious trio—whose memories will be cherished in the South as long as the Blue Mountains of Virginia look down upon fields consecrated by their blood and made immortal by their bravery.

They tell me that Stuart went into battle, his last battle singing,
"Soon with Angels I'll be marching
With bright laurels on my brow."
X X X X X X X X X X X X X X X
"Who will care for Mother now."

When I announced his death to the couriers those brave men bowed their heads and wept like children and the religious services which our Chaplain held in the woods by the light of the camp fire were among the most solemn and touching that I have ever attended.

Sunday, May 15th.—The loss of General Stuart breaks up our circle at Headquarters of Cavalry Corps and scatters the staff. The enemy disappeared from our front last evening. Severe storm, thunder and lightning. We certainly are having all the elements of horror around about us here. I've had but one quiet day since I rejoined the Army. McClellan and Venable returned from Richmond tonight and gave us the sad particulars of poor Stuart's death. He gave his favorite horse to Venable and remembered to leave his spurs to my good young friend, Lillie [Lily] Lee of Shepherdstown who brought them in from the far West for him at the beginning of the war.[58]

Sunday May 15th 1864

My Dear Wife [Mrs. Roberta Powers]—

The Sabbath morn opens upon us sadly this morning. And with a heart depressed with deep and bitter grief I long to commune with some heart which can sympathize with me. We heard yesterday of the death of our noble leader, Genl. Stuart and the news has thrown a gloom upon us all. Since the death of the lamented Jackson, no event, no disaster, has so affected me. Jackson was a great loss to his country and to the cause. Genl. Stuart is a great loss to his country. But to us, who have been intimately associated with him—and to me in particular—his loss is irreparable, for in him, I have lost my best Friend in the army.

I cannot realize that he is <u>gone</u>, that I am to see his gallant figure nor hear his cheering voice, no more. 'God's will be done,' a great man has fallen, and his faults are now swallowed up and forgotten in the recollection of his eminent virtues—his glorious valor and patriotism. May God in his mercy comfort his poor widow. My heart sorrows for her, as for one very near to me.

The Corps organization of the Cavalry is suspended for the present—The personal Staff being assigned temporarily to the different cavalry Divisions. Our Q.M. Department remains as it is at least for the present.

The two armies here still confront each other in line of battle, though there had been no serious engagement since Thursday, when Genl [Edward] Johnson's Division was repulsed and himself and many of his men captured, the position and some of the artillery was recovered, but not the prisoners—though in the same day we repulsed every other attack.

It has been raining for three days and you can hardly imagine how uncomfortable we are lying in the mud, and wet every day. Fortunately my neuralgia attack has worn itself out and affects me but very slightly—though I am worn out and wearied in mind with continued anxiety. Oh if it could all end, and this terrible turmoil cease! For nearly two weeks our men have been in line of battle—exposed to all the inclemency of the weather—first the insufferable heat and now the drenching rains. And yet they stand and fight.

And the wounded and the maimed and the dying lie around on the cold wet ground. No dear ones near to minister to their wants—and the last breath is caught by the passing breeze and no listening ear of affection ever hears the sound. How long will a merciful God permit this war?—And will this wail of woe that rises from bloody battle fields never cease?

[Brig. Gen. John D.] Imboden has repulsed the enemy in the Valley and driven them to the Potomac.[59] All other army news you can hear from the papers much better than I can.

I saw brother James yesterday—He is very well. I cannot hear of Harty.

I have written you repeatedly since our move, but fear the letters will hardly reach you. I received yours of the 6th. Direct hereafter to the camp of Major N. R. [Norman R.] FitzHugh, Chf. Qr. Mr. Cav Corps ANVa.

I am rejoiced that during all this turmoil and excitement in Richmond you are in a place so far removed from the scene of danger—And hope you are getting along comfortably—Love to the children and kisses for the babes—little Kate may certainly <u>now</u> retain her name of "Stuart." As it bears no tarnish, but speaks of imperishable fame, and spotless honor.

God be with you, my good wife.

Ever Yours
P. H. Powers

━━◆━━

Near Spottsylvania
[Spotsylvania] CH
Tuesday May 17, 1864

My Dear Wife [Mrs. Roberta Powers],

I write hurriedly to send by a courier just going off. We have had no fighting of any importance since last Thursday, of which I have written you. The weather continues wet and the mud unfathomable—You may imagine our discomfort.

Sunday the enemy shifted his position, moving nearer to the Fredericksburg RR. and in the evening I rode over the deserted lines and positions of the battle field. A more awful sight never met my eyes. The enemy's dead were lying thick as they had fallen three days before in every stage of corruption. They had made no effort to bury hundreds of them. Grant cares not for his men—that is evident from the way he fights them— And his barbarism in leaving his dead and many of his wounded on the field.

Our Army is now said to be nearly equal to his. And all seem confident of final success over him. I pray that it may be so, but ever since the loss of our beloved General, I confess that I feel unusually despondent. It is natural I reckon. All my associations in this war are intimately connected with Genl Stuart. In times of gloom and danger, his cheering voice & his hopeful spirit have always infused hope and courage in those around him. We miss him sadly, but in his own language "God's will be done." All is right.

Our military family is broken up and scattered—And no Corps commander has been appointed yet. Who will take command I am unable to conjecture—

I rejoice that you are not in Richmond during these troubles.

We rarely get papers now, and know not what is going on there. Doubtless you are as well informed even of our own army as I am. As it is almost impossible to get correct information just in the rear of the army. A thousand conflicting rumors are circulated. At one time Grant is retreating across the river—And the next moment advancing towards Richmond. My own impression is another and a decisive battle will be fought in this vicinity. We have official intelligence of Seigel's [Maj. Gen. Franz Sigel] defeat in the Valley.

Of myself I am glad to say I am better in health if not better in spirits.

Direct your letters care Maj NR [Norman R.] FitzHugh HdQrs Cav Corps—through Genl Lee's HdQrs—

Love to all.

Yours
P. H. Powers

Stuart had been mortally wounded on May 11. He died on the twelfth. On the thirteenth, he was buried in Hollywood Cemetery. Those members of his staff who could attend rode in carriages behind the hearse, which was pulled by four white horses. After the ceremony, the staff officers left the city one by one or in small groups. Some knew where they were going. Others waited until orders were issued. They had served Stuart and the cavalry well. But now that the reason for their being together was gone, they went their separate ways, some never to meet again. Each probably felt much like Philip H. Powers when he wrote, "I cannot realize that he is gone, that I am to see his gallant figure nor hear his cheering voice, no more."

APPENDIX

THE POETRY OF CAPT.
WILLIAM WILLIS BLACKFORD

ALONG WITH HIS MANY OTHER ACCOMPLISHMENTS, WILLIAM W. BLACKFORD was a poet. Though he may not rank with the famous authors of literature, his poetry is important, telling of the men and events that surrounded him as he passed through the war that divided his nation and forced him and others to take sides. He could form verses with a comic or lively air, but most of what he penned reflects the more melancholy aspects of the conflict. The word pictures he painted bring to life the emotions, happy and sad, that he experienced. If not for their literary merit, then for the stories they tell, his "lines written on a bale of smoking tobacco" deserve to be remembered.

Lines written on a bale of smoking
tobacco presented to my Comrade, Mess-mate,
and Friend, Major Norman R. FitzHugh,
of Stuart's Staff, before the battle of Fredericksburg

> When first Sir Walter Raleigh drew
> A whiff, with Indian Chieftains round,
> The gallant Knight but little knew
> The wondrous weed that he had found
>
> Let swag'ring Comrades snuff and chew
> But this battle 'eve will you and I
> E'en puff in peaceful pipes Fitz Hugh
> This golden bale of "cut and dry"
>
> And while the smoke to heaven ascends
> Our frosty moon-bright prayer shall be
> For him whose soul tomorrow sends
> A sacrifice to Victory

The Cavalier's Glee
Air—"The Pirates Glee" by Wm. W. B.

Spur on! Spur on! We love the bounding
of barbs that bear us to the fray;
"The Charge!" our bugles now are sounding,
And our bold Stuart leads the way.
The path of honor lies before us,
Our hated foemen gather fast;
At home bright eyes are sparkling for us—
We will defend them to the last.

Spur on! Spur on! We love the rushing
Of steeds that spurn the turf they tread
When through the invaders ranks they're crushing
With our proud battle flag o'erhead.
The path of honor lies before us,
Our hated foemen gather fast;
At home bright eyes are sparkling for us—
We will defend them to the last.

Spur on! Spur on! We love the flashing
Of blades that battle to be free
'Tis for our sunny South they're clashing
For household, God and liberty.
The path of honor lies before us,
Our hated foemen gather fast;
At home bright eyes are sparkling for us—
We will defend them to the last.

The Cavalier's Dirge
Wm. W. B.

My sabre hangs by Chamber wall
The hilt with crape is wound,
No more 'tis drawn at "bugle call,"
Nor clanks to charger's bound.
For heaven has quenched the battles' light
And stilled the cannon's roar
Though lost our Cause we've honor bright
We're home again once more.

It mourns the Cause we loved so well,
And friends who wore the gray,
Who by Stuart rode and Pelham fell,
In Lee's hard pressed array.
For heaven has quenched the battles' light
And stilled the cannon's roar
Though lost our Cause we've honor bright
We're home again once more.

Virginia's war-won battle ground
Their blood long since has blest;
Proud memories dwell forever round,
Our "rebel" heroes' rest.
For heaven has quenched the battles' light
And stilled the cannon's roar
Though lost our Cause we've honor bright
We're home again once more.

Stuart at Manassas
July 1861

Throughout the restless morning long
Dismounted there we lay
Watching all the shifting scenes
Of that eventful day.
Now here, now there the batteries move
And troops are hurried past,
While louder roars the musketry,
And thunder cannon fast.
A canopy of smoke enfolds
The field from anxious eye,
Save glimpses now and then between
Where upward rolling from the scene
The clouds come drifting by.
The order comes at last to press
Where hottest is the fray,
And lightly to the saddle spring
The riders in the gray.

From champing bit the charger flings
The foam flakes frothing free
O'er glossy breast, and tossing crest,
With neigh of ecstasy.
He "snuffs the battle from afar,"
And "mocketh he at fear,"
"His glory's in his nostril wide"
When danger's hour is near.
Disdainfully he spurns the earth
Impatient in his might,
With fiery glance on battle bent,
And kindling in its light.
Moving to the front, we halt
'Neath bordering forest shade,
Awaiting there some chance to strike
By fate of fortune made.
From out the thicket Stuart views
The progress of the day,
Where Jackson rears his first Stonewall
And holds the foe at bay.

But see! to turn his flank they come:
 Our forces still delay;
Oh God! for one brief moment more
 Their onward march to stay.
Right ahead in gaudy red
Trim Zouave lines appear
With swaying "quick-step" moving fast
And glittering light from bayonets cast
As on to the grim Stonewall they past
 Our woodland covert near.

Then Stuart's sabre waves "the Charge!"
 The bugles ring; a cheer,
A dash, a flash, a whirlwind's crash
 Of steeds in mad career.
Along their line a sheet of flame
Darts out, like serpent's tongue
And many a gallant horse and man
 Upon the turf is flung.

But through their smoke we on them broke
 And through their ranks we tore,
Like lightning stroke that rends the oak
 And scatters all before.
Wheeling to the "left about,"
We charged them through again,
And many a Zouave soldier lay
 Hoof trodden on the plain.

Disconcerted, checked and foiled,
They from the sudden blow recoiled;
Moments now like hours move;
Delay the victory may prove.

Beckham's guns then Stuart placed,
 The flank to enfilade,
And still, with cavalry support,
 The threatened movement stayed;
Until our battle front extending,
 Infantry the flank defending;
Early sweeps with banners dancing,
 Full upon the foe advancing.

But while the conflict rages high,
Its fate yet veiled in doubt;
Look! they break! Oh! what a sight!
Like bees they swarm o'er fields in flight
In panic stricken rout.

Forward dart the cavalry,
Like arrow from a bow,
And eager strain, with spur and rein,
To strike a parting blow.
We then, with race and glorious chase,
And wild excitement burn;
Till captured prisoners choke the way,
And fading light of closing day
Warns that we pursuit must stay
Reluctant still to turn.

The Death of Pelham

His tent stands deserted,
No more shall we hear
When battle is raging
The young cannoneer.

And pawing unnoticed
His steed neighs in vain,
A kindly caress
From his master to claim.

For the angel of death
Our hero has ta'en
From fields of his glory
All fresh with his fame.

Rappahannock's stained waters
Ne'er bore to the sea
The blood of a gentler
Nor bolder than he.

Virginia has placed
Her wreath on his bier,
By beauty and valor
Bedewed with a tear.

And Alabama now clasps
To her bosom once more,
Regretted and honored,
The son that she bore.

Fleetwood Fight
June 9th 1863—by Col. Wm. W. Blackford

It was a sultry eve in June
On Fleetwood's shady height
And the leader of our cavalry
Had halted for the night.
Like cavalier of olden time
A sable plume he wore
And ne'er curbed knight more skillfully
A charger's wrath before.

His stalwart form fatigue defied
And joyous was his mood
In camp or bower—In council bold,
In action fierce and shrewd.
For Stuart seemed one born to rule
In danger's trying hour
And brave men knew and proudly too,
Acknowledged then his power.

The evening sun a martial scene
Now lights with golden ray
Where dashes Rappahannock's wave
O'er mossy rocks away.
For miles along those shady banks
White tents like snow flakes shine,
And kindling camp-fires rising smoke,
Where o'er the dark green wood it broke,
In wreathing eddies twine;
Till caught in upper currents sway,
Southward wafting floats away
On the horizon's decline.

Tethered o'er the grassy plain
Ten thousand horses neigh
Of royal race and trained to war
In many bloody fray.
From Maryland and Georgia,
From Carolina's shore;

And Old Virginia's hunting ground,
So merry once with horn and hound,
 They here their riders bore.

With closing day the camp-fires throw
 Their ruddy light around
While song, and din of anvil's ring
 And martial music sound.
 Silently each murmur dies,
 And flickers faint the light,
And save the restless tramp of steeds,
 The camp is hushed in night.

 Dawn had scarce a rosy tint
 O'er Cedar Mountain flung
When bursting through the fog which lay
 Along the rivers winding way,
 With star bespangled banners gay,
 Bold Buford's Legions come.
And there with brilliant staff array
 Chief of all their host that day
 With them rides Pleasonton.
Through river ford and outpost,
 The furious riders rush
And eager dashing onward seek
 Our sleeping camp to crush.

No time there was for mounting then,
 No time to hitch a gun;
On foot each southron fought them as
 From grassy couch he sprung
Again, and yet again, they charge,
 Our forming ranks to break;
But what surprise has failed to win,
 Attack can never take.

High above us shown [*sic*] the sun,
 And waning seemed the fight,
When gathering clouds of cavalry
 Appear upon the right.

Gregg leads the way, Kilpatrick's sword
Is flashing in the sun
And there Sir Percy Wyndham waves
His glittering squadrons on
To Fleetwood hill they're moving,
Commanding all the plain:
To meet them now at Fleetwood
We turn with slackened rein.

A cheer to charge then Stuart gave
And out leaped bright their blades
As thundering to the shock he lead [sic]
His fiery light brigades

Harmon first his sabre dyes
Deep red in foeman's gore
And full upon them thick and fast
Our White's battalion pour

There Hampton spurs across the field
Our Southern Bay and he,
Whose plume ere leads in thickest fray
To deeds of chivalry.

Like billows capped with sparkling foam
In squadrons front deploy
And flags to battle breezes flung
Dash Baker, Waring, Black and Young
And Lomax and Flournoy.

At sweeping gallop rumbling rolls
Through dusty clouds its way
Beckham's Horse Artillery there
On battle front to play

Twice a thousand men in blue
And twice a thousand gray
Are pricking fast the space between
And ne'er a finer sight was seen
And ne'er a bolder band I ween
Than rode in that array

Around the good old Mansion house
In flowery paths they meet
And bloody brushed the roses bloom
Neath foaming charger's feet.

Terrific was the shock, the shiver
The lines of battle rocked
Horse to horse and hand to hand
Swaying back and forth they stand
In deadly conflict locked.

Tarnished is the sabre's gleam
By many a bloody stroke
And dimly fades the fray from view
In dust and cannon smoke.

Steeds with empty saddles strain
Around the field in fright
Pause and snort toss back their mane
And with look bewildered neigh again
For comrades in the fight.

O'er their battery sweep the waves
Of hottest action and
Triumphant now we wrest the prize
The proudest in a soldiers eyes
Of captured cannon won

Beaten backward, Stubborn still
Back from bloody Fleetwood hill
Oft sound their bugles in retreat
For counter charges fierce to meet
Defiant still the bugles blew
With lines unbroken they withdrew.

Where Duffie's distant column moves
To strike upon our rear
Butler bravely bars the way
And unsupported holds at bay
The threatened danger near.

Then Lee, the Gallant Rooney charged
Where Buford still he holds
And back across the river bank
The tide of battle rolls.

The gorgeous rays of setting sun
Upon our banners play
But brighter round them far the glow
Of glorious victory.

Appomattox
Wm. W. B.

Surrendered! You say? The Army Surrendered?
The soldier his knapsack unslung
And bitterly thought of the Cause long defended
As he heavily leaned on his gun.

The past like a dream o'er his memory steals,
In the dark rising war clouds are leaping,
Echoes afar from the thundering peals,
Where Sumter grim vigil is keeping.

On the shore of events, by passion's wave cast,
Gathering multitudes tread,
And whirl-winds of battle o'er fields sweeping fast
Their glorious memories shed.

In the sun's setting light a grave horseman rides by,
The soldiers farewell is a cheer,
The gray charger returns a proud toss of the head,
On the cheek of the rider's a tear.

Devoted and brave he has lead the lost cause,
Through success, and reverse in the past,
But fortune can change not the victory won
O'er Lee's countrymen's hearts in the last.

NOTES

INTRODUCTION

1. Peter W. Hairston, *The Cooleemee Plantation and Its People* (Winston-Salem, NC: Hunter Publishing Company, 1986), pp. 33, 44–45, 55, 57; Robert J. Trout, *They Followed the Plume: The Story of J. E. B. Stuart and His Staff* (Mechanicsburg, PA: Stackpole Books, 1993), pp. 72–75.

2. Trout, *They Followed the Plume*, pp. 213–17.

3. *Ibid.*, pp. 94–99.

4. *Ibid.*, pp. 218–24.

5. *Ibid.*, pp. 232–41.

6. *Ibid.*, pp. 89–94.

7. *Ibid.*, pp. 251–56.

8. *Ibid.*, pp. 224–32.

9. *Ibid.*, pp. 68–72.

1861

1. Adele H. Mitchell, ed., *The Letters of Major General James E. B. Stuart* (Stuart—Mosby Historical Society, 1990), p. 194.

2. *Ibid.*, p. 199.

3. Betty and Sammy (Elizabeth Perkins and Samuel) were Hairston's children by his first wife, Columbia, Stuart's sister, who died in 1857 giving birth to their third child, who lived only long enough to be baptized. Agnes Wilson was Fanny and Peter's first child, just a baby at this time. "Cooleemee" was located south of Winston-Salem. Hairston, *The Cooleemee Plantation and Its People*, pp. 33, 55.

4. Though Hairston gives Stuart's rank as that of colonel, he was actually a lieutenant colonel until July 16, 1861, when he was promoted to colonel.

5. Winfield Scott (June 13, 1786–May 29, 1866) was born on his father's farm near Petersburg, Virginia. He had seen service in the War of 1812 and the Mexican War. That he was a distinguished soldier cannot be argued. He remained with the Union and did not join with other Virginians who embraced the Confederate cause. This action fostered the opinion

271

expressed by Hairston and others. His "Anaconda Plan" as adapted to Federal strategy eventually brought the war to a successful conclusion for the North. Scott lies in Post Cemetery, West Point, New York. Ezra J. Warner, *Generals in Blue* (Baton Rouge: Louisiana State University Press, 1964), pp. 429–30.

6. Brig. Gen. John Buchanan Floyd (June 1, 1806–August 26, 1863) had served as governor of Virginia from 1848 to 1852. He also served as secretary of war under President James Buchanan, resigning on December 29, 1860. He joined the Confederate army, becoming a brigadier general on May 23, 1861. His role in the Fort Donelson Campaign led to his being relieved of command on March 11, 1862. Floyd was physically exhausted and his health broke. He died of natural causes on August 26, 1863. He is buried in Sinking Springs Cemetery at Abingdon, Virginia. Patricia L. Faust, ed., *Historical Times Illustrated Encyclopedia of the Civil War* (New York: Harper & Row, Publishers, 1986), p. 265.

7. Hairston gave George to Stuart, but the horse was not up to the strenuous demands Stuart made on all his horses throughout the war and after six months was sold.

8. Charles Frederick Fisher (December 26, 1816–July 21, 1861) was Fanny Hairston's brother-in-law, having married her older sister, Ruth. He became colonel of the 6th North Carolina Infantry and was killed at 1st Manassas. Fisher is buried in the Old Lutheran Cemetery, Salisbury, North Carolina. Hairston, *The Cooleemee Plantation and Its People*, p. 58; Robert K. Krick, *Lee's Colonels* (Dayton: Morningside House, Inc., 1991), p. 140.

9. Stuart had taken John Brown's Bowie knife after Brown was captured in the fire engine house at Harpers Ferry and had given it to Hairston.

10. Joseph cannot be identified except to state that he was another of the Hairstons' servants.

John was John Goolsby, Hairston's servant, who accompanied him to war and carried letters back and forth between Peter and Fanny. Hairston, *The Cooleemee Plantation and Its People*, p. 57.

11. The Confederate forces abandoned Harpers Ferry on June 15, 1861. *The War of the Rebellion: The Official Records of the Union and Confederate Armies* (Washington, DC: U.S. Government Printing Office, 1880–1901. Reprint, Harrisburg, PA: National Historical Society, 1971), Ser. I, Vol. 2, p. 472.

12. Hairston spent about four months in Europe over the winter of 1843–44. He accompanied his brother, George, who took the trip to help his ailing health. While in Paris, he had the opportunity to meet and talk with some of Napoleon's old soldiers, as well as see formations of France's current army. Hairston, *The Cooleemee Plantation and Its People*, p. 25.

13. From a Greek legend involving the followers of Achilles, a myrmi-
don is any follower who carries out orders without question.

14. Mr. Giles was Jesse Giles, one of the overseers at "Cooleemee."
Hairston, *The Cooleemee Plantation and Its People*, p. 71.

15. Turner Ashby (October 23, 1828–June 6, 1862) had been Jackson's
cavalry commander. He had been a farmer before the war and was a natural cavalry leader. For most of his time under Jackson, he led units that were
eventually combined to form the 7th Virginia Cavalry. Ashby was promoted
to brigadier general on May 23, 1862, just a few days before his death at
Harrisonburg, Virginia. He is buried in Stonewall Cemetery, Winchester,
Virginia. Ezra J. Warner, *Generals in Gray* (Baton Rouge: Louisiana State
University Press, 1959), pp. 13–14.

16. Robert Patterson (January 12, 1792–August 7, 1881) did not hold
a commission in the Federal forces but was commander of the Pennsylvania volunteers. Born in Ireland, he had served in the Pennsylvania militia
and the 32nd U.S. Infantry from 1812 to 1815. During the Mexican War,
he was a major general of volunteers. He was appointed a major general of
Pennsylvania volunteers on April 15, 1861, and was mustered out on July
27, 1861. Patterson is buried in Laurel Hill Cemetery, Philadelphia, Pennsylvania. Faust, ed., *Historical Times Illustrated Encyclopedia of the Civil War*,
pp. 561–62.

17. *O.R.*, Ser. I, Vol. 2, p. 471.

18. Green Grief Mason was an overseer who had been hired in 1843.
He remained at "Cooleemee" until after the war in 1865. Hairston, *The
Cooleemee Plantation and Its People*, p. 23.

19. Mr. Orrender was another of the overseers at Cooleemee. *Ibid.*, p. 67.

20. Latin for "in times of war the laws are silent."

21. Luke Tiernan Brien (December 22, 1827–November 25, 1912) as
a Marylander gave up a great deal to serve the Confederacy. He was one
of the first three staff officers selected by Stuart upon becoming a general in
September 1861. He served on Stuart's staff from October 2, 1861, until
April 23, 1862. In the army reorganization of April 1862, Brien was elected
lieutenant colonel of the 1st Virginia Cavalry, a position he assumed with
Stuart's blessing. In October of that same year, he resigned because of ill
health and accepted Peter W. Hairston's invitation to live at "Cooleemee"
plantation in exchange for his help as an overseer. Brien returned to the
war in 1864 as assistant adjutant general to W. H. F. Lee. After the war, he
worked on the railroad. Brien is buried in St. Ignatius–Loyola Catholic
Church Cemetery, Urbana, Maryland. Trout, *They Followed the Plume*, pp.
72–75.

Robert Swan, a veteran of the Mexican War, became major of the 1st Virginia Cavalry, but he was unpopular and was not reelected in the elections of April 1862. He never held any other rank except as a volunteer aide and spent 1864 and 1865 under arrest by the Federals in Maryland. Robert K. Krick, *Lee's Colonels*, 3rd Edition (Dayton: Press of Morningside Bookshop, 1991), p. 364.

22. Anson Burlingame was a congressional representative from Massachusetts. Lincoln appointed him minister to Austria, but the Austrian government found him unacceptable because of his opinion on Hungary and Sardinia. Lincoln then appointed him minister to China. Roy P. Basler, ed., *The Collected Works of Abraham Lincoln* (New Brunswick, NJ: Rutgers University Press, 1953), Vol. IV, p. 293.

23. Clement Laird Vallandigham (July 29, 1820–June 16, 1871) was an Ohio Democrat who opposed the Lincoln administration and the war against the southern states. Banished to the Confederate states, he managed to anger President Jefferson Davis and was expelled from the Confederacy. He lived in Canada until June 1864. Mark Mayo Boatner III, *The Civil War Dictionary* (New York: David McKay Company, Inc., 1959), p. 864.

The Pierce referred to is the former U.S. president Franklin Pierce, who was also an opponent of Lincoln and the war.

24. The 8th Pennsylvania was a three-month regiment. There is no mention of the capture of Lt. Col. Samuel Bowman in any of the reports of the campaign. That he was taken prisoner is verified, however, by the fact that he was exchanged on September 21, 1862, for Lt. Col. Francis Redding Tillou Nicholls of the 8th Louisiana Infantry, a future brigadier general and postwar governor of Louisiana. *O.R.*, Series II, Vol. 3, pp. 131–32, 147, 689, 739–40; Series II, Vol. 4, pp. 395, 400, 577; Faust, *Historical Times Illustrated Encyclopedia of the Civil War*, pp. 197–200; Warner, *Generals in Gray*, pp. 224–25.

25. George Henry Thomas (July 31, 1816–March 28, 1870) was a Virginian who remained in the U.S. Army, rising to the rank of major general. In June 1862, Thomas was commanding the 2nd U.S. Cavalry and his subsequent career proved that he was not quite the "fat old man who can not ride without holding on to the pommel of the saddle" as Hairston claims. He eventually was transferred to the western theater of the war and earned the sobriquet "Rock of Chickamauga" for his stand in the battle of the same name. He went on to defeat Confederate general John B. Hood at Franklin and Nashville, virtually destroying Hood's army as a fighting force. Thomas is buried in Oakwood Cemetery, Troy, New, York. Warner, *Generals in Blue*, pp. 500–502.

26. Richard Caldwell was Fanny's brother. Hairston, *The Cooleemee Plantation and Its People*, p. 57.

27. The attack on Romney occurred on June 13, 1861, and was conducted by Col. Lewis "Lew" Wallace's 11th Indiana Infantry. Wallace's report makes no mention of the depredations Hairston claims occurred, though he did arrest a Maj. Isaac Vandever, who was supposedly "exciting rebellion, organizing troops, and impressing loyal citizens." Col. Ambrose P. Hill with the 13th Virginia Infantry and Col. Simeon B. Gibbon's 10th Virginia Infantry were sent by Johnston to check the enemy's advance. Johnston's report does not refer to any acts against the citizens of Romney. *O.R.*, Ser. I, Vol. 2, pp. 123–24, 471.

28. Ambrose Powell Hill (November 9, 1825–April 2, 1865) was a United States Military Academy graduate in the class of 1847. He had fought in the Mexican War and against the Seminole Indians in Florida. He resigned in March 1861 to join the Confederacy. Hill entered the Confederate army as the colonel of the 13th Virginia Infantry and rose in rank to be a lieutenant general. Unwell physically at times, he was nevertheless one of Lee's finest combat officers. He was killed while riding to rally his troops following the breaking of Lee's lines at Petersburg. Hill is buried in Richmond, Virginia. Warner, *Generals in Gray*, pp. 134–35.

29. A roundabout was another name for a short jacket that came down to the waist. A more military term for the same garment was a shell jacket.

30. Little has been written concerning this short-lived Federal offensive. Neither side seemed to be willing to put the other to the test, with the result that both were resigned to the defensive. *O.R.*, Ser. I, Vol. 2, pp. 471, 698, 700–703.

31. At this time, Stuart was still wearing his blue undress U.S. Army coat. Riding out of the woods, he came upon a company of forty-six men, which he later identified as being members of the 15th Pennsylvania (a three-month regiment), along with one private of the 1st Wisconsin Volunteers (Pvt. Solomen Wyse of Company K), and two privates of the 2nd U.S. Cavalry. Ordering them to dismantle a fence that separated them, Stuart watched as the confused soldiers obeyed. By the time the fence was down, the bold cavalryman had been joined by others of the 1st Virginia, who helped take the shocked Federals prisoner. That Stuart's capture of some soldiers occurred is supported by the Confederate record of the action. But there is no mention in the Federal reports that the 15th Pennsylvania Infantry was ever engaged at Falling Waters. The 1st Wisconsin was supported by the 11th Pennsylvania, but between the two regiments only one man was reported missing. Col. P. Jarrett of the 11th Pennsylvania did not re-

port a man missing. From what unit Stuart took the majority of his prisoners is unknown. For his success at Falling Waters, Stuart received his colonel's
commission. *Ibid.*, pp.179–86.

32. Powers had married Roberta Macky Smith of Clarke County on
December 28, 1852. They had four children at the beginning of the war,
and would have twins in March 1864 and four more children after the war.
Trout, *They Followed the Plume*, p. 213.

33. The "only Negro" may have been James Humbles, who served as
a bugler in Company C of the 1st Virginia. He had enlisted at Lexington
in April 1861. He was a free man, and his record states that "For some
time he carried his musket and saw active service." Robert J. Driver, *1st
Virginia Cavalry* (Lynchburg, VA: H. E. Howard, Inc., 1991), p. 188.

34. Capt. William Augustine Morgan (March 30, 1831–February 14,
1899) commanded Company F (the Shepherdstown Troop) of the 1st Vir-
ginia Cavalry. Some of the men in this company evidently lived near
Powers's family, as Shepherdstown was in the county bordering Clarke
County, where Powers resided. Morgan is buried in Elmwood Cemetery,
Shepherdstown, West Virginia. Driver, *1st Virginia Cavalry*, pp. 124, 210;
Lee A. Wallace Jr., *A Guide to Virginia Military Organizations 1861–1865*
(Lynchburg, VA: H. E. Howard, Inc., 1986), p. 40.

35. Elizabeth Stuart was J. E. B. Stuart's mother.

36. Hairston is referring to Napoleon's 1812 campaign in which he
invaded Russia. His army, much reduced in numbers, captured Moscow,
where he hoped to spend the winter. The Russians, having already destroyed
considerable property and food while Napoleon advanced on their capital,
now set fire to the city, forcing the French emperor into a disastrous retreat
that virtually annihilated his army.

37. Samuel Harden Hairston (April 1822–April 27, 1870) was a cousin
of Peter's. In July 1861, he was a sergeant with the 11th Mississippi Infantry. In May 1862, he joined Stuart's staff as quartermaster with the rank of
major. He resigned in March 1863. He was killed in the collapse of the
gallery in the Virginia state capitol building. Hairston is buried at "Berry
Hill" in Pittsylvania County, Virginia. Trout, *They Followed the Plume*, pp.
173–76.

38. James Thomas Watt Hairston (January 26, 1835–January 19, 1908)
was a captain in the 11th Mississippi Infantry. Plagued by rheumatism, he
was forced to resign his commission in the infantry, but because he held a
second commission, as a lieutenant, he was able to serve as commandant of
Libby Prison until his health improved enough for him to join Stuart's staff
as adjutant in January 1862. He remained with Stuart until his health again
caused him to resign in March 1863. He saw no further service in the war.

Hairston lies in the family cemetery at "Beaver Creek," Henry County, Virginia. *Ibid.* pp. 165–69.

39. Edmund Kirby Smith (May 16, 1824–March 28, 1893) was an 1848 graduate of the United States Military Academy. As an infantry officer, he won two brevets in the Mexican War. He then taught mathematics at West Point for several years, after which he fought Indians on the Texas frontier. When Florida seceded from the Union, he resigned his commission and entered the Confederate army as a lieutenant colonel. Promoted to brigadier general in June 1861, Smith was seriously wounded at 1st Manassas. Successive promotions brought him to the rank of general in February 1864. His service was mainly in the western theater of the war. After the war, he was in business for a short time, but he soon returned to education and held a professorship in mathematics at the University of the South from 1875 until his death. Smith is buried in Sewanee, Tennessee. Warner, *Generals in Gray*, pp. 279–80.

40. Robert Seldon Garnett (December 16, 1819–July 13, 1861) was defeated and killed by forces under the command of Maj. Gen. George B. McClellan in a rear-guard skirmish at Corrick's Ford on the Cheat River on July 13, 1861. He was the first general officer on either side to be killed in battle. Garnett is buried in Greenwood Cemetery, Brooklyn, New York. *Ibid.*, p. 100.

41. The battery mentioned was most probably Capt. Robert Conway Stanard's 3rd Richmond Howitzers.

42. William Willis Blackford (March 23, 1831–April 30, 1905) received his education at the University of Virginia where he studied to be an engineer. His first position was with the Virginia and Tennessee Railroad. Following his marriage to Mary Trigg Robertson, daughter of former Virginia governor Wyndham Robertson, on January 10, 1856, he went to work for his father-in-law in a plaster mine. At the start of the war he became the first lieutenant of the Washington Mounted Rifles, which later became part of the 1st Virginia Cavalry. Blackford remained with the regiment until the army's reorganization, when he was defeated in the election for officers. A commission as captain in the engineers followed, and in June 1862 he received orders to report to Stuart. He served on the staff until January 1864. At that time he was promoted and assigned to the newly organized 1st Regiment of Engineers. By the end of the war Blackford was a lieutenant colonel. His postwar career included a professorship at Virginia Polytechnic Institute, an engineer position with the Baltimore and Ohio Railroad, and a stint as an oyster farmer. Trout, *They Followed the Plume*, pp. 63–67.

43. Richmond cannot be identified further, but considering the reference, he most likely was a family servant.

44. This was the Methodist Episcopal Church on the Sudley Farm near Sudley Springs, where a portion of the Federal army crossed Bull Run in an attempt to outflank the Confederates. The hospital was established by Assistant Surgeon D. L. Magruder under the orders of Surgeon William S. King, U.S. Army medical director. When the hospital was captured by Stuart's cavalry, six doctors remained to continue to care for the wounded. They were Surgeon Foster Swift and Assistant Surgeon G. A. Winston of the 8th New York Militia, Assistant Surgeons Charles C. Gray and George M. Sternberg of the Regular Army, and Doctors Joseph M. Homiston and William F. Swalm of the 14th New York State Militia. There is a possibility that a seventh doctor was also captured, as one report listed Assistant Surgeon C. S. DeGraw of the 8th New York State Militia as having been taken prisoner by Stuart's cavalry. *O.R.*, Vol. 2, pp. 344–45, 388.

45. The number of Union troops engaged was actually 28,452, of which there were 2,645 casualties. The Confederates had 32,232 troops and suffered 1,981 casualties.

46. The Kneller mentioned was most probably Lewis Kneller of Company D, 1st Virginia Cavalry. He enlisted at Harpers Ferry on April 25, 1861, and served with the 1st Virginia until his company was transferred to the 6th Virginia Cavalry in September 1861. He later reached the rank of corporal and on March 24, 1865, transferred to Thomson's Battery of the Stuart Horse Artillery battalion. Driver, *1st Virginia Cavalry*, p. 195.

47. Roberta Powers's brother was William Smith.

48. Blackford is referring to two of his brothers, Capt. Charles Minor Blackford (October 17, 1839–March 10, 1903) of Company B, 2nd Virginia Cavalry, and Capt. Eugene Blackford (April 11, 1839–February 4, 1908) of the 5th Alabama Infantry. Charles is buried in Spring Hill Cemetery, Lynchburg, Virginia, and Eugene rests in Pikesville, Maryland. W. W. Blackford, *War Years with Jeb Stuart* (New York: Charles Scribner's Sons, 1945), pp. x–xi, 45.

49. Randolph H. McKim (April 16, 1842–July 15, 1920) was a private in Company H, 1st Maryland Infantry, C.S.A. He later served on the staff of Brig. Gen. George H. Steuart as aide-de-camp. He was a minister after the war. McKim is buried in Greenmount Cemetery, Baltimore, Maryland. "Rev. Randolph H. McKim, D.D.," *Confederate Veteran*, Vol. XXVIII, p. 351.

50. The identity of this officer is unknown. There was no "Genl. Stewart," and George H. Steuart of Maryland was not promoted to general's rank until March 1862.

51. Thomas Lafayette Rosser (October 15, 1836–March 29, 1910) attended West Point but resigned just two weeks before he would have gradu-

ated. In the Confederate army he would rise from the rank of captain of artillery to major general of cavalry under Stuart. After the war, he was chief engineer for the Northern Pacific and Canadian Pacific Railroads and a farmer. In 1898, during the Spanish-American War, he was appointed brigadier general of U.S. Volunteers by President William McKinley. Rosser is buried in Riverview Cemetery, Charlottesville, Virginia. Warner, *Generals in Gray*, pp. 264–65.

52. William Nelson Pendleton (December 26, 1809–January 15, 1883) was a captain of an artillery battery. A West Point graduate, he had resigned his U.S. Army commission to study for the ministry. At the outbreak of the war, he had been elected captain of the Rockbridge Artillery. He rose to the rank of brigadier general of artillery during the war. Pendleton is buried in the Stonewall Jackson Cemetery, Lexington, Virginia. *Ibid.*, pp. 234–35.

The Reverend Dabney Ball (May 1820–February 15, 1878), better known as the "Fighting Parson," was a Marylander who came south to join the 1st Virginia as chaplain. Quickly earning a reputation for fearlessness in battle as well as delivering fine sermons, Ball caught Stuart's attention and became the cavalry's first commissary officer. He later resigned but returned to the staff in the quasi-official position of chaplain to the Cavalry Corps. Ball lies in Mount Olivet Cemetery, Baltimore, Maryland. Trout, *They Followed the Plume*, pp. 49–56.

53. Robert C. Puryear was a delegate from North Carolina to the Provisional Congress of the Confederate Congress that convened in Richmond on July 20, 1861.

54. Former North Carolina governor Thomas Morehead was also a representative to the Provisional Congress.

55. William Starke Rosecrans (September 6, 1819–May 17, 1907) drove Robert E. Lee and the Confederate forces under his command from the northwestern part of Virginia, which eventually allowed the state of West Virginia to be formed in 1863. Rosecrans later would rise to command the Army of the Cumberland in the western theater. In September 1863, he was defeated at the Battle of Chickamauga; this ended his military career. In the postwar period, he resided in California, became involved in politics, and served in Congress. Rosecrans is buried in Arlington National Cemetery, Arlington, Virginia. Warner, *Generals in Blue*, pp. 410–11.

56. Julius Caldwell was Fanny's brother.

57. Irvin McDowell (October 15, 1818–May 4, 1885) graduated from West Point in 1838 and taught tactics there from 1841 to 1845. Brevetted for gallantry during the Mexican War, McDowell served the following years until 1861 in the adjutant general's department. After his failure at First

Manassas, he commanded a corps in the Army of the Potomac under McClellan and in Pope's Army of Virginia. He had been promoted to major general in March 1862. His subsequent service was relegated to secondary theaters of the war. McDowell remained in the army after the war, retiring in 1882. He is buried in the Presidio, San Francisco, California. Warner, *Generals in Blue*, pp. 297–99.

58. Captain Fauntleroy was most probably Capt. Charles M. Fauntleroy of the Confederate Navy who was in charge of the naval batteries attached to the army.

59. This "commission" would eventually lead to Ford's arrest and imprisonment, a circumstance that was certainly not in Stuart's mind when he wrote it.

60. On August 28–29, Maj. Gen. Benjamin F. Butler, commanding a force of about 900 men, made a successful attack on Confederate batteries at Hatteras Inlet, North Carolina. He captured 715 prisoners, 1,000 stands of small arms, 30 cannons, and one ten-inch Columbiad. He also took possession of several ships and boats loaded with supplies. This is undoubtedly the "foray" to which Hairston is referring. *O.R.*, Vol. 4, pp. 579–86.

61. Although some have speculated whether Antonia Ford actually did perform her daring little mission, Hairston certainly believed it. As for the bouquet of flowers sent to Rosser, Hairston, as he records, saw it himself. The possible romance between Rosser and Ford suggested by Hairston was not to be. In 1863 Ford was arrested as a spy working for Stuart and John S. Mosby. During her imprisonment, she met Maj. Joseph Willard of the family that owned the Willard Hotel in Washington. The two fell in love and married on March 10, 1864. Rosser had married Miss Betty Winston of "Courtland" on May 28, 1863. Linda J. Simmons, "The Antonia Ford Mystery," *Northern Virginia Heritage*, p. 3; Jean Geddes, "Love Story 1862–64," *Virginia Cardinal*, pp. 18–19; Millard K. Bushong and Dean M. Bushong, *Fightin' Tom Rosser, C.S.A.* (Shippensburg, PA: Beidel Printing House, Inc., 1983), p. 43.

62. Ephraim Elmer Ellsworth (April 11, 1837–May 24, 1861) of the 11th New York Fire Zouaves was killed on May 24, 1861. Upon leading his regiment into Alexandria, he had noticed a Confederate flag flying from the Marshall House Hotel. He climbed to the roof and tore down the flag. As he descended the stairs, he was shot by James T. Jackson, the hotel's proprietor. Jackson was killed moments later by Pvt. Francis Brownell of Ellsworth's regiment. Faust, *Historical Times Illustrated Encyclopedia of the Civil War*, p. 240.

63. Henry Toole Clark was governor of North Carolina from July 7, 1861, until January 1, 1863, when he was succeeded by Zebulon B. Vance.

64. The skirmish took place at Great Falls, Maryland. The Confederate forces fired about fifty rounds from their artillery, to which the Federals were unable to reply as their guns were not in position. No casualties were reported. *O.R.*, Ser. I, Vol. 5, pp. 127–28.

65. The action that Hairston mentioned was just a rumor.

66. The rumor was false. In fact, on the night of July 21, Davis met with Beauregard and Johnston. During the meeting, he learned from his generals that no troops were in pursuit of the enemy at that time. The president was greatly surprised and ordered troops under the command of Brig. Gen. Milledge L. Bonham to pursue the retreating Federal army at dawn. Beauregard changed the orders, and no pursuit occurred. Hudson Strode, *Jefferson Davis: Confederate President* (New York: Harcourt, Brace and Company, 1959), pp.123–24.

67. The force consisted of the 79th New York State Militia, four companies of the 1st U.S. Chasseurs, two companies of the 3rd Vermont Regiment, five companies of the 19th Indiana, four guns of the 5th U.S. Artillery (Capt. Charles Griffin's Battery), and fifty regular and forty volunteer cavalry. *O.R.*, Ser. I, Vol. 5, p. 169.

68. Stuart had with him 305 men of the 13th Virginia Volunteers, a section of the Washington Artillery, and a detachment of the 1st Virginia Cavalry. *O.R.*, Ser. I, Vol. 5, p. 183.

69. Though a portion of the Federal column did retreat rather rapidly and in slight disarray, it was because of an order given to avoid being cut off and captured. There is no indication in any of the Federal or Confederate reports that what Hairston wrote occurred. *O.R.*, Ser. I, Vol. 5, pp. 167–84.

70. Judge Thomas Ruffin was a friend of the Hairstons.

71. General Floyd was attacked by Brig. Gen. William S. Rosecrans at Carnifax Ferry, Virginia (now West Virginia), on September 10, 1861. *O.R.*, Ser. I, Vol. 5, pp. 146–48.

72. Mrs. Bradley Johnson was the wife of Lt. Col. Bradley Tyler Johnson (September 29, 1829–October 5, 1903), commander of the 1st Maryland Infantry (Confederate). A graduate of Princeton, Johnson was active in politics before the war. At its outbreak he was prominent in recruiting the 1st Maryland Infantry (Confederate) and served as its major and later its colonel. He became a brigadier general on June 28, 1864. For a time, he commanded cavalry under Brig. Gen. John McCausland, but he ended the war in charge of a prison stockade in Salisbury, North Carolina. After the war, he was a lawyer, politician, and writer. Johnson is buried in Loudoun Park Cemetery, Baltimore, Maryland. Warner, *Generals in Gray*, pp. 156–57.

73. The identity of the "foraging parson" is unknown. The regiment

to which Hairston referred was most likely the 1st Maryland Infantry (Confederate).

74. Samuel Harden Hairston was at this time a member of the 11th Mississippi Infantry. He would be discharged on October 3, 1861, for chronic rheumatism. There is no record of his affiliation with any battery. He may have been trying to raise one in the hope of transferring from the infantry because of poor health. His discharge would have made that unnecessary. Trout, *They Followed the Plume*, pp. 173–76.

75. Robert Wilson was a friend of the Hairstons.

76. Theophilus Hunter Holmes (November 13, 1804–June 21, 1880) had been in command of Confederate troops in the vicinity of Fredericksburg, Virginia. Holmes had graduated from West Point in 1829 and had served with the 8th U.S. Infantry in Mexico, earning a brevet for gallantry. He entered the Confederate army and rose to the rank of lieutenant general by October 1862. Following the Seven Days Campaign, he was assigned to the Trans-Mississippi Department and later commanded the District of Arkansas. He was a farmer after the war. Holmes is buried in Fayetteville, North Carolina. *O.R.*, Ser. I, Vol. 2, p. 907; Warner, *Generals in Gray*, p. 141.

77. Nathaniel Prentiss Banks (January 30, 1816–September 1, 1894) was given command of the Department of the Shenandoah on July 19, 1861. He had previously been in command of the Department of Annapolis. After his expulsion from the Valley and his defeat at Cedar Mountain, he was transferred to the West, where he commanded the ill-fated Red River Campaign. He was a U.S. congressman after the war. Banks is buried in Grove Hill Cemetery, Waltham, Massachusetts. *O.R.*, Ser. I, Vol. 2, pp. 171, 675; Warner, *Generals in Blue*, pp. 17–18.

78. Sam and Alexander Wilson were friends of the Hairstons.

79. Redmond Burke's (?–November 25, 1862) career as a scout and aide to Stuart would make fascinating reading except that very little is known about him or his exploits. Unlike John S. Mosby and Frank Stringfellow, Burke did not survive the war to write his memoirs. He was killed in an ambush on November 25, 1862, in Shepherdstown, Virginia (West Virginia). Hairston's admiration for Burke was well placed. He was an excellent scout and a fearless fighter on whom Stuart relied for information in the early months of the war. Burke lies in Elmwood Cemetery, Shepherdstown, West Virginia. Trout, *They Followed the Plume*, pp. 75–79.

George Freaner (January 20, 1831–November 10, 1878) would become a major and serve on Stuart's staff as an assistant adjutant and inspector general from December 7, 1863, until Stuart's death at Yellow Tavern on May 12, 1864. Freaner had demonstrated his many talents in his prewar careers, which included practicing law, editing a newspaper, and being elected to Maryland's House of Representatives, though he did not serve. Until his appointment to Stuart's staff, he served with the 1st Virginia Cavalry and as adjutant in the brigade to which the 1st Virginia belonged. Freaner is buried in Rose Hill Cemetery, Hagerstown, Maryland. *Ibid.*, pp. 128–32.

80. On September 25, 1861, Federal brigadier general William F. Smith made a reconnaissance in force with 5,250 infantry and cavalry and sixteen pieces of artillery toward Lewinsville, Virginia, the site of Stuart's brush with the enemy on September 11. According to Smith's report, after an exchange of artillery fire, both sides retired. There was no Confederate report of this action, so Kershaw's participation can not be confirmed. It is, however, the only skirmish that fits the date to which Hairston referred. *O.R.*, Ser. I, Vol. 5, pp. 215–17.

Joseph Brevard Kershaw (January 5, 1822–April 13, 1894) had been a lawyer before the war. His only military experience came as a lieutenant of infantry during the Mexican War. He also served two terms in the South Carolina Legislature. At the commencement of the war, he was the colonel of the 2nd South Carolina Infantry. Promoted to brigadier general in February 1862, Kershaw remained at that rank until May 1864, when he was commissioned a major general. After the war, he returned to his law practice and held a judgeship for sixteen years. Kershaw is buried in the Quaker cemetery in Camden, South Carolina. Warner, *Generals in Gray*, p. 171.

81. Hairston erroneously attributes the Confederate victory at Lexington, Missouri, on September 20, 1861, to McCulloch, when in actuality the Confederate forces were commanded by Maj. Gen. Sterling Price. *O.R.*, Ser. I, Vol. 3, pp. 185–88.

82. Lee's conduct of the Cheat Mountain Campaign to which Hairston indirectly referred came under censure from many sources. The *Richmond Examiner* reported that Lee had sent an elaborate plan of his intended campaign to the Confederate War Department and criticized him accordingly when it failed. However, no such plan was ever presented by the War Department or the *Examiner*. Lee did send a letter to President Davis in which he explained the campaign's failure. He took no blame himself, nor did he blame others, which was to become typical of Lee's reports. Douglas Southall Freeman, *R. E. Lee, A Biography* (New York: Charles Scribner's Sons, 1962), Vol. I, pp. 571–78.

83. French for "Who goes there?" It was the challenge made by pickets while on outpost duty.

84. William Edmondson "Grumble" Jones (May 9, 1824–June 5, 1864) became one of Stuart's most irascible subordinate officers. Though Stuart would proclaim him his finest outpost officer, their two personalities clashed

repeatedly, and in the end Jones was assigned to the department of Southwestern Virginia and East Tennessee. He was killed at the Battle of Piedmont on June 5, 1864, and was buried in the yard of Old Glade Spring Presbyterian Church, Washington County, Virginia. Warner, *Generals in Gray*, pp. 166–67.

85. There appears to be no report of this action elsewhere, being most likely another outpost skirmish.

86. On the evening of September 28, 1861, the 69th and 71st Pennsylvania Infantry regiments were advanced by Brig. Gen. William F. Smith toward Munson's Hill. Deploying in the dark, the troops fired into each other. The casualties were one killed and two wounded from the 69th, and four killed and fourteen wounded from the 71st. There were no Confederate troops engaged. *O.R.*, Ser. I, Vol. 5, pp. 218–20.

87. There is no mention of this action in any of the Federal or Confederate reports.

88. Jubal Anderson Early (November 3, 1816–March 2, 1894) graduated from the United States Military Academy in the class of 1837. He spent some time fighting the Seminoles, and then resigned his commission to study law. He established a practice in Rocky Mount, Virginia, and also served as a member of the Virginia House of Delegates and commonwealth attorney. During the Mexican War, he was a major of Virginia volunteers. At the outbreak of the war, he became the colonel of the 24th Virginia Infantry, which he led at First Manassas. He was promoted to brigadier general in July 1861 and major general in January 1863. He commanded A. P. Hill's corps during the Battle of the Wilderness and was promoted to lieutenant general in May 1864. Heavily outnumbered, he fought in the Shenandoah Valley and came close to Washington before falling back to the Valley. There he engaged Sheridan in several battles until finally defeated. After the war, he fled to Mexico. but soon returned to practice law in Lynchburg. His subsequent years were filled with controversy involving a number of Confederate generals, most notably James Longstreet. Early is buried in Lynchburg, Virginia. Warner, *Generals in Gray*, pp. 79–80.

89. William Dorsey Pender (February 6, 1834–July 18, 1863), a West Point graduate with the class of 1854 (the same as Stuart), would rise in rank to major general and gain a reputation as one of Robert E. Lee's finest officers. He died of a wound he suffered on July 2, 1863, at Gettysburg. Pender is buried the yard of Cavalry Church, Tarboro, North Carolina. *Ibid.* pp. 233–34.

90. Minnie Scales was wife of Alfred Moore Scales (November 26, 1827–February 8, 1892), who succeeded Pender as colonel of the 13th North Carolina. A lawyer and politician before the war, Scales rose to the rank of

brigadier general and was severely wounded on the first day at Gettysburg. He rode in the same ambulance as Pender as they left Pennsylvania. Scales, however, recovered from his wound and fought in the 1864 campaign. After the war, he resumed his law practice and reentered politics. He is buried in Green Hill Cemetery, Greensboro, North Carolina. *Ibid.*, pp. 268–69.

91. William Henry Chase Whiting (March 22, 1824–March 10, 1865) graduated from the United States Military Academy in 1845 with the highest grades ever attained to that time. He entered the Confederate army as an engineer but was transferred and promoted to brigadier general in the infantry. Whiting fought for a time in Virginia but was then sent to North Carolina, where he developed Fort Fisher. After another stint with the Army of Northern Virginia at Petersburg, Whiting, now a major general, returned to Fort Fisher, where he was severely wounded when the fort was finally taken. He died of his wounds and was buried in Oakdale Cemetery, Wilmington, North Carolina. *Ibid.*, pp. 334–35.

92. There is no report of this action.

93. John Charles Fremont (January 21, 1813–July 13, 1890) was not court-martialed and later fought in the Valley Campaign against Stonewall Jackson. Fremont had been a famous explorer and the 1856 Republican presidential candidate. His war career did not match the success of his early life. After the war, he was the territorial governor for Arizona for nine years. Fremont is buried in Rockland Cemetery, Piermont-on-the-Hudson, New York. Warner, *Generals in Blue*, pp. 160–61.

94. William Thompson Martin (March 25, 1823–March 16, 1910) rose from the rank of captain to major general. His early service was with Stuart and the Confederate forces in the East, but after his commission as brigadier general in December 1862, he was sent west, where he eventually served with Gen. Joseph Wheeler's cavalry. Martin rests in City Cemetery, Natchez, Mississippi. Warner, *Generals in Gray*, pp. 214–15.

95. Fitzhugh Lee (November 19, 1835–April 28, 1905) was a nephew of Robert E. Lee. A graduate of West Point (class of 1856) and a fine cavalry officer in his own right, Fitz rose to the rank of major general and eventually commanded the cavalry of the Army of Northern Virginia when Hampton, Stuart's successor, was sent south to North Carolina in January 1865. After the war, he was elected governor of Virginia in 1885 and served as major general of U.S. Volunteers during the Spanish-American War in 1898. Lee is buried in Hollywood Cemetery, Richmond, Virginia. *Ibid.*, pp.178–79.

96. Robert Ransom Jr. (February 12, 1828–January 14, 1892), a graduate of the United States Military Academy (class of 1850), had resigned his commission in the U.S. Army and joined the Confederate Army as colonel

of the 1st North Carolina Cavalry. With his promotion to brigadier general in March 1862, he switched branches of service to command an infantry brigade under Longstreet. He was later transferred to North Carolina and promoted major general. He retired in the fall of 1864 because of declining health. Ransom is buried in Cedar Grove Cemetery, New Bern, North Carolina. *Ibid.*, pp. 253–54.

97. *O.R.*, Ser. I, Vol. 5, pp. 413–21, 437–51; *Supplement to the Official Records of the Union and Confederate Armies* (Wilmington, NC: Broadfoot Publishing Company, 1994), Vol. 1, pp. 407–9.

98. Roger Williams Steger (1834–November 24, 1877) had been a schoolteacher before the war. He joined the Amelia Dragoons, which became part of the 1st Virginia Cavalry under Stuart. Having been unable to join Stuart's staff, Steger returned to his company. He was captured near Fredericksburg during the winter of 1863. Exchanged in early 1865, he rejoined the 1st Virginia and served until the war's end. He was a farmer after the war. Steger is buried in Hollywood Cemetery, Richmond, Virginia. Trout, *They Followed the Plume*, p. 250.

99. The process of filling a bond involves obtaining the names of individuals who are willing to stand financially behind the officer to cover the expense of material lost, stolen, or misused while under that officer's charge. Since the officer most likely would not have the money to cover extensive losses, he asked other individuals to back him.

100. Abraham Charles Myers (May 1811–June 20, 1889) graduated from West Point in 1833, taking five years rather than the usual four because of poor grades. Assigned to the 4th U.S. Infantry, he fought in the Seminole Wars in Florida and in Mexico, where he earned two brevets for gallantry. Myers had transferred to the quartermaster department while he was stationed in Baton Rouge during the Seminole War. He entered Confederate service in April 1861 and was immediately assigned to the quartermaster corps. Promoted to colonel on February 15, 1862, Myers held that rank until a dispute with President Davis caused him to resign his commission in February 1864. Faust, ed., *Historical Times Illustrated Encyclopedia of the Civil War*, p. 519.

101. The Reverend Edmund Harrison was a private in the 4th Virginia Cavalry. He eventually was detailed to the Nitre Department in Richmond.

102. Accotink is in the vicinity of Pohick Church along the Telegraph Road.

103. The raccoon is mentioned by John Esten Cooke in *Wearing of the Gray*. John Esten Cooke, *Wearing of the Gray* (Bloomington: Indiana University Press, 1977), pp. 185–86.

104. There is no report of this action.

105. George Washington Custis Lee (September 16, 1832–February 18, 1913) was the eldest son of Gen. Robert E. Lee. He graduated from West Point with Stuart in 1854. He remained on President Davis's staff and eventually rose to the rank of major general in the Confederate Army. In the closing months of the war, he did command troops in the field. Lee is buried in the Lee mausoleum in Lexington, Virginia. Warner, *Generals in Gray*, p. 179.

106. John Letcher (March 29, 1813–January 26, 1884) was a lawyer and U.S. congressman before being elected Virginia's governor in 1859. He was not originally a supporter of secession, but when Virginia did secede, he gave all his support to the Confederate government. His term expired in 1864, and he retired to Lexington. He was ruined financially by the war and spent six weeks in prison. Letcher returned to practicing law after the war and served two years in Virginia's state legislature. Faust, ed., *Historical Times Illustrated Encyclopedia of the Civil War*, pp. 433–34.

107. Charles William Field (April 6, 1828–April 9, 1892), a Kentuckian, had graduated from West Point in 1849. He resigned his commission in the U.S. Army in May 1861 and became colonel of the 6th Virginia Cavalry soon thereafter. On March 9, 1862, he was promoted to brigadier general and transferred to the infantry, where he served for the remainder of the war, rising to the rank of major general. Field is buried in Loudoun Park Cemetery, Baltimore, Maryland. Warner, *Generals in Gray*, pp. 87–88.

108. *O.R.*, Ser. I, Vol. 5, pp. 451–56, 470–95; *Supplement to the O.R.*, Ser. I, Vol. 1, pp. 407–9.

109. William Eskridge Towles (March 15, 1837–February 19, 1863) was a lawyer in Louisiana when the war began. He entered 7th Louisiana Infantry but soon transferred to what became the 21st Mississippi Infantry to be with his brother. His brother died of typhoid fever in September 1861 and Towles again transferred, this time to the Washington Artillery of New Orleans. Shortly after, he accepted a position as voluntary aide to Stuart, to whom he was related. Towles expected that the post would become permanent, and when that did not happen as quickly as he had anticipated, he left the staff and rejoined the Washington Artillery. He was killed in a train accident while traveling home on furlough. Towles lies in the Towles Family Cemetery, West Feliciana Parish, Louisiana. Trout, *They Followed the Plume*, pp. 260–62.

110. "Vaucluse" was the Dabney family's home near Lynchburg, Virginia.

111. *O.R.*, Ser. I, Vol. 5, p. 495.

1862

1. *O.R.*, Ser. I, Vol. 5, pp. 503–4, 510–11.

2. *Ibid.*, pp. 518–20, 524, 531, 550–51, 1098, 1101–2.

3. Warrenton Juncton is now Calverton.

4. *O.R.*, Ser. I, Vol. 12, Part 1, pp. 412–17.

5. John Pelham (September 7, 1838–March 18, 1863) was the commander of the Stuart Horse Artillery. He had attended the United States Military Academy, leaving just a few weeks before he would have graduated. Making his way south to Alabama, he offered his services to the Confederacy. A gifted artillerist, he was mortally wounded at the Battle of Kelly's Ford on March 17, 1863. Pelham is buried in City Cemetery, Jacksonville, Alabama. Trout, *They Followed the Plume*, pp. 204–13.

6. Mr. Ballard was John P. Ballard, a cousin of Major Powers and owner of the Ballard-Exchange, a famous Richmond hotel. Sis F. was Jane Frances Powers, nicknamed Fanny, a sister of Major Powers and the wife of John P. Ballard. Willie is William Hazard Powers, brother of Major Powers.

7. Alice was Alice Burnett Powers (1854–1934), the major's daughter.

8. The home of James Barbour was a half mile north of Brandy Station. The house was built by Coleman Beckham as a wedding present to his daughter, Fannie, upon her marriage to James Barbour in 1857. It was named "Beauregard" after Gen. P. G. T. Beauregard at the request of Maj. Roberdeau Wheat of the Louisiana Tigers. The house suffered extensive damage during the war but was restored. Culpeper Historical Society, Inc., *Historic Culpeper* (Culpeper Historical Society, Inc., 1974), p. 38.

9. Though Stuart had been impressed with Harrison (see Stuart letter of November 11, 1861), Powers's opinion was honored, and Harrison did not get the appointment as Powers's assistant.

"Entre nous" means "between us."

10. Lelia was Lelia Harrison, wife of Zebulon Montgomery Pike Powers, another brother of Major Powers.

11. Powers is referring to the Battle of Kernstown, fought on March 23, 1862.

12. James Lansing Powers was another brother of Major Powers.

13. William Ballard, the son of John Ballard ("Mr. B.") and his wife, Fanny, Powers's sister, was serving in the army.

14. Mr. Lobban was the husband of Kitty Lobban of Charlottesville, with whom Roberta Powers was staying at this time.

15. Mary was the wife of Major Powers's brother, William.

16. John Evans Johnson (September 1814–June 11, 1905) was colonel of the 9th Virginia Cavalry. He was dropped during the army's reorgani-

zation in April and later served as a voluntary aide to Gen. Richard S. Ewell. Krick, *Lee's Colonels*, p. 210.

17. Williams Carter Wickham (September 21, 1820–July 23, 1888), a Virginia lawyer, planter, and politician before the war, rose to the rank of brigadier general and commanded a brigade in Stuart's cavalry corps. Twice wounded, Wickham resigned his commission and assumed a seat in the Confederate Congress, to which he had been elected shortly after the Battle of Chancellorsville. He was a businessman and politician after the war. Wickham is buried in Hanover County, Virginia. Warner, *Generals in Gray*, pp. 335–36.

18. *O.R.*, Ser. I, Vol. 11, Part 1, pp. 444–45.

19. *Ibid.*, pp. 570–75.

20. William Downs Farley (December 19, 1835–June 9, 1863) received his education at the University of Virginia. Before the war, he helped his father run the family business, took an interest in politics, and became a strong advocate of secession. His first service was with the 1st Carolina Regiment of Infantry, but when his enlistment expired, he became an independent operator. After serving on the staff of Milledge L. Bonham and as a scout for Beauregard, Farley joined Stuart as a voluntary aide and independent scout. Everything he needed to wage war he took from the enemy. His daring became legendary, and John Esten Cooke wrote of a number of his adventures. Farley was mortally wounded at the Battle of Brandy Station and died within a few hours. He is buried in Fairview Cemetery, Culpeper, Virginia. Trout, *They Followed the Plume*, pp. 106–14.

21. Hugh Legare Farley was a sergeant in Company G, 3rd South Carolina Infantry.

22. Farley was mistaken as to the regiment to which the captain belonged. The 47th New York was not engaged at Williamsburg, being in South Carolina at the time. *O.R.*, Ser. I, Vol. 11, Part 1, p. 450.

23. This was Col. Christopher Haynes Mott (June 22, 1826–May 5, 1862) of the 19th Mississippi Infantry. Krick, *Lee's Colonels*, p. 282.

24. The names of the color bearers were Color Sergeant Peebles, who was first wounded; Pvt. William P. Meaders, who was wounded next; Pvt. John Halloran, who was not wounded; and Lt. Columbus F. Jones, also not wounded. There is no mention of Farley in the report of Lt. Col. Lucius Q. C. Lamar of the 19th Mississippi, and only two of the bearers were wounded. *O.R.*, Ser. I, Vol. 11, Part 1, p. 599.

25. Four guns, one caisson, and forty horses belonging to Battery H of the 1st U.S. Artillery commanded by Capt. Charles H. Webber were captured. *Ibid.*, p. 471.

26. Stuart's report confirms this incident. *Ibid.*, p. 571.

27. This engagement took place at West Point or Eltham's Landing. The Federals reported their losses as 48 killed, 110 wounded, and 28 captured. *Ibid.*, p. 618.

28. Powers is referring to Stonewall Jackson's victory at the Battle of McDowell on May 8.

29. Louisa Ann (actually Ann Louisa) was a friend of the Powers family. Mrs. Powers stayed with her and Mrs. Housen at their home, "Kalorama," near Staunton.

30. *O.R.*, Ser. I, Vol. 11, Part 1, pp. 941, 994.

31. Hardeman Stuart's friend was Capt. Robert Eggleston Wilbourn, who served on the staffs of Gustavus W. Smith, Richard S. Ewell, and Thomas J. Jackson.

32. Oscar J. E. Stuart was Hardeman's brother. He served in the 18th Mississippi Infantry.

33. Robertson's father, Wyndham Robertson, was ex-governor of Virginia.

34. Robertson had returned to the family's home, "The Meadows," near Abingdon, Virginia, to recuperate from his illness.

35. Sam was Robertson's servant.

36. *O.R.*, Ser. I, Vol. 11, Part 1, pp. 1004–46.

37. William Latané (January 16, 1833–June 13, 1862) had been a physician in Essex County before the war. He had graduated from Richmond Medical College in 1853 and after taking postgraduate courses in Philadelphia, he returned to his home to establish his practice. At the war's commencement he joined the Essex Light Dragoons, which later became Company F of the 9th Virginia Cavalry. He was elected third lieutenant of the company at its initial organization. When the company was reorganized in spring 1862, Latané was elected captain. He is buried at Summer Hill Plantation in Hanover County. Robert K. Krick, *9th Virginia Cavalry* (Lynchburg, VA: H. E. Howard, Inc., 1982), p. 85; William Campbell, "Stuart's Ride Around McClellan," *Confederate Veteran* V, pp. 53–54.

38. William Henry Fitzhugh Lee (May 31, 1837–October 15, 1891), known as "Rooney," was Robert E. Lee's second son. In 1857 he went from the halls of Harvard directly into the U.S. Army as a second lieutenant, not having been able to enter West Point because of an injured hand. He resigned to take up farming. With the coming of the war, he entered Confederate service and rose rapidly to colonel. In September he was commissioned a brigadier general. Seriously wounded at Brandy Station June 9, 1863, he was captured while recuperating and did not rejoin the army until March 1864. He was promoted to major general during his imprisonment.

After the war, he returned to farming and also served in the Virginia Senate and in the U.S. Congress. Lee is buried in the Lee mausoleum in Lexington, Virginia. Warner, *Generals in Gray*, pp. 184–85.

39. *O.R.*, Ser. I, Vol. 11, Part 2, pp. 513–18.

40. Cooke is referring to the Battle of Gaines's Mill, otherwise known as the Battle of First Cold Harbor. The Confederates under Ambrose P. Hill, James Longstreet, Daniel H. Hill, and Jackson faced the corps of Fitz John Porter and Henry W. Slocum. Lee had planned for Jackson to outflank Porter along Beaver Dam Creek, but Stonewall was delayed, and A. P. Hill's and Longstreet's attacks were repulsed with heavy loss. Just before dark, the Federals were driven from their positions by the first coordinated Confederate assault of the day. Losses were 6,837 for the Federals and 8,751 for the Confederates. Boatner, *The Civil War Dictionary*, p. 321.

41. Philip St. George Cooke (June 13, 1809–March 20, 1895) was Stuart's father-in-law. A Virginian, Cooke remained in the U.S. Army and commanded the Federal cavalry in the Peninsula Campaign. His singular failure to capture his son-in-law during the Chickahominy Raid plus what was felt were other shortcomings in his performance led to his assignment to courts-martial duties for the remainder of the war. Cooke lies in Elmwood Cemetery, Detroit, Michigan. Warner, *Generals in Blue*, pp. 89–90.

42. Nat was Nathaniel Cooke, son of Philip Pendleton Cooke, John Esten's brother. John O. Beaty, *John Esten Cooke, Virginian* (Port Washington, NY: Kennikat Press, n.d.), p. 78.

43. Lt. D. T. Webster was serving on the staff of Brig. Gen. Robert E. Rodes and was killed in a charge.

Brisco Gerard Baldwin was also serving on Rodes's staff and acted as the lieutenant colonel of the 6th Alabama. He would later serve on Robert E. Lee's staff as chief of ordnance. *O.R.*, Ser. I, Vol. 11, Part 2, pp. 631–35.

44. James Walkinshaw Allen (July 2, 1829–June 27, 1862) was a Virginia Military Institute graduate in the class of 1849. Before the war, he was a farmer and served on the VMI faculty. He became colonel of the 2nd Virginia on April 28, 1861, and was wounded at 1st Manassas. He is buried at Liberty, Virginia. Krick, *Lee's Colonels*, p. 32.

45. "Memoranda" appears here because this entry, although dated July 7, actually describes events of June 27 and 28.

46. "Orapax" was the home of Mrs. Sarah "Sal" Dandridge Cooke Duval in New Kent County, Virginia. Mrs. Duval was John Esten Cooke's sister. Beaty, *John Esten Cooke, Virginian*, p. 141.

47. Talcott Eliason (1826–October 22, 1896) was Stuart's staff surgeon. Born in Beaufort, North Carolina, he was the son of William Alexander Eliason, who had graduated first in his class at the United States Military

Academy in 1821. Talcott did not follow in his father's footsteps, choosing instead to enter the medical profession. He graduated from Jefferson Medical College in Philadelphia in 1847. When the war began, Eliason entered the army, became a surgeon for the 1st Virginia Cavalry, and joined Stuart's staff in January 1862. He served with Stuart until his health forced him to resign in October 1863. He died on October 22, 1896, in Hancock, Maryland. Eliason is buried in the Presbyterian Cemetery, Hancock, Maryland. Trout, *They Followed the Plume*, pp. 99–102.

48. Lawrence O'Bryan Branch's (November 28, 1820–September 17, 1862) brigade was engaged along Beaver Dam Creek during the fighting on the twenty-sixth (Battle of Mechanicsville). Branch, a graduate of Princeton, was a lawyer and U.S. congressman before the war. He was killed at the Battle of Sharpsburg and was buried in Raleigh, North Carolina. Warner, *Generals in Gray*, p. 31.

49. The "bucktails" to which Cooke referred were the men of the 13th Pennsylvania Reserves (also known as the 1st Pennsylvania Rifles, the Kane Rifle Regiment, and the 42nd Regiment of the Line), raised initially in McKean, Elk, and Cameron counties of Pennsylvania. Their sobriquet came from the fact that the soldiers of the regiment wore deer tails or pieces of deer hide shaped like tails on their caps. The regiment had seventy-five men reported as missing after the Battle of Mechanicsville on the twenty-sixth and another ninety-six men missing after the Battle of Gaines's Mill on the twenty-seventh. Undoubtedly it was some of these men that Cooke saw as prisoners. O. R. Howard Thompson and William H. Rauch, *History of the "Bucktails"* (Philadelphia: Electric Printing Company, 1906), pp. 9–11, 96–121.

50. Thomas Reade Rootes Cobb (April 10, 1823–December 13, 1862) had resigned from the Confederate Provisional Congress to recruit what became the Cobb Legion, the unit he led during the Seven Days Battles. Promoted to brigadier general in November 1862, Cobb was mortally wounded on December 13, 1862, while defending the "sunken road" during the Battle of Fredericksburg. He lies in Oconee Hill Cemetery, Athens, Georgia. Warner, *Generals in Gray*, p. 56.

51. The batteries that came to assist Pelham were those of Capt. John Bowyer Brockenbrough (2nd Maryland Battery), Capt. James McDowell Carrington (Charlottesville Battery), and Capt. Alfred Ranson Courtney (Henrico Artillery). No guns were reported damaged or disabled by these batteries. *O.R.*, Ser. I, Vol. 11, Part 2, p. 560.

52. Lt. Jones Rivers Christian (1834–May 20, 1895) of the 3rd Virginia Cavalry had served as a guide for Stuart during the Chickahominy Raid. A native of New Kent County, Virginia, Christian was very familiar with the

topography of the Peninsula and was of great assistance to Stuart throughout the Seven Days Battles. He was captured on May 8, 1864, in the Wilderness and became one of the "Immortal 600." Christian was a post office clerk in Richmond after the war. He is buried in Hollywood Cemetery, Richmond, Virginia. Trout, *They Followed the Plume*, pp. 85–86.

53. The guns that were captured belonged to the following batteries (not all the guns of each battery were taken): the 5th U.S. Artillery, Battery C, commanded by Capt. Henry V. De Hart, who died as a result of wounds received while trying to save his guns; the 1st Pennsylvania Light Artillery, Battery A, commanded by Capt. Hezekiah Easton, who was killed defending his guns; the 1st Pennsylvania Light Artillery, Battery B, commanded by Capt. James H. Cooper; and the 1st Pennsylvania Light Artillery, Battery G, commanded by Capt. Mark Kerns, who was wounded in the action. *O.R.*, Ser. I, Vol. 11, Part 2, pp. 32, 400–402, 407–12, 989–90.

54. Johann August Heinrich Heros von Borcke (July 23, 1835–May 10, 1895) was one of the most colorful individuals on Stuart's staff. A Prussian who had come to fight for the Confederacy, von Borcke built a reputation as a fighter equal to his six-foot-four, 240-pound frame. He had joined Stuart in time for the Battle of Seven Pines on May 31 and by June 20 was a captain on the staff. He reached the rank of major before he was terribly wounded in the throat at the Battle of Middleburg on June 19, 1863. He was unable to return to active duty with Stuart. Von Borcke is buried in Berlin, Germany. Trout, *They Followed the Plume*, pp. 273–80.

55. Pvt. J. H. Carson was detached from the Jeff Davis Legion and was serving in Stuart's escort during this time. *O.R.*, Ser. I, Vol. 11, Part 1, p. 1040.

56. This was probably Pvt. William H. Patterson (1836–April 20, 1863) of Company E, 1st Virginia Cavalry, who served as a courier for Stuart from September 1861 to February 1863. Driver, *1st Virginia Cavalry*, p. 214.

57. This was probably 1st Lt. David Algenon Timberlake (1833–1901) of Company G, 4th Virginia Cavalry. He was attached to Stuart's headquarters as a scout because of his familiarity with the area in which the army was operating. Kenneth L. Stiles, *4th Virginia Cavalry* (Lynchburg, VA: H.E. Howard, Inc., 1985), p. 119.

58. Jasper Strong Whiting was serving as Jackson's assistant adjutant general.

59. Cooke is probably referring to Pvt. James P. Riely of Company D, 6th Virginia Cavalry. Michael P. Musick, *6th Virginia Cavalry* (Lynchburg, VA: H. E. Howard, Inc., 1990), p. 149.

60. This was Lt. William Dabney Waller. Robert K. Krick, *9th Virginia Cavalry* (Lynchburg: H. E. Howard, Inc., 1982), pp. 104, 125.

61. Mrs. Stanhope Crump was not the wife of Dr. Crump.

62. Betty was the daughter of Cooke's sister, Sarah Dandridge Cooke Duval. Ben may have been Cooke's servant.

63. Sal was Cooke's sister, Sarah Dandridge Cooke Duval.

64. Though this appears as Evelington in most texts, Evelynton is correct.

65. O.R., Ser. I, Vol. 12, Part 2, pp. 518–21.

66. Laurence Simmons Baker (May 15, 1830–April 10, 1907) was colonel of the 1st North Carolina Cavalry. He was promoted to brigadier general in July 1863, but because he was suffering from numerous wounds he received during his service, he was assigned departmental command in North Carolina in 1864. Baker was a railroad agent after the war. He is buried in Cedar Hill Cemetery, Suffolk, Virginia. Warner, Generals in Gray, pp. 14–15.

67. Stuart makes no mention of the use of rockets on Evelynton Heights. O.R., Ser. I, Vol. 11, Part 2, p. 520.

68. O.R., Ser. I, Vol. 11, Part 2, pp. 520–21.

69. O.R., Ser. I, Vol. 12, Part 2, pp. 98–101, 102–3.

70. Blackford, War Years with Jeb Stuart, pp. 87–88; Heros von Borcke, Memoirs of the Confederate War for Independence (Dayton: Morningside House, Inc.), Vol. 1, pp. 87–89.

71. O.R., Ser. I, Vol. 11, Part 2, pp. 924–25.

72. Francis Engle Patterson (May 7, 1821–November 22, 1862) was the son of Gen. Robert Patterson. He had served in Mexico and remained in the army after the war until he resigned in May 1877. When war erupted, he rejoined the army and became colonel of the 17th Pennsylvania Infantry. Promoted to brigadier general in April 1862, Patterson served in Joe Hooker's division of the III Corps. He was under investigation for an unauthorized retreat when he was killed by the accidental discharge of his pistol. Patterson is buried in Laurel Hill Cemetery, Philadelphia, Pennsylvania. Warner, Generals in Blue, pp. 362–63.

73. Von Borcke tells of this somewhat embarrassing and comical incident in his memoirs. Apparently he thought he had captured a Yankee but had actually latched onto a trooper of the 9th Virginia Cavalry dressed in a captured blue uniform. The trooper thought that von Borcke was a Federal because of his German accent. The confusion was cleared up when von Borcke brought his "prisoner" into camp. Stuart continued the Prussian's embarrassment by asking von Borcke from time to time, "How many prisoners of the 9th Virginia have you taken lately?" Borcke, Memoirs of the Confederate War for Independence, Vol. 1, pp. 77–78.

74. This was either James Thomas Watt Hairston or his brother, Samuel Harden Hairston. Both were on Stuart's staff at this time. Trout, They Followed the Plume, pp. 165–69, 173–76.

75. Edward Stuart was Hardeman's brother.

76. The "Misses Price" were Elizabeth Winston and Anne (Nannie) Overton Price, the daughters of Dr. and Mrs. Lucien Bonaparte Price of "Dundee" near Hanover Court House. Adele H. Mitchell, ed., *Southern Cavalry Review* (Stuart-Mosby Historical Society, March 1985), Vol. 2, No. 5, p. 1.

77. This was probably Capt. Benjamin K. Barker, who worked in the harness shops in Richmond. Barker later commanded Company D of the 1st (Armory) Battalion Virginia Infantry, local defense troops. Wallace Jr., *A Guide to Virginia Military Organizations 1861–1865*, pp. 179–80.

78. Norman Richard FitzHugh (December 8, 1831–May 13, 1915) had joined Stuart's staff officially on June 24 but was well known to the cavalry's commander before that date from his service with the 9th Virginia. FitzHugh began as the cavalry's adjutant general but later in the war became its quartermaster. He was twice captured, first on August 18, 1862, at Verdiersville, and again on December 1, 1864, at Stoney Creek south of Petersburg while serving as quartermaster on Wade Hampton's staff. He was an orange grower after the war. FitzHugh is buried in Evergreen Cemetery, Jacksonville, Florida. Trout, *They Followed the Plume*, pp. 114–19.

79. This incident was also mentioned by von Borcke, though he dated it as occurring on the twenty-sixth. Borcke, *Memoirs of the Confederate War for Independence*, Vol. 1, pp. 90.

80. John Pope (March 16, 1822–September 23, 1892) was one of the North's more controversial generals. A West Point graduate (class of 1842), his first service of the war was in the western theater, where he made a name for himself Island No. 10 and opening the upper Mississippi River in March and April 1862. His failure against Lee in August of that same year relegated him to virtual oblivion in the Department of the Northwest. Pope is buried in Bellefontaine Cemetery, Saint Louis, Missouri. Warner, *Generals in Blue*, pp. 376–77.

81. *O.R.*, Ser. I, Vol. 12, Part 2, pp. 118–26.

82. John Landstreet (April 23, 1818–November 21, 1891) was chaplain of the 1st Virginia Cavalry and during the Seven Days Battles had been a voluntary aide to Stuart. He continued in the ministry after the war. Landstreet lies in Green Hill Cemetery, Martinsburg, West Virginia. Trout, *They Followed the Plume*, pp. 191–97.

83. "Gay Mont" was the home of William Robertson Bernard, a relative of Frank Smith Robertson, who would become the assistant engineer officer on Stuart's staff in early 1863. Stuart's visit is chronicled in the diary of Helen Struan Bernard Robb, which is housed at the College of William and Mary.

84. This incident is mentioned by both von Borcke and Blackford in their reminiscences although the latter stated that the watch belonged to Cye, "the old carriage driver." Blackford, *War Years with Jeb Stuart*, p. 94; Heros von Borcke, *Memoirs of the Confederate War for Independence*, Vol. 1, pp. 92–93.

85. Von Borcke wrote at length about his encounter with one of the largest specimens of the American rattlesnake. Heros von Borcke, *Memoirs of the Confederate War for Independence*, Vol. 1, pp. 93–95.

86. The Blakeley was a rifled cannon designed by Capt. Alexander T. Blakeley of the British Army. It came in a variety of sizes and calibers. Primarily a Confederate weapon that was smuggled through the blockade, the Blakeley was popular with the horse artillery. Faust, ed., *Historical Times Illustrated Encyclopedia of the Civil War*, p. 66; Boatner, *The Civil War Dictionary*, p. 68.

87. Ambrose Everett Burnside (May 23, 1824–September 13, 1881) graduated from the United States Military Academy in 1847. He was relegated to garrison duty during the Mexican War. He resigned his commission in 1853 to enter into the manufacturing of a breech-loading rifle that bore his name. His efforts failed, but he found success in other areas. When the war began, he became the colonel of the 1st Rhode Island Infantry. He commanded a brigade at First Manassas and was promoted to brigadier general in August 1861. In March 1862 he was commissioned major general, and he commanded a corps in a number of major battles in the East. He was appointed the commander of the Army of the Potomac and led it in the disaster at Fredericksburg in December 1862. He was sent to command the Department of the Ohio but eventually returned to the Army of the Potomac. His failure at the Battle of the Crater in July 1864 ultimately caused him to resign in April 1865. After the war, he was active in business and politics, being elected governor of Rhode Island three times. Burnside is buried in Swan Point Cemetery, Providence, Rhode Island. Warner, *Generals in Blue*, pp. 57–58.

88. *O.R.*, Ser. I, Vol. 12, Part 2, p. 184.

89. Dabney is referring to the Battle of Cedar Mountain, which took place on August 9, 1862.

90. Stuart did make a wager with one of the officers. He won a hat, which he lost at Verdiersville on the eighteenth.

91. John Bell Hood (June 1, 1831–August 30, 1879) graduated from the United States Military Academy with the class of 1853. After serving in Texas and California, he resigned his commission in April 1861 to join the Confederate army. Hood distinguished himself at all levels, rising rapidly from regimental command to major general by October 1862. After suf-

fering a serious arm wound at Gettysburg and losing a leg at Chickamauga, he received a promotion to lieutenant general in February 1864 and then to full general in July 1864 (though this rank was only temporary). As an army commander, Hood never achieved the success he had experienced at brigade and divisional levels of command, and after the disaster at the Battle of Nashville, he was relieved of command at his own request. He is buried in Metairie Cemetery, New Orleans, Louisiana. Warner, *Generals in Gray*, pp. 142–43.

92. Beverly Holcombe Robertson (June 5, 1827–November 12, 1910) was a career soldier. After graduating from West Point in the class of 1849, he served on the frontier with the 2nd Dragoons. He was dismissed from the army in August 1861 because of his having been appointed a captain in the Confederate army. He was soon made colonel of the 4th Virginia Cavalry and, in June 1862, was promoted to brigadier general. His relationship with Stuart deteriorated after the Battle of Brandy Station in June 1863, and he ended the war in the Department of South Carolina. He sold insurance after the war. Robertson is buried on Rock Castle Farm in Amelia County, Virginia. *Ibid.*, pp. 259–60.

93. Franz Sigel (November 18, 1824–August 21, 1902) was born in Sinsheim, Germany. He attended a military academy and upon graduation became a subaltern under Grand Duke Leopold. Joining in the revolution of 1848, he was forced to flee to Switzerland when the Prussians were victorious. He emigrated to America and settled in New York, where he made a living as a teacher. In 1861 he was in Saint Louis, where he was director of schools. Commissioned a brigadier general in August 1861 and a major general in March 1862, Sigel owed his quick rise to political connections and an ability to rally German-Americans to the colors, not to military talent. He fought in both the western and eastern theaters and suffered a humiliating defeat at the Battle of New Market on May 15, 1864, after which he was removed from field command. He ultimately resigned on May 4, 1865. He was a politician after the war. Sigel is buried in Woodlawn Cemetery, New York City, New York. Warner, *Generals in Blue*, pp. 447–48.

94. George Wythe Randolph (March 10, 1818–April 3, 1867) was a lawyer before the war. He organized the Richmond Howitzers, commanding them in early 1861. He was commissioned brigadier general on January 12, 1862, and served as Confederate secretary of war until he resigned in November 1862. Discovering he had tuberculosis, he resigned his generalship to go to France in hopes of a cure. He returned to Virginia after the war. Randolph rests at "Monticello," the home of his maternal grandfather. Warner, *Generals in Gray*, pp. 252–53.

95. Stephen Dill Lee (September 22, 1833–May 28, 1908) graduated from the United States Military Academy with Stuart in the class of 1854. He had an amazing career in the Confederate army. Entering as a captain, he rose through the ranks until, on June 23, 1864, he was commissioned a lieutenant general. He served in all branches of the army and was at the very beginning of the war on the staff of Gen. P. G. T. Beauregard. After the war he was a farmer, state senator, and president of Mississippi State College. Lee is buried in Friendship Cemetery, Columbus, Mississippi. *Ibid.*, pp. 183–84.

96. *O.R.*, Ser. I, Vol. 12, Part 2, pp. 725–28.

97. Col. Fontaine was Edmund Fontaine, father of John B. Fontaine, Stuart's future chief surgeon. Beaver Dam was the name of the Fontaine home, located near Beaver Dam Station.

98. *O.R.*, Ser. I, Vol. 12, Part 2, pp. 729–31.

99. *Ibid.*, p. 733.

100. *Ibid.*, pp. 641–48.

101. Trout, *They Followed the Plume*, pp. 251–56, 362.

102. *O.R.*, Ser. I, Vol. 12, Part 2, pp. 538, 743, 749.

103. This Flint Hill was closer to today's Oakton and should not be confused with the present Flint Hill west of Warrenton.

104. *O.R.*, Ser. I, Vol. 12, Part 2, pp. 744–45.

105. Price's mother, Mrs. Thomas Randolph Price Sr., was the former Christian Elizabeth Hall, granddaughter of the second bishop of Virginia, Richard Channing Moore, after whom Price was named. Trout, *They Followed the Plume*, p. 218.

106. Andrew Reid Venable (December 2, 1832–October 15, 1909), was at this time the assistant commissary of subsistence in the 1st Regiment of Virginia Artillery under Col. John Thompson Brown. He joined Stuart's staff after the Chancellorsville Campaign. Price and Venable had served together in the 3rd Richmond Howitzers in the fall of 1861. After the war, Venable returned to his estate, "Milnwood," near Farmville, Virginia, to take up farming. He is buried in College Cemetery, Hampden-Sidney, Virginia. *Ibid.*, pp. 218, 270.

107. Lt. Charles Minnigerode Jr. was the son of Dr. Charles Minnigerode, rector of St. Paul's Church in Richmond, where President Jefferson Davis and his family worshiped. Young Minnigerode was aide-de-camp to Gen. Fitzhugh Lee.

108. Price is mistaken. Hardeman Stuart's old regiment, the 18th Mississippi, was not engaged at Second Manassas. He had joined either the 4th or 5th Texas. Trout, *They Followed the Plume*, p. 362.

109. *O.R.*, Ser. I, Vol. 19, Part 1, pp. 416, 816, 823.

110. *Ibid.*, pp. 818–21.

111. *Ibid.*, pp. 823–24.

Lafayette McLaws (January 15, 1821–July 24, 1897) graduated from the United States Military Academy in the class of 1842. His career in the U.S. Army was undistinguished, but when he resigned in March 1861, he was commissioned a colonel in the Confederate army and took command of the 10th Georgia Infantry. Promoted to brigadier general in September 1861 and major general in May 1862, McLaws fought well under his old West Point classmate James Longstreet. After the disappointing Nashville Campaign, however, Longstreet relieved McLaws of his command for alleged failures in the preparation of and assault on Fort Sanders. Reinstated and given his old command by President Davis, McLaws and Longstreet clashed again, and the former was transferred to Georgia. At the last he was serving under Joe Johnston and surrendered with that officer at Greensboro, North Carolina. In the postwar period, he was in the insurance business and also worked as an internal revenue collector and postmaster. McLaws is buried in Savannah, Georgia. Warner, *Generals in Gray*, pp. 204–5.

112. The cavalry at Crampton's Gap was under the command of Col. Thomas Munford. He also had regiments of Brig. Gen. William Mahone's Brigade (6th, 12th, and 16th Virginia Infantry and the 10th Georgia Infantry), under Col. William A. Parham, as well as Capt. Roger Preston Chew's Horse Artillery Battery and a section of naval howitzers belonging to Capt. John H. Thompson's Portsmouth Light Artillery. Brig. Gen. Howell Cobb finally responded to Colonel Munford's pleas for reinforcements and committed his regiments. Unfortunately, this was done in piecemeal fashion, and before Brig. Gen. Paul J. Semmes's Brigade could intervene, the battle was lost. Munford was critical of Cobb in his report but praised Parham, Chew, and the 2nd and 12th Virginia Cavalry. Cobb, for his part, had behaved gallantly when his lines were broken, at one point grabbing the flag of a regiment in an attempt to rally the fleeing soldiers. His brother-in-law and volunteer aide, Col. John B. Lamar, was mortally wounded at his side, after which he left the field with his men. The episode of Stuart rallying the fugitives from Cobb's command is supported by Heros von Borcke's account of the same event. *O.R.*, Ser. I, Vol. 19, Part 1, pp. 818–19, 826–28, 870–71; John Michael Priest, *Before Antietam: The Battle for South Mountain* (Shippensburg, PA: White Mane Publishing Company, Inc., 1992), pp. 272–304; von Borcke, *Memoirs of the Confederate War for Independence*, Vol. 1, pp. 216–19.

113. David Rumph "Neighbor" Jones (April 5, 1825–January 15, 1863) graduated from West Point with the class of 1846. His wife was a niece of President Zachary Taylor, and he was cousin to Jefferson Davis. He served

in the Mexican War and was Gen. P. G. T. Beauregard's chief of staff during the attack on Fort Sumter at the beginning of the war. Commissioned a brigadier general on June 17, 1861, he was promoted to major general on March 10, 1862. Though he was not wounded at Sharpsburg, he developed a serious heart condition soon after, which led to his death. Jones is buried in Hollywood Cemetery, Richmond, Virginia. Warner, *Generals in Gray*, pp. 163–64.

William Edwin Starke (1814–September 17, 1862) was a cotton broker before the war and lived in New Orleans. After a short time as staff officer, he received command of the 60th Virginia Infantry and was promoted to brigadier general on August 6, 1862. He was killed at Sharpsburg and rests in Hollywood Cemetery in Richmond. *Ibid.*, p. 289.

Lewis Addison Armistead (February 18, 1817–July 5, 1863) had been a cadet at West Point but was dismissed in 1836. Nevertheless, he received an army appointment and served in the Mexican War, being brevetted twice for gallantry. At the beginning of the war, he commanded the 57th Virginia Infantry. He was commissioned brigadier general on April 1, 1862. He is best known for his participation in Pickett's Charge during the Battle of Gettysburg, in which he was mortally wounded. Armistead lies in St. Paul's Churchyard, Baltimore, Maryland. *Ibid.*, pp. 11–12.

Samuel Garland Jr. (December 16, 1830–September 14, 1862) had attended both the Virginia Military Institute and the University of Virginia. Graduating from the latter with a law degree in 1851, Garland established his offices in Lynchburg. At the beginning of the war, he was commissioned colonel of the 11th Virginia Infantry. He was promoted to brigadier general on May 23, 1862. Garland is buried in Lynchburg, Virginia. *Ibid.*, pp. 98–99.

William Dabney Stuart (September 30, 1830–July 30, 1863) was a graduate of the Virginia Military Institute with the class of 1850. He was a teacher and school official in Richmond before the war. At the time of Sharpsburg, he was commanding the 56th Virginia Infantry. He was mortally wounded at Gettysburg and rests in Thornrose Cemetery, Staunton, Virginia. Krick, *Lee's Colonels*, p. 362.

114. Price's figures are accurate. The Federal cavalry's escape was led by Col. Benjamin Franklin "Grimes" Davis of the 8th New York Cavalry. He was later killed at the Battle of Brandy Station on June 9, 1863. *O.R.*, Ser. I, Vol. 19, Part 1, pp. 796, 955.

115. Brig. Gen. Julius White was the only Federal general captured at Harpers Ferry.

116. There were two George Woodbridges attached to Stuart's headquarters: George Woodbridge of Company E of the 4th Virginia Cavalry

and George N. Woodbridge of Company I. Because their dates of service at cavalry headquarters are unknown, it is impossible to ascertain which one Price is referring to. Trout, *They Followed the Plume*, p. 326.

117. Pvt. Walker Keith Armistead of the 5th Virginia Cavalry was attached to Stuart's headquarters from August 18, 1862, to January 1863, when he applied for a cadet warrant. He was the son of Brig. Gen. Lewis Armistead, on whose staff he later served as aide-de-camp.

118. Francis Henry Deane was a courier attached to Stuart's headquarters from the 5th Virginia Cavalry.

119. According to Stuart's report, only the 2nd and not the 3rd Richmond Howitzers were involved in this demonstration. The other battery that sent a section of guns was the Salem Artillery. *O.R.*, Ser. I, Vol. 19, Part 1, p. 820.

120. The Federal forces engaged in this action, which actually occurred on the nineteenth and twentieth, consisted of Brig. Gen. George Sykes's 2nd Division of the 5th Corps and Col. James Barnes's 1st Brigade of the 1st Division of the 5th Corps. Brig. Gen. William N. Pendleton, Lee's chief of artillery, had forty-four guns in position overlooking the ford, which was picketed by two brigades of infantry barely numbering 300 men. The Federals swept across the river, capturing four pieces of artillery (one each from the batteries of Capt. Victor Maurin, Capt. John Milledge Jr., Capt. Marmaduke Johnson, and Capt. Charles T. Huckstep). On the morning of the twentieth, Stonewall Jackson sent A. P. Hill's Division to drive the Federals back, which they promptly did. Hill admitted to 30 killed and 231 wounded. The Union forces suffered 71 killed, 161 wounded, and 131 captured. *O.R.*, Ser. I, Vol. 19, Part 1, pp. 174–75, 204, 339–40, 351–52, 830–35, 982.

121. *O.R.*, Ser. I, Vol. 19, Part 2, pp. 10–14; Blackford, *War Years with Jeb Stuart*, pp. 162–63; von Borcke, *Memoirs of the Confederate War for Independence*, Vol. 1, pp. 272–76.

122. *O.R.*, Ser. I, Vol. 19, Part 2, pp. 55–56.

123. Thomas Taylor Munford (March 28, 1831–February 27, 1918) graduated from the Virginia Military Institute with the class of 1852. He was a farmer until the outbreak of the war, when he was appointed lieutenant colonel of the 2nd Virginia Cavalry. Promoted to colonel on April 25, 1862, Munford rendered efficient service at that rank for the remainder of the war, even though he often commanded a brigade and at times a division and was repeatedly recommended for the rank of brigadier general. After the war, he was a cotton planter and businessman. Munford is buried in Lynchburg, Virginia. Faust, ed., *Historical Times Illustrated Encyclopedia of the Civil War*, p. 517.

124. Walter Quarrier Hullihen (June 14, 1841–April 8, 1923) had joined the staff as an aide-de-camp in August 1862. At the start of the war, he was enrolled in the University of Virginia with the goal of being a minister. After some service with the 2nd Richmond Howitzers, he secured a cadetship and ended up on Stuart's staff, where he remained until November 1863. At that time he was promoted to captain and assigned as assistant adjutant general to Brig. Gen. Lunsford Lomax. Twice wounded during the war, he finished his military career on the staff of Brig. Gen. William H. F. Payne. After the war, he continued his education and became a minister in the Episcopal church. Trout, *They Followed the Plume*, pp. 179–86.

125. The Federal force guarding White's Ford was three companies of the 99th Pennsylvania Infantry under Lt. Col. Edwin R. Biles. *O.R.*, Ser. I, Vol. 19, Part 2, pp. 49–51.

126. See Lee's report, *O.R.*, Ser. I, Vol. 19, Part 2, p. 51.

127. Benjamin Stephen White (March 11, 1828–March 21, 1891) was a Marylander who became attached to the staff during the raid because of his intimate knowledge of the White's Ford area. As reward for his services he was made an aide-de-camp, and he also did some scouting for Stuart in Loudoun and neighboring counties. Severely wounded in the neck at the Battle of Brandy Station on June 9, 1863, White was given charge of the cavalry horse infirmary. His service there led to his promotion to major on January 5, 1864. He lived in Maryland after the war and is buried in Monocacy Cemetery, Beallsville, Maryland. Trout, *They Followed the Plume*, pp. 280–83.

128. The horses were Skylark and Lady Margrave. Bob managed to rejoin Stuart, but as far as is known, the horses were never recovered. Blackford, *War Years with Jeb Stuart*, pp. 178–79; Mitchell, ed., *The Letters of Maj. Gen. James E. B. Stuart*, p. 283.

129. Charles James Faulkner Sr. lived in his home, "Boydsville," near Martinsburg. He served on Stonewall Jackson's staff as assistant adjutant general. At one time he was the United States minister to France.

130. *O.R.*, Ser. I, Vol. 19, Part 2, pp. 82–97.

131. *Ibid.*, pp. 97–101.

132. *Ibid.*, p. 141.

133. Flora Stuart (November 14, 1857–November 3, 1862) was born in Leavenworth, Kansas, while Stuart was serving in the U.S. Army. She died of a fever in Lynchburg, where she first was buried. She now lies in Hollywood Cemetery, Richmond, Virginia. Adele H. Mitchell, "Descendants of General J. E. B. Stuart," *Civil War Times* Vol. 1, No. 10, p. 46.

134. *O.R.*, Ser. I, Vol. 19, Part 2, p. 102.

135. *Ibid.*, pp. 140–45; Blackford, *War Years with Jeb Stuart*, p. 183.

William Gaston Delony (September 8, 1826–October 2, 1863) had graduated from the University of Georgia in 1846 and took up the practice of law. He became the captain of Company C, Cobb's Georgia Legion on August 1, 1861. Promoted to lieutenant colonel on November 1, 1862, Delony was mortally wounded on September 23, 1863, at Brandy Station and died in a U.S. hospital in Washington City. He is buried in Oconee Hill Cemetery, Athens, Georgia. Krick, *Lee's Colonels*, p. 117.

136. Lewis Frank Terrell (September 12, 1836–April 14, 1864) held the position of inspector on Stuart's staff but was used primarily for court-martial duty, a circumstance that eventually led to a break with Stuart. Terrell wanted action, but Stuart wanted to use his ability as a lawyer, which Terrell had been before the war. An attempt to keep Terrell by assigning him to the Stuart Horse Artillery failed, and he left the staff in May 1863. He served briefly with Maj. Gen. Isaac R. Trimble during the Gettysburg Campaign. Following the army's return to Virginia, Terrell accepted an appointment as commander of the Light Artillery Brigade for the Department of South Carolina, Georgia, and Florida but seems to have never actually taken command. His last post was artillery commander under Brig. Gen. William B. Taliaferro in Florida. While performing his duties, he contracted typhoid fever, and died on James Island, South Carolina. Terrell is buried in Hollywood Cemetery, Richmond, Virginia. Trout, *They Followed the Plume*, pp. 256–60.

137. Hampton crossed the river at Kelly's Mill. *O.R.*, Ser. I, Vol. 21, p. 15.

138. Price is in error as to the identity of the unit. It was the 3rd Pennsylvania Cavalry. The post was under the command of Capt. George Johnson. The Federals admitted to a loss of five officers and seventy-seven men. They estimated Hampton's force at between 700 and 800 when in actuality he had only a little over 200. *Ibid.*, pp. 13–16.

139. Price is referring to Stuart's son, James Ewell Brown Stuart Jr.

140. *O.R.*, Ser. I, Vol. 21, pp. 23–27.

Thomas Conway Waller (December 9, 1832–December 23, 1895) had been a farmer and politician before the war. At the war's outbreak he became captain of Company A, 9th Virginia Cavalry, and rose through the ranks until he was promoted to colonel on January 5, 1865. Waller is buried at "Grafton" near Garrisonville, Virginia. Krick, *Lee's Colonels*, p. 386.

141. Robert Archelaus Hardaway (February 2, 1829–April 27, 1899), like Pelham, was from Alabama. In May 1861 he became captain of the battery that carried his name. Eventually he rose to the rank of lieutenant

colonel and commanded a battalion. After the war, he was a civil engineer and a professor at the University of Alabama and at Auburn. *Ibid.*, p. 178.

142. Mr. Lawler is most probably Francis Lawley, correspondent for the *London Times,* who visited both Lee and Jackson in addition to Stuart during December.

143. Mrs. Lily Parran Lee had been the wife of Lt. Col. William Fitzhugh Lee, who had been killed at First Manassas. Stuart and Lee had served together on the frontier and had remained close friends. Mrs. Lee had given Stuart one of his two pairs of gold spurs, which Stuart asked to be returned to her as he lay dying after his mortal wounding at Yellow Tavern. Mitchell, ed., *The Letters of Maj. Gen. James E. B. Stuart,* pp. 282, 420.

144. *O.R.,* Ser. I, Vol. 21, pp. 28–29.

145. *Ibid.,* pp. 689–91.

146. Mathis Winston Henry (November 28, 1838–November 28, 1877) attended the United States Military Academy, graduating with the class of 1861. He served briefly in the U.S. Army but resigned to join the Confederate service. He served in the cavalry and then in the horse artillery. Promoted to major in the artillery, he commanded a battalion in Hood's Division until his transfer to the western army. After the war he was involved in mining in Nevada. Henry is buried in Old Chapel Cemetery, Clarke County, Virginia. Krick, *Lee's Colonels,* p. 190.

147. *O.R.,* Ser. I, Vol. 21, p. 547.

148. William Barksdale (August 21, 1821–July 3, 1863) had served in the Mexican War and was a member of the U.S. Congress from 1852 until he resigned when Mississippi seceded. He became colonel of the 13th Mississippi Infantry and because of his distinguished service was promoted to brigadier general on August 12, 1862. He was mortally wounded at Gettysburg on July 2, 1863, during Longstreet's attack on the Union army's left flank anchored on Little Round Top. Barksdale lies in Greenwood Cemetery, Jackson, Mississippi. Warner, *Generals in Gray,* pp. 16–17.

149. George Edward Pickett (January 28, 1825–July 30, 1875) had the dubious honor of graduating last in the class of 1846 at West Point. He went on to gain two brevets for gallantry in the Mexican War and afterward served on the Texas frontier until 1855. Transferred to Washington Territory, Pickett remained there until 1861. His first commission in the Confederate army was that of colonel. He was promoted to brigadier general in January 1862 and to major general in October of the same year. He was known for commanding the famous charge that bears his name at the Battle of Gettysburg, but his subsequent service was in secondary theaters of the war until Grant struck at Petersburg. Pickett's inability to hold the

Confederate position at Five Forks in April 1865 led to his being relieved of command by Lee. After the war, he was an insurance agent. Pickett is buried in Hollywood Cemetery, Richmond, Virginia. *Ibid.*, pp. 239–40.

150. William Johnson Pegram (June 29, 1841–April 1, 1865) was a student at the University of Virginia at the commencement of the war. His earliest service was with the 21st Virginia Infantry, but he was soon commissioned a lieutenant and transferred to the Purcell Artillery. His ability to fight artillery was quickly recognized, and he was promoted until he reached the rank of colonel on February 18, 1865. Pegram was killed at the Battle of Five Forks. He is buried in Hollywood Cemetery, Richmond, Virginia. J. C. Goolsby, "Col. William Johnston [*sic*] Pegram," *Confederate Veteran*, VI, pp. 270–271; Krick, *Lee's Colonels*, p. 302.

Lt. James Ellett commanded a section of Capt. William G. Crenshaw's Battery. *O.R.*, Ser. I, Vol. 21, p. 645.

151. The Napoleon was perhaps the most famous gun of the war, though not necessarily the best. Technically a gun howitzer, the Napoleon was named for the French emperor Napoleon III, who sponsored its development. The 1857 model of the gun had a 66-inch bronze tube weighing 1,227 pounds, with a smoothbore of 4.62 inches. Later in the war there was a shortage of bronze, and the Confederacy manufactured some Napoleons of iron. The gun had a range of 1,680 yards when firing a solid shot but was most effective between 800 and 1,200 yards. It could also fire grape shot, spherical case shot, and shell. Faust, ed., *Historical Times Illustrated Encyclopedia of the Civil War*, p. 520; Boatner, *The Civil War Dictionary*, p. 578.

152. Pelham never filed a report of his actions in the battle, or if he did, it has not been found. He was, however, mentioned in other reports. *O.R.*, Ser. I, Vol. 21, pp. 547, 553, 631, 638, 645, 666.

153. John Thompson Brown (February 6, 1835–May 6, 1864) had attended the University of Virginia and had practiced law until the outbreak of the war. He was a member of the Richmond Howitzers before the war and was made a lieutenant in that organization on April 21, 1861. Brown was commissioned a captain the following month and major in September of the same year. His rapid rise continued with his promotions to lieutenant colonel in the spring of 1862 and to colonel on June 2, 1862. His responsibility grew with his rank, until he commanded the 2nd Corps Artillery Reserve. He was killed by a sharpshooter during the Battle of the Wilderness. Brown is buried in Maplewood Cemetery, Charlottesville, Virginia. S. H. Pendleton, "Col. John Thompson Brown," *Confederate Veteran*, Vol. VIII, pp. 25–26; Krick, *Lee's Colonels*, p. 72.

154. Reuben Lindsay Walker (May 29, 1827–June 7, 1890) graduated from the Virginia Military Institute in 1845. Before the war, he was a civil

engineer and a farmer. When the war began, he received command of the Purcell Battery and with it participated in the Battle of First Manassas. Commissioned major in March 1862, then lieutenant colonel, and finally colonel, Walker commanded the artillery of A. P. Hill's 3rd Corps until the end of the war. He was promoted to brigadier general on February 18, 1865. After the war, he returned to farming for a short period, then was superintendent of a railroad and later a construction engineer. Walker is buried in Hollywood Cemetery, Richmond, Virginia. Warner, *Generals in Gray*, pp. 322–23.

155. Lt. James S. Utz was a member of the 3rd Richmond Howitzers.

156. The Parrott gun was invented by Robert Parker Parrott, who was a graduate of West Point in the class of 1824. From 1836 to 1867, he ran the West Point Foundry in Cold Spring, New York. The guns of his design were iron, rifled muzzle loaders with a distinctive reinforcing band around the breech. Manufactured in sizes ranging from 3-inch (10 pound) to 10-inch (250 pound), the Parrott gun saw extensive service throughout the war. Faust, ed., *Historical Times Illustrated Encyclopedia of the Civil War*, p. 558; Boatner, *The Civil War Dictionary*, p. 621.

157. George Dashiell Bayard (December 18, 1835–December 14, 1862) graduated from West Point in 1856 and served in the cavalry on the frontier in Kansas and Colorado before the war. Shortly after the commencement of the war, Bayard was appointed colonel of the 1st Pennsylvania Cavalry. He led this unit until promoted to brigadier general and chief of cavalry of the 3rd Corps on April 28, 1862. Bayard is buried in Princeton, New Jersey. Warner, *Generals in Blue*, p. 26.

Conrad Feger Jackson (September 11, 1813–December 13, 1862) had fought in the Mexican War as captain and afterward worked for the Reading Railroad. During that time he was a member of the "City Guard," which became part of the 9th Pennsylvania Reserves (later the 38th Pennsylvania Infantry) at the beginning of the war. Jackson became colonel of the regiment on July 27, 1861. He fought Stuart at the Battle of Dranesville in December 1861. For this and other services, he was promoted to brigadier general on July 17, 1862. Jackson is buried in Allegheny Cemetery, Pittsburgh, Pennsylvania. *Ibid.*, pp. 246–47.

158. John Rogers Cooke (June 9, 1833–April 10, 1891) was the brother of Flora Cooke, Stuart's wife. He was commissioned a second lieutenant in the U.S. Army immediately after his graduation from Harvard. Like his brother-in-law, Cooke went with the Confederacy at the outbreak of the war, causing further tension in the already divided family. He was elected colonel of the 27th Virginia Infantry in April 1862 and promoted to brigadier general in November of the same year. He was wounded seven times

before his wounding at Fredericksburg. After the war, he was a merchant in Richmond and helped found the Confederate Soldiers' Home there. Cooke is buried in Hollywood Cemetery, Richmond, Virginia. Warner, *Generals in Gray*, p. 61.

159. Major Brown was most likely Maj. Ridgley Brown (November 12, 1833–June 1, 1864) from Montgomery County, Maryland, who was at this time involved in organizing the 1st Maryland Cavalry. He was killed at South Anne River and rests at "Elton" in eastern Montgomery County. Krick, *Lee's Conlonels*, p. 72.

160. *O.R.*, Ser. I, Vol. 21, pp. 695–97.

161. *Ibid.*, pp. 697–701, and 702–4.

162. *Ibid.*, pp. 705–42.

163. Bob was Robert Wren Powers, brother of Philip.

164. Juliet Fox Carlton was the wife of Robert Powers.

165. Robert Hall Chilton (February 25, 1815–February 18, 1879) was Lee's chief of staff and inspector general of the army. A graduate of West Point with the class of 1837, Chilton served as a captain in the dragoons and in staff positions. He resigned his U.S. Army commission on April 29, 1861. He recieved a lieutenant colonel's commission in the Adjutant and Inspector General's Department. He rose to the rank of brigadier general. After the war, he was a president of a manufacturing company. Chilton is buried in Hollywood Cemetery, Richmond, Virginia. Warner, *Generals in Gray*, p. 49.

166. James Lawrence Corley was Robert E. Lee's chief quartermaster.

167. John Boursiquot Fontaine (April 1, 1840–October 1, 1864) had trained for medicine before the war but had practiced only a little more than a year when Virginia seceded. He offered his services, becoming the surgeon for the 4th Virginia Cavalry. Fontaine married Elizabeth Winston Price of "Dundee" in January 1863. He became Stuart's medical director in October 1862. He was mortally wounded in action while going to the aid of Brig. Gen. John Dunovant in a cavalry action southwest of Petersburg. Fontaine is buried in the family cemetery near Beaver Dam Station, Virginia. Trout, *They Followed the Plume*, pp. 119–24.

168. Samuel Granville Staples (November 29, 1821–August 6, 1895) served with Stuart as a voluntary aide only briefly during the Peninsula Campaign. A lawyer before the war, it was to that profession that he returned in postwar years. He was twice elected to a judgeship and also worked in Washington for the Department of the Interior. Staples is buried in Fairview Cemetery, Roanoke, Virginia. *Ibid.*, pp. 247–49.

169. James Louis Clark (1841–September 4, 1910) practiced law in Baltimore before the war. His first military service was with the 1st Mary-

land Infantry (C.S.A.) as the quartermaster for the regiment. As such he held a captain's rank. Though he was unable to file his bond he continued in the position until June 1862, when he resigned. Though his affiliation with Stuart is somewhat clouded, it appears that he was attached to the staff while trying to raise a company for the Stuart Horse Artillery. When this failed, he accepted a captaincy in the 12th Virginia Cavalry, and then served with Harry Gilmor's 2nd Maryland Cavalry. Captured in August 1864, Clark was incarcerated until February 1865, when he was exchanged. He rejoined the army and was paroled at Appomattox. He resumed his law career after the war. Clark lies in Loudon Park Cemetery, Baltimore, Maryland. *Ibid.*, pp. 86–89.

Richard Edgar Frayser (October 1830–December 22, 1899) was in the merchantile business before the war. Joining the 3rd Virginia Cavalry in June 1861, Frayser served as a private until he was promoted to captain in the Signal Corps in September 1863. What had triggered this rapid rise was his service as a scout for Stuart during the Chickahominy Raid. Frayser continued to serve on the staff until May 12, 1864, when he was captured in the Wilderness. It was the same day Stuart died in Richmond. He was one of the "Immortal 600" and remained a prisoner until February 1865, when his poor health brought his exchange. He worked in the newspaper and publishing business after the war. Frayser is buried in Hollywood Cemetery, Richmond, Virginia. *Ibid.*, pp. 124–28.

William Henry Hagan (April 6, 1821–June 18, 1895) entered the war as a member of the Shepherdstown Troop, which became Company F in Stuart's 1st Virginia Cavalry. He was attached as a corporal to regimental headquarters, where he served as commander of Stuart's escort. His courage and daring were mentioned frequently by Stuart in his reports. Promoted to lieutenant in April 1862, Hagan held the position of aide-de-camp on the staff and the unofficial post of chief of couriers. After Stuart's death, he served on Wade Hampton's staff until the end of the war. In the postwar period, he ran a hotel and was president of the Potomac Cement Mills for many years. Hagan rests in Elmwood Cemetery, Shepherdstown, West Virginia. *Ibid.*, pp. 162–65.

James Marshall Hanger (November 12, 1833–August 26, 1912) was a lawyer in the firm of Baylor and Hanger when the war erupted. He joined the 1st Virginia Cavalry's Company E and was detailed to the brigade quartermaster. In October 1862 he was promoted to captain and was eventually assigned to Stuart as assistant quartermaster. He held this position under Stuart and Wade Hampton until the capture of Norman FitzHugh in December 1864, when he became the cavalry's quartermaster. He then served under W. H. F. Lee and Fitz Lee, being promoted to major in February

1865. After the war, he had a successful career as a lawyer, representative in Virginia's House of Delegates, and consul to Bermuda. Hanger is buried in Thornrose Cemetery, Staunton, Virginia. *Ibid.*, pp. 176–79.

William J. Johnson (February 3, 1828–October 4, 1895) is one of the least known of Stuart's staff. His prewar vocation is unknown, but at the war's outbreak, he immediately joined Company C of the 1st Virginia Cavalry. He was soon quartermaster sergeant and in October 1861 was commissioned captain in the commissary department. When Dabney Ball resigned as Stuart's commissary of subsistence, Johnson was called to the post, which he held until Stuart's death. He later served under Hampton and Fitz Lee. After the war, he became successful in the wholesale grocery business. Johnson is buried in Hollywood Cemetery, Richmond, Virginia. *Ibid.*, pp. 186–88.

Thomas Baynton Turner (May 8, 1843–April 29, 1863) had a short career as a clerk before the war. When Virginia seceded, his Alexandria militia company became part of the 17th Virginia Infantry. Turner was able to secure a cadetship and reported to Stuart in September 1862. His stay was brief in that he was captured during the aftermath of the Battle of Sharpsburg. When released, he rejoined Stuart in mid-November and remained with the staff until March 1863. Stuart granted him his desire to join Mosby, and he served with the great partisan ranger until mortally wounded on April 25, 1863. Turner lies in the family cemetery at "Kinloch" in Fauquier County, Virginia. *Ibid.*, pp. 263–68.

1863

1. James Alexander Walker (August 27, 1832–October 20, 1901) was colonel of the 13th Virginia Infantry. At this time, he was commanding Gen. Jubal Early's brigade, while Early commanded the division in the absence of Gen. Richard S. Ewell, who was recovering from a wound he had suffered at Second Manassas. Walker eventually rose to the rank of brigadier general. He became a lawyer and politician after the war. He is buried in East End Cemetery, Wytheville, Virginia. Warner, *Generals in Gray*, p. 319.

2. Powers is referring to the the Conscription Act of April 16, 1862, and the supplementary act of October 11, 1862.

3. Alice was Powers's daughter. She had been staying with his brother, Robert, and wife, Juliet, to attend school.

4. Pink was David Pinckney Powers, another of Philip's brothers.

5. Matthew Calbraith Butler (March 8, 1903–April 14, 1909) had been a lawyer and a member of the state legislature of South Carolina before the

war. At the time of the Dumfries Raid, he was in command of 2nd South Carolina Cavalry. He lost his right foot at the Battle of Brandy Station on June 9, 1863. Promoted to brigadier general and then major general, Butler had a distinguished career. After the war, he served in the U.S. Senate and was a major general of volunteers during the Spanish-American War. Butler is buried in Willowbrook Cemetery on his family's plantation near Edgefield, South Carolina. Warner, *Generals in Gray*, pp. 40–41.

6. James Winston Watts (April 19, 1833–December 3, 1906) left his farm near Lynchburg at the beginning of the war and entered the service as a lieutenant in Company A of the 2nd Virginia Cavalry. He rose in rank until he was lieutenant colonel. At the Battle of Aldie on July 17, 1863, he was wounded and disabled for further service in the field. After the war, he was in the hardware business and for a time in banking. Krick, *Lee's Colonels*, pp. 388–89; Gen. Clement A. Evans, Ed., *Confederate Military History* (Dayton: Press of Morningside Bookshop, 1975), Vol. III, pp. 1242–43.

7. Bullock had been severely wounded in the engagement, but his death wound came when he was struck the second time while being carried from the field by a companion. Borcke, *Memoirs of the Confederate War for Independence*, Vol. 2, p. 169.

8. James Henry Drake (June 9, 1822–July 16, 1863) had been a plasterer and mechanic before the war. Enlisting in the 1st Virginia Cavalry's Company A in April 1861 as the commissary of the company, he rose through the ranks until he became colonel in May 1863. At the time of Stuart's raid, he was a major but was commanding the regiment, as Price indicated. He died of wounds he received at Kearneysville and is buried in the Lutheran Churchyard, Stephens City, Virginia. Driver, *1st Virginia Cavalry*, p. 169; Krick, *Lee's Colonels*, p. 123.

9. Price's account compares well with the Federal reports of the action. About 150 men of the 2nd Pennsylvania under Capt. Charles Chauncey and 100 to 150 men of the 17th Pennsylvania Cavalry under Maj. Reuben Reinhold were involved. The various accounts agree that the Federals were routed but only after attempting to rally at least four separate times during the retreat. *O.R.*, Ser. I, Vol. 21, pp. 708–13.

10. Samuel Peter Heintzelman (September 30, 1805–May 1, 1880) was a graduate of the United States Military Academy with the class of 1826. His service with the army before the Mexican War was routine garrison, recruiting, and quartermaster duty. During the war with Mexico, he earned a brevet for gallantry. In 1851 he earned another brevet to lieutenant colonel for services in the Southwest. At the beginning of the war, he was commissioned colonel of the 17th Infantry on May 14, 1861. He did not

command the regiment very long, being promoted to brigadier general just three days later. On May 5, 1862, he was made a major general and led the 3rd Corps during the Peninsula Campaign. His unsatisfactory performance caused his transfer to secondary theaters of the war for its duration. He retired from the army in 1869, and after a brief period as a businessman in New York, he retired. Heintzelman is buried in Forest Lawn Cemetery, Buffalo, New York. Warner, *Generals in Blue*, pp. 227–28.

11. It was while at this telegraph station that Stuart sent his famous message to U.S. Army quartermaster general Montgomery Meigs complaining about the poor quality of the mules with which he had to pull the captured wagons.

12. *O.R.*, Ser. I, Vol. 21, p. 718.

13. James Barlow's home was called "Sully." His wife, Maria, spent the whole morning feeding "Rooney" Lee, Hampton, and their staffs along with Stuart's staff. *The Cannoneer*, Vol. 12, No. 1 (July 1993), pp. 9–10.

14. William Morrell McGregor (November 18, 1842–December 28, 1908) was an Alabamian like Pelham. His first service had been with the 10th Alabama Infantry. It took him almost a year to recover from the leg wound he had suffered. He rose to the rank of major and was in command of a battalion of horse artillery by war's end. After the war, he was a lawyer and owner of a newspaper before his death in Cameron, Texas, where he is buried.

15. Price is referring to the Battle of Murfreesboro (in Tennessee) fought between Bragg's Army of the Tennessee and the Army of the Cumberland under Rosecrans on December 31, 1862, and January 2, 1863.

Braxton Bragg (March 22, 1817–September 27, 1876) was an 1837 graduate of West Point. After campaigning against the Seminole Indians in Florida, he fought in the Mexican War. In 1856 he resigned from the U.S. Army to become a planter in Louisiana. He was a lieutenant colonel at the time. In March 1861 he was commissioned a brigadier general in the Confederate Army. In April 1862 he was promoted to full general. He fought in the western theater of the war until November 1863, when he gave up his command and came to Richmond to work under President Davis. After the war, he was the chief engineer of the state of Alabama. Bragg is buried in Magnolia Cemetery, Mobile, Alabama. Warner, *Generals in Gray*, pp. 30–31.

Samuel Cooper (June 12, 1798–December 3, 1876) graduated from the United States Military Academy in the class of 1815. He remained in the army, eventually becoming the adjutant general in 1852. When the war began, he resigned and was immediately commissioned a brigadier general in the Confederate army and its adjutant general. Cooper soon rose to the rank of general. He was a farmer after the war. Cooper is buried in Christ Church Cemetery, Alexandria, Virginia. *Ibid.*, pp. 62–63.

16. Price is in error concerning the Federal commanders involved in this expedition. The force was led by Col. James Barnes, who commanded the 1st Division of the 5th Corps. Under him as brigade commanders were Col. Charles A. Johnson, Col. Jacob B. Sweitzer, and Col. Henry A. Weeks. *O.R.*, Ser. I, Vol. 21, pp. 742–43, 930–31.

17. Price was correct concerning the regiment but not its commander. Sir Percy Wyndham commanded the 1st New Jersey Cavalry, not the 3rd Pennsylvania Cavalry. That regiment was led by Col. John B. McIntosh. Federal brigadier general William Averell commanded the brigade that included the 3rd Pennsylvania and did move to within a mile of Kelly's Ford on the thirty-first but does not seem to have advanced west toward Warrenton. *Ibid.*, pp. 742–44, 922–23.

18. *Ibid.*, pp. 749–51.

19. Mary Robertson (April 14, 1834–May 22, 1866) was the daughter of Wyndham Robertson and the sister of Frank Smith Robertson. She and her husband suffered the loss of an infant daughter in 1857. On December 17, 1862, their son, Landon Carter Blackford, died. Tragedy would strike Blackford again shortly after the war, when Mary died from complications after the birth of another daughter, who preceded her in death.

20. Price's brother, Thomas Randolph Price Jr.

21. Jeremy Francis Gilmer (February 23, 1818–December 1, 1883) was an army engineer before the war, having graduated from the United States Military Academy with the class of 1839. After he resigned in June 1861, he offered his services to the Confederacy and was appointed chief engineer for Gen. Albert Sidney Johnston. He was wounded at Shiloh. Promoted from colonel of engineers to major general, he served as the chief engineer of the Confederate War Department. In the postwar period, he was the president of the Savannah Gas Light Company. He is buried in Laurel Grove Cemetery, Savannah, Georgia. Warner, *Generals in Gray*, p. 105.

22. Alfred Landon Rives was the assistant chief engineer under Gilmer.

23. French for "between us."

24. Frank and his father evidently took Stuart's advice, as a letter dated February 27, 1863, to Frank from the Confederate War Department appointed him an assistant engineer with orders to report for duty to Stuart.

25. *O.R.*, Ser. I, Vol. 25, Part 1, pp. 4–5.

26. Obadiah Jennings Wise, son of ex-governor of Virginia Brig. Gen. Henry Alexander Wise, was killed on Roanoke Island on February 8, 1862. Cooke's brief biography of him appeared in "Outlines from the Outpost,"

which was printed during the war in the *Southern Illustrated News*. Wise is buried in Hollywood Cemetery, Richmond, Virginia.

27. Cooke used this as a pseudonym at times during the war when he sent letters and articles to newspapers.

28. James Dearing (April 25, 1840–April 26, 1865) resigned from West Point when the war began. He served with the artillery, rising from second lieutenant to major. He was selected to replace Robert F. Beckham as commander of the Stuart Horse Artillery Battalion, but he refused the appointment, as it came with the rank only of lieutenant colonel. His decision was rewarded by promotion first to colonel and then brigadier general of cavalry. He was mortally wounded on April 6, 1865, at High Bridge. Dearing is buried in Spring Hill Cemetery, Lynchburg, Virginia. Warner, *Generals in Gray*, pp. 69–70.

29. Alexander Swift Pendleton (September 28, 1840–September 22, 1864), better known as "Sandie," was the son of Brig. Gen. William N. Pendleton, Lee's chief of artillery. He graduated from Washington College in 1857, and taught there for two years before enrolling at the University of Virginia. When the war began, he entered the army as a lieutenant in the engineers and a week later reported to Col. T. J. Jackson. In July 1861 Jackson requested that Pendleton be assigned to him as ordnance officer, and in this capacity he served until Jackson's death. Jackson's successor, Richard S. Ewell, made Pendleton his chief of staff with the rank of lieutenant colonel. He also served on Jubal Early's staff. He was mortally wounded at Fisher's Hill and is buried in Stonewall Jackson Cemetery, Lexington, Virginia. Faust, ed., *Historical Times Illustrated Encyclopedia of the Civil War*, pp. 569–70.

Charles James Faulkner Sr. served as Jackson's assistant adjutant general and chief of staff and was primarily concerned with writing the reports of Jackson's battles. He had a brilliant prewar career that included eight years as a U.S. congressman and three years as minister to France. Faulkner resigned from the staff on July 23, 1863. Frank Vandiver, *Mighty Stonewall* (New York: McGraw-Hill Book Company, Inc., 1957), pp. 442–43; Burke Davis, *They Called Him Stonewall* (New York: Rinehart & Company, Inc., 1954), pp. 384–85.

30. The "Old Brigade" is a reference to the "Stonewall" Brigade, and the men mentioned were members of it.

31. Richard Heron Anderson (October 7, 1821–June 26, 1879) graduated from the United States Military Academy in 1842. He served in the Mexican War, earning the brevet of first lieutenant. After resigning from the U.S. Army, he was commissioned a major of infantry in the Confederate army, and four months later he was promoted to brigadier general. He fought

in the Peninsula Campaign and was commissioned a major general on July 14, 1862. When Longstreet was wounded in the Wilderness, Anderson was given the command of the 1st Corps and the temporary rank of lieutenant general. He ended the war in charge of a portion of the defenses of Richmond. After the war, he struggled against poverty, serving as phosphate agent for South Carolina. Anderson is buried in the Saint Helena Episcopal Churchyard, Beaufort, South Carolina. Warner, *Generals in Gray*, pp. 8–9.

32. Aldrich was a sergeant in the ordnance department assigned to Cooke as a clerk. Trout, *They Followed the Plume*, p. 299.

33. Felbert was Dabney's servant.

34. Ephraim was undoubtedly the servant Price had long asked for.

35. Hugh Mortimer Nelson (October 20, 1811–August 6, 1862) had been a lawyer in Baltimore before the war. He was elected captain of Company D, 6th Virginia Cavalry, in July 1861, but was not reelected in April 1862. He served for a time as a volunteer aide-de-camp to Gen. Richard S. Ewell until commissioned a major of cavalry. Nelson died of typhoid fever. He is buried in Old Chapel Cemetery, Clarke County, Virginia. Driver, *1st Virginia Cavalry*, p. 212.

36. Micah Jenkins (December 1, 1835–May 6, 1864) graduated from the South Carolina Military Academy in 1854. He then helped organize the King's Mountain Military School in Yorkville, South Carolina, and remained with that institution until the outbreak of the war. Elected colonel of the 5th South Carolina Infantry, Jenkins later organized the Palmetto Sharpshooters and led them until promoted to brigadier general in July 1862. He was severely wounded at Second Manassas. Along with Lt. Gen. James Longstreet, his commander, he was shot accidentally by Confederate infantry during the Battle of the Wilderness. Jenkins is buried in Magnolia Cemetery, Charleston, South Carolina. Warner, *Generals in Gray*, p. 155.

37. Cobb was killed in the Battle of Fredericksburg, and Brig. Gen. William Tatum Wofford (June 28, 1824–May 22, 1884) took command of his brigade. Wofford was a lawyer before the war and had fought in the Mexican War as a captain of a battalion of Georgia mounted volunteers. His first Confederate service was as the colonel of the 18th Georgia Infantry. Wofford remained with the 1st Corps until almost the end of the war. After the war, he became involved in the organization of railroads and civic matters, and he served on the boards of several educational institutions. Wofford is buried in Cassville Cemetery, Cass Station, Georgia. Warner, *Generals in Gray*, pp. 343–44.

38. Cooke seems to be confusing McLaws's Division with that of Maj. Gen. Richard H. Anderson. Wofford was in McLaws's Division, as was Kershaw.

39. The weapon, a Calisher and Terry breech-loading, bolt-action carbine of .54 caliber (#4928) manufactured in England, was the gift of a Capt. Bushby.

40. Briscoe Gerard Baldwin (?–September 28, 1898) was serving as chief of ordnance on Robert E. Lee's staff. He is buried in Bryan, Texas. "Monument to Col. Baldwin," *Confederate Veteran*, Vol. XXXVI, 1928, p. 469.

41. *O.R.*, Ser. I, Vol. 25, Part 1, pp. 6–9.

42. John W. Gleason was from the 9th Virginia Cavalry's Company F. He was first detached as a courier to cavalry headquarters, then promoted to sergeant and assigned to the ordnance department under Cooke. Robert K. Krick, *9th Virginia Cavalry* (Lynchburg, VA: H. E. Howard, Inc., 1982), p. 74.

43. The two girls were the daughters of Robert Mercer Taliferro Hunter (April 21, 1809–July 18, 1887) of "Fonthill" in Essex County, Virginia. Hunter served as the Confederate secretary of state from July 24, 1861 to February 22, 1862. Before the war, he had been a member of the Virginia House of Delegates and the U.S. Senate. Arrested after the war and incarcerated in Fort Pulaski, Hunter was not freed until January 1866. He later served as Virginia's state treasurer from 1874 to 1880. He is buried at "Fonthill." Faust, ed., *Historical Times Illustrated Encyclopedia of the Civil War*, pp. 376–77.

44. Bradshaw Beverley Turner (1841–1910) was from the 9th Virginia Cavalry, Brig. Gen. W. H. F. Lee's old regiment. Turner was on sick leave from November 1862 to February 1863. Shortly after his return, he was transferred to the ordnance department. He would later serve as a staff officer under W. H. F. Lee. Krick, *9th Virginia Cavalry*, p. 103.

45. Buck was Cooke's horse.

46. Francis Lawley was the Richmond correspondent for the London *Times*.

47. Dabney is not referring to the Union army but rather is using the old name for the Confederate army formed when Gen. Pierre G. T. Beauregard's army at Manassas combined with Gen. Joseph E. Johnston's army from the Shenandoah Valley. Later Beauregard was transferred, and when Johnston was wounded at the Battle of Seven Pines, Lee took command and changed the name of the army to the Army of Northern Virginia.

48. James Ewell Brown Stuart Jr. (June 26, 1860–November 28, 1930), the only son of General Stuart and his wife, Flora, was affectionately known as "Jimmy." He had originally been named Philip St. George Cooke Stuart after his grandfather, Flora's father, but when his namesake remained in the Federal army, Stuart felt the boy's name should be changed. Educated at Norwood Academy, Episcopal High School in Alexandria, and the Vir-

ginia Military Institute, he engaged in various fields of endeavor, including surveying, banking, real estate, and insurance. He was also a U.S. marshal, collector of Customs at Newport News, and a captain in the commissary department during the Spanish-American War. He is buried in Arlington National Cemetery, Virginia. Adele H. Mitchell, "James Ewell Brown Stuart II (Jr.)," *Southern Cavalry Review*, Vol. V, No. 3, pp. 1–4.

49. Lewis Guy Phillips (June 9, 1831–1887), a British soldier of the Grenadier Guards stationed in Canada, was well liked by the officers at Stuart's headquarters. He had arrived before the Battle of Fredericksburg to visit and stayed for some time. In addition to Stuart's gift of "Canada oak," Phillips also presented John Pelham with a necktie to wear during the battle, which he did and then returned to the Englishman as a souvenir of the engagement. Phillips returned to England in September 1864 and retired from the army in July 1885 with the honorary rank of brigadier general. Charles G. Milham, *Gallant Pelham* (Gaithersburg, MD: Butternut Press, Inc., 1985), pp. 207–10; Col. Barrie Almond, "Capt. Lewis Guy Phillips," *The Cannoneer*, Vol. 11, No. 3 (November 1992), pp. 6–7.

50. Conway Robinson Howard was an engineer officer on the staff of Maj. Gen. A. P. Hill.

Robert Murphy Mayo (April 28, 1836–March 29, 1896) commanded the 47th Virginia Infantry in Hill's division. He was on the staff of the Virginia Military Institute before the war. After the war, he served in the Virginia Legislature and the U.S. Congress. Mayo is buried at Yeocomico Church, Westmoreland County, Virginia. Krick, *Lee's Colonels*, p. 268.

51. The Federal forces involved were elements of the 3rd Pennsylvania Cavalry, 4th Pennsylvania Cavalry, 16th Pennsylvania Cavalry, 4th New York Cavalry, 1st Rhode Island Cavalry, and 124th New York Infantry. *O.R.*, Ser. I, Vol. 25, Part 1, pp. 21–26; Rev. Frederic Denison, Chaplain, *Sabres and Spurs: The First Regiment Rhode Island Cavalry in the Civil War, 1861–1865* (Baltimore: Butternut and Blue, 1994), pp. 200–206.

52. *O.R.*, Ser. I, Vol. 25, Part 1, pp. 38–40.

53. Lieut. Bumpo was probably Cooke's nephew Nathaniel.

54. Cooke had met William Makepeace Thackeray, the famous English novelist, in the 1850s.

55. Walter Herron Taylor (June 13, 1838–March 1, 1916) served as Robert E. Lee's assistant adjutant general. A graduate of the Virginia Military Institute in the class of 1855, Taylor engaged in merchandising until the outbreak of the war. He became attached to Lee's staff early in the war and served there until the end. After the war, he was the president of the Marine Bank of Norfolk, Virginia, and a state senator. He is buried in Elmwood Cemetery, Norfolk, Virginia. Rev. Giles B. Cook, "Col. W. H.

Taylor, A.A.G. Army of Northern Virginia: An Appreciation," *Confederate Veteran*, Vol. XXVI, 1916, pp. 234–35.

56. William Hoxton (March 30, 1844–May 31, 1876) was in Capt. James Breathed's Battery of the Stuart Horse Artillery. Before the war, he was a student at William and Mary. He would rise to the rank of captain by the war's end. Hoxton attended the Virginia Theological Seminary after the war to study for the ministry, and graduated in 1868. He is buried in Hollywood Cemetery, Richmond, Virginia.

57. The true identity of Cooke's "Capt. Edelin" is somewhat of a mystery. The only individual who fits the facts given by Cooke is Capt. Charles Columbus Edelin, who commanded Company B in the 1st Maryland Infantry for the first twelve months of the war. Cooke states in his sketch that Edelin was killed on the Blackwater in North Carolina. This Edelin did go to North Carolina when his first term of enlistment expired, but he was not killed there. He returned to fight on the Peninsula in June 1862. There is no record of any other Captain Edelin in the 1st Maryland and no record of any Lemeul Cooper.

58. John Singleton Mosby (December 6, 1833–May 30, 1916) was arguably the best partisan commander of the war. A graduate of the University of Virginia and a lawyer, Mosby enlisted in the 1st Virginia Cavalry early in the war. He quickly caught Stuart's eye and was used extensively as a scout until he requested and received an independent command, which grew into the 43rd Battalion of Virginia Cavalry. His forays behind Federal lines created havoc and consternation at all levels of Union command. Having entered the war a private, he left it a colonel. He had been mentioned in Robert E. Lee's reports more than any other officer. In the postwar period, Mosby's friendship with U. S. Grant and his Republican politics caused his ostracism in the South. Nevertheless, even his enemies had to grant him the fact that he was among the Confederacy's finest fighters. He is buried in Town Cemetery, Warrenton, Virginia.

59. *O.R.*, Ser. I, Vol. 25, Part 1, pp. 41–44.

60. Price is correct, as Hairston did resign because of poor health. He had been suffering from rheumatism almost since the war's commencement. Trout, *They Followed the Plume*, pp. 165, 168.

61. FitzHugh owned a farm, "Forest Hall," just south of the U.S. Ford. Part of the reason he was taking a month's furlough was to relocate his family in Albemarle County out of harm's way. *Ibid.*, p. 118.

62. The surgeon was Dr. William B. Davis and the officer was Lt. Edward W. Horner. Both were mortally wounded.

63. Lizzie was Elizabeth Winston Price of "Dundee." She and Fontaine had been married in January, and her husband had just returned to the army

from his honeymoon. Channing Price was related to Elizabeth. Trout, *They Followed the Plume*, p. 123.

64. Sam was Robertson's servant. The two horses that Robertson finally received from home were Miranda and Bostona.

65. Robert Huston Milroy (June 11, 1816–March 29, 1890) had graduated from Captain Partridge's Academy in Norwich, Connecticut, in 1843. After a brief period of service with a company of Indiana Volunteers, he studied law, which, except for a short term as a judge, he practiced until the war. His early service was as colonel of the 9th Indiana Infantry. Promotions first to brigadier general and then to major general followed. Milroy participated in the Valley Campaign against Jackson and remained in the Winchester area afterward, much to the dismay of the populace, who despised him. Completely outgeneraled by Richard S. Ewell during the Gettysburg Campaign, Milroy faced a court of inquiry and held only a minor position at the close of the war. After the war, he was a trustee of the Wabash and Erie Canal Company and an Indian agent. He is buried in the Masonic Cemetery, Olympia, Washington. Warner, *Generals in Blue*, p. 326.

66. Henry Clay Pate (April 21, 1832–May 11, 1864) was editor of the Petersburg *Bulletin* at the beginning of the war. He had been a captain of a company that eventually was merged into the 5th Virginia Cavalry. He rose to be lieutenant colonel of six companies of scouts that he raised, known as the 2nd Virginia Cavalry or Pate's Battalion. Stuart requested that four more companies be added to form a regiment (5th Virginia Cavalry) and gave the regiment to Tom Rosser. Pate was angered and upset at the turn of events. He later wrote to Stuart accusing Rosser of drunkenness. Stuart turned the letter over to Rosser, who brought charges of insubordination against Pate. Stuart's support of Rosser made Pate Stuart's enemy until the Battle of Yellow Tavern, when the two men shook hands and made up. Pate was killed minutes later. He is buried in Hollywood Cemetery, Richmond, Virginia. Krick, *Lee's Colonels*, p. 299.

67. Paul Hamilton Hayne (1830–1886) of Charleston, South Carolina, was a poet and an acquaintance of Cooke's.

68. William Woods Averell (November 5, 1832–February 3, 1900) had worked as a drug clerk before his appointment to West Point. He graduated in 1855 and had a service record that included garrison duty, a stint at the Carlisle Cavalry School, and two years on the frontier. He was severely wounded during the latter and was an invalid for almost two years. He recovered just as the war began, and after First Manassas he was commissioned colonel of the 3rd Pennsylvania Cavalry. He reached the rank of brigadier general and was a brevet major general by war's end. After the

war, he served as the U.S. consul general to British North America. He is buried in Bath, New York. Warner, *Generals in Blue*, pp. 12–13.

69. H. B. McClellan, *I Rode with J. E. B. Stuart* (Bloomington: Indiana University Press, 1958), pp. 205–17; *O.R.*, Ser. I, Vol. 25, Part 1, pp. 47–64.

70. Milham, *Gallant Pelham*, pp. 227–33; Trout, *They Followed the Plume*, pp. 209–10.

71. Ellie was Ellie Bull, wife of James.

72. Mildred Ballard was the wife of Reuben Sidney Powers, another of Philip's brothers.

73. *O.R.*, Ser. I, Vol. 25, Part 1, p. 60.

74. Peter Fontaine (1840–1908) was attending the University of Virginia when the war began. He joined the Hanover Light Dragoons, which became part of the 4th Virginia Cavalry. His talents were recognized early, and he served on the staffs of Williams C. Wickham and Rosser. He recovered from his wound at Kelly's Ford and returned to duty with Rosser, remaining with him until the war's end. After the war, he returned to the University of Virginia and completed his study in the law. "The Last Roll," *Confederate Veteran*, Vol. XVI, 1908, p. 587.

75. Joseph Lee Minghini (March 1, 1837–January 14, 1919) was a member of Company D, 12th Virginia Cavalry. He is given credit by some for having been the individual who brought Pelham's body off the field, but according to Price's account, which came from Minghini himself, he only brought the ambulance that conveyed Pelham to the Shackelford's home. Minghini was a resident of Martinsburg, West Virginia, after the war. He is buried in the Episcopal and Masonic Cemetery, Middleway, West Virginia. Dennis E. Frye, *12th Virginia Cavalry* (Lynchburg, VA: H. E. Howard, Inc., 1988), p. 152.

76. *O.R.*, Ser. I, Vol. 25, Part 1, pp. 67–70; 74–75

77. James Alexander Seddon (July 13, 1815–August 19, 1880) was Confederate secretary of war from November 1862 to February 1, 1865. He was a graduate of the University of Virginia, and his prewar political experience included four years in the House of Representatives. He held the office of Confederate secretary of war the longest because he deferred to President Davis's authority, whereas his predecessors had opposed the president on certain issues. Seddon rests in Hollywood Cemetery, Richmond, Virginia. Faust, ed., *Historical Times Illustrated Encyclopedia of the Civil War*, pp. 664–65.

78. George Hume Steuart (August 24, 1828–November 22, 1903) was a graduate of West Point with the class of 1848. His prewar army service

was entirely on the frontier. He resigned in April 1861 and accepted a captain's commission in the Confederate army. When the 1st Maryland Infantry was formed, Steuart became the regiment's lieutenant colonel and shortly after First Manassas its colonel. Promoted to brigadier general in March 1862, he fought in the Valley Campaign and was seriously wounded at Cross Keys. He returned to duty, led a brigade at Gettysburg, and fought in the Wilderness, where he was captured on May 12, 1864. He was exchanged and eventually surrendered at Appomattox. After the war, he was a farmer. Steuart is buried in Green Mount Cemetery, Baltimore, Maryland. Warner, *Generals in Gray*, pp. 290–91.

79. Robert Franklin Beckham (May 6, 1837–December 5, 1864), like Pelham, attended the United States Military Academy, graduating with the class of 1859. His army service was with the Corps of Topographical Engineers. At the war's outbreak, he resigned his commission and became a lieutenant in the artillery, reporting to Grove's Culpeper Battery. A fine showing at First Manassas took Beckham away from the battery and into the reserve artillery corps, where he languished until called to staff duty by Maj. Gen. Gustavus W. Smith. His promotion to major soon followed. Beckham served with Smith until that officer resigned from the army in January 1863. Then he again was an officer without a command or a general. Within days of Pelham's death, Stuart ended Beckham's doubtful status by nominating him to command the Stuart Horse Artillery, which he did magnificently until February 1864. He was then promoted to colonel and sent to the Army of Tennessee. On November 29, 1864, he was mortally wounded at the Battle of Columbia, suffering a wound almost exactly like Pelham's. Beckham is buried in St. John's Church Cemetery, Ashwood, Tennessee. Trout, *They Followed the Plume*, pp. 56–62.

80. Robert Henry Goldsborough (January 15, 1841–April 6, 1865) left his home in Maryland to join the Confederate army. His first service was with Capt. William H. Chapman's Virginia Light Artillery, which he joined just eight days before it was virtually destroyed at the Battle of Sharpsburg. He next enlisted in Company B of the 39th Virginia Cavalry Battalion, which served as bodyguard for Gen. Richard S. Ewell. On May 2, 1863, he was discharged from the company in order to accept Stuart's offer. When he reported for duty in late May, his inexperience led to his capture at the Battle of Brandy Station on June 9, 1863. He remained in prison until February 20, 1865, when he was exchanged. He became a staff officer to Gen. G. W. C. Lee and was killed at the Battle of Sayler's Creek during the retreat to Appomattox. Goldsborough rests in the family cemetery at "Ashby" in Talbot County, Maryland. *Ibid.*, pp. 145–49.

81. Thomas Stuart Garnett (April 19, 1825–May 4, 1863) attended the

Virginia Military Institute and graduated from the University of Virginia. He was a doctor before the war and served as a lieutenant in the Mexican War. He was the captain of the 9th Virginia Cavalry's Company C, then became lieutenant colonel of the 48th Virginia Infantry. He was promoted to colonel in October 1862 and probably would have succeeded Jones had he not been killed at the Battle of Chancellorsville. Garnett is buried in Hollywood Cemetery, Richmond, Virginia. Krick, *Lee's Colonels*, p. 151.

John Robert Jones (March 12, 1827–April 1, 1901) graduated from the Virginia Military Institute in 1848. Before the war, he ran a military school in Urbana, Maryland. At the outbreak of the war he raised a company of infantry, which became part of the 33rd Virginia Infantry. He fought with this regiment through the Valley Campaign and rose to the rank of lieutenant colonel. Jones was promoted to brigadier general in June 1862 on the recommendation of Stonewall Jackson. Through his actions at Chancellorsville, he faced a court-martial for cowardice but was acquitted. Despite the acquittal, he never held command of troops again. Captured in July 1863 at Smithburg, Tennessee, he was a prisoner of war for over two years before he was released. He was a businessman after the war. Jones is buried in Woodbine Cemetery, Harrisonburg, Virginia. Warner, *Generals in Gray*, p. 165.

82. John Montgomery Preston became captain of Company B of the 48th Virginia Infantry and served in that capacity until wounded during the Mine Run Campaign late in 1863. "The Last Roll," *Confederate Veteran*, XXXVI, 1928, p. 469.

83. Charles Read Collins (December 7, 1836–May 7, 1864) graduated from the United States Military Academy with the class of 1859. He served in the Corps of Topographical Engineers until June 10, 1861, when he resigned. His first Confederate commission was as a lieutenant in the artillery, but he soon became a captain in the engineers and was on the staffs of several generals before being transferred to North Carolina. At the time he relieved Blackford, he was a major in the 15th Virginia Cavalry. He rose to the rank of colonel of the regiment, and was killed at the Battle of Todd's Tavern. Collins is buried in St. John's Episcopal Churchyard, King George Court House, Virginia. Krick, *Lee's Colonels*, p. 96; John Fortier, *15th Virginia Cavalry* (Lynchburg, VA: H. E. Howard, Inc., 1993), p. 127.

84. "Beaver Dam" was the home of Edmund Fontaine, father of Dr. John B. Fontaine.

85. George Stoneman (August 22, 1822–September 5, 1894) served in the 1st U.S. Dragoon Regiment after his graduation from West Point with the class of 1846. He saw no service in the Mexican War, having participated in the "Mormon Battalion" march from Leavenworth, Kansas, to San

Diego. At the outbreak of the war, Stoneman was a captain in the 2nd U.S. Cavalry. He was promoted to major and served on McClellan's staff in West Virginia. When McClellan gained command of the army, Stoneman was commissioned brigadier general and given command of the cavalry. A major generalcy followed, along with a transfer to the infantry. He was back as chief of the cavalry when Hooker replaced Burnside as commander of the Army of the Potomac. Replaced after the Battle of Chancellorsville, Stoneman was assigned first to Washington and then to the 23rd Corps in the West. He again returned to the cavalry as commander of the Cavalry Corps of the Army of the Ohio until captured in July 1864. Exchanged, he served the rest of the war in North Carolina, eastern Tennessee, and southwestern Virginia. Remaining in the army until 1871, he then retired on disability. His postarmy career included the governorship of California. He is buried in Lakewood, New York. Warner, *Generals in Blue*, pp. 481–82.

86. *O.R.*, Ser. I, Vol. 25, Part 1, pp. 83–89; 1066–68; Stephen Z. Starr, *The Union Cavalry in the Civil War* (Baton Rouge: Louisiana State University Press, 1979), pp. 352–55.

87. *O.R.*, Ser. I, Vol. 25, Part 1, p. 1045.

88. William Todd Robins (November 22, 1835–October 28, 1906) had enlisted in W. H. F. Lee's company of cavalry at the war's commencement. The company was attached to the 9th Virginia Cavalry, of which Lee became colonel. Robins served as the regiment's sergeant major before being commissioned its adjutant. When Lee was promoted to brigadier general, Robins became the assistant adjutant general and chief of staff of Lee's brigade. By the war's end, Robins was a colonel commanding the 24th Virginia Cavalry. He is buried in Ware Episcopal Churchyard, Gloucester County, Virginia. Maryus Jones, "William Todd Robins," *Southern Historical Society Papers*, Vol. XXXIV (1906), pp. 275–77.

89. John Randolph Chambliss Jr. (January 23, 1833–August 16, 1864) had graduated from the United States Military Academy in the class of 1853. After only a year of army service, he resigned to become a planter and was thus still engaged when the war began. He was the colonel of the 41st Virginia Infantry before taking command of the 13th Virginia Cavalry as its colonel. He was promoted to brigadier general on December 19, 1863, and was killed in fighting along the Charles City Road outside of Richmond. Chambliss is buried in Emporia, Virginia. Warner, *Generals in Gray*, pp. 46–47.

90. Richard Lee Turberville Beale (May 22, 1819–April 21, 1893) was a lawyer and politician before the war. On its outbreak, Beale became a lieutenant in a company that was known as "Lee's Legion." The company was attached to the 9th Virginia Cavalry, and Beale rose through the ranks

until as colonel he commanded the regiment. He was commissioned a brigadier general on January 6, 1865. After the war, he again practiced law and politics and was elected to Congress in 1878. His final resting place is about one and a half miles north of Hague at Hickory Hill, Westmoreland County, Virginia. *Ibid.*, pp. 20–21.

91. "Winded" means that a cannonball passed so close to an individual that it created an effect in air pressure similar to the concussion caused by an explosion.

92. Powers reenlisted in Company G on April 26, 1863. Driver, *1st Virginia Cavalry*, p. 217.

93. John Henry Winder (February 21, 1800–February 7, 1865) not only graduated from West Point, but also taught tactics there for a time. He fought in the Mexican War, earning two brevets for gallantry. He resigned his commission to become a brigadier general in the Confederate army in June 1861. At the same time, he was appointed provost marshal of Richmond. He was disliked by the citizens of Richmond because of his police powers and despised by the North for what they claimed was the starvation of Union prisoners. In fact, he did the best with what he had. Winder is buried in Green Mount Cemetery, Baltimore, Maryland. Warner, *Generals in Gray*, pp. 340–41.

94. John Mason Lee was Gen. W. H. F. Lee's assistant adjutant general. Charles Waite was Lee's quartermaster.

95. On the night of April 25, Turner and a few other Mosby men were on a scouting mission to Warrenton. They had stopped at the home of Charles H. Utterback about three miles from the town. While conversing with Utterback, the party was attacked by troopers of the 8th Illinois Cavalry, led by Capt. Elon J. Farnsworth. It was Farnsworth who shot Turner as he tried to flee. Turner was taken to his family's home, "Kinloch," where he lingered until the twenty-ninth. He was twice visited by Federal cavalry and roughly handled on at least one occasion, which may have contributed to his death. Trout, *They Followed the Plume*, p. 268.

96. The "Vineyard" was the home of the family of Cooke's brother Philip Pendleton Cooke, who had died in 1850. It was located in the lower Shenandoah Valley.

97. Buff was the facing color (used on collars and cuffs) of the Confederate engineer corps. As a second lieutenant, Robertson would have had one row of gold lace on his coat sleeve.

98. Alpheus Starkey Williams (September 20, 1810–December 21, 1878) attended Yale University and studied law, opening an office in Detroit. He served for a period as a judge before fighting in the Mexican War as a lieutenant colonel of a Michigan regiment. He was also Detroit's postmaster

for a time. When the war began, he was a brigadier general of state volunteers and was quickly commissioned with the same rank in the U.S. Army. Early in the war, he fought primarily in the eastern theater, but after Gettysburg was transferred to the West. After the war, he was elected to the U.S. Congress. Williams is buried in Elmwood Cemetery, Detroit, Michigan. Warner, *Generals in Blue*, pp. 559–60.

99. Alfred Pleasonton (July 7, 1824–February 17, 1897) graduated from the United States Military Academy in the class of 1844. He fought in Mexico, where he gained a brevet for bravery, on the Indian frontier, and in Florida. His early service in the war was with the 2nd U.S. Cavalry, and after distinguishing himself in the Peninsula Campaign, he gained a promotion to brigadier general of volunteers. A major generalcy followed in June 1863, but he soon fell from favor because of a poor performance in the Gettysburg Campaign and a disagreement with Lincoln's administration over the Kilpatrick-Dahlgren Raid in February 1864. U.S. Grant replaced Pleasonton with Phil Sheridan in March 1864. Pleasonton was assigned to the Department of Missouri for the duration of the war. He remained in the army after the war until his retirement in 1888. Pleasonton is buried in the Congressional Cemetery, Washington, D.C. *Ibid.*, pp. 373–74.

100. Henry Brainerd McClellan (October 17, 1840–October 1, 1904) joined the staff as Maj. Norman R. FitzHugh's replacement when that officer was transferred to the position of quartermaster. McClellan was born and raised in Philadelphia and attended college in Massachusetts. He lived in the South for only three years before the war, working as a schoolteacher. McClellan joined the 3rd Virginia Cavalry at the outbreak of the war. His talent and education (he had graduated with four degrees at the age of seventeen) brought him a lieutenant's commission and the position of regimental adjutant. By May 1863 he was a major and on Stuart's staff. After Stuart was killed, McClellan served on the staffs of Robert E. Lee and Wade Hampton. After the war, he returned to education, becoming the headmaster of the Sayre Female Institute in Lexington, Kentucky. He was a cousin to Federal major general George B. McClellan. Henry McClellan is buried in Lexington Cemetery, Lexington, Kentucky. Trout, *They Followed the Plume*, pp. 197–204.

101. This was the 6th New York Battery, commanded by Capt. Joseph W. Martin. Three guns were captured but had been disabled by bursting (gun exploded during firing), wedging (placing a shell in the barrel so as to jam it partway down), or spiking (driving a metal spike or headless nail into the vent). Out of the thirty-six men Martin took into the engagement, twenty-one were casualties. The battery fired a total of 263 rounds. *O.R.*, Ser. I, Vol. 27, Part 1, pp. 1023–26.

102. Pierce Manning Butler Young (November 15, 1836–July 6, 1896) had been a cadet at West Point when the war began. Resigning when his native state, Georgia, seceded, he accepted an appointment as a lieutenant in the artillery. Joining Cobb's Georgia Legion, he rose to the rank of lieutenant colonel in command of the cavalry. He ultimately reached the rank of major general. After the war, he entered politics, serving as a congressman. He is buried in Oak Hill Cemetery, Cartersville, Georgia. Warner, *Generals in Gray*, p. 348.

103. The Federals lost 936 officers and men, of whom 486 were prisoners. Stuart's total loss was 523 officers and men. McClellan, *I Rode with J. E. B. Stuart*, pp. 292–93. Pleasonton reported a loss of 866; Stuart listed his as 485. *O.R.*, Ser. I, Vol. 27, Part 1, p. 170; Ser. I, Vol. 27, Part 2, p. 719.

104. Elijah Viers White (August 29, 1832–January 11, 1907) commanded the 35th Virginia Cavalry Battalion. At the war's beginning he had served in the 7th Virginia Cavalry as a private, but he soon organized his own company for border service. Wounded several times, White survived the war. He was a banker and farmer after the war. He is buried in Union Cemetery in Leesburg, Virginia. Krick, *Lee's Colonels*, p. 392.

105. Lunsford Lindsay Lomax (November 4, 1835–May 28, 1913) graduated from West Point in 1856. He had been doing routine frontier duty with the U.S. Cavalry when the war began. After resigning from the army, he was commissioned a captain in the Virginia state forces and served for a time on the staffs of various generals. Promoted to lieutenant colonel, he was assigned the post of inspector general for the Army of West Tennessee. Another promotion to colonel brought him the command of the 12th Virginia Cavalry and a transfer to the Army of Northern Virginia. Lomax was promoted to brigadier general in July 1863 and to major general in August 1864. He ended the war fighting in North Carolina with Wade Hampton against Sherman. He was a farmer and president of Virginia Polytechnic Institute after the war. Lomax is buried in Town Cemetery, Warrenton, Virginia. Warner, *Generals in Gray*, pp. 190–91.

106. The Federals lost 305 men at Aldie and 214 of the 1st Rhode Island's 298 at Middleburg. Confederate losses were 119. Wilbur S. Nye, *Here Come the Rebels* (Dayton: Morningside Bookshop, 1984), pp. 181, 185.

107. The two officers were Maj. William R. Sterling, of Hooker's staff, and Capt. Benjamin F. Fisher, acting chief signal officer of the Army of the Potomac. *O.R.*, Ser. I, Vol. 27, Part 3, p. 192.

108. Henry Saxon Farley (February 11, 1840–June 3, 1927) had the distinction of being the first West Point cadet to resign over the growing tension between North and South. His first action in the war was to fire

the first shot on Fort Sumter in Charleston Harbor. He held commissions in the infantry and artillery simultaneously, though most of his early war service was in the artillery. The time he spent on Stuart's staff was brief, lasting only about three months. He then commanded the dismounted cavalry during the siege of Petersburg. His postwar life was varied and included teaching, editing a newspaper, gold mining, public speaking, and acting in movies. He was the brother of William D. Farley. Henry Farley is buried in Flushing Cemetery, New York, New York. Trout, *They Followed the Plume*, pp. 102–5.

Harry W. Gilmor (January 24, 1838–March 4, 1883) served on Stuart's staff for one day as a volunteer aide, but it was the day of the Battle of Kelly's Ford and Pelham's death. His life before the war was not overly eventful. He tried farming and homesteading, with little enthusiasm or success. When the war came, he immediately left his home in Maryland for Virginia, where he joined the 12th Virginia Cavalry as a private. Several times wounded, Gilmor ended the war a prisoner, having been captured in February 1865. After the war, he was the police commissioner for the city of Baltimore. Gilmor rests in Loudon Park Cemetery, Baltimore, Maryland. *Ibid.*, pp. 140–45.

George St. Leger Ommanney Grenfell (May 30, 1808–March 6, 1868) had led an adventurous life before coming to Stuart's staff in September 1863. Born in England and educated in Holland, he became involved with the French Revolution of 1830, was the principal figure in the failing of a bank in Paris for which he was tried and convicted *in absentia*, and traveled to such places as Gibraltar, Morocco, Turkey, and Argentina. He gained some military experience along the way, and after the war came, he made his way to the Confederacy, ending up with John Hunt Morgan. From Morgan he went to Stuart and then to Joe Wheeler's cavalry. Grenfell finally left the Confederacy, traveled north, and became involved in the "Northwest Conspiracy." Grenfell was captured, tried, and imprisoned on the Dry Tortugas. It is believed that he drowned attempting to escape, and his body was never recovered. *Ibid.*, pp. 157–62.

Richard Byrd Kennon (November 10, 1835–December 14, 1892) was studying to be a doctor when the war broke out. He enlisted in the 4th Virginia Cavalry, becoming a lieutenant, and served as a courier for Stuart at First Manassas. He resigned from the cavalry in September 1861 to accept a commission in the Adjutant General's Department. Kennon was assigned to the 8th Virginia Cavalry and was serving with it when he was called to Stuart's staff. During Stuart's ride in the rear of the Federal army in June 1863, Kennon performed the outstanding feat of twice swimming the mile-wide Potomac River at Rowser's Ford to find out if it was fordable. Upon leaving the staff, he became brigade inspector for Gen. Thomas L. Rosser, a position he held until the end of the war. He was a farmer in the postwar period. Kennon is buried in St. Luke's Episcopal Church Cemetery in Northampton County, North Carolina. *Ibid.*, pp. 188–91.

109. Charles Grattan (December 8, 1833–June 20, 1902) was a member of the Virginia State Legislature and was attending law lectures at the University of Virginia when the war began. He enlisted in the 1st Virginia Cavalry but actually served as assistant quartermaster to Maj. John A. Harman, who was Stonewall Jackson's quartermaster. He gave up his position and took his seat in the Virginia Legislature in December 1861. At the close of the session, he took the ordnance exam, was commissioned a lieutenant, and was assigned to Col. Henry C. Cabell's battalion of artillery. Later he was transferred to the 2nd Corps Artillery, where he served until he replaced John Esten Cooke as Stuart's ordnance officer in October 1863. After Stuart's death, he served with Hampton and Fitz Lee. He was a lawyer and judge after the war. Grattan rests in Thornrose Cemetery, Staunton, Virginia. *Ibid.*, pp. 149–57.

Garland Mitchell Ryals's (May 27, 1839–September 13, 1904) prewar vocation is unknown. At the start of the war, he joined the 3rd Virginia Cavalry and became a sergeant. During his military career, he served as ordnance officer to Gen. John C. Breckinridge's cavalry brigade and aide to Gen. Benjamin H. Helm in the western theater of the war. Upon his return to the Army of Northern Virginia in September 1862, he served first as ordnance officer and then provost marshal for Gen. Fitz Lee. His transfer to Stuart's staff followed in June 1863. After Stuart's death, Ryals went to Hampton's staff. He prospered in the mercantile business after the war. Ryals is buried in Bonaventure Cemetery, Savannah, Georgia. *Ibid.*, pp. 241–47.

1864

1. *O.R.*, Ser. I, Vol. 33, pp. 103, 107–8.

2. Blackford was promoted to the rank of major and transferred to the newly formed 1st Regiment of Engineers. Stuart used his influence to help Blackford attain the position and the promotion. Blackford, *War Years with Jeb Stuart*, p. 249.

3. The two men referred to were John Esten Cooke and Norman R. FitzHugh. Blackford may have forgotten about a third member of the staff who had also been with Stuart from the time he had joined the staff: William "Henry" Hagan. Trout, *They Followed the Plume*, pp. 328–29.

4. Robert Emmett Rodes (March 29, 1829–September 19, 1864) was

a graduate of the Virginia Military Institute with the class of 1848. He taught at the institute from that time until 1851, when he became a civil engineer. His first command during the war was as colonel of the 5th Alabama Infantry. Rodes was promoted to brigadier general in October 1861 and to major general following the Battle of Chancellorsville. His death was the result of wounds received during the Battle of Winchester. He is buried in Presbyterian Cemetery, Lynchburg, Virginia. Warner, *Generals in Gray*, p. 263.

5. The Battle of Cross Keys (June 8, 1862) was one of the actions in Jackson's Valley Campaign.

6. George Gordon Meade (December 31, 1815–November 6, 1872) graduated from West Point with the class of 1835 but resigned from the army one year later to take up civil engineering. In 1842 he rejoined the army as a lieutenant in the Corps of Topographical Engineers. Meade remained in the engineers until 1861 except for the time he served in the Mexican War. Shortly after the war began, he was commissioned a brigadier general of volunteers. He fought in many of the eastern battles and was severely wounded during the Seven Days Battles. He was given command of the Army of the Potomac on June 28, 1863, and led it until the war's end, though he was under U. S. Grant after he was appointed commander in chief of all the U.S. armies. Meade remained in the army after the war until his death. He is buried in Laurel Hill Cemetery, Philadelphia, Pennsylvania. Warner, *Generals in Blue*, pp. 315–17.

7. The reason for the meeting of McClellan and his brother was that their sister had died in Philadelphia. Trout, *They Followed the Plume*, pp. 197–200.

8. Francis Harrison Pierpont (January 25, 1814–March 24, 1899) was the governor of the new state of West Virginia and had been the primary force behind the formation of the state. Cooke was evidently commenting on the conscription officers who would have placed Andrew in the Federal army had they managed to catch him. Faust, ed., *Historical Times Illustrated Encyclopedia of the Civil War*, pp. 584–85.

9. Pvt. Sampson D. Sweeney was Stuart's famous banjo player. He had originally been a member of Company H, 2nd Virginia Cavalry, but Stuart had him transferred to his headquarters company. Sweeney died of smallpox on January 13, 1864. Theodore Stanford Garnett, *Riding with Stuart: Reminiscences of an Aide-de-Camp* (Shippensburg, PA: White Mane Publishing Co. Inc., 1994), pp. 114–15.

10. Pvt. Charles D. Lowndes had been detached from Company E, 4th Virginia Cavalry to Stuart's headquarters company as a courier. *Ibid.* p. 118.

11. *O.R.*, Ser. I, Vol. 33, Part I, pp. 139–40.

12. *Ibid.*, pp. 140–41.

13. Benjamin Franklin Stringfellow (July 18, 1840–June 8, 1913) had been a member of the 4th Virginia Cavalry before being detailed as a scout to Stuart in June 1862. Young and frail looking, Stringfellow proved to be one of the war's most daring and resourceful scout-spies as he ventured behind Federal lines in uniform and in disguise. His adventures make for thrilling reading. He emerged from the war with a $10,000 price on his head and fled to Canada for two years. Returning in 1867, Stringfellow studied for the ministry and graduated from Episcopal Seminary in 1876. He served churches in Powhatan and Middlesex counties in Virginia but still found time to write and give talks about his adventures. He is buried in Ivy Hill Cemetery, Alexandria, Virginia.

14. "Marshfield," located about two miles from Richmond and about one quarter of a mile outside the fortifications, was the home of John P. Ballard (of the Ballard House, a famous hotel in Richmond) and his wife, Powers's sister, Jane Frances "Fanny" Powers. Roberta Powers was staying there with the Ballard family's servants.

15. William M. Pegram was detached from Company K, 4th Virginia Cavalry, and was serving at headquarters as a clerk for Maj. H. B. McClellan. Garnett, *Riding with Stuart*, p. 114.

16. James Byron Gordon (November 2, 1822–May 18, 1864) was engaged in a mercantile business and farming before the war. He also served as a member of the North Carolina Legislature in 1850. Enlisting as a private when the war began, he was elected lieutenant and then captain of his company. An appointment as major in the 1st North Carolina Cavalry followed. Commissioned a brigadier general in September 1863, Gordon led his North Carolina brigade in most of the cavalry actions in the latter part of the year. In May 1864 he rode in pursuit of Sheridan toward Richmond. He was mortally wounded at Meadow Bridge on May 12, the day after Stuart's mortal wounding at Yellow Tavern. Gordon is buried in St. Paul's Episcopal Churchyard, Wilkesboro, North Carolina. Warner, *Generals in Gray*, pp. 110–11.

17. Dabney had been promoted captain in the Adjutant General's Department and transferred to Gordon's staff on November 19, 1863. Apparently Gordon was pleased with the young officer. Trout, *They Followed the Plume*, p. 96.

18. "Kennons," located in Amelia County, Virginia, was the home of the family of John H. Steger, father of Roger W. Steger, who had been on Stuart's staff in 1861. Cooke's sister, Mary, had married one of John Steger's sons. Beaty, *John Esten Cooke, Virginian*, pp. 89, 111; Trout, *They Followed the Plume*, p. 250.

"Glenmore," located in Albemarle County about seven miles from Charlottesville, was the home of Benjamin H. Magruder, father of John Bowie Magruder, former colonel of the 57th Virginia Infantry. He had been mortally wounded at Gettysburg during Pickett's Charge on July 3. He died on the fifth, and his body was returned to his father and buried at the family home. Col. William H. Stewart, "Col. John Bowie Magruder," *Southern Historical Society Papers*, Vol. XXVII (1899), pp. 205–10; Krick, *Lee's Colonels*, p. 260.

19. 'N'Importé was actually Tallulah Hansell, the fiancee of William Pelham, John Pelham's older brother. Peggy Vogtsberger, "Who Was N'Importe?," *The Cannoneer*, Vol. 3, No. 2 (September 1984), p. 6.

20. Sally Dandridge was engaged to Pelham.

21. Ulric Dahlgren (April 3, 1842–March 2, 1864) had been a student of law and civil engineering before the war. When the war began, his first service was as a staff officer for Franz Sigel. A daring and resourceful officer, Dahlgren had lost a leg during the Confederate withdrawal from Gettysburg. Promoted to colonel, he was back in the war and ready for a new assignment by the beginning of 1864. Dahlgren was killed in an ambush while trying to lead his men away from Richmond to safety. He is buried in Philadelphia. Faust, ed., *Historical Times Illustrated Encyclopedia of the Civil War*, pp. 202–3.

22. O.R., Ser. I, Vol. 33, Part I, pp. 168–224.

23. George Armstrong Custer (December 5, 1839–June 25, 1876) graduated last in his class at West Point in June 1861. His early service was mostly as a staff officer, but he managed to participate in every fight he could find and gained the eye of senior officers. His efforts paid off handsomely when on June 29, 1863, he was jumped from his temporary rank of captain to brigadier general. His career both during and after the war was controversial, but no one could ever accuse him of cowardice or the inability to inspire the men under his command. Custer finished the war a major general of volunteers. His subsequent army service was as lieutenant colonel of the 7th U.S. Cavalry, fighting Indians in the West. His actions and death at the Battle of the Little Bighorn, like his life, have been the topic for heated debate among historians for decades. He rests in the cemetery at West Point. Warner, *Generals in Blue*, pp. 108–10.

24. O.R., Ser. I, Vol. 33, Part I, pp. 161–68.

25. The papers found on Dahlgren's body included plans to penetrate Richmond's defenses and free Federal prisoners held in various parts of the city. Along with this operation, the city was to be put to the torch and President Jefferson Davis and his cabinet were to be killed. The South was outraged, and the North denied the legitimacy of the papers, basically stat-

ing that Dahlgren wrote them. Except for the authenticity of the papers, which has been proven, their origin is still a subject of argument, some historians feeling that Dahlgren was a convenient scapegoat. Faust, ed., *Historical Times Illustrated Encyclopedia of the Civil War*, p. 203.

26. *O.R.*, Ser. I, Vol. 33, Part I, pp. 240–46.

27. Garnett, *Riding with Stuart*, pp. 47–48.

28. John Sedgwick (September 13, 1813–May 9, 1864) taught school for two years before entering West Point, from which he graduated in 1837. He fought in the Mexican War, earning two brevets. At the start of the war he was a colonel, but he was soon commissioned brigadier general of volunteers. He participated in most of the battles in the eastern theater of the war and was wounded several times. He was promoted to major general in July 1862. He was shot in the head and killed by a sniper during the Battle of Spotsylvania. Sedgwick is buried in Cornwall Hollow, Connecticut. Warner, *Generals in Blue*, pp. 430–31.

29. Latin for "with laughter."

30. Scratches is a leg problem of horses stemming from constant wet feet and might be compared to the chapping of human hands and feet. It appears most often on the pasterns and heels and can degenerate into serious and painful scabs if left untreated.

31. David B. Bridgford was the provost marshal of the Army of Northern Virginia.

32. *O.R.*, Ser. I, Vol. 33, Part I, pp. 314–15.

33. Theodore Stanford Garnett Jr. (October 28, 1844–April 27, 1915) was a student at Episcopal High School in Alexandria, Virginia, at the outbreak of the war. His reaction to the news was to journey home and enlist in the Hanover Artillery. His youth was brought to the attention of Robert E. Lee, President Davis's military advisor at the time, who promptly sent the disappointed Garnett home. He ended up as a clerk in the Navy Department, where he toiled for eighteen months, until Stuart requested the secretary of the navy to send him someone with a "good hand." Garnett got the job, arriving at cavalry headquarters sometime in late April or early May 1863. Stuart soon recognized that Garnett had more going for him than his penmanship and in March 1864 had the young clerk commissioned a lieutenant and his aide-de-camp. After Stuart's death, Garnett served on the staffs of Generals W. H. F. Lee and William P. Roberts. In the postwar period, he was a lawyer and a judge. He is buried in Elmwood Cemetery, Norfolk, Virginia. Trout, *They Followed the Plume*, pp. 132–39.

34. Lee's wife, Charlotte Wickham, had died on December 26, 1863, while her husband was a prisoner of war.

35. James Franklin Hart (February 13, 1837–April 20, 1905) graduated

from the South Carolina Military Academy in 1857. He was a teacher for the next two years, after which he studied law. In June 1861 he became a lieutenant of artillery in Wade Hampton's Legion. By December he was captain of the battery that thereafter bore his name. He lost a leg at Burgess Mill in October 1864, but he returned to accept a commission of major and commanded a battalion of artillery until the war's end. After the war, he was a lawyer. Hart is buried in Rose Hill Cemetery, York, South Carolina. Krick, *Lee's Colonels*, p. 186.

36. "Sister Willie" was Miss Willie Anne Burwell, the wife of Cooke's brother, Philip Pendleton Cooke.

37. Blackford's father, William Mathews Blackford (1801–April 14, 1864) had just died in Lynchburg.

38. William Lee Church was the adjutant and inspector general of Brig. Gen. Pierce M. B. Young's Brigade.

Farley was at this time attached to Young's Brigade, though his exact duties are unclear. Trout, *They Followed the Plume*, p. 104.

39. Spanish for "Who knows?"

40. Carter Moore Braxton (September 5, 1836–May 27, 1898) began the war as captain of the Fredericksburg Artillery. His lieutenant colonel's commission was dated February 27, 1864. After the war, he was a civil engineer. Krick, *Lee's Colonels*, p. 68.

41. Armistead Lindsay Long (September 3, 1825–April 29, 1891) graduated from West Point in 1850. He served in the U.S. artillery until just before the outbreak of the war, when he was appointed to staff duty. Resigning his commission in June 1861, he became a major of artillery in the Confederate army. After a time as a staff officer to Gen. William W. Loring, Long reported to Robert E. Lee. When Lee took command of the Army of Northern Virginia, Long became his military secretary and was promoted to colonel. He was commissioned brigadier general in September 1863 and assigned to command the artillery of the 2nd Corps. For a few years after the war he was a civil engineer, but he became blind in 1870 and spent much of his life afterward writing. Long is buried in Maplewood Cemetery, Charlottesville, Virginia. Warner, *Generals in Gray*, pp. 191–92.

42. Sainty was Edward St. George Cooke, John Esten's brother, who died in adolescence.

43. Boteler was mistaken concerning several of the individuals. Cooke was not Grattan's assistant and, in fact, outranked him. Grattan was not a major nor is there evidence he ever achieved that rank. Chiswell Dabney and Hullihen had been promoted and were no longer on Stuart's staff, though they may have been visiting the headquarters of their former com-

mander. Finally, Stuart's pet name for Hullihen was "honey-bun." Trout, *They Followed the Plume*, pp. 89–99, 149–57, 179–86.

44. Judge John Perkins (July 1, 1819–?) graduated from Yale in 1840 and after studying law established a practice in New Orleans. In 1851 he was appointed judge of the circuit court. The following year, he was elected to the U.S. Congress as a representative from Louisiana. During the war, he served as a representative in the Confederate Congress. "Louisiana in Confederate Congress," *Confederate Veteran*, Vol. XXXV, 1927, pp. 220–21.

45. Gouverneur Kemble Warren (January 8, 1830–August 8, 1882) received an appointment to the United States Military Academy at the age of sixteen. He graduated second in his class four years later. His entire service before the war was with the Corps of Topographical Engineers and as an instructor at West Point. In May 1861 he was appointed lieutenant colonel of the 5th New York Infantry and in August became its colonel. He commanded a brigade in the Peninsula Campaign but was not promoted to brigadier general until September 1862. At Gettysburg his quick action saved Little Round Top on the second day of the battle. In August 1863 he was commissioned major general. He was relieved of command of his corps by Maj. Gen. Philip Sheridan on April 1, 1865, for supposed incompetence. He was eventually exonerated of any blame in association with Five Forks. Warren is buried in Island Cemetery, Newport, Rhode Island. Warner, *Generals in Blue*, pp. 541–42.

Winfield Scott Hancock (February 14, 1824–February 9, 1886) graduated from West Point in 1844. He earned a brevet for gallantry during the Mexican War, and then saw service against the Seminoles. At the beginning of the war, he was commissioned a brigadier general of volunteers. He was promoted to major general in November 1862. Hancock fought in most of the major battles in the East and was seriously wounded at Gettysburg during Pickett's Charge. He recovered and returned to lead his corps until his wound reopened and he was forced to relinquish command. He remained in the army after the war and ran for president in 1880. Hancock is buried in Montgomery Cemetery, Norristown, Pennsylvania. *Ibid.*, pp. 202–4.

46. Garnett, *Riding with Stuart*, pp. 49–53; O.R., Ser. I, Vol. 36, Part I, p. 773.

47. John Marshall Jones (July 26, 1840–May 5, 1864), an 1841 graduate of West Point, had been an instructor there during the Mexican War and had not participated in that conflict. He resigned his commission as a captain in the 7th U.S. Infantry and accepted the same rank in the Confederate service. For a time, he was the assistant adjutant general and adjutant

and inspector general to a number of general officers. He rose to the rank of lieutenant colonel before jumping to brigadier general in May 1863 and taking a field command. He survived two wounds, including a serious one at Gettysburg, before leading his brigade into the Wilderness fighting. Jones is buried in Maplewood Cemetery, Charlottesville. Warner, *Generals in Gray*, pp. 164–65.

Leroy Augustus Stafford (April 13, 1822–May 8, 1864) was a planter in Louisiana before the war. He served as a private in a volunteer company during the Mexican War. At the beginning of the war, he helped raise a company and was elected its captain. In October 1861 he was appointed colonel of the 9th Louisiana Infantry and with it fought in many of the major battles in the eastern theater of the war. Commissioned brigadier general in October 1863, he was given command of the 2nd Louisiana Brigade. He was mortally wounded on May 5, 1864, while leading his command. Stafford is buried at his family's home, "Greenwood," near Cheneyville, Louisiana. *Ibid.*, pp. 287–88.

48. William Wellford Randolph (February 20, 1837–May 5, 1864) attended the University of Virginia before the war. He was elected to the Virginia Legislature for 1863–64. He became the lieutenant colonel of the 2nd Virginia Infantry on April 26, 1864. Randolph is buried at Old Chapel Cemetery, Clarke County, Virginia. Krick, *Lee's Colonels*, p. 314.

49. Junius Daniels (June 27, 1828–May 13, 1864) graduated from the United States Military Academy in 1851. Resigning from the army in 1858, he took charge of his father's plantation in Louisiana. When the war erupted, he was elected colonel of the 14th North Carolina Infantry. He was promoted to brigadier general in September 1862. He was mortally wounded on May 12, 1864, at the Battle of Spotsylvania Court House. Daniels is buried in Old Colonial Graveyard, Halifax, North Carolina. Warner, *Generals in Gray*, pp. 66–67.

John Brown Gordon (February 6, 1832–January 9, 1904) trained to be a lawyer, but when the war broke out, he was attempting to develop coal mines in Georgia. At the beginning of the war, he was elected captain of an infantry company. He rose to the rank of lieutenant general—a most remarkable achievement for someone who had no previous military training. After the war, he entered politics and served three terms in the U.S. senate and one term as governor of Georgia. Gordon was also very active in the Confederate Veterans Association and commanded that body from 1890 until his death. He is buried in Oakland Cemetery, Atlanta, Georgia. *Ibid.*, p. 111.

50. Henry Heth (December 16, 1825–September 27, 1899) attended West Point, graduating with the class of 1847. From that time until the

war, he remained on routine frontier duty. After his resignation, he was commissioned colonel of the 45th Virginia Infantry. In January 1862 he was promoted to brigadier general but joined Lee's army only in February 1863. Heth was commissioned major general in May 1863 and was severely wounded in the head at Gettysburg. He returned to the army and served with it until Appomattox. He was in the insurance business after the war. Heth is buried in Hollywood Cemetery, Richmond, Virginia. *Ibid.*, p. 133.

Cadmus Marcellus Wilcox (May 29, 1824–December 2, 1890) received an appointment to West Point in 1842 and graduated four years later. He served in the Mexican War, earning a brevet of first lieutenant. After his resignation from the U.S. Army, he became colonel of the 9th Alabama Infantry and received a promotion to brigadier general in October 1861. Wilcox fought in virtually all the battles in the eastern theater of the war. His record earned him a major generalcy in August 1863. He remained with Lee's army until the end. After the war, he served in the Federal Land Office in Washington. Wilcox is buried in Oak Hill Cemetery, Washington, D.C. *Ibid.*, pp. 337–38.

51. The identity of "General Peyton" is unknown. There was no officer by that name in the Confederate service. Boteler may have been referring to Brig. Gen. Abner M. Perrin (February 2, 1827–May 12, 1864), who commanded a brigade in Anderson's Division. Perrin was conspicuous for his bravery during the Battle of the Wilderness and was killed while leading his brigade at the Battle of Spotsylvania. He is buried in Confederate Cemetery, Fredericksburg, Virginia. *Ibid.*, p. 235.

52. A general order to this effect was issued by Meade on May 10, 1864. *O.R.*, Ser. I, Vol. 33, Part II, p. 598.

53. Henry Harrison Walker (October 15, 1832–March 22, 1912) graduated from West Point in 1853 and served in Kansas up until the war. He resigned in May 1861 and was appointed a captain in the Confederate army. In a short time he was elected lieutenant colonel of the 40th Virginia Infantry and fought on the Peninsula, where he was twice wounded. He was promoted to brigadier general in July 1863 and led his brigade until wounded at Spotsylvania. His service thereafter was limited. Walker was an investment broker after the war. He rests in Evergreen Cemetery, Morristown, New Jersey. Warner, *Generals in Gray*, p. 318.

Harry Thompson Hays (April 14, 1820–August 21, 1876) graduated from St. Mary's College in Baltimore, Maryland, and afterward studied law there. He established a practice in New Orleans, Louisiana, and became involved in politics. Hays served with distinction in the Mexican War, and during the 1850s he was a prominent politician in Louisiana. At the beginning of the war, he became colonel of the 7th Louisiana Infantry and fought in Jackson's Valley Campaign, being severely wounded at the Battle of Port Republic. Upon his return to the army, he was promoted to brigadier general in July 1862. Hays was again wounded at Spotsylvania and afterward was transferred to the Trans-Mississippi Department, where he served under Gen. Kirby Smith, who appointed him a major general. He was a lawyer after the war. Hays is buried in Lafayette Cemetery #1, New Orleans, Louisiana. *Ibid.*, p. 130.

54. Edward Johnson (April 16, 1816–March 2, 1873) graduated from West Point in 1838. He fought in the Seminole War and in Mexico, being brevetted twice for bravery. His native state, Virginia, also honored him with a sword. At the start of the war, he was appointed colonel of the 12th Georgia Infantry. Johnson was promoted to brigadier general in December 1861 and was wounded in Jackson's Valley Campaign. In February 1863 he was commissioned a major general and served until he was captured at Spotsylvania. After his exchange, he was transferred to the Army of Tennessee and was again captured at the Battle of Nashville. Johnson remained a prisoner of war until July 1865. He was a farmer after the war. Johnson is buried in Hollywood Cemetery, Richmond, Virginia. *Ibid.*, pp. 158–59.

55. Boteler has misdated this entry, as Stuart was not at Spotsylvania on the tenth but had actually left at about three o'clock on the afternoon of the ninth. The events Boteler described occurred on that date. Garnett, *Riding with Stuart*, pp. 57–63.

56. Channing Meade Smith (May 22, 1842–November 8, 1932) enlisted in the "Black Horse Troop" from Warrenton, Virginia, on April 25, 1861. This famous unit eventually became Company H of the 4th Virginia Cavalry. Sometime after September 1862, Smith began his scouting activities when he was detached from his company. His service with Stuart began in May 1863. Smith was resourceful and daring. During one scouting expedition behind Federal lines he visited the headquarters and talked with the staff officers of Gen. Gouverneur K. Warren. When he returned to make his report, he carried with him a flag from Gen. John Sedgwick's Corps, which he had "captured" while in the Federal camp. In August 1864 Smith transferred to Mosby's command and was promoted to lieutenant. He served with the "Gray Ghost" until the end of the war. He was a farmer after the war. Trout, *They Followed the Plume*, pp. 294–98.

57. Philip Henry Sheridan (March 6, 1831–August 5, 1888) should have graduated from West Point in 1852, but a suspension because of an argument with another cadet set him back a year. From his graduation in 1853 until the war, he served on the frontier. His earliest war service was as a quartermaster and commissary, but on May 25, 1862, he was appointed colonel of the 2nd Michigan Cavalry. Sheridan became a brigadier general

in September 1862 and a major general in March 1863. His general's commissions took him away from the cavalry to the infantry. His fighting capabilities caught the attention of U. S. Grant, who brought Sheridan east with him when he was appointed commander in chief of all the Federal armies. Sheridan was given command of the cavalry of the Army of the Potomac and was later entrusted with a separate command in the Shenandoah Valley, where he fought and defeated Jubal Early. His cavalry forces contributed significantly in the pursuit of Lee to Appomattox. After the war, he remained in the army and eventually reached the rank of full general. Sheridan is buried in Arlington National Cemetery. Warner, *Generals in Blue*, pp. 437–39.

58. Stuart gave the horse, a gray named "General," on which he was riding when mortally wounded, to Venable. His other horse, a small bay he called his "pony," he gave to McClellan. The gold spurs had been a gift to Stuart from Lily Parren Lee. Her husband, William Fitzhugh Lee, lieutenant colonel of the 33rd Virginia Infantry and a friend of Stuart's, had owned the spurs. He had been mortally wounded at First Manassas, after which his wife had presented the spurs to Stuart.

59. John Daniel Imboden (February 16, 1823–August 15, 1895) attended Washington College in Lexington, Virginia. After his graduation, he taught school, then studied law and opened an office in Staunton. Imboden entered politics and twice was elected to the state legislature. At the beginning of the war, he became captain of the Staunton Artillery. He later organized what became the 62nd Virginia Mounted Infantry. Imboden was promoted to brigadier general in January 1863. He performed vital service for Lee during the Gettysburg campaign. He fought in Jubal Early's Valley Campaign but was forced to relinquish field command after contracting typhoid fever in the fall of 1864. For the remaining months of the war, he was on prison duty in South Carolina. After the war, he resumed his law practice. Imboden is buried in Hollywood Cemetery, Richmond, Virginia. Warner, *Generals in Gray*, p. 147.

BIBLIOGRAPHY

MANUSCRIPTS

University of Chicago Library, Department of Special Collections
    Wyndham Robertson Papers (Frank S. Robertson)
Duke University
    John Easton Cooke Papers
The Huntington Library
    Dabney Ball Papers
Library of Congress
    William Elizabeth Brooks Collections (Alexander R. Boteler)
Mississippi Department of Archives and History
    James Hardeman Stuart Papers
Library of the University of North Carolina at Chapel Hill, Southern Historical
    Collection
    Blackford Family Papers
    Peter Wilson Hairston Papers
    R. Channing Price Papers
Virginia Historical Society
    Saunders Family Papers (Chiswell Dabney)
United States Army Military History Institute
    Lewis Leigh Jr. Collection, Philip H. Powers Papers
Privately Owned Papers
    Staige D. Blackford: Poetry of William W. Blackford
    Mrs. Robert E. Osth: Philip H. Powers Papers
    Philip H. Powers Jr.: Philip H. Powers Papers
    Mrs. Isabel Smith Stewart: Farley Family Papers

SECONDARY SOURCES

Basler, Roy P., ed. *The Collected Works of Abraham Lincoln*. New Brunswick, NJ: Rutgers University Press, 1953.
Beaty, John O. *John Esten Cooke*. Port Washington, NY: Kennikat Press, n.d.
Blackford, W. W. *War Years with Jeb Stuart*. New York: Charles Scribner's Sons, 1945.
Boatner, Mark M. III. *The Civil War Dictionary*. New York: David McKay Company, Inc., 1959.
Bushong, Millard K., and Dean M. Bushong. *Fightin' Tom Rosser, C.S.A.* Shippensburg, PA: Beidel Printing House, Inc., 1983.
Confederate Veteran. 40 vols. Wilmington, NC: Broadfoot Publishing Company, 1893–1932.
Cooke, John Esten. *Outlines from the Outpost*. Chicago: The Lakeside Press, 1961.
———. *Wearing of the Gray*. Bloomington: Indiana University Press, 1977.
Crute, Joseph H. Jr. *Confederate Staff Officers*. Powhatan, VA: Derwent Books, 1982.
Culpeper Historical Society, Inc. *Historic Culpeper*. Culpepper, VA: Culpeper Historical Society, Inc., 1974.

Davis, Burke. *Jeb Stuart: The Last Cavalier*. New York: Bonanza Books, 1957.
————. *They Called Him Stonewall*. New York: Rinehart & Company, Inc., 1954.
Denison, Rev. Frederic. *Sabres and Spurs: The First Regiment Rhode Island Cavalry in the Civil War, 1861–1865*. Baltimore: Butternut and Blue, 1994.
Dickinson, Jack L. *8th Virginia Cavalry*. Lynchburg, VA: H. E. Howard, Inc., 1986.
Douglas, Henry Kyd. *I Rode with Stonewall*. Greenwich, CT: Fawcett Publications, Inc., 1961.
Downey, Fairfax. *Clash of Cavalry: The Battle of Brandy Station*. New York: David McKay Company, Inc., 1959.
Driver, Robert J. Jr. *1st Virginia Cavalry*. Lynchburg, VA: H. E. Howard, Inc., 1991.
Evans, Gen. Clement A., ed. *Confederate Military History*. Dayton: Press of Morningside Bookshop, 1975.
Faust, Patricia L., ed. *Encyclopedia of the Civil War*. New York: Harper & Row, 1986.
Fortier, John. *15th Virginia Cavalry*. Lynchburg, VA: H. E. Howard, Inc., 1993.
Freeman, Douglas Southall. *Lee's Lieutenants*. 3 vols. New York: Charles Scribner's Sons, 1942–44.
————. *R. E. Lee: A Biography*. New York: Charles Scribner's Sons, 1962.
Frye, Dennis E. *12th Virginia Cavalry*. Lynchburg, VA: H. E. Howard, Inc., 1988.
Garnett, Theodore Stanford. *Riding with Stuart: Reminiscences of an Aide-de-Camp*. Shippensburg, PA: White Mane Publishing Co., Inc., 1994.
Goldsborough, W. W. *The Maryland Line in the Confederate Army*. Gaithersburg, MD: Olde Soldier Books, Inc., 1987.
Hairston, Peter Wilson. *The Cooleemee Plantation and Its People*. Winston-Salem, NC: Hunter Publishing Company, 1986.
Hubbell, Jay B., ed. "The War Diary of John Esten Cooke," *The Journal of Southern History*, VII (1941): 526–40.
Krick, Robert K. *Lee's Colonels, 3rd Edition*. Dayton: Press of Morningside Bookshop, 1991.
————. *9th Virginia Cavalry*. Lynchburg, VA: H. E. Howard, Inc., 1982.
McClellan, H. B. *I Rode with Jeb Stuart*. Bloomington: Indiana University Press, 1958.
Milham, Charles G. *Gallant Pelham: American Extraordinary*. Gaithersburg, MD: Butternut Press, 1985.
Mitchell, Adele H., ed. *The Letters of Major General James E. B. Stuart*. Stuart-Mosby Historical Society, 1990.
Musick, Michael P. *6th Virginia Cavalry*. Lynchburg, VA: H. E. Howard, Inc., 1990.
Nye, Wilbur S. *Here Come the Rebels*. Dayton: Press of Morningside Bookshop, 1984.
Priest, John Michael. *Before Antietam: The Battle for South Mountain*. Shippensburg, PA: White Mane Publishing Co., Inc., 1992.
Ramey, Emily G., and John K. Gott, eds. *The Years of Anguish: Fauquier County, Virginia 1861–1865*. Annandale, VA: Bacon Race Books, 1965.
Southern Historical Society Papers. 49 vols. [1876–1944.] Reprint, Millwood, NY: Krause Reprint Co., 1977.
Starr, Stephen Z. *The Union Cavalry in the Civil War*. Baton Rouge: Louisiana State University Press, 1979.
Stiles, Kenneth L. *4th Virginia Cavalry*. Lynchburg, VA: H. E. Howard, Inc., 1985.
Strode, Hudson. *Jefferson Davis: Confederate President*. New York: Harcourt, Brace and Company, 1959.
Supplement to the Official Records of the Union and Confederate Armies. Wilmington, NC: Broadfoot Publishing Company, 1994.
Thomason, John W. Jr. *Jeb Stuart*. New York: Charles Scribner's Sons, 1930.
Thompson, O. R. Howard, and William H. Rauch. *History of the "Bucktails."* Philadelphia: Electric Printing Company, 1906.

Trout, Robert J. *They Followed the Plume: The Story of J. E. B. Stuart and His Staff.* Mechanicsburg, PA: Stackpole Books, 1993.

U.S. War Department. *The War of the Rebellion: The Official Records of the Union and Confederate Armies.* 128 vols. Washington, DC: U.S. Government Printing Office, 1880–1901. Reprint, Harrisburg, PA: National Historical Society, 1971.

Vandiver, Frank. *Mighty Stonewall.* New York: McGraw-Hill Book Company, Inc., 1957.

Von Borcke, Heros. *Memoirs of the Confederate War.* Dayton: Morningside House, Inc., 1985.

Wallace, Lee A. Jr. *A Guide to Virginia Military Organizations 1861–1865.* Lynchburg, VA: H. E. Howard, Inc., 1986.

Warner, Ezra J. *Generals in Blue.* Baton Rouge: Louisiana State University Press, 1964.

———. *Generals in Gray.* Baton Rouge: Louisiana State University Press, 1959.

Wise, Jennings Cropper. *The Long Arm of Lee.* New York: Oxford University Press, 1959.

INDEX